Recent Trends in the Economics of Copyright

The International Library of Critical Writings in Economics

Series Editor: Mark Blaug

Professor Emeritus, University of London, UK
Professor Emeritus, University of Buckingham, UK
Visiting Professor, University of Amsterdam, The Netherlands

This series is an essential reference source for students, researchers and lecturers in economics. It presents by theme a selection of the most important articles across the entire spectrum of economics. Each volume has been prepared by a leading specialist who has written an authoritative introduction to the literature included.

A full list of published and future titles in this series is printed at the end of this volume.

Wherever possible, the articles in these volumes have been reproduced as originally published using facsimile reproduction, inclusive of footnotes and pagination to facilitate ease of reference.

Recent Trends in the Economics of Copyright

Edited by

Ruth Towse

Professor of the Economics of Creative Industries
Erasmus University Rotterdam, The Netherlands
and Bournemouth University, UK

and

Richard Watt

Associate Professor, Department of Economics
University of Canterbury, New Zealand

THE INTERNATIONAL LIBRARY OF CRITICAL WRITINGS IN ECONOMICS

An Elgar Reference Collection
Cheltenham, UK • Northampton, MA, USA

Published by
Edward Elgar Publishing Limited
The Lypiatts
15 Lansdown Road
Cheltenham
Glos GL50 2JA
UK

Edward Elgar Publishing, Inc.
William Pratt House
9 Dewey Court
Northampton
Massachusetts 01060
USA

A catalogue record for this book is available from the British Library

Library of Congress Control Number: 2008927683

ISBN 978 1 84720 045 7

Printed and bound in Great Britain by MPG Books Ltd, Bodmin, Cornwall

Contents

Acknowledgements

The editor and publishers wish to thank the authors and the following publishers who have kindly given permission for the use of copyright material.

American Economic Association for articles: Michele Boldrin and David Levine (2002), 'The Case Against Intellectual Property', *American Economic Review, Papers and Proceedings*, **92** (2), 209–12; Josh Lerner and Jean Tirole (2005), 'The Economics of Technology Sharing: Open Source and Beyond', *Journal of Economic Perspectives*, **19** (2), Spring, 99–120.

William J. Baumol for his own article: (2004), 'The Socially Desirable Size of Copyright Fees', *Review of Economic Research on Copyright Issues*, **1** (1), 83–92.

Blackwell Publishing Ltd for articles: Justin Pappas Johnson (2002), 'Open Source Software: Private Provision of a Public Good', *Journal of Economics and Management Strategy*, **11** (4), Winter, 637–62; Ruth Towse (2006), 'Copyright and Artists: A View From Cultural Economics', *Journal of Economic Surveys*, **20** (4), 567–85.

Elsevier Ltd for articles: Amit Gayer and Oz Shy (2006), 'Publishers, Artists and Copyright Enforcement', *Information Economics and Policy*, **18**, 374–84; Martin Peitz and Patrick Waelbroeck (2006), 'Piracy of Digital Products: A Critical Review of the Theoretical Literature', *Information Economics and Policy*, **18**, 449–76.

Harvard Law School for article: Stan J. Liebowitz and Stephen Margolis (2005), 'Seventeen Famous Economists Weigh in on Copyright: The Role of Theory, Empirics and Network Effects', *Harvard Journal of Law and Technology*, **18** (2), Spring, 435–57.

Justin P. Johnson and Michael Waldman for their own article: (2005), 'The Limits of Indirect Appropriability in Markets for Copiable Goods', *Review of Economic Research on Copyright Issues*, **2** (1), June, 19–37.

William M. Landes and Richard A. Posner for their own article: (2003), 'Indefinitely Renewable Copyright', *University of Chicago Law Review*, **70** (2), Spring, 471–518.

Ivan P. L. Png for his own article: (2006), 'Copyright: A Plea for Empirical Research', *Review of Economic Research on Copyright Issues*, **3** (2), 3–13.

Fabrice Rochelandet and Wendy J. Gordon for article: Fabrice Rochelandet (2003), 'Are Copyright Collecting Societies Efficient Organisations? An Evaluation of Collective Administration of Copyright in Europe', in Wendy J. Gordon and Richard Watt (eds), *The*

Economics of Copyright, Chapter 10, Cheltenham, UK and Northampton, MA, USA: Edward Elgar, 176–97.

Arthur Snow, Lisa N. Takeyama and Wendy J. Gordon for article: Arthur Snow and Richard Watt (2005), 'Risk Sharing and the Distribution of Copyright Collective Income', in Lisa N. Takeyama, Wendy J. Gordon and Ruth Towse (eds), *Developments in the Economics of Copyright*, Chapter 2, Cheltenham, UK and Northampton, MA, USA: Edward Elgar, 23–36.

Every effort has been made to trace all the copyright holders but if any have been inadvertently overlooked the publishers will be pleased to make the necessary arrangement at the first opportunity.

In addition the publishers wish to thank the Library of Indiana University at Bloomington, USA and the Library of the University of Warwick, UK, for their assistance in obtaining these articles.

General Introduction

Ruth Towse and Richard Watt

This collection of articles is designed for readers who are familiar with the principles of economics and who have a basic knowledge of the principles of copyright law. For those who wish to review their knowledge, there are several accessible surveys that cover all aspects of the field: Besen (1998) and Raskind (1998). The aim of this collection is to give a flavour of the progress in this growing field over the last ten years or so. This Introduction briefly lays out the structure of the book, which is in five parts; each part is preceded by a more comprehensive introduction that puts in context the choice of articles reprinted here. We have purposefully kept the number of articles to a minimum so as to keep within one volume.

The last decade has seen a flourish of interest in many issues to do with copyright and it is therefore not surprising that this includes economic aspects among them. This interest has been fostered by the formation of the Society of Economic Research in Copyright Issues (www.serci.org), which since 2004 has published a journal specialising in the economics of copyright, *The Review of Economic Research on Copyright Issues* (*RERCI*). While there is a literature on the economics of copyright that goes back to the early twentieth century (and scattered writings from even earlier – see Hadfield, 1992; Scotchmer and Maurer, 2004), the acceleration of interest effectively began in the 1980s, stimulated by the problems associated with the development of copying technologies, such as photocopying, cassette and video recorders. Thus the 1980s saw the development of two strands of analysis – that on the economic analysis of copying, and that concerning copyright law, predominantly written by economists and lawyers specialising in law and economics. The former group are well represented by Besen and Kirby (1989), Johnson (1985), Novos and Waldman (1984), Liebowitz (1985); the latter by Landes and Posner (1989), Gordon (1982) and Koboldt (1995). (See Liebowitz and Watt (2006) and Handke, Stepan and Towse, forthcoming, for reviews of this literature.) These articles were published in a range of economics and law journals, perhaps without a sense of there being a field of the economics of copyright; most of these now 'classic' articles are reprinted in Towse and Holzhauer (2002), which also includes the comprehensive survey by Gordon and Bone (1998).

The same acceleration of interest has taken place in the last ten years with the development of far more powerful digitalised technologies, especially P2P and MP3, and the Internet as a new means of distributing what has come to be called 'content'. Content provision – the creative works supplied by individual creators and by the industries now often referred to as the 'creative industries' – is distinguished from its distribution for mass consumption via various media. The works produced by these creators and their industry counterparts, the film studios and sound recording labels, the publishers and broadcasters, the software and game producers, are all protected by copyright law and this has led to the identification of these industries as 'based on copyright'. These developments have in turn produced three distinct trends in the economics of copyright: theoretical analysis of the economic organisation of these industries; empirical studies of their economic growth and contribution to national incomes and studies that attempt to estimate the economic significance of unauthorised use of copyright material, popularly known as 'piracy'; and a third trend, the theoretical comparison between copyright law and other alternatives as efficient means of guaranteeing participation in creative endeavours, i.e. bundling, network effects, open source, indirect appropriability. While the macroeconomic studies are important for policy purposes, they do not challenge economists except in terms of getting access to the necessary data and therefore we do not include any papers on that topic here but instead refer the reader to a special issue of the *RERCI* (2004), **1** (1), devoted to this topic. On the other hand, trying to sort out the econometric problems of studying the effects of 'piracy' has been challenging and unsurprisingly, though by the time of writing (2007), there have been many attempts at the subject, there is not yet a consensus on the extent to which unauthorised copying has displaced legitimate trade in copyright works. We reprint here a small selection of this literature in Part II; Johnson and Waldman (**II, 4**), Peitz and Waelbroeck (**II, 5**) and Png (**II, 6**). We also include in Part II the article by Boldrin and Levine (**II, 7**), in which they argue against the case for copyright and indeed for all intellectual property law; in this they follow a well-established tradition in the early economics of copyright that argues there is not only no need for regulation but that it is undesirable (see Plant, 1934).

Economists have also been interested since the 1980s in the economics of collective rights management by copyright collection societies. They too are being affected by digitalisation partly because of their members' independent ability to collect royalties and other remuneration from their copyright works and partly because the operation of the collecting societies in particular and collective rights management in general are affected by the worldwide nature of digital distribution by Internet, and by the use of digital technologies to manage rights through digital rights management. These changes make it even more important to understand the economics of how collecting societies work and their economic rationale, particularly as their operations tend to attract the attention of anti-trust authorities from time to time.

Copyright collecting societies are interesting economic institutions because they are mostly private, non-profit membership organisations that have developed to enable individual rights-holders (the authors and subsequent holders of copyrights) to collect royalties cooperatively. They typically do this by the issue of blanket licences for specific bundles of rights, negotiating the terms with bodies representing the various users. A recent survey by Handke and Towse (2007) shows the scope of this literature. In this volume, we reprint three papers on topics in the administration of copyright in Part III: the article by Baumol (**III, 8**) deals with the question of what royalty rate should be set in a non-market setting and advocates the use of efficient component pricing; the article by Snow and Watt (**III, 9**) develops an analytical model of the distribution of royalty income in a copyright collective, and the third article by Rochelandet (**III, 10**) is a comparative study of the relative efficiency of the organisational arrangements of collecting societies.

Part IV presents a rather different view of the economics of copyright as the focus here is on copyright as a measure for protecting the work of creative and performing artists. The article by Gayer and Shy (**IV, 11**) considers the incentive to artists rather than to the record label of enforcing copyright, and the article by Towse (**IV, 12**) provides a survey of aspects of copyright law – moral rights, *droit de suite* (artists' resale rights) and performers' rights – that are of particular interest in cultural economics, in which the study of artists' labour markets includes the role of copyright as an incentive to artistic work.

Part V discusses the development of interest by economists in open source questions that have interested lawyers for some time now, led in particular by Stanford Law School professor, Lawrence Lessig. Open source is a system under which software is distributed along with full disclosure of its source code (the written programming instructions comprising the software), so that any downstream users may freely appropriate this programming code for their own use. This, of course, seems at first sight to be diagonally opposed to copyright – rather than going to lengths to protect and hide software code, it is fully exposed and others are openly invited to use it at will. Open source, however, relies heavily on copyright law (Leveque and Meniere, 2007), because while downstream use is encouraged, it is restricted (for example, most open source licences do not allow code to be taken from the open source commons and then sold on for economic gain in any way). However, the basic idea behind open source is that the huge community of programmers that is available on the Internet will ensure that bugs in programmes are quickly found and fixed, and that more and better software is made generally more available than would be the case under a fully commercial system.

The law and economics literature on open source software is certainly huge, and growing very quickly, which means that there is an enormous pool of papers from which we had to choose only a few for this volume. Our final choice reflects the two most important issues that have interested economists – the reasons why programmers would participate in open source projects, when their efforts are not directly rewarded by any royalty mechanism (Lerner and Tirole (**V, 13**), which also provides a good summary of the literature up to 2005), and the interconnections between the open source community and markets for commercial software, including an analysis of the relative efficiencies of each model of software development and distribution (Johnson (**V, 14**)).

Overall, the last ten years have been fruitful in producing important research in the economics of copyright with economists still questioning, though possibly less than previously, the merits of copyright law. With demands for longer and stronger copyright protection for commercially valuable copyrights becoming increasingly pressing, the political economy of copyright is correspondingly increasingly important, and it is clear that economists will continue to play an important role in analysing the costs and benefits of copyright. This work will undoubtedly proceed in terms of theoretical development but economists also have a fundamental role to play in doing empirical research. We hope this volume has made the case for both aspects of the economics of copyright.

References

Besen, Stanley M. (1998), 'Intellectual property', in Peter Newman (ed.), *New Palgrave Dictionary of Law and Economics*, **2**, London: Macmillan, pp. 348–51.

Besen, Stanley M. and Sheila Nataraj Kirby (1989), 'Private copying, appropriability and optimal copying royalties', *Journal of Law and Economics*, **32**, 255–80.

Gordon, Wendy J. (1982), 'Fair use as market failure: a structural and economic analysis of the Betamax case and its predecessors', *Columbia Law Review*, **82**, 1600–57.

Gordon, Wendy J. and Robert Bone (1998), 'Copyright', Entry 1610 in B. Bouckaert and G. De Geest (eds.), *Encyclopedia of Law and Economics*, Cheltenham, UK and Northampton, MA, USA: Edward Elgar, pp. 189–215.

Hadfield, Gillian K. (1992), 'The economics of copyright: A historical perspective', *Copyright Law Symposium* (ASCAP), **38**, 1–46.

Handke, Christian and Ruth Towse (2007), 'Economics of Copyright Collecting Societies', *International Review of Intellectual Property and Competition Law*, 8/2007 (**38**), 937–57. Also available at www.serci.org.

Handke, Christian, Stepan, Paul and Ruth Towse (forthcoming), 'Development of the Economics of Copyright' to be published in Josef Drexl (ed) *Competition Law and Intellectual Property*, Cheltenham, UK and Northampton, MA, USA: Edward Elgar.

Johnson, William R. (1985), 'The Economics of Copying', *Journal of Political Economy*, **93** (1), 158–74.

Koboldt, Christian (1995), 'Intellectual Property and Optimal Copyright Protection', *Journal of Cultural Economics*, **19** (2), 131–55.

Landes, William M. and Richard A. Posner (1989), 'An Economic Analysis of Copyright Law', *Journal of Legal Studies*, **18** (2), 325–63.

Leveque, Francois and Yann Meniere (2007), 'Copyright Versus Patents: The Open Source Software Legal Battle', *Review of Economic Research on Copyright Issues*, **4** (1), 27–46.

Liebowitz, Stan J. (1985), 'Copying and Indirect Appropriability', *Journal of Political Economy*, **93** (5), 945–57.

Liebowitz, Stan J. and Richard Watt (2006), 'How Best to Remunerate Creators in the Market for Music: Copyright and its Alternatives', *Journal of Economic Surveys*, **20**(4), 513–45.

Novos, Ian E. and Michael Waldman (1984), 'The Effects of Increased Copyright Protection: An Analytic Approach', *Journal of Political Economy*, **92** (2), 236–46.

Plant, Arnold (1934), 'The Economic Aspects of Copyright in Books', *Economica*, **1**(2), 167–95.

Raskind, Leo (1998), 'Copyright', in Peter Newman (ed.), *New Palgrave Dictionary of Law and Economics*, London: Macmillan, **1**, pp. 478–83.

Scotchmer, Suzanne and Stephen A. Maurer (2004), 'Institutions: A Brief Excursion Through History', chapter 1 of Scotchmer, Suzanne (ed.) (2004), *Innovation and Incentives*, Cambridge, MA, MIT Press, pp. 1–29.

Towse, Ruth and Rudi Holzhauer (2002), *Economics of Intellectual Property*, Cheltenham, UK and Northampton, MA, USA: Edward Elgar.

Part I
Economic Aspects of the Copyright Term

Introduction to Part I

Part I focuses on the term of copyright only; other copyright doctrines have also been subject to detailed economic analysis (see, for example, Novos and Waldman, 1984; Raskind, 1998; Gordon and Bone, 2000). We have chosen to concentrate on this apparently simple feature of copyright because of the recent (and possibly ongoing) controversy surrounding the term or duration of copyright and because these three papers show both the power of economics in understanding the issues and also demonstrate that the economics of copyright is a specialised field such that general economic principles only take one so far.

Long before the modern study of law and economics got underway, Thomas Babington Macaulay famously stated (in a speech to the House of Commons, 5th February 1841):

> Copyright is a monopoly and produces all the effects which the general voice of mankind attributes to monopoly ... the effect of a monopoly is to make articles scarce, to make them dear, and to make them bad ... It is good that authors be remunerated; and the least exceptional way of remunerating them is by a monopoly. Yet monopoly is an evil; for the sake of good, we must submit to evil; but the evil ought not to last a day longer than is necessary for the purpose of securing the good.

Quite so – but how long is this necessary period of time? In England and the USA, the term was originally fixed in relation to the creation of the work: in England, the 1709 Statute of Anne set it at 14 years renewable for a further 14 years and in the USA the 1790 Federal law made the same provision. However, the term has been increased several times in the ensuing years; being gradually altered to 50 years after the death of the author (the convention in European author's rights legislation, adopted with the Berne Convention) and then to 70 years in all the countries of the European Union and in the USA (and elsewhere too). Connecting copyright to the author's lifetime considerably extended its duration in some cases: for example, a work produced by an author at the age of 25 who died at age 75 would be protected for 50 years during the life of the author and for 70 subsequent years, making the effective term 120 years – a significant extension over the original 28 years maximum duration envisaged by the US Founding Fathers and the English Parliament.

All economists who support the principle of copyright law have taken more or less the same stance as Macaulay - that copyright is a trade-off between the beneficial incentive and the 'evil' of higher prices with consequent loss of access by users; copyright must therefore be limited in duration while lasting long enough to be an effective incentive. The answer to how long that actually should be is studiously avoided. The 1989 article by Landes and Posner is generally regarded as the fundamental article on the law and economics of copyright law; in it, they changed the emphasis of the analysis away from the trade-off between *price* and incentive to the cost of access by later creators because they regard the more damaging effect of the monopoly to be its inhibition of future creativity. In their model, the cost of expression is the variable to be balanced against the incentive to create, where the cost of expression includes tracing costs of later creators who need to check they do not infringe or who need to seek authorisation to create a derivative work. In Landes and Posner (1989), therefore, the cost of tracing is the variable that is emphasised as determining the duration of the copyright term. They considered the point that different types of work and authors need different strengths of protection and so, in principle, the copyright term should vary, but recognise that it would be administratively unworkable and so support the existence of a uniform term for all copyrightable works. However, subsequent developments have caused Landes and Posner to revise their view that the copyright term should be limited and they now propose, in the paper that we reproduce (**I, 3**) of this book, that copyright should be indefinitely renewable.

The first article reprinted in this book has a curiosity value over and above its contribution to the debate on the economically efficient term of copyright. It was a joint submission of a brief to the US Supreme Court by 17 leading US economists, including several Nobel Prize winners (the list is included in the document), as *amici curiae* in support of the petitioner(s); with George Akerlof as the first author alphabetically, the brief is sometimes referred to as Akerlof et al. (2002) reproduced here as (**I, 1**). The occasion was the case *Eldred v. Ashcroft* (the US Attorney General) that reached the US Supreme Court in 2002; it challenged the Copyright Term Extension Act of 1998 (the CTEA or, as it is popularly known, the 'Sonny Bono extension') that increased the term of copyright in the USA from 50 to 70 years after the author's death and in addition, made it retrospective – a cardinal sin especially to economists – and it was that feature of it that was the basis of the Eldred case. Eldred, a non-commercial Internet publisher, along with several other such publishers, wished to publish works that had recently come into the public domain upon the expiry of the 50 year plus life rule without paying a royalty; but with the extension of the term to 70 years plus life, the works reverted to being in copyright. In their amici brief, the '17 economists' in fact mostly adopted a very similar argument to that of Macaulay, dwelling on social cost of monopoly in contrast to the insignificant extra incentive offered by the extension of 20 years (due to discounting far into the future), emphasising its negligible increase in value due to discounting of an extra 20 years' revenues. However, as the next article in Part I demonstrates, the economic analysis of copyright has moved on some considerable way from the statements by Macaulay and first principles alone are no longer adequate to the task.

The article by Liebowitz and Margolis (**I, 2**) essentially points out that the '17 economists' had not taken on board the specific features of the economics of copyright, rather relying as they did on basic economic principles without considering the nature of the cultural industries in which copyright law plays such a major role. They emphasise the effect of the extension on the elasticity of supply, something, however, about which little is known empirically (though Liebowitz has a notable record of doing empirical research on the impact of copyright). They point out that while copyright protects vast numbers of works, very few of these ever have commercial value and fewer still remain on the market long enough to outlive the duration of the copyright term and enter the public domain: this winner-takes-all feature of what are sometimes called the 'copyright-based' industries must be taken into account in assessing the optimal term of copyright.

Landes and Posner in (**I, 3**) also make use of detailed empirical research on the effect of the term of copyright on the commercial status of various types of works. Their main concern, however, is something that has received little attention in the previous literature of the economics of copyright: the role of rent-seeking in lobbying legislators for extensions of copyright (and, of course, for other aspects of copyright law, such as its scope). The CTEA, which included an extension to 95 years for works for hire (essentially those works created by corporations) was strongly lobbied for by, among others, the Disney Corporation, owners of the Mickey Mouse copyright, which without the extension would soon have entered the public domain. Rent-seeking is viewed by economists as akin to the 'deadweight' loss of monopoly in being wasteful: use of the concept of rent intentionally signals wasteful use of resources, economic rent being the amount in excess of the outlay needed to induce an effort on the part of producers. Rent-seeking essentially means looking for a handout that has no incentive effect – in this case, an extra 20 years' revenue that was not anticipated at the time of the creation of the protected work. Landes and Posner take the view here that with any fixed term for copyright (even when the term is 'fixed' in relation to the life of the author), there will be an incentive on the part of copyright holders to seek an extension and so resources will inevitably be wasted in lobbying. To avoid that, they favour no limit to the copyright term, proposing indefinitely renewable copyright (similar to the indefinite term of trade marks), something against which almost every economist and lawyer previously had made a strong case.

References

Gordon, Wendy and Robert Bone (2000), 'Copyright', Entry 1610 in B. Bouckaert and G. De Geest (eds), *Encyclopedia of Law and Economics*, Cheltenham, UK and Northampton, MA, USA: Edward Elgar, pp. 189–215.

Landes, William M. and Richard A. Posner (1989), 'An Economic Analysis of Copyright Law', *Journal of Legal Studies*, **XVIII** (2), June, 325–66.

Novos, Ian E. and Michael Waldman (1984), 'The Effects of Increased Copyright Protection: An Analytical Approach', *Journal of Political Economy*, **92** (2), April, 236–46.

Raskind, Leo (1998), 'Copyright', in *New Palgrave Dictionary of Law and Economics*, London: Macmillan.

[1]

No. 01-618

In the Supreme Court of the United States

ERIC ELDRED *et al.*,

Petitioners,

v.

JOHN D. ASHCROFT, ATTORNEY GENERAL,

Respondent.

On Writ of Certiorari to the United States Court of Appeals for the District of Columbia Circuit

BRIEF OF GEORGE A. AKERLOF, KENNETH J. ARROW, TIMOTHY F. BRESNAHAN, JAMES M. BUCHANAN, RONALD H. COASE, LINDA R. COHEN, MILTON FRIEDMAN, JERRY R. GREEN, ROBERT W. HAHN, THOMAS W. HAZLETT, C. SCOTT HEMPHILL, ROBERT E. LITAN, ROGER G. NOLL, RICHARD SCHMALENSEE, STEVEN SHAVELL, HAL R. VARIAN, AND RICHARD J. ZECKHAUSER AS AMICI CURIAE IN SUPPORT OF PETITIONERS

ROY T. ENGLERT, JR.
Counsel of Record
Robbins, Russell, Englert, Orseck & Untereiner LLP
1801 K Street, N.W.
Suite 411
Washington, D.C. 20006
(202) 775-4500

May 20, 2002

TABLE OF CONTENTS

TABLE OF AUTHORITIES

Page(s)

Statute

Miscellaneous

TABLE OF AUTHORITIES—Continued

Brief as Amici Curiae in Support of Petitioners

INTEREST OF THE AMICI CURIAE[1]

Amici are professors and scholars who teach and write on economic issues and are concerned about the role of government in promoting economic progress. They are George A. Akerlof, Kenneth J. Arrow, Timothy F. Bresnahan, James M. Buchanan, Ronald H. Coase, Linda R. Cohen, Milton Friedman, Jerry R. Green, Robert W. Hahn, Thomas W. Hazlett, C. Scott Hemphill, Robert E. Litan, Roger G. Noll, Richard Schmalensee, Steven Shavell, Hal R. Varian, and Richard J. Zeckhauser. Various amici have taught, researched, and published analyses of the economics of innovation and the effect of government policy on the incentive to create new works. A summary of the qualifications and affiliations of the individual amici is provided at the end of this brief. Amici file this brief solely as individuals and not on behalf of the institutions with which they are affiliated. Amici represent neither party in this action, and offer the following views on this matter.

SUMMARY OF ARGUMENT

This brief provides an economic analysis of the main feature of the Copyright Term Extension Act of 1998 ("CTEA"), a twenty-year extension of the copyright term for existing and future works.[2] An economist's perspective may be helpful to the Court as it considers Congress's reasons for passing the CTEA, particularly with respect to the extension for existing works.

---

[1] The parties have consented to the submission of this brief, and their letters of consent have been filed with the Clerk of this Court. This brief was not written in whole or in part by counsel for a party. Amici and their counsel were not compensated in any way; the Stanford Institute for Economic Policy Research defrayed printing costs.

[2] Copyright Term Extension Act of 1998, Pub. L. No. 105-298, 112 Stat. 2827. In addition, this brief analyzes one ancillary economic effect of the CTEA, a longer term in Europe for U.S. copyright holders under Europe's "rule of the shorter term."

2

One possibility is that Congress sought a policy that confers a net economic benefit, after subtracting the expected costs. The main economic benefit from copyright protection is to give an author an incentive to create new works. The size of this economic incentive depends upon the "present value" of compensation, as anticipated by the author at the time of creation.

The two components of the CTEA differ markedly in their economic effect. The longer term for *new* works provides some increase in anticipated compensation for an author. Because the additional compensation occurs many decades in the future, its present value is small, very likely an improvement of less than 1% compared to the pre-CTEA term. This compensation offers at most a very small additional incentive for an economically minded author of a new work. The term extension for *existing* works makes no significant contribution to an author's economic incentive to create, since in this case the additional compensation was granted after the relevant investment had already been made.

The CTEA has two further effects on economic efficiency. First, the CTEA extends the period during which a copyright holder determines the quantity produced of a work, and thus increases the inefficiency from above-cost pricing by lengthening its duration. With respect to the term extension for new works, the present value of the additional cost is small, just as the present value of incremental benefits is small. By contrast, the cost of term extension in existing works is much larger in present value, especially for works whose copyrights would soon or already have expired but for the CTEA.

Second, the CTEA extends the period during which a copyright holder determines the production of derivative works, which affects the creation of new works that are built in part out of materials from existing works. Where building-block materials are copyrighted, new creators must pay to use those materials, and may incur additional costs in locating and negotiating with copyright holders. Such transaction costs are especially large where the copyright holders whose permissions are required are numerous or difficult to locate. By reducing the set of building-block materials freely available for new works, the CTEA raises the cost of producing new works and reduces the number created.

Taken as a whole, it is highly unlikely that the economic benefits from copyright extension under the CTEA outweigh the additional costs. Moreover, in the case of term extension for existing works, the sizable increase in cost is not balanced to any significant degree by an improvement in incentives for creating new works. Considering the criterion of consumer welfare instead of efficiency leads to the same conclusion, with the alteration that the CTEA's large transfer of resources from consumers to copyright holders is an additional factor that reduces consumer welfare.

ARGUMENT

I. IT IS HIGHLY UNLIKELY THAT THE ECONOMIC BENEFITS FROM COPYRIGHT EXTENSION UNDER THE CTEA OUTWEIGH THE COSTS

A. The CTEA Provides At Most A Very Small Benefit To Innovation

1. Copyright solves a special problem in the technology of production of creative works

To the extent that a concern for economic values motivates copyright policy, it is important to understand its main benefits and costs. In basic terms, copyright protection grants a monopoly over the distribution and sale of a work and certain new works based upon it. The copyright monopoly has several costs, which are described at pages 10-12 and 12-15 below. In addition, copyright protection provides a benefit to society by providing incentives for the production of new creative works.

4

The main economic rationale for copyright is to supply a sufficient incentive for creation.[3] To produce a new book, film, or other creative work, an author must make a substantial up-front investment.[4] For the resulting work to be profitable overall, the author must recoup her initial investment through sales of the work to consumers. An economically minded author will recognize this and invest in creation only if the expected returns, after paying per-unit (or "marginal") costs, are larger than the up-front investment; otherwise the author would lose money overall.

The recovery of up-front costs is a general concern for many producers, but authors face a special kind of economic problem, due to the technology of production for creative works. To understand this, consider the position of a second competitor, who wishes to make the same product as the first entrant into a market. For products generally, the second competitor must incur the same kinds of costs as the original entrant in order to participate in the market. Books, films, and other creative works are different: without legal protection, an author cannot prevent others from appropriating the fruits of the initial investment. Here, a second competitor can quickly enter the market by simply copying the work and offering it for sale, without incurring similar development costs. Without the ability to exclude, entry may be easy and quick, the resulting fall in prices to marginal cost can be rapid, and non-recovery of initial investment by the author is very likely. In this

[3] For two classic accounts, see William M. Landes & Richard A. Posner, *An Economic Analysis of Copyright*, 18 J. LEGAL STUD. 325 (1989); Stephen G. Breyer, *The Uneasy Case for Copyright: A Study of Copyright in Books, Photocopies, and Computer Programs*, 84 HARV. L. REV. 281 (1970).

[4] The incentives of copyright affect publishers as well as authors, but the same arguments apply to the initial publisher as to the author.

5

environment, an author has less of an incentive to produce new works.[5]

In economic terms, then, copyright provides incentives for creation by solving the special problem of non-excludability of creative works, assuring authors an opportunity to recoup their initial investment in creation. The economic value of a change in copyright policy depends upon the extent to which it increases incentives for creation. The CTEA lengthens the copyright term by twenty years, for both new works and existing works. As the economic value differs for the two kinds of extension, each case is considered in turn.

2. The CTEA's longer copyright for new works provides at most a very small additional incentive

The CTEA lengthens the copyright term for new works from life-plus-fifty years to life-plus-seventy years for individual authors, and from seventy-five years to ninety-five years for works for hire. Thus, the additional compensation from term extension accrues over a number of years. To evaluate and compare the magnitude of cash flows that occur in the future, economists use concepts of "present value" and "future value."

For a given amount of money today, future value is the amount that money would be worth at some point in the future. For example, if the interest rate is 7%, $1 today has a future value of $1.07 a year from now. Present value is the reciprocal of future value; thus $1.07 next year has a present value of $1 today. One dollar, received a year from now, has a present value of approximately $0.93 ($1/1.07). Similarly, $1.14 two years from now has a present value of $1, and $1 in two years

---

[5] See Kenneth J. Arrow, *Economic Welfare and the Allocation of Resources for Invention*, *in* THE RATE AND DIRECTION OF ECONOMIC ACTIVITY: ECONOMIC AND SOCIAL FACTORS 609 (National Bureau of Econ. Research ed., 1962).

6

is equivalent to approximately \$0.87 today. The further away in time it is paid, the less that payment is worth in present value.[6]

The twenty years of copyright term added by the CTEA provide a flow of additional benefits that is very far into the future, and hence very small in present value. To illustrate, suppose that an author writes a book and lives for thirty more years. In this case, under the pre-CTEA copyright regime, the author or his assignee would receive royalties for eighty years. If the interest rate is 7%, each dollar of royalties from year eighty has a present value of \$0.0045. Under the CTEA, this same author will receive royalties for one hundred years. Each dollar of royalties from year one hundred has a present value of \$0.0012.

In this example, the present value of total additional revenues under the CTEA can be calculated by adding up the present values of revenues from year eighty-one through year one hundred. Suppose that the work produces a constant stream of revenues, and assume once again that the interest rate is 7%. In this case, the present value of the total return from years eighty-one to one hundred is 0.33% of the present value from years one to eighty.[7] Put differently, under these assumptions, the additional compensation provided by the CTEA amounts to a 0.33% increase in present-value payments to the author, compared to compensation without the twenty-year term extension.[8]

---

[6] In general, given an interest rate of r, \$1 today grows to $(1+r)^n$ in n years. So \$1, n years in the future, has a present value of $1/(1+r)^n$ today.

[7] The present value of \$1 each year for eighty years is \$14.22 (at a 7% interest rate). The present value of \$1 each year from years eighty-one to one hundred is \$0.047, which is 0.33% of \$14.22.

[8] Analogously, the present value of additional compensation for a new work for hire is 0.47%.

7

The conclusion above is based on two assumptions: a constant stream of revenues and a 7% interest rate.[9] The assumption of a constant revenue stream for one hundred years is very conservative, that is, it tends to overstate the amount of compensation, because most works lose economic value over time. As evidence, only a small percentage of copyright registrants bother to renew their works, although renewal costs only a few dollars,[10] and only a fraction of renewed copyrights continue to be valuable to copyright holders.[11] If depreciation of value is taken into account, the additional compensation provided by the CTEA is likely to be much less than 0.33%.

The second assumption is the choice of an interest rate. In general, much as investors require higher compensation for riskier investments, a higher interest rate is appropriate for the purpose of evaluating highly uncertain revenue streams. Seven percent is meant to be illustrative, but it is a realistic estimate, perhaps even conservative, given the high degree of uncertainty about the revenues resulting from the production of a creative work. Appendix B reports the present value of additional compensation at different rates; the magnitude remains very small over a range of plausible rates.

---

[9] Here, 7% is a real interest rate, defined as the rate of return on capital, net of inflation.

[10] A study of renewals prior to the 1976 Act found a renewal rate of less than 15%. Barbara A. Ringer, *Renewal of Copyright*, *in* STUDIES ON COPYRIGHT 503, 616-20 (Arthur Fisher Memorial ed. 1963).

[11] A pre-CTEA Congressional Research Service study examined a sample of renewed copyrights, finding that 11% of copyrights in books, 12% in musical works, and 26% in motion pictures had some commercial value in 1998. Edward Rappaport, *Copyright Term Extension: Estimating the Economic Values*, Congressional Research Service Report 98-144E (1998).

3. The CTEA's extension of copyright in existing works provides no significant incentive to create new works

The analysis so far has suggested that, under a range of plausible assumptions, the CTEA's term extension for new works provides only a very small economic incentive to create new works, namely much less than one percent. The CTEA's extension of copyright in existing works by twenty years provides essentially no incentive to create new works. By the time of the CTEA's passage, pre-CTEA authors had already made initial investments in creation. Once a work is created, additional compensation to the producer is simply a windfall.

The CTEA's extension for existing works could in theory have an effect on creators of new works, by creating an expectation that, in the future, Congress would extend copyright even more, and that this extension would apply retroactively to existing works. The maximum impact on incentives from this effect, however, is trivial because the current copyright term already has nearly the same present value as an infinite copyright term. Granting a perpetual copyright would increase compensation by at most 0.12% (at a 7% interest rate),[12] or less once declining revenues are taken into account. The actual effect on incentives would be even smaller, if further extensions are not a certainty.[13]

One might argue that the windfall to authors of existing copyrights has a positive consequence, by providing them with

---

[12] At a 7% interest rate, the present value of $1 annually for one hundred years is $14.27, and the present value of $1 annually in perpetuity is $14.29, an increase of 0.12%. For a fuller discussion, see Linda R. Cohen & Roger G. Noll, *Intellectual Property, Antitrust and the New Economy*, 62 U. PITT. L. REV. 453, 471 (2001).

[13] Indeed, if the extension for existing works creates an expectation that the future term could be adjusted downward as well as upward, this could have a negative effect on incentives.

more resources for additional creative projects. However, this argument ignores the profit maximization decision of a producer, which takes into account the producer's cost of capital for a given investment. In general, a profit-maximizing producer should fund the set of projects that have an expected return equal to or greater than their cost of capital. If a producer lacks the cash on hand to fund a profitable project, the producer can secure additional funding from financial institutions or investors. If the producer has resources remaining, after funding all the projects whose expected returns are higher than the cost of capital, this remainder should be invested elsewhere, not in sub-par projects that happen to be available to the firm. If a producer pursues the same set of projects in any event, then its incentives will not be improved from the mere fact of a windfall from consumers.[14]

Aside from its effect on the creation of new works, it is also possible as a logical matter that a term extension could affect a copyright holder's incentive to make investments in existing works. Such cases would occur in at most a small subset of copyrights, since extension has an incremental effect only after many years of copyright, and (as suggested above) most works lose their economic value to the initial copyright owner after a very few years. The same will tend to be true of improvements. For those remaining works where post-creation investments might be thought a significant factor, a twenty-year copyright extension will tend to have little or no incremental effect. For investments such as branding, other legal instruments such as trademark and rights of publicity already protect the investment. For other improvements, such as translations, a separate

[14] The analysis in the text applies to media companies and other producers with substantial resources or access to U.S. capital markets. For a starving artist who lacked resources or access, more resources might permit the artist to fund a larger set of projects. But, for an extension in existing term to help with this, the artist would have to already own an existing copyright about to expire under the pre-CTEA term, which is unlikely.

copyright in the improvement is available. Overall, a twenty-year extension seems unlikely to have a significant effect on post-creation incentives.

B. The CTEA Increases The Social Cost Of Monopoly

A full economic analysis of the CTEA's incremental effects requires an evaluation of its benefits and costs, compared to the effects of the pre-CTEA term. As discussed above, the benefits, in the form of additional incentives to create new works, are at most very small in the case of extended copyright for new works, and insignificant with respect to existing works. For the CTEA to make economic sense as an efficiency-enhancing measure, the costs should be similarly small. The remainder of the brief considers two sources of cost that are affected by the CTEA: misallocations due to inefficient pricing and the effective tax that copyright extension imposes upon the creation of new works.

The economic story of inefficient pricing under monopoly is a familiar one. In a competitive market, sellers undercut one another, with the consequence that price tends to fall to marginal cost. A price equal to marginal cost ensures an efficient allocation of resources, since all consumers who value the good at more than its marginal cost will purchase the good at that price. By contrast, a monopolist can set price above marginal cost for a sustained period of time. At this higher price, some consumers will be unwilling to purchase the good, although they would have purchased it at a price equal to marginal cost.

These missed opportunities for selling give rise to an inefficient allocation, since some consumers value the good more than its marginal cost of production, but less than the higher price charged by the monopolist. The consequences for allocation are important in the case of creative works because marginal costs are very low. Production and distribution of an additional unit are relatively cheap, once the work is created. If copyright gives a producer substantial market power, the price may be well above marginal cost, in which case a large number of consumers may be excluded.

Since the CTEA lengthens the term of copyright by twenty years, it permits above-cost pricing for a longer period of time, and thus it imposes an incremental burden on society. But it is important to note when these higher costs are incurred. As discussed in the previous section, the increase in incentives to create is very small in present-value terms, because it is so far in the future. By contrast, the additional burden of the CTEA is composed of the effect from extension in existing works, as well as an effect in the future from works not yet created.

The extension for existing works accounts for the bulk of the economic cost. (For works not yet created, the additional cost of term extension is small in present value, just as the additional compensation for creating new works is small in present value.) Again, a present-value analysis helps to underscore this point. The closer to copyright expiration a work was under the pre-CTEA regime, the larger the present value of the additional cost imposed by the CTEA. For works whose copyrights were near expiration when the CTEA was passed, this effect is especially large: a deadweight loss experienced today is 224 times as large in present value as a deadweight loss eighty years from now (at a 7% interest rate).

Given the economic benefits and costs described so far, it is difficult to understand copyright term extension as an efficiency-enhancing measure. Moreover, it is especially difficult to understand the CTEA's extension for existing works by reference to efficiency. For existing works, particularly those whose pre-CTEA copyrights were about to expire, the social cost of monopoly pricing is at a maximum, and here the extension provides no counter-balancing increase in the incentive to produce new works.

The analysis so far has focused upon efficiency. The CTEA can also be understood in terms of its impact upon consumer welfare. A consumer-welfare-based analysis of monopoly takes notice of an additional consequence of the copyright holder's monopoly, namely the substantial transfer of resources from consumers to producers that results from prolonging the period of monopoly pricing. Given the redistribution from consumers to producers, the consequences for consumer welfare are more negative than the consequences for efficiency.[15]

II. THE CTEA REDUCES INNOVATION BY RESTRICTING THE PRODUCTION OF NEW CREATIVE WORKS THAT MAKE USE OF EXISTING MATERIALS

A copyright holder has two kinds of monopoly power, each of which is a potential source of producer profit and social cost. First, as discussed above, copyright imparts control over the quantity produced of a work, permitting the holder to maintain a price higher than marginal cost. Second, copyright provides control over the production of derivative works based in part on copyrighted material. In certain circumstances described below, this control results in higher costs and lower production of new creative works.

Many new creative works are built in part out of materials from existing works. For example, new fiction re-tells old stories, new documentaries re-use historical footage, and new music re-mixes and transforms old songs. Improvements in the technology of search and recombination continue to expand the economic importance of new creation based upon old materials.

If building-block materials are copyrighted, there are two sources of inefficiency to consider. If the later innovator must

---

[15] The twenty-year increase in European protection of U.S. copyrights will have an additional effect, a transfer of resources from European consumers to the owners of U.S. copyrights. This windfall to U.S. copyright holders is in addition to the transfer from U.S. consumers, and in general will not lower the profit-maximizing price charged to U.S. consumers, or lessen the inefficiency (and transfers from U.S. consumers) resulting from a producer's exercise of market power.

pay for use of the earlier work, this will raise the innovator's cost of making new works, reducing the set of new works produced. In addition, if the process of bargaining and contracting is itself costly, a copyright holder's control over derivative works imposes an additional tax on innovation.

In many cases efficient exchange is hampered by the presence of several kinds of transaction costs. First, a new creator may have difficulty locating an earlier copyright holder, particularly in the case of very old works that have been under copyright for a long time. Uncertainties about the identity of the original author or subsequent assignee of the copyright deepen the difficulty. When copyright holders are difficult to locate, it is costly to track them down, and, if it is even more difficult to locate copyright holders of older works, then transaction costs will increase disproportionately for these works.

Second, for documentaries and many other works, a new creator must negotiate with a large number of previous copyright holders, often for minimal uses of their works. When copyright holders are numerous, it is costly to negotiate and reach agreements with all of them. One result is a "tragedy of the anti-commons": when too many parties have actual or potential vetoes on the creation of an economically valuable object, that object will tend to be under-produced.[16] The resulting costs to society take two forms: the expenditure of resources to organize and complete these agreements, and a reduction in works created due to the higher costs of producing them.

As Ronald Coase and many others have pointed out,[17] economic efficiency is best promoted by legal arrangements that

---

[16] See James M. Buchanan & Yong J. Yoon, *Symmetric Tragedies: Commons and Anti-Commons*, 43 J.L. & ECON. 1 (2000).

[17] See Ronald H. Coase, *The Problem of Social Cost*, 3 J.L. & ECON. 1 (1960).

minimize transaction costs. Here, a limit on the duration of control rights over derivative works tends to reduce transaction costs. To the extent that the duration of derivative rights is expanded instead, there will tend to be an increase in wasteful expenditures to locate and bargain with copyright holders, as well as a reduction in the creation of new works based upon earlier copyrighted works. Here, the CTEA increases transaction costs by lengthening the rights over derivative works by twenty years, thus shrinking the pool of public domain materials available for recombination into new works.

This conclusion is subject to the condition that the owner of the original copyright is not somehow the most efficient creator of the subsequent work. Although sometimes applied to patent, this argument has little application to copyright. In copyright, diverse, "abundant" expression is the source of value, not successive refinements with respect to an agreed-upon metric of quality,[18] and a large number of disparate innovators may be better at producing abundance. Moreover, in the two situations described above, existing copyright holders are certainly not at an advantage. If the copyright holder is unaware of the copyright (for example, a descendant of the original author) or its value for creating derivative works, he is unlikely to explore possible derivative works in a vigorous way. And, when many existing works have to be pooled and recombined to create a new work, the owner of a single existing work is at no practical advantage in creating the new work, as she still must negotiate with all the other owners. In the case of this single owner, too, transaction costs are minimized when the later innovator has a right to use earlier materials.

In short, a lengthened copyright term under the CTEA keeps additional materials out of new creators' hands. Would-be new creators face increased transaction costs: the necessity to engage in costly locating (especially for very old works, the

---

[18] See Paul Goldstein, *Infringement of Copyright in Computer Programs*, 47 U. PITT. L. REV. 1119, 1123 (1986).

very ones that would be in the public domain but for the CTEA) and bargaining with multiple parties. These higher costs give new creators less incentive to produce. As a result, the CTEA imposes two kinds of burden on society, fewer new works produced and higher transaction costs in the creation of some works.

CONCLUSION

Comparing the main economic benefits and costs of the CTEA, it is difficult to understand term extension for both existing and new works as an efficiency-enhancing measure. Term extension in existing works provides no additional incentive to create new works and imposes several kinds of additional costs. Term extension for new works induces new costs and benefits that are too small in present-value terms to have much economic effect. As a policy to promote consumer welfare, the CTEA fares even worse, given the large transfer of resources from consumers to copyright holders.

Respectfully submitted.

ROY T. ENGLERT, JR.
Counsel of Record
Robbins, Russell, Englert,
Orseck & Untereiner LLP
1801 K Street, N.W.
Suite 411
Washington, D.C. 20006
(202) 775-4500

Counsel for Amici Curiae

May 20, 2002

APPENDIX

1a

APPENDIX A

LIST OF SIGNATORIES TO THE BRIEF

George A. Akerlof
Goldman Professor of Economics, University of California, Berkeley
Nobel Memorial Prize in Economic Sciences, 2001

Kenneth J. Arrow
Joan Kenney Professor of Economics (emeritus), Stanford University
Nobel Memorial Prize in Economic Sciences, 1972

Timothy F. Bresnahan
Professor of Economics, Stanford University
Co-Director, Center for Research on Employment and Economic Growth, Stanford University

James M. Buchanan
Advisory General Director, Center for Study of Public Choice, George Mason University
Nobel Memorial Prize in Economic Sciences, 1986

Ronald H. Coase
Clifton R. Musser Professor of Economics (emeritus), University of Chicago Law School
Nobel Memorial Prize in Economic Sciences, 1991

Linda R. Cohen
Professor of Economics, University of California, Irvine
Professor of Social Science and Law, University of Southern California Law School

Milton Friedman
Senior Research Fellow, Hoover Institution
Nobel Memorial Prize in Economic Sciences, 1976

2a

Jerry R. Green
John Leverett Professor in the University and David A. Wells Professor of Political Economy, Harvard University

Robert W. Hahn
Director, AEI-Brookings Joint Center for Regulatory Studies

Thomas W. Hazlett
Senior Fellow, Manhattan Institute for Policy Research

C. Scott Hemphill
Kapnick Fellow in Economics, Stanford University

Robert E. Litan
Vice President and Director of Economic Studies, Brookings Institution
Co-Director, AEI-Brookings Joint Center for Regulatory Studies

Roger G. Noll
Morris M. Doyle Centennial Professor of Public Policy, Stanford University

Richard Schmalensee
John C. Head III Dean, Sloan School of Management, Massachusetts Institute of Technology

Steven Shavell
Professor of Law and Economics, Harvard Law School
Director, John M. Olin Center for Law, Economics, and Business, Harvard Law School

Hal R. Varian
Dean, School of Information Management and Systems, University of California, Berkeley
Class of 1944 Professorship, Department of Economics, University of California, Berkeley

Richard J. Zeckhauser
Frank P. Ramsey Professor of Political Economy, John F. Kennedy School of Government, Harvard University

3a

APPENDIX B

PRESENT VALUE OF ADDITIONAL COMPENSATION

For an individual author:*

Interest Rate	*Compensation, Years 1-80*	*Additional Compensation, Years 81-100*	*Percent Increase*
5%	$19.60	$0.25	1.28%
7%	$14.22	$0.05	0.33%
10%	$10.00	$0.00	0.04%

For a work for hire:

Interest Rate	*Compensation, Years 1-75*	*Additional Compensation, Years 76-95*	*Percent Increase*
5%	$19.48	$0.32	1.65%
7%	$14.20	$0.07	0.47%
10%	$9.99	$0.01	0.07%

* Individual author calculations assume authorship thirty years prior to death, which implies eighty years of copyright without the CTEA, one hundred years of protection with the CTEA.

Calculations assume a constant annual revenue stream. For ease of exposition, annual payments are assumed to be $1, but the percentage increases are unchanged for larger or smaller constant annual streams.

[2]

Harvard Journal of Law & Technology
Volume 18, Number 2 Spring 2005

SEVENTEEN FAMOUS ECONOMISTS WEIGH IN ON COPYRIGHT: THE ROLE OF THEORY, EMPIRICS, AND NETWORK EFFECTS

Stan J. Liebowitz & Stephen Margolis***

TABLE OF CONTENTS

I. INTRODUCTION

On May 20, 2002, seventeen economists, including five Nobel laureates, presented an amicus curiae brief discussing the economics of copyright extension in support of the petitioners in *Eldred v. Ashcroft*, a Supreme Court case challenging the constitutionality of the Sonny Bono Copyright Term Extension Act of 1998 ("CTEA").[1] The economists' amicus brief was unusual in several respects, not least in that it brought together a group of economists almost as notable for its diversity of opinion (spanning the ideological spectrum from Kenneth Arrow to Milton Friedman) as for its academic distinction.[2]

---

* Professor of Managerial Economics, School of Management, University of Texas at Dallas.

** Professor of Economics, College of Management, North Carolina State University.

1. Brief of George A. Akerlof et al. as Amici Curiae in Support of Petitioners at 12, Eldred v. Ashcroft, 537 U.S. 186 (2003) (No. 01-618).

2. The signatories to the amicus brief are: George A. Akerlof, Kenneth J. Arrow, Timothy F. Bresnahan, James M. Buchanan, Ronald H. Coase, Linda R. Cohen, Milton Fried-

When such a distinguished and broad panel of economists appears to agree on a subject, it would be reasonable to assume that they reflect the profession's views as a whole. Further, it would be natural to expect that any document signed by these economists would meet the same exacting standards normally associated with their works. Also, that this document was used in an important legal matter reasonably merits an even higher degree of confidence in its integrity. In short, readers would have every reason to believe that the arguments set forth in this document are sound down to the smallest details. Yet this is not the case.

The *Eldred* case is now resolved; the Supreme Court has found against the petitioners. Nevertheless, active debates in both the legal and economic literatures raise questions regarding the particulars of copyright law and its underlying principles. Thus, the issues raised in the economists' brief remain important. Critics of copyright are making bold claims, in some instances even advocating its abolition.[3] Scholars in the fields of law and economics will continue to address the economics of copyright duration in the foreseeable future, so it is important that they understand the imperfections in the economists' brief. This Article provides a counterweight to the amicus brief, identifying some points the economists ignored, clarifying some discussions they did not quite get right, and providing data that runs counter to some assumptions they made.

II. BACKGROUND

The CTEA has two major provisions: First, it extends the term of copyright protection for a given work from fifty years after the author's death to seventy years after the author's death, or, in the case of institutional authors, from seventy-five to ninety-five years.[4] Second, it applies this extension retroactively to works produced prior to its enactment.

The CTEA was criticized vigorously from a number of perspectives, but most forcefully from an active academic community advocating expansion of an "information commons."[5] *Eldred v. Ashcroft* became one of the vehicles for this opposition to copyright extension

man, Jerry R. Green, Robert W. Hahn, Thomas W. Hazlett, C. Scott Hemphill, Robert E. Litan, Roger G. Noll, Richard Schmalensee, Steven Shavell, Hal R. Varian, and Richard J. Zeckhauser. Akerlof et al., *supra* note 1, at 1.

3. Michele Boldrin & David Levine, *The Case Against Intellectual Property*, AM. ECON. REV., May 2002, at 209–12 (suggesting that no protection of intellectual property, either de facto or de jure, is needed); *see also* Raymond S.R. Ku, *The Creative Destruction of Copyright: Napster and the New Economics of Digital Technology*, 69 U. CHI. L. REV. 263 (2002) (suggesting that intellectual property protection is unnecessary for digital products).

4. 17 U.S.C. § 302 (1998).

5. *See, e.g.*, Creative Commons, *at* http://creativecommons.org (last visited Mar. 15, 2005).

and became a *cause celebre* in the online and academic communities. The litigation was coordinated at the Berkman Center for Internet and Society and argued before the Supreme Court by Lawrence Lessig, a leading advocate for expansion of the public domain.

Eric Eldred publishes literary works on the Internet that have entered the public domain. The CTEA prevented certain works from entering the public domain that he intended to provide on his website. Eldred claimed that the CTEA was unconstitutional on two grounds: First, he argued that it violated the Patent and Copyright Clause of the Constitution, which specifies that patents and copyrights are provided for a limited time and that they are authorized in order to promote the "Progress of Science and the useful Arts."[6] Second, Eldred claimed that the CTEA was a violation of free speech. The Supreme Court has now ruled on the case, rejecting Eldred's claims.

While legal briefs do not always provide balanced views, the prominence of the *Eldred* economists appears to lend their brief substantial credibility. Without appropriate scrutiny, their brief could be taken by scholars and the general public as expressing the definitive view on the costs and benefits of copyright. This Article argues not that the CTEA extensions are clearly efficient, but that the case is not as one-sided as the economists' brief suggests.

There are important aspects of the economics of copyright that are ignored or not fully considered by the *Eldred* economists. They overlook factors, such as the elasticity of supply of creative works, which might reverse their conclusion about the impact of copyright extension on the creation of new works. They neglect the possibility that network effects in the market for derivative works might make a copyright commons inefficient, independent of any impact on supply. Finally, they avoid the difficult empirical work needed to support their conclusion.

III. BASIC POINTS IN THE BRIEF

The amicus brief makes two points:

(1) The portion of the law making the copyright extension retroactive makes little economic sense. The Constitution provides for copyright to provide incentives for authors to create. Yet there can be no incentive impact when copyright is extended on items that have already been created under a previous copyright regime.

(2) Extending copyright from life plus fifty years to life plus seventy years affects creation only through incremental revenues that accrue many years in the future. The impact of these incremental

6. U.S. CONST. art. I, § 8, cl. 8. A portion of the clause reads, "to promote the Progress of Science and useful Arts by securing for limited Times to Authors and Inventors the exclusive Right to their respective Writings and Discoveries."

revenues on present values is so small that it can have little incentive effect. Copyright extension brings about incremental deadweight losses that are incurred far in the future and discounted heavily. Although both factors are likely to be very small, the *Eldred* economists argue that copyright should not be extended, because copyright imposes current costs on the creators of new copyrighted items who reuse old material in their new works.

This Article agrees with the *Eldred* economists on the first point, if the analysis is restricted to incentives to create. It argues at length below, however, that there are other important considerations that might reverse this conclusion. The economists' second point is not as clear-cut and is incompletely explored in the brief. The following sections consider each of these points in reverse order. Finally, the Article presents data relevant to the evaluation of copyright extension.

IV. New Works: Comparisons of Costs and Benefits

The optimal length for copyright is not something that anyone can define with certainty. Although there have been claims in the literature that the optimal length is so short that copyright is unnecessary, there has been very little recent and serious examination of this issue.[7] Putting aside for now the matter of efficient management of existing works, how much can be said about the efficiency of copyright extension?

To make a full determination of the costs and benefits of copyright extension, economists need to know more about these markets than they currently do. Economists are far from alone in this ignorance; the information requirements are severe. The data that economists would need, but do not have, include (1) the number and value of new works created as a result of extensions of copyright duration (i.e., the elasticity of supply of creative works and the surplus created by additional works); (2) the reduction of surplus for reproductions of copyrighted materials under extended copyright, relative to the surplus that would be generated if copyright protection were less lengthy (i.e., the increased unnecessary deadweight losses). The general structure of the tradeoff between creation and use is well known. Nevertheless, commentators rarely consider a detailed construction of the values they compare. This Article presents such a construction. First, it identifies a shortcut that the economists took that caused them to understate the potential benefit of copyright extension. Next, it argues that a portion of the "deadweight loss" that is identified in the monopoly model of copyright is properly understood as a necessary cost of

7. Some of the earlier claims include Arnold Plant, *The Economic Aspects of Copyright in Books*, 1 ECONOMICA 167 (1934); Robert M. Hurt & Robert M. Schuchman, *The Economic Rationale of Copyright*, AM. ECON. REV., May 1966, at 421.

providing incentives for creation. This discussion sets the stage for presenting a diagrammatic model of the market for creative works. Using that model, this Article illustrates an instance in which copyright extension is beneficial. The model also permits identification of the various factors that one must account for to assess properly the merits of copyright extension.

A. The Gains and Losses from Extending Copyright

The *Eldred* economists use a shortcut to describe the benefits from an extension of copyright — they talk about the additional royalties generated by the extension. With such payments far in the future, the present value of extending copyright from, say, ninety to one hundred years, is likely to be very small. The *Eldred* economists emphasize the small present value of additional payments to authors in order to suggest that these payments can have only very limited effects on the creation of additional works. The benefits to society, however, are not the same as the present value of payments going to the copyright owners.[8]

Yet small increases in payment need not have small impacts on the creation of additional works. There is a possibility that for some authors, in some range of income and propensity to create, a small increase in present value could make an important difference in creative output, perhaps because they reach a point where they switch to full-time writing.[9]

At the conceptual level adopted by the amicus brief, it is certainly possible that there might be many potential authors with similar opportunity costs who, at the current copyright length, are on the margin of writing books. Figure 1 presents a very tight distribution of opportunity costs for authors. Even a trivial increase in the present value of royalty payments, such as the increase from royalties R to royalties S, might lead to a substantial increase in the number of works if the costs-of-creation distribution is dense at those magnitudes. If this is the case, small increases in payments from an expansion of copyright might result in large increases in the number of

8. *See* Wendy J. Gordon, *Authors, Publishers, and Public Goods: Trading Gold for Dross*, 36 LOY. L.A. L. REV. 159 (2002).

9. An example might be Charles Ives, working at his insurance job by day and writing music in his spare time. *See* Microsoft Encarta, Charles E(dward) Ives, *available at* http://encarta.msn.com/encyclopedia_761551849/Ives_Charles_E(dward).html (last visited Apr. 23, 2005).

Figure 1: Distribution of Authors' Costs

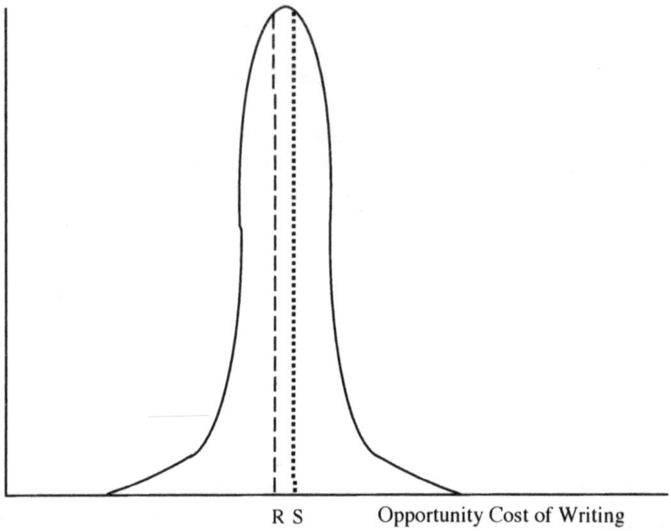

creative works, which in turn produces significant social benefits.[10]

Thus, the *Eldred* economists' focus on the royalty streams is incorrect. They should have focused instead on the impact of copyright changes on the value of forthcoming works. Section C will demonstrate that this error is not harmless. First, however, the next section reviews briefly the economic impacts of changes in the term of copyright.

B. Productive and Unproductive Deadweight Loss

Calling a deadweight loss "productive" might seem oxymoronic. However, some deadweight losses serve a useful function if they are unavoidable consequences of an incentive system for which there is no better alternative. Copyright engenders a deadweight loss as a byproduct of the incentives to create that it provides. A system of private

10. We assume that this large increase in works also leads to a large increase in surplus. We also assume that the new works do not decrease the surplus generated from older works. It is possible, of course, that the potential surplus for copyrighted works is limited, and that the increased surplus from these new works comes at the expense of decreased surplus for works that would otherwise have been consumed in place of the new works.

ownership providing the incentive for creation cannot give a reward to the creator without also having an apparent deadweight loss in the consumption market.[11]

While it is misleading to refer to a copyright as equivalent to a monopoly, the monopoly model is the easiest to apply and is the standard vehicle illustrating these issues.[12] Moreover, the monopoly model is the framework for the arguments in the amicus brief. When the following text refers to "books," readers should note that "books" stand in for any creative work.

Figure 2 is the standard textbook treatment of monopoly. Assume it represents the market for reproductions of a particular book title for some period of time. The demand for this title lasts for multiple time periods, each identical to the first.

The perfectly competitive solution is a price of Pc and quantity Qc, which yields no profit in the reproduction market with which to pay the creator of the title. This maximizes the surplus in the reproduction market (the sum of areas 1–5) for this title. However, the title will not be produced if the creator requires a positive payment to induce creation, which implies that no surplus at all will occur without some copyright protection. This is one of the problems Arrow identifies in his classic 1962 article.[13]

Though it is not ideal, a copyright provision that results in a monopoly output level still is likely to produce a positive value for society compared to no production at all. If copyright induces creation of works, society benefits from the production of copies of this title in the amount of 1+2+3+4, less the fixed costs of creation. Area 5 is normally called a deadweight loss, because one imagines that in a competitive market, it would be consumer surplus.[14] However, being able to imagine an improvement is not the same as being able to bring it about, as Demsetz points out in his classic response to Arrow.[15] Once a copyright regime is adopted as the mechanism to stimulate

11. Perfect price discrimination can avoid the deadweight loss, and various approximations to such price discrimination can reduce this loss. Such measures, however, provide only imperfect relief.

12. Although copyright provides a monopoly over the particular title, there might be many close substitute titles available. This monopoly is no different than the fact that every firm has a monopoly on the name of its product. Kia and Mitsubishi have a monopoly over automobiles with their names, although few would argue that they have monopoly power in the automobile market. *See* Edmund W. Kitch, *Elementary and Persistent Errors in the Economic Analysis of Intellectual Property*, 53 VAND. L. REV. 1727, 1729 (2000).

13. *See* Kenneth J. Arrow, *Economic Welfare and the Allocation of Resources for Invention*, *in* THE RATE AND DIRECTION OF INVENTIVE ACTIVITY: ECONOMIC AND SOCIAL FACTORS 609 (R. Nelson ed., 1962).

14. This also assumes that copyright owners cannot perfectly price discriminate, because the ability to do so would convert area 5 into producers' surplus.

15. *See* Harold Demsetz, *Information and Efficiency: Another Viewpoint*, 12 J.L. & ECON. 1 (1969).

Figure 2: The Market for Reproductions of a Title

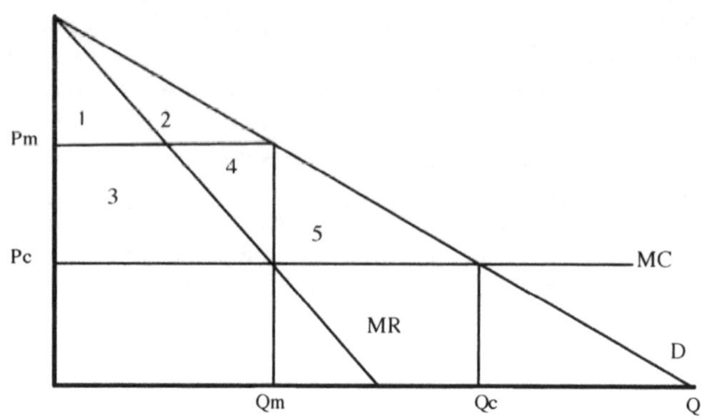

production of creative works, area 5 is no longer a feasible component of the surplus and thus is not really a deadweight loss. Area 5 can be thought of as a "productive" deadweight loss, or the cost of copyright, since it is required in order to generate any surplus at all.

The disagreement between Demsetz and Arrow largely hinged on defining the term "efficient." Was the efficient output the theoretical ideal, as Arrow suggested, or was it the best that could be actually achieved, as Demsetz proposed? Although the Authors believe that Demsetz won that point, this Article does not need to answer that question for the purpose of evaluating copyright length. Once one accepts copyright as the mechanism to provide incentives for creative works, and agrees that all books are given the same copyright term, then the "productive" deadweight losses are best understood as irrelevant to welfare considerations, since there is no other manner in which they could become part of the surplus within the confines of the chosen copyright mechanism.

The analysis further suggests that deadweight losses need to be treated carefully in a determination of the optimal copyright duration. For example, if one were to adopt a methodology of comparing the gains to the losses when extending copyright, a proper cost-benefit analysis would not contrast the sum of areas 1 through 4 with area 5, since area 5 is not a loss. In other words, even if area 5 were larger than the sum of areas 1 through 4, it would be incorrect to conclude that society would be better off not having this good produced at all.

Of course, this diagram now illustrates gains (of copyright extension) with no balancing losses. How then could one arrive at any optimal length of copyright less than infinity? The answer is that once a creator has received sufficient payment to generate creation, any further payment is unnecessary. Therefore, any further deadweight losses are no longer productive and are thus unnecessary.

If the creator receives a payment in the first period (the sum of areas 3 and 4) that fully covers the cost of creation, then, in the second period, area 5 is an old-fashioned deadweight loss. In this second period, the cost of copyright extension is not mitigated by a balancing benefit, since the author would have created the book anyway, based only on first period revenues.

Who would argue that all deadweight losses should be treated alike? Unfortunately, such a conclusion might occur to the casual reader of the economists' amicus brief, which states:

> First, the CTEA [Copyright Term Extension Act of 1998] extends the period during which a copyright holder determines the quantity produced of a work, and thus increases the inefficiency from above-cost pricing by lengthening its duration. *With respect to the term extension for new works, the present value of the additional cost is small, just as the present value of incremental benefits is small.*[16]

The *Eldred* economists talk about additional costs from extending the term of copyright, but neglect to explain how these costs are calculated, save for a brief discussion of the harm brought about by the monopoly restrictions on quantity. They make no attempt to distinguish those deadweight losses that are productive (i.e., necessary to bring about additional creative works) from those that are not.

Even more troublesome is their claim that the present value of additional benefits is necessarily small. The parallel construction between the benefits and costs in the italicized sentence incorrectly implies that both benefits and costs occur far into the future, which leads to their being heavily discounted and thus small. The logic is correct for the increased costs of copyright extension, which only begin to occur when the current copyright term expires, but it is not true for all benefits. The present value of additional *revenues* to authors might be heavily discounted (and small), but this need not imply that the impact of these revenues on the creation of works is small, since evaluators need to know something about the elasticity of creation before making any such statements. Further, the benefits from any additional creative works begin to accrue immediately; they are not discounted far into the future, the way that incremental revenues and incremental costs are.

16. Akerlof et al., *supra* note 1, at 1 (emphasis added).

C. An Example of Beneficial Copyright Extension

Figure 3 shows how copyright extension might lead to large benefits even with a lengthy original term of copyright. This diagram assumes that all titles have equal costs of reproduction and equal value to consumers, but have different costs of writing. The horizontal axis has new titles, aligned in increasing order by the cost of creation. All the dollar values are discounted to present values.

Figure 3: The Market for Titles

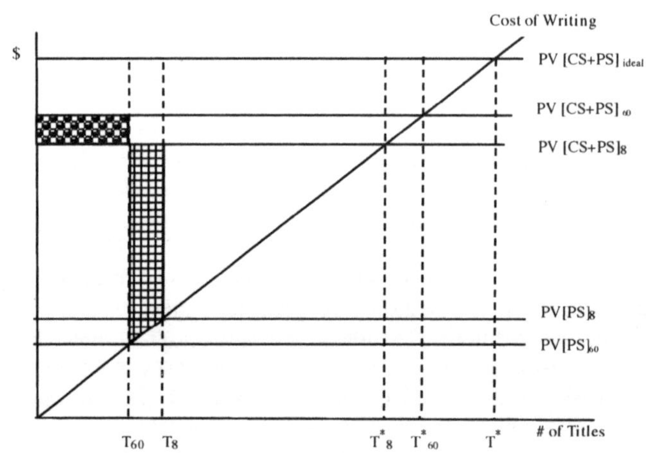

The opportunity cost of creation is represented by the upward-sloping "Cost of Writing" curve. This example assumes a linear curve to indicate a constant increase in titles as payments to authors increase. Books will be written as long as the (discounted) rewards to the author are greater than the costs of writing the book, where writing costs are stipulated to include editing, design, and any other fixed costs of creation that are avoided by follow-on publishers. These costs of writing are not included in the calculation of consumers' and producers' surpluses in the reproduction market, which are modeled in this diagram. The model assumes that the market for publishers' acquisition of titles is perfectly competitive, so that the author captures the entire producers' surplus in the market for the reproductions of a single title.

Since each title is assumed to have identical values to consumers and identical costs of reproduction, the present value of the sum of producer and consumer surplus is the same for each book and can be represented by a horizontal line for any potential copyright regime. The ideal value of each title (e.g., perfect price discrimination by the publisher selling copies of titles, the present value of areas 1–5 in Figure 2) is represented by the highest horizontal line labeled $PV[CS+PS]_{ideal}$. For any number of titles, the area under this line represents the potential value of the titles to society — that is, the total value of the titles if each were exploited to exhaust all possible gains from trade before the costs of creation are considered.

T^* represents the optimal number of titles that would be produced in this ideal world, since all titles to the left have a potential surplus in the market for reproductions that is greater than the cost of writing the book, and all titles to the right have a creation cost greater than the potential surplus.

In a world of copyright, the surplus in the reproduction market is less than ideal, however. Figure 3 represents two cases: an infinite copyright life (represented by 8) and a sixty year copyright life, indicated by the subscripts. Although the extension of copyright length proposed by the CTEA was far less than infinity, this Article uses the assumption of infinite life for illustration.

The present values of the realized total surplus (producer plus consumer surpluses) under the copyright regimes are shown in the diagram as $PV[CS+PS]_{60}$ and $PV[CS+PS]_{8}$ for a sixty year and infinite copyright life, respectively. Assuming that the demand for each book title persists for more than sixty years, the present value of the total surplus in the reproduction market is less with an infinite copyright than with a sixty-year copyright since the reproduction market would never achieve its efficient (non-monopoly) output under an infinite copyright regime. The vertical difference between these two horizontal lines might be quite small. This is because the surpluses after sixty years are highly discounted in present value terms, as the *Eldred* economists argued, although this Article draws them as having a non-negligible difference in value.

The payments received by authors are the present values of the producer's surplus in the reproduction market, and are reflected by horizontal lines PV[PS], with obviously smaller values than the total surplus.

Next, how does a change from a sixty-year term to an infinite term affect the market? The increase in unnecessary deadweight loss for the books that would have been written with a copyright length of sixty years (those books to the left of T_{60} in Figure 3) is given by the rectangle with the embedded spheres. This area reflects the lower surpluses in the reproduction market that result from the increased life of the monopoly restriction (from sixty years to infinity).

The change in the number of new titles depends on the additional reward received by authors *and* on the elasticity of creation with respect to reward. Figure 3 assumed a constant elasticity throughout, although Figure 1 illustrated a case where the elasticity was particularly large at the original copyright length.[17] A greater elasticity would increase the value from copyright extension. The value to society from the increase in titles is given by the cross-hatched area, which is drawn to be larger than the harm from the unnecessary deadweight loss. In this example, it is clear that an infinite copyright is better than a sixty-year copyright. This is a straightforward possibility that is short-changed by the *Eldred* economists.

Note: (1) that the optimal number of titles in Demsetz' sense under either copyright regime is greater than the actual number of titles, because authors only receive part of the surplus, and (2) that the optimal number of titles declines as copyright term increases, because total surplus decreases. Note as well that the optimal number of titles is always less than the ideal number of titles (in Arrow's sense), because the total potential surpluses are not realized under any real-world copyright regime.

The full benefits from copyright extension include the consumer and producer surpluses, starting immediately and continuing into the future, resulting from any additional works generated by the copyright extension. These benefits are not all highly discounted. It is these full benefits — not the relatively minor incremental revenues that the *Eldred* economists discussed — that must be traded off against the additional deadweight losses that occur far in the future.[18]

A correct assessment of copyright extension balances the present value of the surpluses generated by the new works resulting from the copyright extension against the heavily discounted, *additional unnecessary* deadweight losses for those works that would be created in the absence of the extension.

Finally, there is the question of how realistic the construction of Figure 3 might be. That depends on many factors. In the real world, how dense is the distribution of opportunity costs otherwise portrayed in Figure 1? Where in that distribution are the points representing pre-extension and extended copyright length and what are the resulting elasticities of supply? How is the surplus divided between authors and readers? The assumption in Figure 3 that all titles are of ex post equal value is clearly false. Are the more valuable titles likely to get produced first? Without additional research, the *Eldred* economists were not in a position to state whether the current copyright length is too long or too short.

17. *See supra* Figure 1 and accompanying text.

18. The amicus brief argues that the deadweight losses are felt immediately. Akerlof et al., *supra* note 1, at 1. However, this is only true for the minority of cases involving aged preexisting works under *retroactive* copyright extension. In these cases, the works that were to enter the public domain in the immediate future instead remain under the control of the copyright owner, generating immediate deadweight losses.

V. RETROACTIVE EXTENSION OF COPYRIGHT TERM

The seventeen economists' claim regarding retroactive extension (point (2) in Part III above) appears obvious, because lengthening the term of copyright can have no effect on the size or quality of the body of creative works that existed at the time that the CTEA was enacted. However, lengthening the term of copyright increases the price for using already-created materials that would otherwise move into the public domain. This price elevation results in the monopoly deadweight loss that occurs where intellectual property is priced above reproduction cost. Since these costs are not balanced by any new creations, the retroactive extension of copyright is clearly socially inefficient.

The *Eldred* economists thus claim that the argument regarding retroactive copyright extension is completely one-sided. However, there are certain features of copyright law that the economists ignored in their brief, inflating their estimation of the costs of copyright. Furthermore, there are social benefits to copyright extension. Therefore, the situation is not as dire as the economists predicted: the costs do not clearly outweigh the benefits.

The amicus brief does acknowledge the possibility that such after-the-fact extensions of copyright might increase the incentives to create for future authors who may expect the same treatment in any subsequent copyright extension. They regard this as a minor influence, however, and this Article agrees.[19]

A. *Efficiency of Ownership*

The political fight over the CTEA appears largely to have been about its impact on already existing works. Indeed, potential revenues in 2110 are probably not a big incentive for Marshall Mathers or Shania Twain to crank out CDs. However, the rights to derivative works are an important matter to current owners of aged works and to non-owners, such as Mr. Eldred, who would now like to use these aged works. Public choice considerations nicely predict the players in the recent controversy — on both sides, they are parties with interests in old works. These interests are worth pursuing because they are not discounted by seventy, eighty, or one hundred years.

Eldred is aggrieved because he is unable to republish works that were written in the 1920s. In support of the CTEA, amicus briefs were submitted by various well-known owners of mature copyrights, such as Dr. Seuss Enterprises, Allene White (owner of E.B. White's copy-

19. The *Eldred* Court did note, however, that Congress has consistently applied copyright extensions retroactively, citing fairness arguments that legislators have repeatedly raised to support that practice.

rights in *Stuart Little* and *Charlotte's Web*), and Barbara and Madeline Bemelmans (owner of Ludwig Bemelmans' copyrights in the Madeline series).

The issue is management of existing creative works. The economists' brief considers only the monopoly deadweight losses — one side of the argument — and concludes that all the weight is against extension. Another issue well-known to economists is not noted in the brief: open access is not a universally preferable way to manage a resource.[20] The tragedy of the commons is thought not to hold for non-rivalrous goods (i.e., the intellectual property itself), since the reading of a story by one person does not prevent others from reading it as well.[21] It is possible, however, that one person's ownership of a copy of a book might alter the utility of another person's ownership, or that one person's creation of a derivative work based on the book might alter the value of another's derivative work. There are several reasons why consumers might want to circumscribe others' access to intellectual property through copyright law.

The Authors are certainly not the first to note a stewardship role in intellectual property protection. Edmund Kitch argues that patent is better understood as a claim-staking system rather than as a monopoly, allowing efficient exploitation of a technological realm.[22] In a recent paper, William Landes and Richard Posner elaborate on the advantages of copyright ownership, noting the possibility of excessive or inappropriate uses of intellectual properties and the role of copyright in avoiding the common access problem.[23]

1. The Possibility of Misuse

Movies, among other derivative works, are large, risky investments that would be made more risky in the absence of the exclusivity

20. The closest the brief comes to mentioning this issue is their acknowledgement that extending copyright might increase the copyright owners' incentives to invest in improvements to the creative work. Akerlof et al., *supra* note 1, at 9. The amici mostly dismiss this as an issue, noting that "a twenty-year copyright extension will have little or no incremental effect." *Id.* Misuse or excessive activity in the creation of derivatives does not appear in their discussion, nor does any role of copyright in addressing such problems.

21. See Denis S. Karjala, Statement of Copyright and Intellectual Property Law Professors in Opposition to H.R. 604, H.R. 2589, and S. 505, The Copyright Term Extension Act 9 (Jan. 28, 1998), *available at* http://homepages.law.asu.edu/%7Edkarjala/OpposingCopyrightExtension/legmats/1998Statementhtml.

22. *See* Edmund W. Kitch, *The Nature and Function of the Patent System*, 20 J.L. & ECON. 265, 266 (1977).

23. William M. Landes & Richard A. Posner, *Indefinitely Renewable Copyright*, 70 U. CHI. L. REV. 471, 485 (2003). Landes and Posner discuss the possibility of copyright externalities, both technological and pecuniary. In turn, they are reacting to a statement in a brief by a group of intellectual property law professors that declares: "There can be no overgrazing of intellectual property, however, because intellectual property cannot be destroyed or even diminished by consumption." Karjala, *supra* note 21.

that copyright law provides. Absent copyright protection, others have every incentive to produce further derivative works. As an example, *The Grinch*, made in 2000, cost over $125 million to produce. How would the prospects for the movie be affected if just before its release, the Grinch character suddenly appeared in pornographic movies or advertising for cigarettes, altering the public's view of the character? As rational actors, motion picture executives would anticipate this situation and possibly might not make the movie in the first place. The copyright owner's role is similar to the private owner of a natural resource that can be subject to crowding. In both cases, the owner tries to prevent dissipation of value through misuse of an asset. A rational owner would approve derivative projects that maximize his or her profits. Copyright policy must balance beneficial restrictions that constitute stewardship over resources against standard monopoly losses.

There are, of course, many expensive derivative works that are based upon creations entirely in the public domain. The question is whether they are produced as regularly or as well as they would be if they were protected by copyright. Further, one must consider whether they are produced under greater secrecy, raising their costs, in order to protect themselves from contemporaneous imitators. This is an empirical question to which economists do not yet have the answer.

Malicious or offensive derivative uses of some creative works might seriously diminish their value without a sufficient offset in the form of public benefit.[24] Of course, the law accepts some damage to the value of creative works when they are subject to parody or criticism. However, these fair-use exceptions to copyright protection exist because they clearly serve a purpose that is expected, in the aggregate, to pass a cost-benefit test.

2. Snob, Veblen, and Aesthetic Network Effects

A second concern for efficient management of intellectual property deals with a particular type of network effect. As currently used, the term "network effects" is almost exclusively associated with positive effects — each user's utility increases with the number of users. But, as congestion externalities show, network effects can also be negative.[25] One of the earliest and most original treatments of network effects (although that term was not yet in use) was the paper by Harvey Leibenstein, who considered both positive effects (i.e., "bandwagon") and negative effects (i.e., "snob" and "Veblen").[26] Snob

24. The existence of a "Madeline Does Dallas" might lead to some awkward questions during bedtime stories.

25. *See* Stan J. Liebowitz & Stephen E. Margolis, *Network Externality: An Uncommon Tragedy*, J. ECON. PERSP., Spring 1994, at 133.

26. Harvey Leibenstein, *Bandwagon, Snob, and Veblen Effects in the Theory of Consumers' Demand*, 64 QUARTERLY J. ECON. 183 (1950).

effects occur when consumers derive more utility as the number of other users of the product decreases, the opposite of the current use of network effects.[27] Veblen effects occur when consumers derive additional utility from a product as its market price gets higher.

Architectural works, which are protected by copyright, are instructive examples of negative network efforts. Builders in housing developments usually offer a variety of elevations of houses of the same floor plan. The practice of building varied elevations cannot be a monopoly restriction to elevate price, since the restriction on any one design does not restrict the total output of a set of very good substitutes. Yet, builders do vary designs and often enter contracts obligating them to do so. The production of different elevations does increase cost, relative to building the same design over and over again, but the total value of a development must increase by more than these additional costs, or builders would discontinue the practice. In tract developments, a builder's ownership of a large number of lots may internalize the negative network effect of visually identical houses. In other instances, a subdivision's covenants and restrictions can internalize them. And of course, copyright can internalize this "aesthetic" network effect (to coin a new term).

These are real external effects, not just pecuniary ones. Many consumers derive less utility if their house looks very similar to all the others in their subdivision. If the market could not internalize consumer preference for variety, total wealth would be reduced. The decisions of individual consumers might lead to a lack of variety, since the harm to others from additional uses of a design does not directly enter the individual decision maker's utility calculus.

The scope of such external effects is quite large and underappreciated. For example, the literature on resale price maintenance suggests a "demonstration" motive by manufacturers who try to keep retailers from charging too low a price.[28] Some retailers may not provide needed demonstration services, relying instead on free-riding on other retailers who do provide it, causing the service to disappear under competitive pressures. An additional explanation, especially for those cases where demonstrations seem unimportant, would be that some retailers do not provide enough of an exclusive aura about their products (snob effect), or some retailers might lower the price to a

27. The term "snob" carries an unfortunate connotation that mischaracterizes many of these network effects. Ordinary consumers often evidence a preference for expressing individuality. An image may delight the eyes if it is seen every now and then, but it may seem absolutely banal if it appears on every telephone pole.

28. *See* Lester G. Telser, *Why Should Manufacturers Want Fair Trade?*, 3 J.L. & ECON. 86, 91 (1960). Since the manufacturer receives the same price from the retailer independent of the retailer's price, it would appear that the manufacturer would be pleased to have the retailer increase total sales without the manufacturer needing to lower his price. Yet, there are numerous cases where manufacturers try to limit retailers from charging too little.

level that distresses other consumers of the product (Veblen effect), in either case lowering the utility for all the other users.

Such external effects also might explain why competition does not lower the prices of high-end items (top-of-the-line automobiles, stereo equipment, appliances, etc.) which are known to have higher margins and yet where monopoly power appears to be missing. Competitors with lower prices for equivalent products would not take customers away from the higher-priced product, and competition would not reduce markups, if the customers derive utility from the fact that the original product is sold to a more exclusive clientele. Such external effects can also explain why customers prefer diamonds to cubic zirconia.

Within the world of copyrighted works, evidence of these aesthetic network effects is plentiful. The practice among artists of numbering prints and publicizing the total number in the series, with a promise not to increase the number of prints, might be a mere monopoly restriction, but it also might be a way of increasing the actual utility that a consumer enjoys. Snob effects might help to explain why original paintings sell for so much more than almost perfect forgeries that seemingly provide the same visual experience.[29] These effects might help explain the behavior and existence of the designer clothing industry and the custom-home building industry. In all these cases, demand itself is a function of the number of users. Where these effects appear, they affect the shape of the demand curve — they are not simply movements along a demand curve.

Where there are technological network effects such as these, it is important that these effects be internalized. Firms producing copies or derivatives of creative works after the copyright expires may be in the position of fisherman on an open access lake. They produce at their own private optima, not taking into account the effects that they have on other producers. Ownership can effectively manage these interactions, and copyright provides that ownership. The difficulty, of course, is distinguishing between pecuniary and real (technological) effects. Internalizing pecuniary effects leads to monopoly; internalizing real effects leads to efficient levels of activity.

These aesthetic network effects may be prevalent for some classes of creative works. They may be important for simple copies of visual works that are publicly displayed, musical and literary works that are used in advertising, and for decorative items. They may also be important for derivative works of all sorts. At a minimum, one needs to know something about the empirical realities of these markets before

29. Obviously, for works still under copyright, a forgery might sell for less, since it violates copyright. For the large number of works in the public domain, however, it is still the case that copies that can only be discerned by experts will not sell for as high a price as the original.

making pronouncements about the efficiency, or lack of efficiency, in the copyright law.

B. The Costs to Current Creators of Derivative Works

A major portion of the economists' *Eldred* brief is devoted to a purported increase in the costs of creation resulting from copyright extension. They claim that because creative works derive inspiration and form from the creative works of the past, copyright stifles new creation, and extended copyright stifles creation unnecessarily. Their discussion is largely misguided in that it fails to take account of some of the special features of copyright.

The economists' brief cites a seminal paper by Landes and Posner that notes the costs and benefits of copyright extension.[30] The economists' brief is largely consistent with the first part of Landes and Posner, which presents a model of copyright, but it neglects a central purpose of their paper. Landes and Posner build a model of an abstract copyright law to illustrate the properties of an optimal level of protection, the determinants of that optimal level of protection, and the trade-off that exists at the optimum. They then use their model as a platform for explaining some of the specific features of actual copyright law. Their approach is summarized as follows:

> [V]arious doctrines of copyright law, such as the distinction between idea and expression and the fair use doctrine, can be understood as attempts to promote economic efficiency by balancing the effect of greater copyright protection — in encouraging the creation of new works by reducing copying — against the effect of less protection — in encouraging the creation of new works by reducing the cost of creating them.[31]

The economists' discussion of the costs of derivative works takes no note of the moderating influences of these features of copyright. There is no question that creators of derivative works have the greatest latitude, and therefore the lowest costs, where the works that they would employ are in the public domain. But the fair use exceptions and the distinction between the idea and the expression provide suffi-

30. William M. Landes & Richard A. Posner, *An Economic Analysis of Copyright Law*, 18 J. LEGAL STUD. 325, 347–61 (1989).

31. *Id.* at 333. If this Article limited its attention to the creation of additional works, it would conclude that retroactive extension of copyright is inefficient.

cient relief from copyright restrictions that a large share of creative reuses of protected works are permitted.[32]

This Article could paraphrase the Landes and Posner discussion of both the idea-expression distinction and fair use, and although it might be a breach of academic etiquette, it would not be a copyright violation. There are two reasons: First, these matters are discussed in a number of places, so it would be difficult to establish that Landes and Posner were the source. Second, while it would reflect the ideas in their discussion, it would not use their expression unless it constitutes a "lazy copy."

Copyright protects expression, not ideas. Many economists have seen *It's a Wonderful Life*, the Jimmy Stewart movie classic, and have read *The Choice*, Russell Roberts' treatment of free trade. Although Roberts uses the plot device of a man who must return to earth to earn his angel's wings, his book does not infringe the movie's copyright. Though clearly an important creative element of the movie, the plot device is not protected by copyright. Television addicts will also note the flock of shows that followed the *Friends* format or the current proliferation of *Survivor*-type shows. Artists do indeed draw on old themes, and they are allowed to do so. On the other hand, they are not allowed to incorporate details of copyrighted works. So the economists are correct in that copyright does raise artists' costs — copyright forces artists to do some work themselves. However, since only specific expressions are protected, extensive parts of the culture are not, as is sometimes claimed, walled off from creative re-use.

Fair use doctrine also includes important exemptions to copyright that further expand the legal reuses of existing works. An important example of fair use is parody, which allows works to be reused in certain kinds of creative transformations, such as comical parodies of books or movies using many recognizable details of the original work.

A recent case that captured a great deal of public attention illustrates that even very extensive borrowing from a creative work can fall under fair use. Alice Randall's novel, *The Wind Done Gone,* prompted objections from the Margaret Mitchell Trust, owners of the rights to *Gone with the Wind.*[33] *The Wind Done Gone* uses the characters and plot elements from the earlier work, but views them from the perspective of the slaves who lived and worked on the plantation.[34]

32. Fair use is a defense against the claim of copyright infringement, and is often used to allow portions of copyrighted works to be copied when the copying is likely not to harm the market. *See generally* Wendy J. Gordon, *Fair Use as Market Failure: A Structural and Economic Analysis of the* Betamax *Case and its Predecessors*, 82 COLUM. L. REV. 1600 (1982).

33. *See* Houghton Mifflin, The Wind Done Gone: Questions and Answers About This Dispute, *at* http://www.houghtonmifflinbooks.com/features/randall_url/qandas.shtml (last visited Mar. 15, 2005).

34. *Id.*

Although an initial injunction delayed publication, the Eleventh Circuit subsequently found that this new perspective both transformed the original work substantially and did so to provide important criticism.[35] Here again, copyright did not bar use of important elements of our culture that were essential to a creative work of social criticism. Critics of copyright deplore that Ms. Randall was forced to defend her fair use in court, but the fact that copyright occasionally imposes legal costs is not a sufficient argument for curtailing it. Additionally, Ms. Randall could have told her story without so directly borrowing the particulars of *Gone with the Wind* and its reservoir of publicity and sentiment, although that might have limited the scope of her market.

VI. What Do Economists Know about Copyright Length?

The CTEA's extension of the copyright term occurs far into the future, relative to the time when a copyrighted work is created. What are the odds that the extension will have any consequence for a creative work? To answer this, one must know something about the longevity of copyrighted works.

The amicus brief reports a Congressional Research Service study that finds that only a small percentage of works copyrighted during the 1920s and 1930s and renewed in the 1950s and 1960s had commercial value in 1998 (eleven percent of copyrights in books, twelve percent in musical works, and twenty-six percent in motion pictures).[36] It also reports that less than one percent of books had their copyrights renewed.[37] This interesting result can be read in a misleading fashion. Copyrighted works do not start life as equals. The great majority of copyrighted works never have much market value. It is well-known that a small percentage of titles account for a large share of sales of copyrighted materials.

In the mid-1980s, Liebowitz conducted an unpublished examination of the longevity of titles, which examined the concentration of sales. In 1986, adult hardbound trade books and book club sales together totaled approximately $1.7 billion.[38] That year, there were approximately 25,000 new hardbound trade titles produced, in addition to the hundreds of thousands of old titles in that category.[39] Best-

35. *See* Suntrust Bank v. Houghton Mifflin Co., 268 F.3d 1257 (11th Cir. 2001).

36. Akerlof et al., *supra* note 1, at 7 (citing Edward Rappaport, Cong. Research Serv., Copyright Term Extension: Estimating the Economic Values 6–14 (1998), *available at* http://countingcalifornia.cdlib.org/crs/pdf/98-144.pdf).

37. Rappaport, *supra* note 36, at 6.

38. The Bowker Annual of Library and Book Trade Information 414 (33rd ed. 1988). Adult hardbound books numbered 1.025 billion and book clubs 0.698 billion.

39. *Id.* at 403–05. There were 41,925 new titles in 1986, including both paperback and hardbound. Approximately 17,000 of those were new paperback titles.

sellers for 1986, which numbered less than 200, therefore represented a small percentage of these titles. Yet, the top 124 best-sellers in 1987 generated combined sales of approximately 35 million copies.[40] The average 1986 price of a hardcover book was thirty-two dollars.[41] Thus, best-sellers were likely to have generated nearly $1 billion in sales out of a total of $1.7 billion.[42] Note that this does not include sales of best-sellers from previous years that were still selling in relatively large numbers. These numbers back up anecdotal evidence — that the distribution of book sales is very highly skewed toward the more successful book titles.

One question, then, is the longevity of those titles that actually have significant market value and make up the majority of sales in the market. To address this question, Liebowitz constructed a small data set consisting of a sample of titles reviewed in Book Review Digest in the 1920s, along with best-sellers. Book Review Digest reviewed approximately twenty-five percent of new titles. Generally, these were the titles attracting the most attention, written by the more important authors and published by the better-known houses. Table 1 gives the number of these titles that were in print after fifty-eight years.

Table 1: Life Expectancies of Titles

	Number Of Titles	Number in Print After 58 Years	Percent in Print After 58 Years
All Books	236.00	97.00	41%
Best-sellers	91.00	49.00	54%
Non-best-sellers	145.00	48.00	33%

More than half of the best-sellers in the sample remained in print for a long enough period of time that the 1976 extension to the copyright law would likely have affected the present value of future book

40. *Id.* at 522–28 (detailing the number of copies sold of the sixty leading titles, and informing that an additional sixty-four titles sold approximately 150,000 copies each).

41. *Id.* at 408. The average price for fiction hardcover titles was seventeen dollars, so if fiction dominated the bestseller sales, the number in the text might need to be adjusted downward, but would still have bestsellers representing a very large component of sales.

42. This could be taken as evidence supporting the idea that optimal copyright length is not very long. If it were the case that best-selling authors derive far more income than their next best opportunity, then for two-thirds of the market, copyright would be longer than necessary. Without further examination of the income distribution of these authors, however, one cannot assert the truth of such a statement.

sales.[43] Even for non-best-sellers, a third still survived after fifty-eight years, indicating that a fairly significant share of other important books would likely be affected by changes in copyright law even when the copyright term is quite long.

Table 2 presents a further breakdown of longevity by category of title. There clearly are large differences among titles in different categories which have the likelihood of remaining in print for fifty-eight years. For some categories, the number of books remaining in print for this period is quite large.

Table 2: Percentage of Titles Surviving More Than Fifty-Eight Years

Category	**All Titles**	**Best Sellers Removed**
Academic	68%	68%
Philosophical	52%	41%
History	51%	43%
Biography	49%	42%
Religion	46%	40%
Poetry	43%	40%
Fiction	36%	40%
Mystery	23%	16%
Comedy	25%	0%
Autobiography	19%	11%
Art	17%	17%
Travel	6%	6%
Sports	0%	0%

What is the importance of these findings for analyzing the *Eldred* case? They indicate that the inferences about depreciation rates of books drawn from overall survival rates are likely to be misleading. The great majority of books are obscure. They never had much market value, and their demise reflects this lack of viability more than it reflects depreciation. They are unlikely to have significant value in the public domain, just as they had insufficient value under copyright to keep them in print. However, for the small number of titles generating the lion's share of economic value, life expectancy is rather long. Extending copyright might have only a small change in expected reve-

43. 17 U.S.C. § 302 (2005). Prior to 1976, the copyright term was twenty-eight years followed by an additional renewal of twenty-eight years. The 1976 law increased this to fifty years after the death of the author.

nues for these books, but not because they have gone out of print or have lost commercial potential.

VII. CONCLUSION

It is amazing that copyright duration, a topic that has brought forth hardly any economic research, could bring together such a strong group of economists. Given both the ideological range and the distinction of this group, readers might well conclude that there is no other side to this issue. Copyright extension thus might seem to join rent control as one of very few things on which economists agree.

Nevertheless, there is another side to the economics of copyright extension, different from the one put forward by this distinguished group. A more complete view requires consideration of the responsiveness of creative efforts to marginal incentives and the function of ownership of intellectual property beyond the incentive to create. A more nuanced view requires attention to the limitations in the exclusionary aspect of copyright law. A more correct view requires an examination of empirical magnitudes that no one has fully undertaken.

[3]

The University of Chicago
Law Review

Volume 70 | Spring 2003 | Number 2

Indefinitely Renewable Copyright

William M. Landes & Richard A. Posner†

INTRODUCTION

In this Article we raise questions concerning the widely accepted proposition that economic efficiency requires that copyright protection should be limited in its duration.[1] The Constitution authorizes Congress to create copyright and patent protection "for limited Times."[2] The first federal copyright act was enacted in 1790 and provided for an initial term of fourteen years plus a renewal term of the same length, provided the author was still living at the end of the initial term.[3] The initial term was lengthened to twenty-eight years in 1831, and the renewal term to twenty-eight years in 1909, to forty-seven years beginning in 1962, and to sixty-seven years beginning in

---

† Landes is the Clifton R. Musser Professor of Law and Economics at The University of Chicago. Posner is a judge of the U.S. Court of Appeals for the Seventh Circuit and a senior lecturer at The University of Chicago Law School. We thank Louis Kaplow, Steven Shavell, and participants in the Harvard Law School's law and economics workshop (where a previous version of this Article was given on March 12, 2002), along with Michael Abramowicz, Scott Kieff, Elisabeth Landes, Lawrence Lessig, and especially Jane Ginsburg and Douglas Lichtman, for extensive and highly valuable comments on a previous draft, and Peter Broadbent, Bryan Dayton, and especially Brian Grill for their excellent research assistance.

1 See, for example, Brief of George A. Akerlof, et al, as Amici Curiae in Support of Petitioners, *Eldred v Ashcroft*, No 01-618, *10–12 (US Sup Ct filed May 20, 2002) (available on Lexis at 2001 US Briefs 618) ("Akerlof Brief") (arguing that extending the copyright term increases the social cost of monopoly).

2 US Const Art I, § 8, cl 8. For a detailed discussion of the history of this provision and specifically its reference to "limited Times," see Edward C. Walterscheid, *Defining the Patent and Copyright Term: Term Limits and the Intellectual Property Clause*, 7 J Intel Prop L 315, 315–64 (2000). For a more general discussion on this clause, see Malla Pollack, *What Is Congress Supposed to Promote? Defining 'Progress' in Article I, Section 8, Clause 8 of the United States Constitution, or Introducing the Progress Clause*, 80 Neb L Rev 754 (2001).

3 Act of May 31, 1790 § 1, 1 Stat 124, 124.

1998.[4] The Copyright Act of 1976 switched from a fixed to a variable, but still limited, term equal to the life of the author plus fifty years, increased to seventy years in 1998 by the Copyright Term Extension Act (popularly known as the "Sonny Bono" Act).[5] Until the 1976 Act, federal copyright protection was largely limited to published works, other works being mainly protected by (state) common law copyright, which had no time limit, although an unpublished work could be federally copyrighted by being registered with the Copyright Office. A substantial fraction of all federally copyrighted works were of this character.[6] Except in the case of works for hire (works in which the employers, or occasionally other hirers, of the actual creators of the works are the copyright owners), publication lost much of its significance under the 1976 Act, which protected works fixed in a tangible form, whether or not they were published. As for works for hire, the 1976 Act fixed a term of seventy-five years from publication or one hundred years from creation, whichever expired first; the Sonny Bono Act extended these terms to ninety-five and one hundred twenty years. The 1976 Act also made works created after January 1, 1978 nonrenewable, but it allowed assignments and other transfers of copyrights to be terminated by the author or his heirs.

The legal significance of the Constitution's phrase "limited Times" is unclear (the motivation—a hostility deeply rooted in Anglo-American law and politics to government-conferred monopoly—is clear enough). Any time short of infinity, which is to say any fixed period of years, is "limited" in the literal sense of the word; and even if "limited" means something *far* short of infinity, this limitation might conceivably be circumvented by allowing repeated extensions of the copyright term. Renewals and extensions of patents and copyrights had been common in England in the eighteenth century, though on an individual rather than on a wholesale basis, and it was English practice

4 Act of Feb 3, 1831 § 1, 4 Stat 436, 436 (twenty-eight year initial term); Act of Mar 4, 1909 § 23, 35 Stat 1075, 1080 (twenty-eight year renewal term); Joint Resolution of Sep 19, 1962, Pub L No 87-668, 76 Stat 555, 555 and eight subsequent statutes cited in Historical and Revision Notes, Extension of Renewal Terms under Prior Law, 17 USC § 304(a) (2000) (preventing subsisting renewal terms from expiring between 1962 and 1976); Copyright Act of 1976 § 304(a)–(b), Pub L No 94-553, 90 Stat 2541, 2573–74 (forty-seven year renewal term); Sonny Bono Copyright Term Extension Act § 102(d), Pub L No 105-298, 112 Stat 2827, 2827–28 (1998), codified at 17 USC § 304(a) (sixty-seven year renewal term).

5 Copyright Act of 1976 § 302(a), 90 Stat at 2572–73, codified as amended by the Sonny Bono Copyright Term Extension Act § 102(b), 112 Stat at 2827, at 17 USC § 302(a) (2000).

6 From July 1, 1974 through September 30, 1977, unpublished works comprised about 30 percent of new copyright registrations. See Copyright Office, *1975 Annual Report of the Register of Copyright* 19 (Library of Congress 1976) (104,006 unpublished works out of 401,274 total registrations); Copyright Office, *1976 Annual Report of the Register of Copyright* 30 (Library of Congress 1977) (31,165 unpublished works out of 108,762 total registrations); Copyright Office, *1977 Annual Report of the Register of Copyright* 34 (Library of Congress 1978) (121,317 unpublished works out of 452,702 total registrations).

that provided the model and inspiration for the Copyright Clause of the Constitution and for the early federal copyright statutes.[7] Then too, common law copyright (now largely preempted by the federal copyright statute) was perpetual; and so it is conceivable that states could recognize copyright after the expiration of federal copyright protection if the federal copyright law disclaimed any intention of preempting state law.[8] And while Congress could not grant perpetual copyright under the authority of the Constitution's Copyright Clause, maybe it could do so under other grants of power to Congress, such as the power to regulate interstate and foreign commerce. That seems unlikely, however, since the Framers clearly intended to limit, as well as confer, congressional authority to grant patents and copyrights. In any event, we are interested in the economics of indefinitely renewing the copyright term and express no view on its legality.[9]

In this Article, we use the term "indefinite renewal" rather than "perpetual" copyright because there is an important economic difference between granting perpetual copyrights and granting copyrights for a limited time with, however, a right to renew the copyright as many times as the owner (including the original owner's heirs and other successors) wants. We recognize that the present system of fixed nonrenewable copyright terms and a system of indefinite renewals are not the only alternatives. In particular, a system of indefinite renewals could have an upper bound: perhaps an initial term of twenty years and a maximum of six renewal terms of ten years each, for a maximum duration of eighty years. We shall consider this alternative to a "pure" system of indefinite renewals at various points in the Article.

Although a copyright that could be renewed indefinitely could turn out to be perpetual, this is unlikely for any but a tiny fraction of all copyrights. In the empirical part of this Article we show that fewer than 11 percent of the copyrights registered between 1883 and 1964 were renewed at the end of their twenty-eight-year term, even though the cost of renewal was small.[10] And only a tiny fraction of the books

---

7 See Walterscheid, 7 J Intel Prop L at 355–56, 363–64 (cited in note 2).

8 Consider *Bonito Boats, Inc v Thunder Craft Boats, Inc*, 489 US 141, 166–67 (1989) (noting that state trade secret laws coexist with the federal patent scheme).

9 Compare *Eldred v Ashcroft*, 2003 US LEXIS 751, *16 (upholding the constitutionality of the Sonny Bono Act).

10 The renewal fee was 50 cents from 1909 to 1928, see Act of Mar 4, 1909 § 61, 35 Stat at 1087; $1 from 1928 to 1948, see Act of May 23, 1928 § 61, 45 Stat 713, 714; $2 from 1948 to 1965, see Act of Apr 27, 1948 § 2, 62 Stat 202, 202; $4 from 1965 to 1977, see Act of Oct 27, 1965, Pub L No 89-297, 79 Stat 1072, 1072; $6 from 1978 to 1990, see Copyright Act of 1976 § 708(a)(2), 90 Stat at 2593; $12 from 1990 to 1992, see Copyright Fees and Technical Amendments Act of 1989, Pub L No 101-318, 104 Stat 287, 287 (1990); $20 from 1992 to 1999, see Copyright Renewal Act of 1992, Pub L No 102-307, 106 Stat 264, 266; $45 from 1999 to 2002, see 37 CFR § 201.3 (2001); and $60 from July 1, 2002 to the present, see 37 CFR § 201.3 (2002). We add that cost might be significant for individuals who are renewing a group of individual works at the same time. To take

ever published are still in print; for example, of 10,027 books published in the United States in 1930, only 174, or 1.7 percent, were still in print in 2001.[11] These data suggest that most copyrights depreciate rapidly and therefore few would be renewed if even a slight fee were required; the sheer bother of applying for renewal appears to be a significant deterrent. The in-print data are indeed merely suggestive, since it costs more to keep a book in print than to renew a copyright and since a copyrighted work's derivative works may have commercial value after the original work has lost it. Nevertheless, it is apparent that even with an unlimited right of renewal the public domain would remain a vast repository of intellectual "property" (in a legal sense, nonproperty) available for use without charge and also usable as free inputs into the creation of new intellectual property. Paradoxically, a system of unlimited renewals might, depending on the length of the initial term and on the fee structure, *expand* the number of works in the public domain, although the average (and conceivably the total) value of the works in the public domain might fall since copyright in the most valuable works would probably be renewed many times.

Furthermore, it is a mistake to treat the public domain as a fixed supply of works from which any enlargement of copyright protection subtracts. The size of the public domain is in part a positive function of the extent of copyright protection, since, as a first approximation, the more extensive copyright protection is, the greater the incentive to create intellectual property—some fraction of which will become a part of the public domain when the copyright expires or, under the system we are suggesting, is not renewed.

The Article is organized as follows. Part I is a critical review of the economic arguments for limiting the duration of copyright protection. Part II questions the conventional view that the public good character of intellectual property implies that once a copyrighted work falls into the public domain, it will be allocated and exploited efficiently; we show that just as an absence of property rights in tangible

---

an example, consider a photographer who might have taken fifty photographs of a particular event and desires to renew the copyright on all fifty pictures. His total renewal fee would be fifty times the statutory fee. Prior to 1992, a copyright holder who wanted to renew his copyright had to file a renewal application during the last year of the initial copyright term. An amendment that year to the Copyright Act made renewals automatic, although there still are some benefits to filing for renewal registration. See Robert A. Gorman and Jane C. Ginsburg, *Copyright: Cases and Materials* 356–57 (Foundation 6th ed 2002).

11 We are indebted for this computation to Lawrence Lessig, who based it on data in library and book annuals. See, for example, W.I. Fletcher, ed, *Co-Operative Index to Leading Periodicals* (F. Leypoldt 1884); *American Library Annual* (R.R. Bowker 1918); Wyllis E. Wright, ed, *American Library Annual* (R.R. Bowker 1956); Wyllis E. Wright, ed, *American Library Annual* (R.R. Bowker 1957); Madeline Miele, ed, *The Bowker Annual of Library & Book Trade Information* (R.R. Bowker 19th ed 1974); Bowker's *Books in Print*, online at http://www.booksinprint.com (visited Feb 28, 2003).

property would lead to inefficiencies, so an absence of copyright protection for intangible works may lead to inefficiencies because of congestion externalities and because of impaired incentives to invest in maintaining and exploiting these works. Part III presents our empirical analysis of the expected duration of copyrights and trademarks, using data on registrations and renewals over the past ninety years. Our interest in trademark renewals derives from the fact that trademarks may be renewed indefinitely for ten-year periods, and an empirical analysis of these renewals may cast light on the likely performance of a system of indefinite renewals for copyrights. We find that both copyrights and trademarks are subject to significant depreciation and have an expected or average life of only about fifteen years, and also that renewal rates are highly sensitive to renewal fees. These findings suggest that a system of indefinite copyright renewals need not starve the public domain.

I. The Economic Rationale of a Limited Copyright Term

Two propositions are widely believed by most economists; it is the unrecognized tension between them that makes the question of a limited versus indefinite copyright term an interesting and difficult one. The first proposition is that so far as is feasible, all valuable resources, including copyrightable works, should be owned, in order to create incentives for their efficient exploitation and to avoid overuse. The second proposition is that copyright should be limited in duration. The reasons for the second proposition are several: (1) tracing costs increase with the length of copyright protection; (2) transaction costs may be prohibitive if creators of new intellectual property must obtain licenses to use all the previous intellectual property they seek to incorporate;[12] (3) because intellectual property is a public good, any positive price for its use will induce both consumers and creators of subsequent intellectual property to substitute inputs that cost society more to produce or are of lower quality, assuming (realistically however) that copyright holders cannot perfectly price discriminate;[13] (4) because of discounting to present value, incentives to create intellectual property are not materially affected by cutting off intellectual-property rights after many years, just as those incentives would not be materially affected if, during the limited copyright term, lucrative new

---

12 This point is emphasized in our previous paper on copyright law. See William M. Landes and Richard A. Posner, *An Economic Analysis of Copyright Law*, 18 J Legal Stud 325, 357 (1989) (arguing for fair use in cases where transaction costs are too high relative to the benefits of a license).

13 The second and third points both rest on the fact emphasized in our paper that creators of intellectual property characteristically build heavily on earlier such property rather than creating *ex nihilo*.

markets for the copyrighted work, unforeseen when the work was created, emerged;[14] (5) in any event, retroactive extensions of copyright should not be granted, because such extensions do not affect the incentive to create works already in existence,[15] but the possibility of such extensions invites rent-seeking.

These five points taken together imply that the optimal term of copyright protection is determined by balancing at the margin the incentive effects of a longer term against both the administrative and the access costs arising from the public goods aspect of intellectual property; by "access costs" we mean both the deadweight losses from limiting output and the transaction costs involved in obtaining a license from the copyright owner granting access to a copyrighted work. Since the incremental incentive to create new works as a function of a longer term is likely to be very small (given discounting and depreciation) beyond a term of twenty-five years or so,[16] access costs will tend to dominate, implying an optimal copyright term considerably shorter than the current term of life plus seventy years. Thus, the second proposition (limited copyright terms) denies the first (valuable resources should be owned) and asserts that copyrightable intellectual property should be taken out of private ownership and placed in the public domain after a period of years no greater than necessary to induce the socially efficient incentives to create new works. But is the second proposition sound? It may be, for there undoubtedly are cases in which property rights cost more than they are worth (a homely example—a spatial counterpart to the temporal limitation of copyright—is shopping malls that do not charge for parking, thus treating their parking lot as a commons). It has seemed so to many students of copyright, but its soundness no longer seems obvious to us.[17]

---

14 One must be cautious, however, in asserting that "unforeseen" opportunities will not affect incentives. A particular new market may be unforeseen or unanticipated yet may be part of a *class* of markets that when the work was created had a foreseen, positive probability of coming into existence, and therefore may have influenced the incentive to create the work. See generally Jane C. Ginsburg, *Copyright and Control over New Technologies of Dissemination*, 101 Colum L Rev 1613 (2001) (when copyright owners seek to exploit a new market that new technology has opened, courts enforce the copyright law to preserve the copyright owners' exclusive rights against innovative upstarts).

15 Not literally zero, because knowledge of the possibility of a future lengthening of the copyright term might have some, though probably very small, incentive effects.

16 For example, suppose a copyright would yield $1 per year in perpetuity at a discount rate of 10 percent. Under a system of perpetual copyright, the present value of this infinite stream of income would equal $10 (=1/*r*). Under a limited copyright term (=*t*) the present value would be $(1-e^{-rt})/r$. Hence if $t=25$ and $r=0.10$, the present value of $1 per year for twenty-five years is $9.18, which is more than 90 percent of the present value of a perpetual copyright. If the value of the copyright depreciates by, say, 5 percent per year, the difference in present value between a perpetual and twenty-five-year copyright is only about 2.5 percent ($6.67 versus $6.51).

17 For a summary of the arguments in favor of a limited term, see Landes and Posner, 18 J Legal Stud at 361–63 (cited in note 12).

A. Tracing Costs

The argument for limiting copyright duration because of tracing costs is superficial except in explaining why common law copyright in unpublished works was (before the 1976 Copyright Act) perpetual: Because there is usually only one copy of such works, the cost of determining the copyright holder's identity is trivial unless the copy has passed through many hands.[18] The argument for limiting duration is superficial in other contexts, not because the costs of tracing the ownership of copyrighted works are inherently slight but because they could probably be made slight by modest institutional reforms. Enormous tracing costs would be incurred by any would-be publisher of a new translation of the *Iliad* if the heirs of Homer could enforce copyright in the work, but that is only because no one knows who those heirs are. Equally immense tracing costs would be required to determine the ownership of a parcel of land if titles to land were not recorded in a public registry. It is not perpetual property rights but the absence of registration that creates prohibitive tracing costs.

Were a system of indefinitely renewable copyright to be instituted today but limited to works created after the system was in place, there need be no great difficulty in identifying copyright owners a century or for that matter a millennium hence if, for example, the law required copyright owners to reregister their copyrights every ten or even twenty-five years in some central registry under the name of the copyright holder and to notify the registry in the event the copyright was transferred. The owner would be required to provide the registry with his address and notify it of any changes of address; a transferee would likewise be required to furnish this information to the registry. Then a search of the registry under the name of the original owner would reveal the address of the copyright holder from whom a license would have to be sought. The analogy is to the registries in which titles to real estate are recorded and to the Uniform Commercial Code registries in which security interests in personal property are recorded. A fee would be charged for renewing a copyright registration in recognition of the costs imposed on the registry itself and on the searchers. The fee could exceed those costs if it were desired to expand the public domain by discouraging renewals of works unlikely to have much commercial value.

---

18 An example is the discovery in the library of Harvard University of an unpublished manuscript entitled *The Inheritance*, written by Louisa May Alcott in 1849. It had been miscatalogued for many years, and no one knew of its existence. Although Alcott was childless, the copyright holders—fourth-generation descendants of Alcott's father—were not difficult to locate. See Lawrence Van Gelder, *Uncovered at Harvard: Alcott's First Novel*, NY Times C15 (May 1, 1996).

Tracing costs could be reduced further by requiring, when feasible, that a notice of copyright be placed on copyrighted works. Such a notice, which would be a precondition of copyright protection, would indicate the name of the copyright holder and the date of the most recent copyright registration or renewal.[19] This would enable a potential user to determine readily whether the work was still protected and with whom to get in touch if a license had to be obtained. Notice would reduce tracing costs because the registry would have to be searched only for the subset of works that were still under copyright.

Under existing law, the point at which copyright protection begins is relatively unimportant because the duration of protection is determined not by that starting point but instead (except in the case of works for hire) by the death of the author. Under a system of renewals, the starting point becomes critical. So our suggested system would require a return to something like the pre-1976 law, where copyright protection generally began with publication or registration; but we do not explore these details in this Article.

We acknowledge a possible concern with joint ownership of copyrights; the more owners there are of a property, the greater will be the tracing and transaction costs. But these problems arise in the case of land and other physical property and are dealt with in a variety of ways, such as by forming a trust or corporation to own or operate the property, or by allowing partition. Problems of joint ownership of copyrights can be solved in similar ways. The counterpart to partition is the right of any joint owner of a copyright to license its use, subject to a duty to account for the profits to the other owners. Tracing and transaction costs reduce the value of property to its owner, thus giving them an incentive to reduce these costs by consolidating ownership or control.

B. Transaction Costs

The transaction costs argument against indefinite renewal (compared to life plus seventy years or a single renewal term) is stronger than the argument from tracing costs but must not be exaggerated. Transaction costs, like tracing costs, might actually be lower under a system of indefinite renewal, though this would depend on how the

---

19 For some works, it is true that up-to-date notices would not be feasible or would be too costly relative to the potential benefits in lowering tracing costs. Suppose, for example, that *A* sells a work of art but retains the copyright. *A* may be unable to place an up-to-date copyright notice on a work that has been out of *A*'s possession for many years. Other problems associated with copyright notices must also be considered. For example, a strict notice requirement might result in cluttering up a work of art with multiple notices that would detract from the artistic merits of the work. Even in this case, it might be possible to place a notice on the back of the canvas or on the back of the pedestal on which a sculpture stands.

system was configured, in particular on the length of the initial and renewal terms and on the renewal fee. Although transaction costs would be incurred each time a copyright was renewed, consisting mainly of the time costs of the copyright holder and the costs of administering the renewal system, these costs would be slight if most copyrights were not renewed—and the longer the initial term and the higher the renewal fee, the fewer would be renewed.

The transaction costs incurred in negotiating for the licensing of that minority of works on which the copyright has been renewed many times would often be higher. In many cases, it is true, a new work that potentially infringes the copyright on a very old one will infringe only on a single work, for example (if there had been indefinitely renewable copyright from the beginning of time) *Ulysses* and the *Odyssey*, the movie *Clueless* and the novel *Emma*, *West Side Story* and *Romeo and Juliet*, *Ragtime* and *Michael Kohlhaas*. And in that event transaction costs should not be very high, provided that copyright protection is narrow and excludes ideas, *mise en scène*, and other aspects of expressive works that go beyond the very specific, narrowly defined form or configuration of the copyrighted work; and provided that there is a broad fair-use doctrine that protects, for example, parodies of copyrighted works from being treated as infringement. But these are settled and economically rational features of copyright law that we would not suggest be changed.

Transaction costs would be greatest for composite works, such as anthologies. Under existing law, the publisher of a collection of the world's greatest poems need obtain copyright licenses for only a subset of the poems—none first published before 1923.[20] Under a regime of indefinitely renewable copyright instituted, say, in 1500 A.D., most of the poems in an anthology of popular poetry might still be under copyright protection, and therefore many more licenses would have to be obtained for a new anthology.

The aggregate transaction costs of a system of indefinite copyright renewals would depend on the number (and possibly the value) of licenses (holding tracing costs constant), the transaction costs per license, and the administrative costs of operating a renewal system (including the time and inconvenience costs that individuals incur in renewing copyrights). Since the number of licenses would depend in part on the total number of works renewed, aggregate transaction

---

20 The copyright on a work first published in 1922 would have terminated after seventy-five years (a twenty-eight-year initial term plus a forty-seven-year renewal term) or in 1997. See 17 USC § 304(b) (1994). The Sonny Bono Act added an additional twenty years' protection to works still protected in 1998. See Sonny Bono Copyright Term Extension Act § 102(b)–(d), Pub L No 105-298, 112 Stat 2827, 2827–28 (1998), codified at 17 USC §§ 302–04 (2000).

costs could actually fall compared to a system of automatic renewals or a single term of life plus seventy years.

We do not wish to be dogmatic about transaction costs, since their magnitude has not been estimated. If they are thought to be very great and especially if they are believed to increase exponentially with increases in copyright duration, this could be a compelling argument for placing an upper bound on the duration of copyright under a system of (finite) renewal. Return for a moment to the example of *West Side Story* and *Romeo and Juliet*. Shakespeare's play copied extensively from an earlier *Romeo and Juliet* which in turn copied the plot from Ovid's story of Pyramus and Thisbe. Had copyright been in force since Ovid's day and if Ovid's heirs had renewed it right up to the present, the producer of *West Side Story* might have to get a license from those heirs as well as from Shakespeare's heirs (and doubtless from the heirs of the author of the earlier *Romeo and Juliet* as well), assuming the license obtained by Shakespeare from Ovid's heirs was limited as it would normally be to Shakespeare's use of Ovid's story in his own works.

C. Public Goods and Discounting to Present Value

The public goods argument for limiting the copyright term is valid but overstated. The argument is best understood with the aid of an example. Suppose the marginal cost of manufacturing and distributing a copy of some novel is $1, there are no fixed production costs (typesetting and editing costs are zero), but the author incurs a cost of $1000 (mainly opportunity cost) to write the book—call this the cost of expression. This is a fixed cost, which, because it does not vary with output, does not influence output. As a result, in the absence of copyright, competition among publishers would expand output to the point at which the price of the book fell to $1, which would just cover the publisher's manufacturing and distribution costs and leave nothing with which to compensate the author for his efforts. The incentive of authors to write books would diminish, and with it the supply of new copyrightable works.[21] Copyright protection enables the publisher to charge a price above $1 without worrying about competition from unauthorized copies. A price of, say, $2 would more than cover the publisher's costs and enable a financial return to the author, encouraging him to create new valuable works. But charging a $2 price generates an offsetting social cost. Potential users who value the copyrighted work at more than $1 but less than $2 substitute other goods. The re-

21 For a discussion of why some works would still be produced, and of alterative ways in which authors might still receive financial compensation in the absence of copyright protection, see Landes and Posner, 18 J Legal Stud at 329–33 (cited in note 12).

sult is a loss of value (deadweight loss) equal to the difference between these users' willingness to pay and the $1 marginal cost. Viewed as an institution for promoting economic efficiency, the copyright system seeks to balance the incentive gains from pricing expressive works above marginal cost against the deadweight loss and other costs. Protection beyond that point would yield additional benefits that were more than offset by the higher costs.

From this standpoint, however, it may seem puzzling that the copyright term is so long today, let alone that we should be suggesting that it might be made even longer by being made renewable indefinitely. On the one hand, the present value of $1,000 in royalties to be received ninety-five years from now (life plus seventy years for a work written twenty-five years before the author's death) is trivial, given any plausible discount rate. On the other hand, such a long term of copyright protection can create access (deadweight plus transaction) costs by reducing the number of works that are in the public domain at any given time and can therefore be appropriated without need to obtain a license.

But this analysis is superficial in two respects. First, just as future revenues must be discounted to present value to determine their value, so future deadweight costs must be discounted to present value to determine their present cost.[22] If the present value of some remote future benefit is trivial, so is the present cost of the equally remote future deadweight loss. Second, because the scope of copyright protection is, as noted earlier, very narrow, the size of the deadweight loss created by copyright protection is likely to be relatively small. The narrower the scope of a property right, the more good substitutes there are, the less the owner's monopoly power is, therefore, and so the smaller is the deadweight loss that the monopoly creates. It has even been argued that the optimal duration of a patent would be infinite if the scope of patent protection were narrowed appropriately.[23] Conceivably the scope of copyright protection is already so narrow that an infinite copyright term would not be a source of significant deadweight loss. But this is merely a conjecture (are there good substitutes, for example, for Shakespeare's plays or Mozart's piano concer-

---

22 But at the same rate? Future benefits should be discounted at the private discount rate because we are concerned with their incentive effect. Future deadweight costs should be discounted at a social discount rate lower than the private rate if it is believed that society has an interest in its future inhabitants greater than individuals have for their remote descendants. We do not pursue this issue in this Article.

23 See Richard Gilbert and Carl Shapiro, *Optimal Patent Length and Breadth*, 21 RAND J Econ 106, 111 (1990) ("If one interprets patent policy broadly enough to include at least one policy instrument that affects the flow of profits from the sale of the patented product, then optimal policy calls for infinitely-lived patents whenever patent breadth is increasingly costly in terms of deadweight loss.").

tos?), and one reason the scope is narrow is that the public domain provides a source of free inputs into the creation of new copyrightable works. If valuable works are withheld from the public domain because the copyright term has been extended, there may be significantly fewer public domain works (weighting number by quality) upon which to draw, which will reduce competition with existing copyrightable works.

Our earlier point about the need to discount future deadweight costs loses most of its force, moreover, if the question is whether to extend the term of existing rather than future copyrights—at least existing copyrights that, unless extended, will soon expire. Suppose a copyright that was about to expire is extended another twenty years. The deadweight costs will begin to accrue immediately. They still must be discounted, but the present cost will be much greater than if the discounting were merely of deadweight costs that were to be incurred in a period beginning seventy-five years from now.[24] The case for a system of indefinite renewals may thus be stronger if it is limited to copyrights obtained after the system is instituted, although a potentially offsetting benefit—reduced rent seeking—of a system not limited to future copyrights will be noted shortly.

The length of the initial and renewal terms, the fee charged for renewal, and the scope of renewal (would it be limited to a single work, or could it cover a group of works?) can be adjusted to produce, as a practical matter, whatever copyright term is deemed socially desirable; nor need the length, fee, or scope be the same for all classes of work (books, software, music, etc.). The shorter the initial grant (it could be as short as five or ten years) and the higher the renewal fee, the shorter the de facto term and so the fewer the number of works that will be protected by copyright. The *composition* of the public domain might well differ under an indefinite-renewal system, because there would be better sorting of works into two categories: (1) valuable works, where the benefits of property rights may exceed the costs, and (2) works of little value, where the costs of administering copyright protection are very likely to exceed the benefits and a stiff renewal fee would discourage the owner from seeking continued copyright protection. We argue that this sorting might produce a more efficient system of copyright than the present system.

---

24 This point is emphasized in the economists' amicus curiae brief in the *Eldred* case. Akerlof Brief at *11 (cited in note 1) (demonstrating that a deadweight loss today has a much larger present value than a deadweight loss eighty years from now).

D. Rent-Seeking

Owners of copyrights on old but still commercially valuable works have an incentive to incur lobbying and related expenses to persuade Congress to extend the copyright term on these works. Retroactive extensions do not enhance incentives to create expressive works, so if those incentives are the only benefits from copyright, such extensions will increase access and transaction costs without producing any offsetting value. Moreover, as we just saw, they can be a potent source of deadweight costs.

Consider Disney's successful efforts to lobby for the Sonny Bono Act that extended its copyrights by twenty years in order to protect its soon-to-expire copyrights on Mickey Mouse and other cartoon characters.[25] The costs of these efforts, and of the unsuccessful efforts of competing interests to oppose the extension, were incurred to obtain and limit economic rents, respectively, and if there are no offsetting social benefits these costs were wasted from a social standpoint.

Rent-seeking activities are a natural consequence of any fixed copyright term, since the Congress that enacts the term cannot prevent future Congresses from increasing the term retroactively. There will always be some copyright holders whose income will be diminished when their works fall into the public domain, and they have an incentive to seek retroactive extensions as the end of the copyright term draws near. The problem of rent-seeking that arises from the possibility of retroactive extensions of copyrights would be solved by indefinite renewals, though an alternative would be to interpret the Copyright Clause of the Constitution to forbid retroactive extensions. Since indefinite renewals would eliminate the prospect of losing the income produced by old but still valuable copyrights, there would be little incentive to lobby for copyright extensions. We say "little" rather than "no" because resources might still be spent lobbying for lower renewal fees and longer renewal terms. But normally it would be cheaper to pay the renewal fee than to try to change the law. Notice, however, that a system of indefinite renewals that was limited to future copyrights would fail to curb the incentive to seek retroactive extensions of existing copyrights. Notice, too, that fixing an upper bound to renewals would leave the rent-seeking problem unsolved, since, as the work approached expiration, if it retained commercial value the copyright holder would have an incentive to lobby for a right of further renewal.

---

25 See Janet Wasko, *Understanding Disney: The Manufacture of Fantasy* 85–86 (Polity 2001). The Act went into effect October 27, 1998, four years before the copyright on Mickey Mouse would have expired. See Sonny Bono Copyright Term Extension Act § 102(b)–(d), 112 Stat at 2827–28.

It might be objected that allowing indefinite renewals would eliminate only one form of rent-seeking, because copyrights have other dimensions of value, notably scope, besides duration. However, whatever incentive there exists for lobbying for expansions of scope exists under the current system; it would not be greater under a system of indefinite renewals.

II. Rationing and Maintaining Intellectual Property

A. Congestion Externalities

If we are correct so far, *average* copyright duration might well be shorter under a system of indefinite renewals than under the current system. Such a system might therefore reduce access costs for most but not all works compared to the present system. (It probably would not reduce deadweight costs, because these presumably are generated mainly by valuable copyrights, which would tend to be renewed.) The public goods argument asserts, however, that whatever the case with regard to costs, there are no efficiency or social benefits from continuing indefinitely to protect even a small number of valuable works. It is this issue that we now take up. The argument assumes that the only justification for copyright protection is the incentives it produces to create new works. This may be wrong, or even anachronistic, since until the 1976 Copyright Act, and in the case of works for hire right up to the present day, federal copyright protection attached at dissemination or registration rather than at creation.

The economic theory of property rights emphasizes not only their incentive effects, that is, the investment that they encourage, but also their effect in optimizing current uses of property. Frank Knight made this argument many years ago, using the example of highway congestion.[26] An example closer to intellectual property is a natural pasture. The purpose of assuming it to be natural rather than cultivated is to abstract from the incentive benefits of recognizing a property right. The natural pasture is not created by human effort and therefore there is no social value in encouraging investments in creating it. But in the absence of property rights the pasture would be overgrazed because none of the users would take account of the cost that his use imposed on the other users by making their cattle graze more to obtain the same amount of food. Thus, property rights would confer a social benefit but it would be unrelated to encouraging the creation of new property.

---

[26] Frank Knight, *Some Fallacies in the Interpretation of Social Cost*, 38 Q J of Econ 582, 586–92 (1924) (arguing that the owner of a toll road would charge a toll that was socially efficient).

Analogous benefits of property rights are recognized in some areas of intellectual property. They are recognized in trademark law, which does not impose any fixed limitation on the duration of a trademark, since confusion would result if the same trademark denoted goods of different provenance and quality, and which, through the concept of "dilution," protects trademark owners from the loss of value resulting from nonconfusing duplication of their trademarks (as where a hot dog stand adopts the name "Tiffany's"). And increasingly they are recognized in the law of publicity rights as well, which prevents others from using one's name or likeness in advertising or other commercial uses without one's permission. The tendency is to make these rights inheritable.[27] The motive is not to encourage greater investment in becoming a celebrity (the incremental encouragement would doubtless be minimal), but to prevent the premature exhaustion of the commercial value of the celebrity's name or likeness.[28]

Recognition of an "overgrazing" problem in copyrightable works has lagged. Typical is the statement of a large group of intellectual property professors in opposition to the Sonny Bono Act:

> The fundamental difference between tangible and intellectual property is that intellectual property is a nondepletable commons, while tangible property necessarily depletes with use. "The tragedy of the commons" is that failure to recognize perpetual and transferable property rights in tangible property leads inevitably to "overgrazing," as soon as an item of property enters the public domain from which everyone may draw freely. Recognition of perpetual property rights leads to economic efficiency, because a rational owner will optimize the balance between present and future consumption.
>
> There can be no overgrazing of intellectual property, however, because intellectual property is not destroyed or even diminished by consumption. Once a work is created, its intellectual content is infinitely multipliable.[29]

27 See Mark F. Grady, *A Positive Economic Theory of the Right of Publicity*, 1 UCLA Enter L Rev 97, 124–26 (1994) (noting the split among courts on the issue of whether publicity rights are inheritable and the legislative activity to make such rights inheritable). Consider Douglas G. Baird, *Does Bogart Get Scale? Rights of Publicity in the Digital Age*, 4 Green Bag 2d 357, 363–64 (2001).

28 See Grady, 1 UCLA Enter L Rev at 103, 126 (cited in note 27) (arguing that an efficient rule would protect valuable publicity rights after death to prevent the value from being dissipated too quickly).

29 Dennis S. Karjala, *Statement of Copyright and Intellectual Property Law Professors in Opposition to H.R. 604, H.R. 2589, and S. 505, The Copyright Term Extension Act* 9 (Jan 28, 1998), online at http://www.law.asu.edu/HomePages/Karjala/OpposingCopyrightExtension/legmats/1998statement.html (visited Feb 28, 2003).

This is overstated, if only because it ignores the trademark and right-of-publicity cases—both examples of intellectual property the value of which can be diminished by consumption. But before proceeding further, we must distinguish between technological and pecuniary externalities. The externality in the pasture case is technological because it imposes a real cost on third parties (the other grazers), rather than merely altering the distribution of wealth. Refusing to recognize inheritable publicity rights could impose either type of externality, or both types. If anyone could use Humphrey Bogart's name or likeness in advertising, the aggregate value of that advertising use might be greater even though Bogart's estate would lose income. Indeed, if the marginal cost of additional copies of his image were zero, the marginal utility would also be zero, even though the total utility could be very great. But the total utility might fall if the lack of excludability and resulting proliferation of the Bogart image led to confusion, the tarnishing of the image, or sheer boredom on the part of the consuming public. Eventually the image might become worthless.

Apparently this is a concern of the Walt Disney Company with regard to its copyrighted characters, such as Mickey Mouse.

> To avoid overkill, Disney manages its character portfolio with care. It has hundreds of characters on its books, many of them just waiting to be called out of retirement. . . . Disney practices good husbandry of its characters and extends the life of its brands by not over-exposing them. . . . They avoid debasing the currency.[30]

FIGURE 1
COPYRIGHT EXTERNALITIES

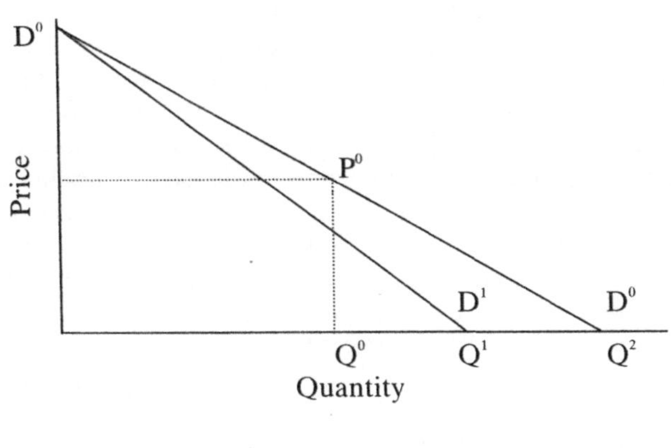

30 Bill Britt, *Disney's Global Goals*, Marketing 26 (May 17, 1990).

Figure 1 illustrates the problem. D^0D^0 is the demand schedule in period t. Assume that the work has been under copyright for so long that if the copyright expired today the expected return to the author would have been sufficient to induce its creation. By assumption, therefore, copyright protection in period t and all future periods would have no effect on whether the work was created in period t=0. It would create a deadweight cost illustrated by the $P^0Q^2Q^0$ triangle in Figure 1, which is caused by the copyright holder's charging a price equal to P^0 although marginal cost is zero. Terminating the copyright in t would eliminate the deadweight loss, as the number of uses of the work would increase to Q^2, that is, until the value of the marginal use equaled zero.

But now suppose that, contrary to the usual assumption about copyrights, additional uses impose technological externalities. Then terminating the copyright will lead not only to a movement along the demand curve but also to a downward shift (say to D^0D^1) in the overall demand, destroying value equal to the difference between the area under the original demand curve D^0D^0 up to P^0 and the area under D^0D^1 up to a zero price. If the externalities are small, the difference between the two demand curves could be negative, so that terminating the copyright at t would increase value. But if they are large, termination would result in a net loss in value. In the limit, additional uses beyond Q^0 might depress the demand curve (as it rotates downward around the point that intersects the vertical axis at D^0) until it coincided with the vertical axis. In that event, terminating the copyright would have destroyed all its previous value—the area under D^0D^0 from the point that intersects the vertical axis to the initial price and quantity of P^0 and Q^0.

But how far is the concern with technological externalities that has been flagged in reference to publicity rights actually applicable to copyright? A book or other copyrightable property is, as we noted earlier, a public good; its use by one consumer does not interfere with its use by any other. This point cannot be decisive, however; a celebrity's name or likeness has public good characteristics as well, yet unlimited reproduction of the name or the likeness could prematurely exhaust the celebrity's commercial value, just as unlimited drilling from a common pool of oil or gas would deplete the pool prematurely. The same could be true of a novel or a movie or a comic book character or a piece of music or a painting, particularly with regard to copyrights on components of completed works rather than on the completed works themselves. If because copyright had expired anyone were free to incorporate the Mickey Mouse character in a book, movie, song, etc., the value of the character might plummet. Not only would the public rapidly tire of Mickey Mouse, but his image would be blurred, as some authors portrayed him as a Casanova, others as catmeat, others as an animal-rights advocate, still others as the henpecked husband of Minnie. In effect, there would be both a movement along and shift downward in the demand curve in Figure 1 until Mickey Mouse's commercial value was zero.[31] To the extent that such appropriations of the Mickey Mouse character were classified as parodies, they would be sheltered by the fair-use doctrine. But not all would be so classified,[32] and in that event the fair-use doctrine would not insulate them from liability under a regime of indefinitely renewable copyright.

We do not wish to press this argument too far. While examples can even be given of works of elite culture that may have been debased by unlimited reproduction (the *Mona Lisa*, the opening of Beethoven's *Fifth Symphony*, and several of Van Gogh's most popular paintings come immediately to mind), there are counterexamples, such as the works of Shakespeare, which seem undiminished by the proliferation of performances and derivative works, some of them kitsch, such as Shakespeare T-shirts and the movie *Shakespeare in Love*.

B. Creation and Copying from the Public Domain

A second economic argument against limiting the duration of copyright is unrelated to congestion or overuse externalities. It returns us to the question of incentives. The conventional economic criticism of unlimited duration draws too sharp a distinction between creation and copying. Imagine a novel published many years ago in which copyright has expired. The novelist is rediscovered and there is a surge in demand for his novels. Since no publisher could establish a property right in them, the incentives of publishers to publish and promote

---

31 In contrast, in the absence of negative technological externalities, terminating the copyright would reduce the marginal value to zero. But since the demand curve would be unchanged, total value would increase because there would be no deadweight cost from termination.

32 The line the law draws in implementing the fair-use defense to copyright infringement is between complementarity and substitution (or between productive and substitutable uses for the copyrighted work), see, for example, Wendy J. Gordon, *Fair Use as Market Failure: A Structural and Economic Analysis of the* Betamax *Case and its Predecessors*, 82 Colum L Rev 1600, 1643–44 n 237 (1982) (giving examples of complementarity and substitution and stating that "complementarity should favor fair use"); or, so far as is relevant to our example, between parody and burlesque, see Richard A. Posner, *When Is Parody Fair Use?*, 21 J Legal Stud 67, 71 (1992) ("[T]he parodist should not be allowed to take so large a fraction . . . of the original work as to make the parody a substitute for that work."). Uses of the Mickey Mouse character that were intended to provide the audience with a substitute for the Disney Corporation's productions incorporating the character would not be considered fair use. Compare *Ty, Inc v Publications International, Ltd*, 292 F3d 512, 517 (7th Cir 2002) ("[C]opying that is complementary to the copyrighted work . . . is fair use, but copying that is a substitute for the copyrighted work . . . is not fair use.").

them might well be inadequate from a social standpoint. Often the demand for particular works of intellectual property is unknown before they actually hit the market.[33] Suppose an enterprising publisher has only a 20 percent chance of success with obscure public-domain authors. He publishes the works of five such authors in order to have one success. In the absence of copyright protection, other publishers can wait and see which author sells and then bring out their own version of his works. Publishers who wait avoid the costs of failure, but their free riding on the market information developed by the first to publish reduces the incentive of any publisher to search for potentially successful public domain works.[34] The tendency would be for only works of already well-known and safe authors whose works were in the public domain to be published.

Granted, a system of indefinite renewals is not a panacea for this problem, since works that were no longer popular would tend not to be renewed many times. This problem would exist even if copyright were perpetual rather than either duration-limited or indefinitely renewable, since owners of a perpetual copyright that they considered worthless would not take even modest steps to assure the continued registration (for example, notifying the registry of changes of address) that a system of perpetual copyrights would require. A complete solution would require that the "resurrectors" of old works on which copyright had expired without renewal, like finders in the law of real property, be allowed to obtain copyright in those works. We consider that possibility later. For now, it is enough to observe that a system of indefinite renewals would—depending on the fee, on whether group renewals were permitted, and on the formalities involved in renewal—somewhat mitigate the problem of incentives to invest in public-domain works.

Another such problem is that a publisher would have an incentive to make changes in any public domain work that he did revive, since he could copyright the changes, but changes made merely to stake a claim are socially inefficient. They may create private value for the publisher, but from a social standpoint they impose higher real

---

33 This has been noted in connection with dolls and other goods portraying dead celebrities. See Ronald Alsop, *Items Portraying Dead Stars Produce Profits, Controversy*, Wall St J 37 (May 10, 1984).

34 In other words,

> a work's public domain status is far from an unqualified incentive for utilizing it. . . . Some of the obvious concerns are whether a copyrighted derivative [work] will have to compete with other, often low-budget, low quality copies and whether the producer of the copyrighted derivative of a public domain work is likely to have anything unique in the long run.

Arthur R. Miller, *Copyright Term Extension: Boon for American Creators and the American Economy*, 45 J Copyright Socy USA 319, 324 (1998).

costs net of any value created by the publisher's changes. In other words, extension of the copyright term might reduce socially excessive product differentiation.[35]

Conversely, if because of its age the novel were in need of an elaborate scholarly apparatus, re-editing, or other costly additions to make it readily accessible to a modern readership, publishers might be reluctant to undertake the needed measures, even if they could copyright the scholarly apparatus (which they could not do to the extent it was deemed a matter of ideas rather than expression), fearing that the cost could not be recouped in the face of competition from cheap, barebones editions of the novel. Reviewers might use the scholarly apparatus, of course without compensation, to explain the book to the public who would then buy the barebones edition.

Shakespeare comes to mind here, because the texts of his plays are notably corrupt; also because it is uncertain that we have all the texts of his plays and poems. There is a considerable industry in trying to improve the accuracy of the texts and discover new works by Shakespeare, but it is entirely academic. Despite Shakespeare's popularity, there does not appear to be a significant commercial market for the "maintenance" required to maximize the value of Shakespeare's works.

A parallel example would be an old movie, on which copyright had expired, that a studio wanted to issue in a colorized version that would be very expensive to prepare. Promoting the colorized version might increase the demand for the black and white version, a close substitute for the colorized version. Since anyone could copy and sell the black and white version, the studio considering colorization would not take into account, in deciding whether to colorize, the increase in demand for the black and white version. As a result, the expected revenue from colorization might be less than the (private) costs and so the movie studio would decide against it.[36] This is a good example of a case in which indefinite renewal might be a complete solution, since, given the public's avidity for movies old as well as new, an old movie

---

35 Two qualifications should be noted. One is that the publisher's changes in the public domain work may be too slight to support a copyright in the derivative work. See *L. Batlin & Son, Inc v Snyder*, 536 F2d 486, 491 (2d Cir 1976) (en banc) (holding that to support a copyright in a derivative work based on a public domain work "there must be at least some substantial variation, not merely a trivial variation such as might occur in the translation to a different medium"). The other qualification is that even if the publisher can copyright the derivative work, a third party can copy the underlying public domain work from the derivative work without infringing the copyright. See, for example, *Feist Publications, Inc v Rural Telephone Service*, 499 US 340, 359 (1991) (stating that copyright in a compilation has no effect on the public domain status of the pre-existing underlying material).

36 The implication of this point—that colorization is less likely for movies in the public domain than for those still under copyright—is empirically testable.

would be quite likely to retain enough value to warrant the expense of renewal.

The essential points are illustrated by the copyright on Mickey Mouse. First, the character has changed in appearance over the years since it was first created,[37] indicating continued investment after the initial creation of the copyrighted work. Second, should the copyright be fated to expire, Disney would have an incentive before expiration to change the character further so that, by copyrighting the changes, it might impede imitations. A further complication is that Mickey Mouse is a Disney trademark,[38] and trademarks have no fixed expiration date. After the copyright expired, copiers would still need to disclaim a Disney origin in order to avoid trademark infringement; such disclaimers, like conspicuous notices on paintings, might in some instances impair the commercial value of the copy.

These examples, unlike the analysis of publicity rights and our extension of that analysis to copyright, show that a case against a definite time limit for copyrights can be based on the traditional incentive-based argument for property rights, though with a new twist. The new twist is recognition that the need to invest in intellectual property to maximize its value is not exhausted in the initial creation of the property. Investment is necessary to maintain the value of the property as well, and also to resurrect abandoned or otherwise unexploited intellectual property.[39]

Magnitudes are critical, and in the absence of them only tentative conclusions are possible.[40] The reader should recall, however, the theo-

---

37 For a long time, the changes were in the direction of making Mickey distinctly more youthful in appearance. See Stephen Jay Gould, *The Panda's Thumb: More Reflections in Natural History* 95–107 (Norton 1980) (providing a graphic on Mickey's evolution). Recently, however, we learn that "Mickey Mouse is getting a makeover, along with other familiar Disney cartoon characters. No more cutesy, innocuous, not-a-care-in-the-world pet mouse. The 70-year-old character is about to become more in tune with his true rodency, the edgier times, and become a harried, 1990s creature." Richard L. Eldredge, *Peach Buzz: Will Some Man Please Call Tyra?; Mickey, Minnie to Cop Edgy Attitude*, Atlanta J & Const 2D (Apr 7, 1998).

38 Indeed, Mickey's "primary role today is as the corporate logo of the [Walt Disney] company." Wasko, *Understanding Disney* at 125 (cited in note 25).

39 This is not an entirely novel point.

> For a work to be commercially successful, it requires effort and investment which, while not "creative," is still necessary to generate value. For example, authors employ literary agents, publishers advertise, etc. With musical compositions and photographs, the collection, arrangement and indexing of the works adds value. With film, preservation requires constant attention. Even the straightforward act of printing a book entails a risk on investment. Arguably, none of these activities will be pursued as vigorously on behalf of public domain works as they are for works with ownership rights. And, from an economic point of view, these activities "create" real value.

Edward Rappaport, *Copyright Term Extension: Estimating the Economic Values* 4 (Congressional Research Service May 11, 1998).

40 Rappaport states that the effect he describes "may be important in some cases but, we

retical reasons to doubt that the extension of the copyright term via renewals is likely to impose large tracing, transaction, or deadweight costs, provided that copyrights already existing when the system of renewals is adopted are not eligible to be renewed, since extensions of existing copyrights, as we noted, can impose very large deadweight costs. On the other side of the balance, besides the unknown significance of congestion externalities in the copyright context, we are told that the Disney corporation has spent tens of millions of dollars refurbishing Mickey Mouse, both by subtle alterations in the character and by situating it in carefully selected entertainment contexts in an effort to increase the appeal of Mickey Mouse to the current generation of young children, who apparently have diminished interest in him. The incentive to make such expenditures would be impaired if the copyright expired, allowing anyone to use the character, though the copier could not copy any newly copyrightable features that Disney had added to the original character.[41] At the same time, however, extending the Mickey Mouse copyright, a highly valuable existing copyright, would be likely to impose substantial deadweight costs, which might well exceed the incentive-promoting and congestion-reducing benefits that we have identified.

We conjecture that the reason so few classical composers are recorded and performed is that it is more costly to produce a musical composition than it is, say, to photograph a painting. The recording company that discovered and revived the works of a forgotten or obscure composer would be risking a substantial amount of money in an uncertain venture that could be imitated if successful. Much less expense would be involved in publishing a book, or even arranging an exhibition of works of a forgotten or obscure painter. The absence of property rights in the music of well-known classical composers may also explain another feature of the recording industry. Many different recording companies record the same public domain works of Beethoven, Mozart, Bach, and other well-known composers. Recording

---

believe, will more often be marginal." Id. But he does not explain the reasoning or evidence that leads him to this conclusion.

41 The public legislative history of the Sonny Bono Act says little about the twenty-year addition to the duration of copyrights on works for hire, such as the Disney copyrights. The main rationale given for the extension for individuals (remember that the Act extended the term for individuals from life plus fifty years to life plus seventy years) is (1) balance of payments and (2) the fact that people are living longer (Irving Berlin being a pertinent example). The second point makes very little sense, since an increase in longevity will automatically increase the length of the copyright term measured from the author's death, unless the concern is with the longevity of his heirs. The first point is mercantilist, reflecting the fact that the United States is a net exporter of intellectual property. One of the committee reports does, however, explain that the extension of the copyright term "will provide the important collateral benefit of creating incentives to preserve existing works." Copyright Term Extension Act of 1996, S Rep No 104-315, 104th Cong, 2d Sess 13 (1996). This is a point similar to our colorization example.

companies differentiate their product by promoting the performer or artist who has signed an exclusive contract with the company. Because the recording company can, for example, copyright the Chicago Symphony Orchestra's recording of Beethoven's *Fifth Symphony*, it has an incentive to promote that version; it has little incentive to promote the public domain work of an unknown composer, since it could not appropriate the benefits of those promotional efforts.

Consider also the effect on the recording of a composer's obscure works when his copyrights expire. Our analysis implies that upon the expiration of Puccini's copyrights, the rate at which his obscure works were recorded fell relative to recordings of the best-known works, since an investment in creating a demand for the obscure works would be more difficult to recoup once the works were no longer under copyright.

If our analysis is correct, Lawrence Lessig's criticism of the retroactive extension of the Mickey Mouse copyright[42] overlooks important though, in the present state of knowledge, inconclusive economic arguments for extended copyright protection that are independent of whether the protection is extended ex ante or ex post.[43] Though, as we have seen, ex post extension involves greater deadweight costs but lower rent-seeking costs. If the method of extension were periodic renewal, then, since Congress could cut off the right of renewal at any time, a law authorizing renewals without limit would be less vulnerable to a constitutional challenge than a grant of perpetual copyright *ab initio*—the latter being flatly inconsistent with granting a copyright for "limited Times." Periodic renewal would also have the superior economizing properties that we have emphasized.

But it would not address the case in which intellectual property that has fallen into the public domain by abandonment is sought to be revived. Suppose Tobias Smollett had copyrighted his books but after a few renewals his heirs had decided the books had no value and so declined to pay the renewal fee. Our analysis implies that a publisher who wants to publish Smollett's books today should be permitted to take out copyright on them, by analogy to the rule that allows finders to obtain title to abandoned (as distinct from merely misplaced) prop-

---

42 See references to these and other retroactive extensions in Lawrence Lessig, *The Future of Ideas: The Fate of the Commons in a Connected World* 107 (Random House 2001):

> More disturbingly, we have come to this expanded term through an increasingly familiar practice in Congress of extending the term of copyright both prospectively (to works not yet created) and retrospectively (to works created and still under copyright) .... Each time, it is said, with only a bit of exaggeration, that Mickey Mouse is about to fall into the public domain, the term of copyright for Mickey Mouse is extended.

43 See id at 197–98 ("[I]ncentives are prospective. Whatever we promise Hawthorne, he isn't going to produce any more work.").

erty. Unfortunately, the efficient implementation of such a rule is considerably more complicated in the case of intellectual than of physical property. In the latter case, allowing abandoned property to be withdrawn from the public domain unproblematically implements the policy that valuable property should be owned in order to create the correct incentives for its exploitation. But imagine a "finder" of intellectual property who claimed to have found, and who sought to obtain copyright in and register, all the books in the British Library on which copyright had expired. Such a claim, if honored, would be tantamount to "banking" trademarks by simply listing all possible combinations of the letters of the alphabet, and would create the rent-seeking and transaction-cost problems that we have elsewhere discussed in the trademark context.[44]

The problem may not be insoluble. One way to deal with it would be to limit the acquisition of copyright in previously created works to works created after the law authorizing such acquisition was passed. Another would be to require the publication of such a work within a specified period of time after copyright was claimed in it. Another would be to charge a stiff fee for registering such a copyright.

We have yet to consider an important though not fatal objection both to indefinite renewals and to allowing even limited copyright protection for "found" public domain works. These measures, as we have seen, would create incentives for firms to expend resources on discovering and disseminating obscure public domain works and on maintaining consumer interest in copyrighted works that were about to fall into the public domain (the Mickey Mouse example). But these are not expenditures on creating expressive works; they are marketing expenditures, which are not within the traditional domain of intellectual-property law. Why should a particular subset of such expenditures be singled out for legal protection? Firms that introduce wine and cigar bars, develop movies about wars in outer space, recognize the potential for health clubs that combine workout and social activities, or introduce baggy trousers or pastel colors for clothing cannot prevent other firms from imitating their marketing innovations. Trademark law may prevent confusingly close imitation and copyright law may protect particular advertising slogans, but these laws do not prevent competitors from free riding on the readily available information developed by the innovators.

44 See William M. Landes and Richard A. Posner, *Trademark Law: An Economic Perspective*, 30 J L & Econ 265, 281–83 (1987) ("[T]he ownership of a vast number of [trademarks], and the aggregate licensing revenues that such ownership would command, would be a magnet drawing resources into the activity of creating brand names, probably beyond the optimal level of such investment.").

However, there are at least three possible economic reasons for singling out the particular marketing expenditures in issue for protection by copyright law. First, the distinction between expressive works and the marketing *of those works* is overdrawn. Consider a record company that develops, promotes, and distributes new pop records. A few of them will be financial successes but the others will lose money. Which will be hits and which will be flops is not known in advance. In the absence of copyright protection—and here we are speaking just of protection against the copying of the sound recordings themselves—unauthorized copying of the hit records will drive their price down to their cost of manufacture and distribution and leave nothing for covering the costs incurred in developing and promoting recordings of new songs and new performers. Copyright protection enables the record company to earn enough money on the hits to cover both their costs and the production and marketing costs of the many failures. In effect, copyright indirectly prevents free riding on marketing and information expenditures that are similar to the expenditures incurred in rediscovering obscure public domain works and in maintaining interest in soon-to-expire copyrighted works.[45] To state this another way, exploring the market for expressive works, the sort of exploration that the measures we are discussing would encourage, is a stage in the creation of intellectual property.

Second, marketing expenditures associated with expressive works differ from those associated with the other examples of new products given above (wine and cigar bars, health clubs, and so forth) because it is easier in the former case to identify the innovator. Many people could probably make credible claims of being the first to come up with the idea of baggy pants or pastel shades of clothing or combining exercise and social opportunities under the same roof. Having the legal system try to sort out these competing claims would involve substantial costs that would usually be avoided when someone was seeking to restore a copyright in an obscure public domain work and would never arise when one was seeking merely to renew an existing copyright.

Third, many new business ideas may now be legally protectable by "business method" patents. Such protection often provides incentives for firms to invest in marketing and promotion that would be subject to free riding in the absence of protection.

---

45 This concern is explicit in the Copyright Act of 1976 § 303, Pub L No 94-553, 90 Stat 2541, 2573, codified as amended at 17 USC § 303(a) (2000), which discourages free riding on marketing and promotion expenditures of previously unpublished works about to fall into the public domain by conditioning an additional forty-five years of protection on publication. Thus, copyright on works unpublished on January 1, 1978, continues until December 31, 2002, but if published by that date, protection continues until December 31, 2047.

III. EMPIRICAL ANALYSIS OF COPYRIGHT REGISTRATIONS AND RENEWALS

Data on copyright registrations and renewals during the past one hundred years bear directly on the subject of this Article. If it turned out that all or most copyrighted works created before the 1976 Copyright Act (which became effective on July 1, 1978) were renewed, the implication would be that a system of indefinite renewals might approach perpetual copyright, though this would also depend on how steep the renewal fee was. Conversely, if renewals are infrequent even under the current system of nominal fees,[46] then probably only a relatively few highly valuable works would remain under copyright beyond the initial term even if indefinite renewals were permitted.

A. The Data

The U.S. Copyright Office publishes data on registrations and renewals.[47] Although the number of registrations is only a proxy for the number of copyrighted works because registration has always been optional, the 1909 and 1976 copyright acts created strong incentives to register a copyright and to register it promptly. Not only is registration (or, under the 1976 Act, an application to register) a prerequisite for filing a suit for infringement,[48] but it must be done before the infringement (or within three months of first publication) if the copyright holder wants to recover statutory damages and attorney's fees.[49] As noted earlier, the 1909 Act fixed the copyright term at twenty-eight years from the date of first publication (or, for works that were copyrighted but not published, from the date of registration), and at the end of the term the copyright could be renewed for an additional twenty-eight years (effectively raised to forty-seven years in 1962 and

---

46 See note 10.

47 See Copyright Office, *Annual Report of the Register of Copyrights* (Library of Congress, various years) (individual reports cited in note 6). See also Barbara A. Ringer, *Renewal of Copyright*, in Copyright Society of the USA, ed, 1 *Studies on Copyright: Arthur Fisher Memorial Edition* 503, 616–20 (Rothman & Co and Bobbs-Merrill 1963) (analyzing Copyright Office renewal data by class of original registration, percentage of works copyrighted, and category of renewal claimant).

48 See 17 USC § 411(a) (2000) ("[N]o action for infringement of the copyright in any United States work shall be instituted until registration of the copyright claim has been made in accordance with this title."). Under the Berne Convention Implementation Act of 1988 § 9, Pub L No 100-568, 102 Stat 2853, 2859, codified as amended at 17 USC § 411(a), the registration requirement only applies to a "United States work"—in other words, a work first published in the United States or where the author is a United States national or lives here. See 17 USC § 101 (2000) (distinguishing between a "Berne Convention work" and a "United States work").

49 See 17 USC § 412 (2000) ("[N]o award of statutory damages or of attorney's fees . . . shall be made for . . . any infringement of copyright commenced after first publication of the work and before the effective date of its registration, unless such registration is made within three months after the first publication of the work.").

to sixty-seven years in October 1998) if the copyright holder applied for renewal within the last year of the initial term.[50] Beginning in 1992 renewal became automatic,[51] so renewal registrations were sure to decline after that, but not to zero because there was still an incentive to file, mainly because a renewal registration is prima facie evidence of the validity of the copyright during its extended term and of the facts stated in the certificate of renewal. Another important change in the law was the extension of federal protection by the 1976 Act from published works to all works fixed in a tangible medium, whether or not they are published. This change could be expected to have increased the number of registrations without any increase in the output of copyrightable works.

Our primary focus is on renewals because they allow us to estimate the expected economic life of a copyright.[52] But we need data on registration as well because the number of initial registrations determines the number of works that are potentially renewable twenty-eight years later. For example, works renewed in 1938 were registered initially in 1910. To obtain the number of 1910 registrations, however, we have to deduct renewal registrations in 1910 (from works first copyrighted in 1882) because the Copyright Office includes renewal registrations in its tabulation of registrations.

B. Copyright Registrations and Renewals

Figures 2, 3, and 4 illustrate registrations, renewals, and the renewal/registration ratio, respectively, over the past century; the renewal/registration ratio in year *t* being simply the number of renewals in *t* divided by the number of initial registrations in *t*-28.

---

50 See note 4 and accompanying text.

51 Remember that these are renewals of copyrights that date from before the effective date of the 1976 Copyright Act, which gave the copyright owner a nonrenewable term of life plus fifty (later seventy) years. See text accompanying note 5.

52 Economists have used patent application and renewal data to estimate the expected life and distribution of patent values. For a summary of these studies, see Jean O. Lanjouw, Ariel Pakes, and Jonathan Putnam, *How to Count Patents and Value Intellectual Property: The Uses of Patent Renewal and Application Data*, 46 J Indus Econ 405, 406–07 (1998) ("[A]pplication and renewal data contain rather direct information on the value of the proprietary rights created by patent laws and policy, that is, on the *value of patent protection*."). See also note 76.

FIGURE 2
COPYRIGHT REGISTRATIONS (EXCLUDING RENEWALS)

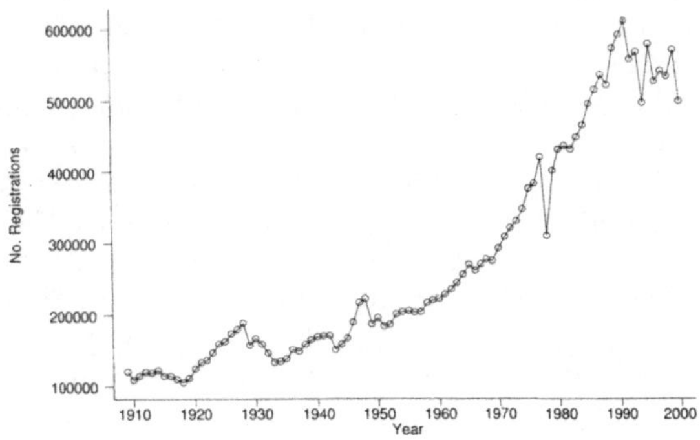

FIGURE 3
RENEWALS IN YEAR *t*

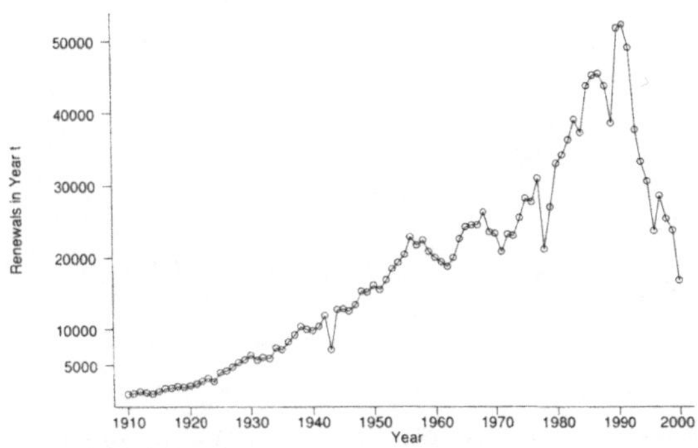

Figures 2 and 3 reveal that copyright registrations and renewals rose rapidly in the twentieth century, but that, as expected, renewals began to decline in 1992 when they became automatic.[53] The rise doubtlessly reflects an increase in the number of copyrightable works brought about by growth in the output of expressive activities, as well as reflecting changes in the copyright law. Why, then, did both registrations and renewals peak in 1991, declining by almost 20 percent by

[53] Recall that the Act of Mar 4, 1909 § 23, 35 Stat 1075, 1080 (effective July 1, 1909) extended the renewal term from fourteen to twenty-eight years. Works that had been renewed for fourteen years in the period 1895 to 1909 were entitled to a further renewal of fourteen years, for a total renewal period of twenty-eight years. Id at § 24, 35 Stat at 1080–81. We do not include the fourteen-year extensions in our count of renewals in the 1910 to 1923 period. Our analysis of renewal data begins with the fiscal year ending June 30, 1910, the first fiscal year of the 1909 Act.

2000, with the decline concentrated in the last year? The answer may be, in part anyway, that the registration fee was doubled in 1991, from $10 to $20, and increased again in 2000, to $30, while the renewal fee was doubled to $12 in 1991, rose to $20 in 1993, and more than doubled, to $45, in 2000. Although these fees seem small in relation to the inconvenience of registering and complying with other requirements of registration, such as submission of a copy of the work to the Copyright Office,[54] Figures 2 and 3 suggest substantial negative responses to higher fees for both original and renewal registrations. The effect on renewals is more ambiguous, of course, because of the automatic renewal amendment in 1992—although the amendment did not eliminate all incentive to register a renewal, since by doing so a copyright holder could recapture rights in already created derivative works.

FIGURE 4
RATIO OF RENEWALS IN *t* TO REGISTRATIONS IN *t*-28

As Figure 4 shows, the fraction of works renewed increased significantly between 1910 and 1991, then plummeted—no doubt mainly because of automatic renewal, though higher fees may also have played a role.[55] Prior to 1992 (the first fiscal year for automatic re-

54 Another reason for the decline in registrations may be that since March 1989, registration has no longer been a condition for bringing an infringement suit for foreign works protected by the Berne Convention and the World Trade Organization, though it remains a prerequisite for seeking statutory damages and attorneys fees. The fact has little quantitative importance, however, because foreign works are only a small fraction of copyright registrations. See text accompanying note 59.

55 We analyze the impact of fee changes in the regression analysis below, see text accompanying note 68, but point out here that it would be a mistake to think that the ratio of renewals to registrations should not change in response to higher fees for *both* renewals and registrations. The mistake lies in failing to note that the ratio of renewals to registrations is calculated from renewals in year *t* and registrations in year *t-28*, and obviously an increase in fees in 1991 could not affect the number of registrations in 1963, the denominator in the 1991 ratio. The only effect

newal), renewal rates ranged from a low of .03 in 1914 to a high of .22 in 1991. Although the full cost of renewal includes both a small renewal fee and the monetary equivalent (probably small) of the inconvenience and other costs associated with renewal,[56] the fact that a small fraction of works are renewed implies that most copyrights have very little economic value after twenty-eight years. Put differently, the decision to renew a copyright depends upon a comparison of the discounted value of the expected future revenues from the copyright compared to the full costs of renewal. If the latter exceeds the former, the copyright will not be renewed. Since only a small fraction of works are renewed, it follows that the expected economic value of the 80 percent or so of copyrighted works that are not renewed is less than the small cost of renewal.

Of course, we cannot dismiss the possibility that some fraction of nonrenewals are due to simple oversight, or careless failure to comply with required formalities. Nonrenewals by corporations or other owners of works for hire might therefore be a better index of decisions not to renew based on lack of commercial value; but we do not have those data.

If, as both the raw data in Figures 2 and 3 and the regression analysis indicate, registrations and renewals respond significantly to modest changes in fees, it is likely that: (1) the size of the public domain will expand under a system of indefinite renewals compared to the present copyright system; (2) the average value of works in the public domain will decline under a system of indefinite renewals; (3) the expected economic life of most copyrighted works is short;[57] and (4) a system of indefinite renewals, at least if limited to works copyrighted after the system is created, will separate valuable works in which continued copyright protection may be socially efficient from works in which the cost of continuing that protection almost certainly exceeds the sum of administrative and access (including transaction) costs.

---

of higher fees on that ratio would come through the effect of a higher renewal fee on the number of renewals that year. Note also that the renewal ratio in Figure 4 is biased downward from 1910 to 1937 because registrations data from 1881 to 1909 include both new registrations and fourteen-year renewal registrations (from works first registered in 1867 to 1895). We account for this bias in our regression analysis.

56 As noted earlier, the full cost of renewal for a person seeking to renew a group of separate works—say, photographs—would be substantial, provided the law required a separate renewal fee for each photograph. See note 10.

57 The actual life of some of these works is longer; an author may err in his estimate of the demand for his work and therefore fail to renew his copyright, though in fact the work has continued value.

C. Depreciation and the Economic Life of Copyrights

Depreciation rates of copyrighted material can be calculated from data on renewals and registrations. Initial registrations constitute one year's stock of copyrighted works. Renewal registrations of those works constitute a different, smaller stock of the same works twenty-eight years later (renewals must be registered in the last year of the initial term). The annual rate at which the first stock shrinks to become the second is the depreciation rate of the first stock. That rate is given by $REN_t = (REG_{t-28})e^{-\delta_t 28}$ where REN_t denotes renewals in t of works registered twenty-eight years earlier ($=REG_{t-28}$) and δ_t equals the annual average depreciation rate for copyrights registered in period t-28. Figure 5 depicts annual depreciation rates, measured in year t, of works registered twenty-eight years earlier. Thus, the depreciation rate of .054 in 1990 (5.4 percent) is the annual depreciation rate of works registered in 1962. The higher the renewal ratio, of course, the lower the depreciation rate, since we are computing the depreciation rate from the fraction of copyrighted works that are renewed.

Figure 5 indicates that the average annual depreciation rate of copyrighted works has ranged from a low of 5.4 percent in 1990 to a high of 12.2 percent in 1914 (for works first registered in 1886), with the overall average being 8.3 percent.[58] The long-term trend (setting to one side the effect, beginning in 1992, of automatic renewal) is toward lower depreciation, implying that copyrightable works have become more valuable. One reason may be the increase, beginning in 1962, in the renewal term from twenty-eight to forty-seven years, which increased the present value of copyrights by extending their potential term. But given discounting, the effect should not have been great, and so it is not surprising that most of the decline in the depreciation rate occurred before 1962.

Why there was *any* decline in depreciation is unclear, however. Even if the demand for copyrightable works has been growing, the supply of new works would be expected to respond at roughly the same rate in order to keep the real value of copyrights roughly constant. One possible reason for the decline in depreciation is that new technologies, such as long-playing records, stereo equipment, radio, and television, have extended the economic life of copyrights. For example, the growth in demand for prerecorded music made possible by technological advances such as radio and television broadcasting, high-quality home stereo systems, and even the automobile (which increases the number of people listening to radio) should have in-

---

58 As noted earlier, estimates of depreciation for the years 1910 to 1937 are biased downward because registration data in the period 1882 to 1909 include renewal registrations. See note 55.

creased the overall demand for copyrighted music. Some of this demand would be satisfied by older though still copyrighted music, resulting in higher renewal rates and hence a lower depreciation rate.

FIGURE 5
ANNUAL DEPRECIATION OF REGISTERED COPYRIGHTS

Here we should mention a complication arising from the fact that as a result of the signing of the Berne Convention by the United States, copyright protection was restored for a number of works that were protected in their country of origin but had fallen into the public domain in this country, mainly because of failure to comply with the requirements of notice or renewal. This has two potential effects on the calculation of depreciation. First, if foreign works were less likely to be renewed (or more likely to fall into the public domain because of improper notice) than U.S. works, depreciation of the latter would be lower than shown in Figure 5. Second, the size of the public domain would be smaller today. These effects are likely to have only a negligible impact on our empirical analysis, however, because we estimate that foreign works constitute only between 1 and 5 percent of copyright registrations.[59]

The reciprocal of depreciation is the average expected life of a copyrighted work. Although the statutory term of copyrighted works first published in the period 1881 through 1972 and renewed for a second term varied from fifty-six to ninety-five years, the commercial life ($=1/\delta$) of the average copyrighted work was much lower, ranging from 8.19 years to 18.5 years for works first registered in 1886 and 1962, respectively. In the first group, 3.3 percent were renewed (in 1914); in the second, 22 percent were renewed (1990).

59 We were able to obtain data on foreign registrations for only some of the years between 1961 and 1977, however.

It is also possible to estimate the number of works registered in 1934 that retain commercial value today. We chose that year because works first published then could be renewed for forty-seven years in 1962, and another twenty years were tacked on in 1998, so that a copyright first registered in 1934 need not enter the public domain until 2029. Yet the estimated depreciation rate of works registered in 1934 is .07, implying that of the works registered that year, 50 percent had fully depreciated by 1944, 90 percent by 1977, and 99 percent by 2000; fewer than 1 in 750 works registered in 1934 will have commercial value in 2030. Had renewals been permitted every five or ten years, then after an initial term of twenty or so years, about 99 percent of the works registered in 1934 would have fallen into the public domain by the year 2000, because by then their commercial value had fallen below the cost and inconvenience of renewal. Of course, the 1 percent that would still be under copyright would mainly be the more valuable and enduring works.

D. Depreciation Rates for Books, Music, and Graphic Arts

The Copyright Office publishes separate data on registrations and renewals for books (including pamphlets—which indeed account for 80 percent of the category), music, and graphic arts (applied art, posters, fine arts, labels, photographs, technical drawings, and maps). As shown in Figure 6, the time trend of these three categories closely tracks the time trend of overall registrations (the correlation is .99). This is not surprising, because these categories account for 70 percent of all registrations.

FIGURE 6
REGISTRATIONS OF ALL COPYRIGHTS, BOOKS, MUSIC, AND GRAPHIC ARTS

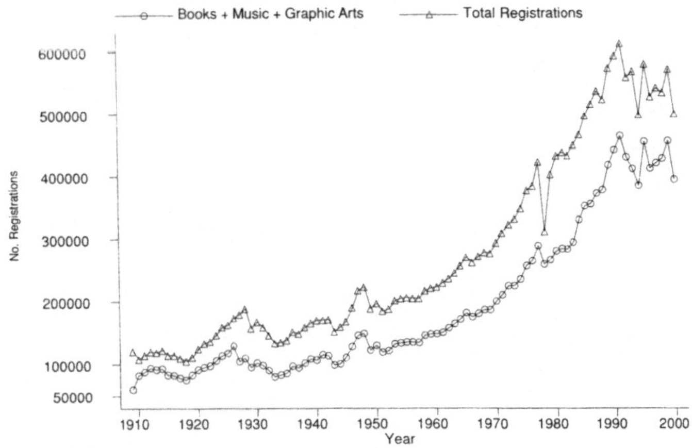

In Figure 7 we see that the number of musical copyrights has grown the fastest, the number of book copyrights the second fastest, and graphic arts the slowest. We estimated simple regressions of the form $log\ y_t = a + rt + u$, where y denotes either book, music, or graphic art registrations, t, time, and u, the residual. The coefficient r, which measures the rate of growth per year, equaled .021 (24.5) for books, .025 (41.5) for music, and .014 (7.44) for graphic arts. The t-statistics (in parentheses) indicate that these growth rates are highly significant.[60] The differences in growth rates between any two of the three categories are also statistically significant.

60 However, books include periodicals for the 1909–26 period, which artificially increases the number of book registrations in that period and so lowers the estimated rate of growth. If we estimate the growth rate from 1927 (rather than 1909) to 2000, the coefficients (and t-statistics) on r are .024 (27.4) for books, .026 (33.3) for music, and .022 (12.8) for graphic arts. Although the growth rates for books and music are much closer, all differences remain statistically significant at the .10 level.

FIGURE 7
SEPARATE REGISTRATIONS FOR BOOKS, MUSIC, AND GRAPHIC ARTS

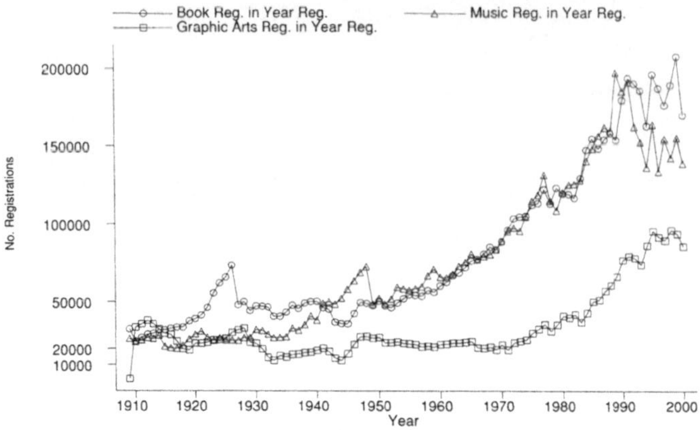

We can also link up renewals with registrations for each of the three categories to estimate category-specific depreciation rates, though since the earliest category-specific registration data we have are for 1909, we can only use renewal data starting in 1937. Figures 8 and 9 graph the renewal ratio and depreciation rates.

FIGURE 8
THE RATIO OF RENEWALS IN *t* TO REGISTRATIONS IN *t*-28

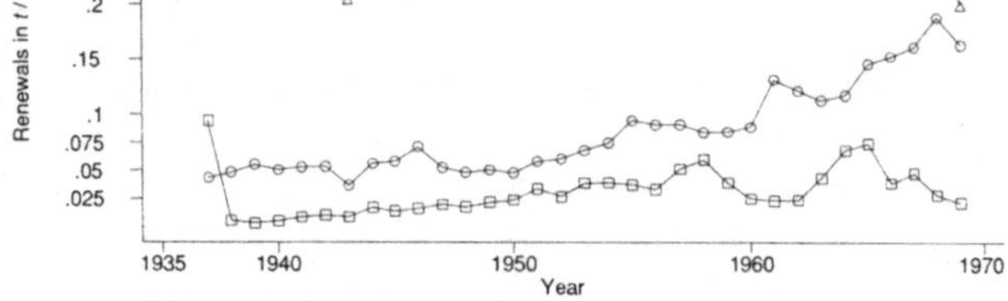

FIGURE 9
DEPRECIATION IN *t* OF REGISTRATIONS IN *t*-28

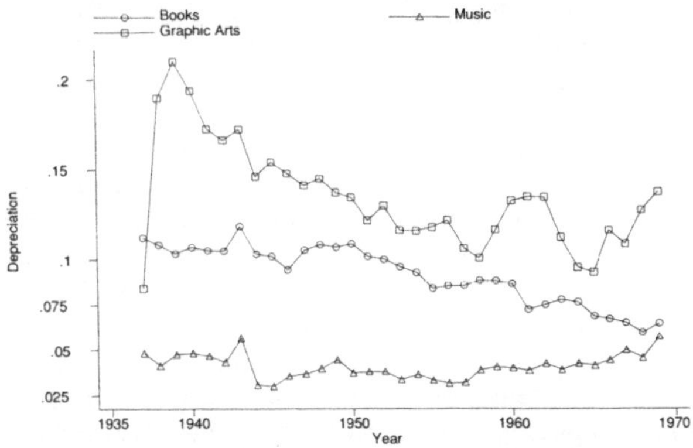

Notice that only about 3 percent of graphic-arts works were renewed after twenty-eight years, compared to 8 percent for books and 32 percent for music, which peaked at more than 40 percent for works renewed in 1944 and 1956. Music renewal rates have been falling sharply since 1956, while book renewal rates have been rising during this period, so that by 1969 renewal rates were greater for books than music for works first copyrighted in 1942. By the same token, depreciation rates are highest for graphic arts (averaging about 14 percent) and lowest for music (about 4 percent), with books in the middle (about 9 percent).[61] We also observe declining depreciation rates for both books and graphic arts, while depreciation of music began to increase in the mid-1950s and by 1969 was just slightly below that of books.

What explains these differences? The graphic-arts category is dominated by commercial art, such as advertising layouts and fabric designs for fashion items, the useful life of which tends to be no longer than the advertising campaign or latest fashion season. (Mickey Mouse is a dramatic exception.) At the other extreme, music written for one use can have many other uses in the future. For example, a song written for a Broadway show might be recorded by many different artists over a long period of time or be used as background music

61 We noted earlier that of 10,027 books published in 1930, only 174 were still in print in 2001. See text accompanying note 11. An annual depreciation rate of 5.7 percent would produce this more than fifty-fold decline. From our data, we estimate a depreciation rate of 8.9 percent for books registered in 1930, but this is the average rate over the period 1930 to 1958 (the date of renewal). Overall, the depreciation rate is 9.2 percent for books registered between 1909 and 1941. The probable explanation for the discrepancy between this rate and the 5.7 percent estimate is the fact, noted in the text, that the book category in our data includes pamphlets and leaflets, which tend to be ephemeral.

in a movie or a television program.[62] In addition, music is less tied to cultural change than purely verbal works, which are often extremely topical and therefore depreciate rapidly. Books are more enduring than most applied art if only because the costs of storing them is relatively low and there is some chance of turning a book into a movie or rekindling interest in the author.

Whatever the reasons for the differences in depreciation rates across these categories, the differences bolster the case for indefinite renewals. Current copyright law does not differentiate among different types of work. All copyrightable works, from computer programs to novels to installation art (which is typically site-specific so that the tangible work lasts only the length of the exhibition), have the identical term despite the large differences in commercial life expectancy. A system of indefinite renewals would automatically distinguish the enduring from the ephemeral. Most works of graphic art probably would not be renewed even if the initial term were only five years. Because books and music are likely to have more lasting value, their renewal rates would be greater. We have seen that it may be socially beneficial to continue property rights in—and only in—intellectual property that retains sufficient value to offset access and administrative costs, because of the investment disincentives and congestion externalities that are likely to result when valuable property is unowned.

E. Regression Analysis

We can use multiple regression analysis to estimate the impact on registrations and renewals of changes in fees, statutory changes in copyright law, and changes in the underlying demand for expressive works. Tables 1 (registrations) and 2 (renewals) present the results of our regression analysis, which provide additional insight into the likely effects of a system of indefinite renewals.

The dependent variable in Table 1 is the logarithm of the annual number of registrations in the period 1910 to 2000. We present both OLS (ordinary least squares) and Cochrane-Orcutt estimates (the latter to correct for significant autocorrelation). The independent variables in equations (1.1) and (1.2) are a time trend (*Year*), the copyright registration or renewal fee (*LogFee*) deflated by the Consumer Price Index (CPI), the expected copyright duration (*LogE(Life)*) computed from our estimates of depreciation, and annual recreation expenditure (*LogRecExp*) that are a proxy for the demand for expres-

62 See Rappaport, *Copyright Term Extension* at 3 n 5 (cited in note 39) (remarking that "in the case of music, . . . its 'timeless' quality allows themes to be recycled endlessly"). Notice, however, that depreciation rates of music rose in the 1956 to 1969 period, suggesting that more recent popular music is less durable than works created in the 1920s and earlier.

sive (and thus often copyrighted) works of music, movies, books, and periodicals,[63] also deflated by the CPI. The registration, fee, duration, and recreational-expenditure variables are in log form; their regression coefficients are therefore elasticities. Equations (1.3) and (1.4) add several dummy variables denoting changes in the copyright statute that are likely to effect the number of registrations. These include the 1962 amendment extending the renewal term to forty-seven years (*1962RenExt*), the extension of copyright protection to sound recordings in 1972 (*1972Sound*), the 1976 Copyright Act, effective in 1978 (*1976Act*), the 1988 ratification of the Berne Convention effective in 1989 (*1988Berne*)[64] and the 1998 (Sonny Bono) Copyright Term Extension Act (*1998BonoExt*), which added twenty years to the copyright term. These variables take a value of 1 for all years in which the given change is in effect and of 0 otherwise.

All four equations reveal a significant growth rate of copyright registrations of about 1 to 2 percent per year. The time trend variable (*Year*) picks up increases in population, income, wealth, and education that are positively correlated with time over the ninety-year period covered by our data and are likely to increase the demand for expressive activities. A positive time trend was visible in Figure 2, but regression analysis enables us to conclude that the trend is the result of (or at least is positively correlated with) an increase in the underlying growth in demand for expressive activities rather than of changes in fees, the law, or other policy variables. Although the regression coefficients on recreation expenditures are positive in all the equations in Table 1, only the OLS estimates (equations (1.1) and (1.3)) are statistically significant.

The most interesting result in Table 1 is the negative and highly significant effect of registration fees (t-statistics between 4.6 and 9.1) on registrations. The coefficients on fees yield a negative elasticity of around .20, implying that a 25 percent increase in fees would reduce copyright registrations by more than 5 percent, even though fees are very small. (For example, the registration fee in 2000 was only $30, and it had averaged only $20.48 in 2000 dollars over the 1910 to 2000 period.) The implication is that most copyrights have negligible expected value, because even very small increases in already very low fees deter

63 We estimate that expenditures on expressive goods account for about 50 percent of the recreation category.

64 The Copyright Act was amended in 1988 (effective in March 1989) to comply with the substantive provisions of the Berne Convention. See Berne Convention Implementation Act of 1988, 102 Stat 2853, codified as amended in various sections of title 17 (2000). The most significant amendment was to make copyright notice optional. See id at § 7, 102 Stat at 2857–58, amending 17 USC § 401(a) ("[A] notice of copyright as provided by this section may [changed from "shall"] be placed on publicly distributed [copies]. . . .") and § 402(a) (same).

many owners of intellectual property from seeking to register it. While registration is now optional rather than a precondition of obtaining a copyright, it confers procedural advantages that should motivate any copyright holder who thinks his work retains significant commercial value to register his copyright.

The number of registrations is also highly responsive to the expected commercial life (*LogE(Life)*) of a work, which for all but a few works is shorter than the statutory copyright term. For example, a 10 percent increase in that expected life leads, other things being equal, to a 3.2 percent increase in registrations in equation (1.4), and this effect is highly significant statistically.[65]

Of the remaining variables, only the 1976 Copyright Act and 1988 Berne Convention dummy variables have statistically significant effects on registrations after we adjust for autocorrelation. Extending the renewal term in 1962 and adding sound recordings to the Copyright Act in 1972 have positive and significant effects on registrations in the OLS but not in the Cochrane-Orcutt estimates. It is not surprising that the term-extension variables (in 1962 and 1998) are insignificant, because the expected commercial life of a copyrighted work is so much shorter than the copyright term, making an increase in the term irrelevant to most potential registrants. Amendments to the Copyright Act that accompanied ratification of the Berne Convention are associated with about a 10 percent increase in registrations. These amendments (for example, notice and the need to record some transfers and licenses became optional) effectively lowered the full cost (including inconvenience costs) of registration, which in turn should increase the number of registrations.[66]

---

65 The only exception to the significant effect of *LogE(Life)* is equation (1.1). But the significance of this equation in our analysis is marginal because it does not adjust for autocorrelation and excludes five important statutory variables.

66 An offset, however, is that registration for Berne Convention and WTO works is no longer a prerequisite to being able to sue for copyright infringement, though registration is still required for certain remedies. See 17 USC § 412 (no award of statutory damages or attorney's fees for non-registered works).

TABLE 1
REGRESSION ANALYSIS OF REGISTRATIONS
(t-STATISTICS IN PARENTHESES)

Independent Variables	*Log Registrations* OLS (1.1)	COREG (1.2)	OLS (1.3)	COREG (1.4)
Year	.013 (3.71)	.018 (5.44)	.005 (1.88)	.018 (4.78)
LogFee	-.31 (9.06)	-.24 (5.57)	-.19 (5.93)	-.20 (4.67)
LogE(Life)	.07 (.79)	.35 (3.79)	.37 (4.01)	.35 (3.57)
LogRecExp	.20 (2.49)	.03 (.50)	.18 (2.56)	.02 (.26)
1962RenExt	-	-	.08 (2.28)	.02 (.39)
1972Sound	-	-	.16 (3.80)	.03 (.48)
1976Act	-	-	.07 (1.77)	-.14 (2.19)
1988Berne	-	-	.12 (2.86)	.11 (1.86)
1998BonoExt	-	-	.02 (.27)	.06 (1.06)
Constant	13.8 (2.43)	-24.1 (5.11)	-.92 (.19)	-24.3 (3.47)
Durbin-Watson	.50	2.25	.87	2.11
rho	-	.84	-	.88
R^2	.97	.72	.98	.66
No. Observations	90	89	90	89

One puzzling result is that the 1976 Act seems, after correction for other factors, to have reduced the number of copyright registrations by about 14 percent. Since the Act eliminated common law copyright and brought unpublished works under the federal statute, one would have expected the number of registrations to increase. The negative coefficient on the 1976 Act is the consequence of a sharp drop in registrations in 1978 (the year the Act took effect)—from more than 420,000 in 1977 to 310,742 in 1978, followed, however, by an increase to more than 400,000 the following year. If equation (1.4) is re-estimated treating fiscal year 1979 rather than fiscal year 1978 as the first full year of the 1976 Act, the coefficient on the *1976Act* variable becomes positive and highly significant (.16 with a t-statistic of 3.08), indicating a 16 percent increase in registrations as a result of the Act. There are no changes in the effect of the other variables when we date fiscal year 1979 as the first year of the 1976 Act.

In Table 2 the dependent variable is the log of the number of renewals per year. Equation (2.1) presents OLS estimates and equation (2.2) Cochrane-Orcutt estimates. Since renewals depend in part on the number of works registered twenty-eight years earlier, we include two registration variables—one for annual registrations from 1882–1910 and the other for annual registrations from 1911–1972—to account for the fact that data on registrations included both new registrations and renewal registrations through (most of fiscal year) 1910. We do not include variables for the 1972, 1976, 1988, and 1998 statutory amendments, as we would not expect them to affect renewals, holding registrations constant. For example, adding twenty years to the renewal term in 1998 increased the expected value (though only slightly) of a renewal but did not affect the incentive to renew because beginning in 1992 renewals had become automatic.

TABLE 2
REGRESSION ANALYSIS OF RENEWALS
(t-STATISTICS IN PARENTHESES)

Independent Variables	*Log Renewals* OLS (2.1)	OREG (2.2)
Year	.018 (2.56)	.023 (2.61)
LogFee	-.09 (1.08)	-.22 (2.13)
LogReg$_{t-28}$*1882–1910*	.95 (10.34)	.86 (5.18)
LogReg$_{t-28}$*1911–1972*	.99 (10.64)	.89 (5.38)
LogRecExp	-.02 (.14)	-.12 (.67)
1962RenExt	-.07 (.69)	-.06 (.48)
1992AutoRen	-.64 (6.37)	-.47 (3.82)
Constant	-36.4 (3.10)	-44.0 (2.99)
Durbin-Watson	1.08	2.12
rho	-	.55
R^2	.98	.90
No. Observations	90	89

Table 2 indicates that renewals are highly responsive to registrations twenty-eight years earlier. Not only are both regression coefficients highly significant, but we cannot reject the hypothesis that the coefficients are both equal to one—that is, for each 1 percent increase in registrations twenty-eight years earlier, renewals increased by 1 percent. As expected, the automatic renewal amendment in 1992 is statistically significant and indicates that renewals fell by about 50 percent after the amendment. Extending the renewal term from twenty-eight to forty-seven years beginning in 1962 had no significant effect on renewals, but this is not surprising. Consider the copyright holder who has to decide whether to renew his copyright after expiration of the initial term of twenty-eight years. Since the expected additional commercial life of such works is likely to be shorter than twenty-eight years, adding nineteen years to the renewal period should not significantly influence the decision whether to renew.

Turning to the *Year* variable, we find a statistically significant increase in renewals of 2 percent per year (holding registrations eligible for renewal constant). This is consistent with a long-term growth in the demand for and hence in the value of expressive activities, since in response to that growth copyright holders would have a greater incentive to renew their copyrights. After adjusting for this upward trend, we do not find any significant effect of recreation expenditures on renewals.[67]

Like initial registrations, renewals are responsive to changes in fees. Although the coefficient on fees is not significant in equation (2.1), autocorrelation in the OLS estimate produces standard errors that are biased. Equation (2.2) corrects for this bias and reveals a statistically significant effect of fees on renewals: A 10 percent increase in the inflation-adjusted renewal fee results in a 2.2 percent decrease in the number of renewals.[68]

F. Trademark Renewal Rates

Additional light is cast on our subject by considering renewal rates for trademarks. A trademark has no fixed expiration date, but maintaining a federally registered trademark (which like a registered copyright confers procedural advantages) requires the owner to file an affidavit during the sixth year after registration, and in every tenth year, stating that the trademark is still in use, and he must also file a renewal application every ten years.[69] Prior to the Trademark Law Revision Act of 1988 (effective November 16, 1989),[70] registrations and

67 This result is expected since there is a .87 correlation between the logarithm of recreation expenditures and *Year*.

68 The reason equations (2.1) and (2.2) do not include an independent variable for the expected life of a copyrighted work is that renewals are used to estimate depreciation and hence expected duration, so that adding the log of expected duration to the right-hand side of the regression equation would place the log of renewals for the same year on both sides of the equation.

69 15 USC § 1058 (2000) ("[T]he registrant shall file . . . an affidavit setting forth those goods or services recited in the registration on or in connection with which the mark is in use in commerce.").

70 See Trademark Law Revision Act of 1988 § 111, Pub L No 100-667, 102 Stat 3935, 3939,

renewals remained in force for twenty-year periods subject to the owner's having to file an affidavit of continued use every ten years.[71] Thus, the Act reduced both the registration and the renewal periods to ten years. Since there is no limit on the number of times a trademark can be renewed, we have in trademark law a model for how a system of indefinite copyright renewals might operate.

Since trademarks can be renewed indefinitely, renewals in period *t* arise from (1) trademarks first registered in *t*-20 and (2) trademarks registered initially in *t*-40, *t*-60, and so on that had been continuously renewed (the last time in *t*-20) and are still in force at time *t*.[72] Assuming a constant rate of depreciation for trademarks in the interval *t*-20 to *t*, we have the following identity: $REN_t = (REG_{t-20} + REN_{t-20})e^{-\delta 20}$ where *REN* and *REG* denote renewals and registrations respectively, *t* denotes time, and δ the depreciation rate.

Figures 10 and 11 plot renewal and depreciation rates for trademarks from 1934 to 1999, the period for which we have data. Trademark renewals averaged 27 percent, annual depreciation was 6.6 percent, and the expected life (equal to the reciprocal of depreciation) was 15.4 years. Trademark renewal rates and the average effective life of a trademark are greater and depreciation lower than the corresponding data for copyrights (see Figures 4 and 5). For an exact comparison, between 1934 and 1991[73] trademark renewals averaged 28 percent, depreciation was 6.4 percent, and the expected life was 15.7 years, while the corresponding figures for copyright renewals were 14 percent, 7.3 percent, and 14 years. Notice that although trademark renewal rates are double copyright renewal rates, the difference in depreciation and in life expectancy is less than 15 percent. The reason is that during that era trademarks were renewed after twenty years but copyrights after twenty-eight years. So we would observe substantially higher renewal rates for trademarks than for copyrights even if depreciation were the same.

---

codified as amended at 15 USC § 1059 (2000) ("each registration may be renewed for periods of 10 years at the end of each successive 10-year period").

71 For the law before the Trademark Law Revision Act, see Act of Oct 9, 1962 § 5, Pub L No 87-772, 76 Stat 769, 770 (providing for a twenty-year period for each trademark renewal).

72 Since our renewal data run through the end of fiscal year 1999 (September 30, 1999), slightly less than a decade after the Trademark Law Revision Act, 102 Stat 3935, went into effect, all renewals in our sample come from trademarks that had been in force for at least twenty years.

73 We use these dates because 1934 is the earliest year for which we are able to calculate trademark renewal rates (which requires that we have renewals from 1914), and 1991 is the last year for accurately estimating copyright renewals because renewals became automatic starting in 1992.

FIGURE 10
THE RATIO OF TRADEMARK RENEWALS IN *t* TO REGISTRATIONS RENEWALS IN *t*-20: 1934–1999

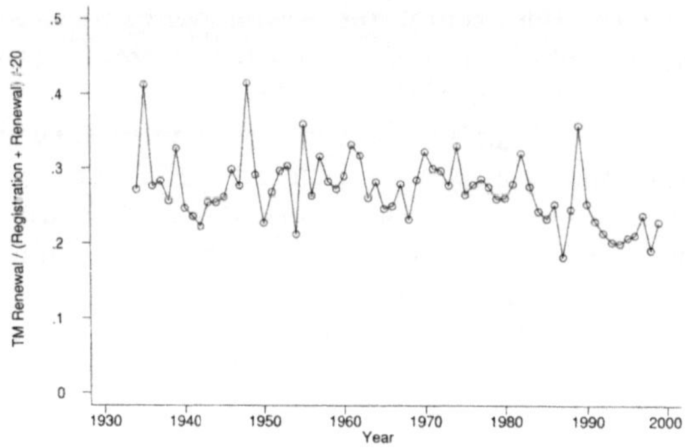

FIGURE 11
DEPRECIATION IN *t* OF TRADEMARK REGISTRATIONS AND RENEWALS IN *t*-20: 1934–1999

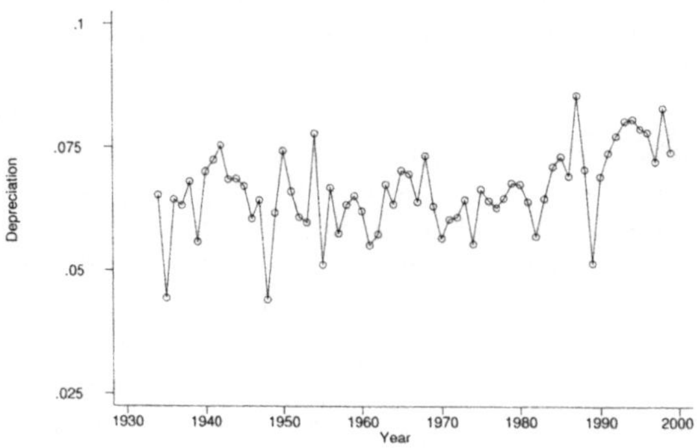

We also regressed (in logs) trademark renewals in *t* on registrations and renewals in *t*-20, a time trend (*Year*), and renewal fees adjusted for the CPI and GNP (*LGNP*) in logs for the period 1935 to 1999. Both registrations and renewals in *t*-20 have positive and highly significant effects on renewals in *t*; renewal fees have a negative though only marginally significant effect (*t*=1.74); and neither time nor

GNP is significant.[74] It is not surprising that the estimated renewal elasticity with respect to fees is relatively small (-.06) and only marginally significant, because there has been very little variation in (nominal) registration fees over the past fifty years. Renewal fees were $15 from 1935 to 1945, $25 from 1946 to 1981, were increased sharply in the next two years (to $150 in 1982, and $300 in 1983), and have remained at $300 since then. There is some evidence that trademark renewal rates declined following the substantial fee increases in 1982 and 1983. Renewal rates averaged .27 in the five-year period of 1977–81 compared to .23 in the five-year period of 1984–88, when the fees were much higher.

The reason depreciation is lower for trademarks than for copyrights is similar to the reason depreciation of copyrighted music is lower than depreciation for books and graphic arts. Like music, a trademark attached to a particular product or service can be extended to new goods and services. A successful trademark embodies the good will and reputation of the producer. Firms have an incentive to capitalize on this good will by introducing new and improved products under the same brand name. The Ford Motor Company initially registered the "Ford" trademark in 1909 for automobiles and parts.[75] Since then, Ford has introduced hundreds of new automobiles under the Ford name. Similarly, Bayer first registered its trademark in 1908 for use on synthetic coal-tar remedies, and later placed the name on numerous pharmaceutical products that did not exist in 1908.

This analysis suggests that the depreciation rate of trademarks is likely to be lower than that of books and graphic arts but not that of musical copyrights, which like trademarks have potential uses, for example in new recordings, beyond their first use. (Of course, some

---

74 The regression equation (t-statistics in parentheses) is

$$\underset{(.66)}{LRen_t = -4.30} + \underset{(11.89)}{.72LReg_{t\text{-}20}} + \underset{(6.05)}{.14LRen_{t\text{-}20}} - \underset{(1.02)}{.005Year} + \underset{(1.74)}{.06LFee_t}$$

$$\underset{(1.45)}{-.40LGNP} + u$$

$R^2 = .91$ Durbin-Watson Statistic = 1.80 n=65

The analysis also supports the assumption that the depreciation rates on registrations and renewals in t-20 are equal. Since the ratio of renewals to registrations averages about .21 over the 1915–79 period (the relevant time period for the dependent variable, which runs from 1935 to 1999), equal depreciation rates imply that the renewal elasticity in the above regression should be about 20 percent of the registration elasticity. This hypothesis is not rejected.

75 The Ford trademark was registered fourteen years after its first use in commerce (1895). For information on Ford's, and other, trademarks, search the database of the United States Patent and Trademark Office, online at http://www.uspto.gov/main/trademarks.htm (visited Feb 28, 2003).

books do too—the novel *Gone With the Wind*, for example, was later made into a very successful movie.) The data support this conjecture. We find, for the period 1934 to 1991, depreciation rates of 13.4 percent for graphic arts, 9.2 percent for books, 6.5 percent for trademarks, and 4.1 percent for music. These differences are all highly statistically significant.

Although trademarks can be renewed indefinitely, we find that their average economic life is only about 15 percent longer than that of the average copyright. The much higher renewal fees for trademarks may explain much of this difference. In 2000, it cost $300 to renew a trademark, compared to only $45 to renew a copyright.[76] However, another factor is that trademarks lapse unless used, and use is expensive, whereas a copyright can for example be renewed for a book that is out of print—the hope being that there will be some future interest in the book. Notice, finally, that the indefinite duration of trademarks is less problematic than would be the case for copyrights, because there are no social benefits to public domain trademarks, except of course generic ones—but trademarks fall into the public domain when they become generic (that is, become names standardly designating a class of products, such as "aspirin").

CONCLUSION

The regression results in Tables 1 and 2 are evidence that copyright registration and renewals are indeed highly responsive to economic incentives, as our theory predicted. The shorter the expected life of a copyright and the higher the registration and renewal fees, the less likely are both registration and renewal. This in turn suggests that a system of modestly higher registration and renewal fees than at present, a relatively short initial term (twenty years or so), and a right of indefinite renewal would cause a large number of copyrighted works

76 Patents have a kind of renewal component too. A patent cannot be renewed after the expiration of its twenty-year statutory term; but even for it to remain in force for the full twenty years the patentee must pay maintenance fees of $890 at three and a half years, $2,050 at seven and a half years, and $3,150 at eleven and a half years after the patent has been issued. 37 CFR § 1.20(e)–(g) (2003). See also 35 USC § 41(b) (2000) (establishing statutory baselines of $830, $1,900, and $2,910, respectively); 35 USC § 41(f) (2000) (authorizing yearly fee adjustments to track the Consumer Price Index). In effect, a patent holder gets to enjoy the full twenty-year term only if he "renews" his patent three times. One study indicates that 82.6 percent of patents were still in force (in other words, had been "renewed") after four years, 57.4 percent after eight years, and 37.1 percent after twelve years. Mark A. Lemley, *Rational Ignorance at the Patent Office*, 95 Nw U L Rev 1495, 1504 (2001) (calculating the percentage of patents for which maintenance fees were paid, by age of patent). We have estimated depreciation rates from these data of 4.8 percent over the first four years after issue, 6.9 percent from five to eight years, and 8.3 percent thereafter. Over the full twenty-year period, the depreciation rate is about 6 percent. Put differently, we estimate an average economic life for a patent (given maintenance fees) of about 16.6 years, which includes a full twenty-year term for about 30 percent of issued patents.

to be returned to the public domain quite soon after they were created. Of course, those would tend to be works of low average commercial value; otherwise, the owner would have renewed. And requiring registration and renewal for copyright protection, rather than, as at present, making these steps optional, would increase the incentive to take them. Nevertheless, a system of indefinite renewals (or one that combines renewals with a maximum duration) may enable society to have its cake and eat it too. More works will be in the public domain, thus minimizing access, transaction, and administrative costs, while those few copyrights that retain their value will remain in copyright protection indefinitely, with the economic advantages, involving investments in maintenance and the avoidance of congestion externalities, that we discussed earlier.

Granted, the more valuable works are also those that confer monopoly power and thus create deadweight loss if the duration of a copyright is extended. But we have given reasons for questioning whether deadweight loss is a serious consequence of extending copyright, at least if the system of indefinite renewals is available only for works created after the system is instituted. However, a benefit of indefinite renewal that should be especially emphasized, but that would be maximized by making the system available to existing copyrights as well, is that it would largely eliminate the rent-seeking problem that is created by the fact that copyright protection expires at a fixed date. Owners of valuable copyrights that are soon to expire will (along with enterprises that would like to appropriate the copyrightable works without charge) expend real resources on trying to persuade (or dissuade) Congress to extend the term.

Part II
Economics of Copying and Copyright Infringement

Introduction to Part II

This book is about copyright, a legal institution that is designed to protect authors from the activities of those who make use of their creations without payment, an activity more popularly known as 'piracy', or simply 'copying'. However, the book would certainly not be complete without a section devoted to the analysis of copying as an economic activity, and to the optimal response of authors to the existence of these activities. Only when we have a proper understanding of what copyright law is supposed to protect from, and what the scenario would likely be in absence of copyright law, can we begin to garner proper understanding of copyright law itself.

The economics of copying is essentially about situations in which one seller must compete with other sellers of very similar (perhaps identical) substitutes. This is, of course, a very common market assumption in much of economic theory, with perfect competition and traditional oligopoly models at the forefront. But for the case of intellectual property, or more particularly for the case of copyright on works of authorship, there is an important difference – the competitor's products are not independent of the first producer's, as they are derived directly from the first producer's output.[1] If there is no 'original', there can be no 'copies'. It is this dependence that affords the producer of originals a range of strategic options that can curb the activities of copiers, perhaps to the extent of complete entry deterrence of competitors, or that can turn the existence of a market for copies to their favour.

It is no coincidence that the economics of copying was born together with, and has lived in parallel with, the economics of copyright. The two are so intimately related, that one literature is almost impossible to conceive without the other. The seminal papers on the economics of copying are normally cited as three cornerstone pieces, all published in the *Journal of Political Economy* in the mid-1980s; Novos and Waldman (1984), Liebowitz (1985) and Johnson (1985). Together these three papers set the stage for a host of others over the next two decades, which have analysed the different strategies of the producer of originals when copying is a possibility, for a number of different theoretical scenarios concerning the exact situation at hand.

Perhaps one of the most important ideas to have emerged from these three seminal papers is that of 'indirect appropriability', which originates in the paper by Liebowitz (1985). Indirect appropriability is a situation in which the seller of originals charges a greater price to consumers who then copy. This type of price discrimination strategy can be shown to appropriate the willingness to pay downstream users in a subsequent copying market, thus rendering copying valuable to the producer of originals.[2] While Liebowitz showed that indirect appropriability seems to have worked well for producers of academic journals since the advent of photocopying, it is not clear whether or not it can also be successfully applied to markets for other intellectual products. The paper by Johnson and Waldman (**II, 4**) addresses this issue by means of a series of simple and easy to follow examples for which indirect appropriation probably will not work. Of course, by elimination, they also provide typologies of markets for which it is more likely to work.

With the advent of digital technologies for producing, storing, delivering and consuming works of authorship, the problem of copying has become even more pressing, and the increased attention of the economics profession to this has been noticeable. The survey paper by Peitz and Waelbroeck (**II, 5**) does a great job of commenting, and providing a sense of order to the theoretical side of this more recent literature.

The so called 'digital revolution' is still in its infancy, and although the enormity of the Internet implies that a huge amount of data on downloading activities can be generated daily, the time frame is still relatively short, perhaps too short for many capital intensive adjustments in the legitimate trade to have taken place. The characteristics of the longer-term equilibrium in the content industries, adjusted for the effects of digitalisation and copying (and sharing) technologies, are still little more than conjecture. The theoretical models that are surveyed by Peitz and Waelbroeck can only venture, albeit with authoritative logic and reasoning, what the future will actually hold, and the really pressing need is for empirical studies. The paper by Ivan Png (**II, 6**) is, by its own admission, a plea for empirical research on the content industries, and above all, on the effects of copying upon these industries.

The very existence of strategies at the disposal of producers of originals, that are a best response to the threat of (or the existence of) copiers, certainly implies that producers of originals are not neutral actors when copyright infringement is a possibility. With or without copyright law, they will take optimal strategic actions, balancing at the margin the costs and benefits to them of these actions. Copyright law will distort this balance, depending on how effective it is, and will also inevitably shift the burden of the costs of this second-best world from the producer of originals to other members of society, most obviously taxpayers, consumers of works of authorship, and even producers of new works of authorship (Landes and Posner, 1989). Much of the literature that attempts to address the issue of what an optimal level of copyright protection would look like generally comes to the conclusion that it should be neither full and absolute, nor should it be totally non-existent. However, a small but notable literature does insist that copyright law at any level is unwarranted, and market-based strategies (most importantly, creative pricing strategies akin to indirect appropriability) are all that are ever required. Perhaps the most outspoken champions of this viewpoint are Michele Boldrin and David Levine, and here we reproduce one of the papers, representative of their general argument, from a set of three or four published between 2002 and 2005.

Notes

1. Quite apart from the fact that the competitor's product may be illegal! The illegality of the competitor's product makes the economics of copyright rather similar to the economics of smuggling (see Bhagwati and Hansen, 1973). The small literature on the economics of recycling and second-hand markets is also relevant (see, for example, Swan, 1980).
2. Indirect appropriability is not restricted to pure copying; it has also been successfully used to explain markets in which consumers of information goods form groups among which units are shared. Again, since the unit that is shared is used to satisfy the consumption desires of more than one user, it can be sold at a higher price (see, for example, Varian, 2000).

References

Bhagwati, J. and B. Hansen (1973), 'A Theoretical Analysis of Smuggling', *Quarterly Journal of Economics*, **87**, 172–87.
Johnson, W.R. (1985), 'The Economics of Copying', *Journal of Political Economy*, **93** (1), 158–74.
Landes, W. and R. Posner (1989), 'An Economic Analysis of Copyright Law', *Journal of Legal Studies*, **XVIII**, 325–63.
Liebowitz, S. (1985), 'Copying and Indirect Appropriability: Photocopying of Journals', *Journal of Political Economy*, **93** (5), 945–57.
Novos, I. and M. Waldman (1984), 'The Effects of Increased Copyright Protection: An Analytic Approach', *Journal of Political Economy*, **92**, 236–46.
Swan, P. (1980), 'Alcoa: The Influence of Recycling on Monopoly Power', *Journal of Political Economy*, **76**, 76–99.
Varian, H. (2000), 'Buying, Sharing and Renting Information Goods', *Journal of Industrial Organization*, **4**, 473–88.

[4]

Review of Economic Research on Copyright Issues, 2005, vol. 2(1), pp. 19-37

THE LIMITS OF INDIRECT APPROPRIABILITY IN MARKETS FOR COPIABLE GOODS

JUSTIN P. JOHNSON AND MICHAEL WALDMAN

ABSTRACT. An extensive literature has developed that argues that in many settings the social welfare costs of copying or piracy are limited because of the presence of indirect appropriability. Indirect appropriability is the idea that original good producers can appropriate some of the value derived by the consumers of copies because of the return that buyers of original units receive from allowing copies to be made. In this paper we discuss the limitations of indirect appropriability, where the two we focus on are the "flooding" of the copy market and substitutability between new units and copies. We also discuss the ramifications of our analysis for real world markets.

1. INTRODUCTION

A crucial issue for understanding the role of copyright protection is understanding the implications of copying or piracy for the profitability of the producers of original works. The traditional argument, that appears, for example, in Arrow (1962) and Hirshleifer and Riley (1979), is that copying deprives producers of original works substantial profits since potential buyers of what we will refer to as new units shift from the new unit market to copying. In turn, because of this decreased revenue or profit flowing to the producers of new works, there is a subsequent decrease in the variety and qualities of original works produced. In the literature this is referred to as the underproduction loss.[1]

Starting with the work of Liebowitz (1985), this basic argument has been challenged on the grounds that the possibility of indirect appropriability changes the implications of copying. Indirect appropriability refers to the idea that buyers of new units receive a return from allowing copies of their new units to be made. In turn, this raises new unit buyers' willingness-to-pay, which subsequently translates into an avenue through which the producers of new works can capture some of the value that consumers of copies place on their copies. In markets where this perspective is correct and important, copying has much different implications for the operation of the market. At a minimum it should decrease the underproduction loss, and at a maximum it could actually increase rather than decrease the variety and qualities of new works produced.

In this paper we discuss the limitations of the indirect appropriability argument. The way we approach the problem is by drawing an analogy between the argument of indirect appropriability and the related argument of Swan (1980) concerning whether or not a durable goods monopolist would want to eliminate the secondhand

[1]The traditional argument is that such markets are also characterized by an underutilization loss, i.e., because original good producers price new units above marginal cost, some individuals for whom it would be efficient to consume new units do not do so.

market for used units. Swan's argument is that, because the price of a new durable unit reflects the prices at which the unit will be traded on the secondhand market in future periods, a durable goods monopolist has an incentive to allow the secondhand market to operate in an unconstrained fashion. This is analogous to Liebowitz's original argument for copying. In each case, because the willingness-to-pay of new unit purchasers reflects the value of future users of the good or future users of copies of the good, the new unit producer has an incentive not to constrain or interfere with what new unit purchasers do with the good after the purchase.

Given this perspective, there are two limitations on the indirect appropriability argument. The first, which is related to the modeling approach taken in Novos and Waldman (1984), is that competition between new unit buyers who offer their goods for copy drives the price these individuals receive for these copies down toward the marginal cost of taking the action (which in many cases is likely close to zero). To see the basic logic, we start with Swan's argument concerning durable goods. Swan's argument depends on the secondhand market for used goods not being "flooded" with used units. That is, if the number of used units on the secondhand market becomes large relative to the number of potential used unit buyers, then the used unit price falls and does not reflect the average value for used units of the buyers of the units. If this were to occur, then a durable-goods monopolist may want to eliminate the secondhand market and sell new units to these buyers directly because their purchases of used units is having little effect on the willingness-to-pay of current new unit buyers.

Although a theoretical possibility, there is no reason to think that the situation described above for durable goods markets is common. Now think about copies as opposed to used units and the indirect appropriability argument. The same argument as above applies. If copies "flood" the market, then the price of new units will not reflect the value consumers of copies place on the copies and the original works producer would be better off eliminating the ability to copy. The difference is that this possibility is much more likely here than in the durable goods case. That is, if as is frequently true each new unit buyer can make multiple copies of his or her new unit, then the flooding of the market for copies is a very realistic possibility.

The second limitation is that, because of the potential substitutability between new units and copies, the availability of copies limits the price that the original durable goods producer receives for new units. To see the logic here, we start again with Swan's argument concerning durable goods. Waldman (1996,1997) and Hendel and Lizzeri (1999) show that this argument is not robust to settings in which quality deteriorates with age and in which individuals consume either zero or one physical unit per period, i.e., used units cannot be combined to form a perfect substitute for a new unit. In such a setting the availability of used units limits the price the durable goods monopolist can charge for new units. In turn, if used unit buyers have a very low valuation for the used units, then this constraint on the new unit price is quite limiting and the monopolist maximizes its profits by eliminating the secondhand market.[2]

[2]In this analysis, as in Waldman (1996,1997), we use the term eliminate the secondhand market to refer to an action that makes used units unavailable for consumption as opposed to one that prohibits trade but does not stop used units from being consumed.

The same logic can be applied to the issue of copying. Suppose that copies are of lower quality than new units and that, in order to focus on this issue, only one copy can be made from each new unit and a copy cannot be used to make another copy. Then the price at which copies are sold serves to limit the price the original works producer receives for new units. Further, if consumers of copies have a sufficiently low valuation for product quality, then the constraint on the price of new units is sufficiently limiting that the original works producer increases its profits by stopping copies from being made. In other words, the possibility of indirect appropriability again fails to make producers better off from consumers having the ability of making copies.

Overall, the analysis of this paper suggests that indirect appropriability may be important for understanding the role of copying for some real world cases such as how the ability to copy impacts libraries, but for many other cases indirect appropriability is an unimportant factor. That is, as we discussed briefly above and in more detail in the following sections, there are multiple reasons for why copying in many real world cases decreases rather than increases revenue and profitability of original works producers. Hence, as argued in the standard view, the likely outcome of copying in many real world markets is decreased variety and quality of original works.

The outline for the paper is as follows. Section 2 discusses the indirect appropriability argument. It starts by discussing the idea of indirect appropriability in durable goods markets, and then discusses the literature that applies the argument to markets in which copying by consumers is feasible. Section 3 analyzes and discusses the first limitation which is based on the possible "flooding" of the market for copies, while Section 4 analyzes and discusses the second limitation which is based on substitutability between new units and copies. Section 5 uses the analysis of Sections 3 and 4 to discuss the circumstances in which indirect appropriability in the market for copies is likely to help producer profitability. Section 6 presents some concluding remarks.

2. Indirect appropriability

The basic argument of indirect appropriability put forth initially in Liebowitz (1985) builds on the earlier argument of Swan (1980) concerning secondhand markets. In this section we start by discussing Swan's contribution and then provide a brief history of the idea of indirect appropriability as applied to copying.

2.1. **Swan's Perspective on Secondhand Markets.** Classic issues in the literature on durable goods are the effect that secondhand markets have on the revenue and profitability of the durable goods producer and the related issue of whether the producer has an incentive to eliminate or otherwise interfere in the operation of secondhand markets.[3] Casual empiricism concerning, for example, behavior in the textbook market suggests that the operation of secondhand markets can hurt authors and publishers, and one of the goals of the introduction of new editions is to kill off the the secondhand market.

For a number of years thinking on this subject was dominated by the work of Peter Swan. His position is stated most clearly in the following quote. "The pure monopolist selling such a durable item as an automobile is paid an amount which

[3]See Waldman (2003) for a general discussion of the durable goods literature.

reflects the net present value of the stream of automobile services to possibly a whole host of future owners. Competitive secondhand auto dealers (or scrap merchants and recyclers in the case of aluminum) can then buy and sell the item idefinitely without in any way restricting the power of the monopolist as the original seller." (Swan, 1980, p. 77) In other words, the buyers of new units realize they will be able to sell those units on the secondhand market in subsequent periods. This realization raises the willingness-to-pay of new unit buyers and so the existence and operation of such secondhand markets cannot hurt producer revenue and profitability.

In a later paper, Rust (1986) formally derives results similar to Swan's discussion. Rust considers a durable goods monopoly model in which each individual consumes either zero or one physical unit of the monopolist's product in every period and the quality of a unit deteriorates as it ages. In Rust's analysis monopoly profitability does not increase if the secondhand market is eliminated and, in fact, monopoly profitability is unchanged by such elimination. But Rust assumes that all consumers are identical and given this assumption his results are not at all surprising. In a setting in which all consumers are identical there is no reason for a unit to trade hands as it ages. So Rust's analysis tells us little about the effects of killing off a secondhand market in a setting in which the secondhand market serves an important allocation role.

2.2. **The Indirect Appropriability Argument in Markets for Copiable Goods.** The argument of indirect appropriability and copying is closely related to Swan's argument concerning secondhand markets. The argument was initially put forth by Stan Liebowitz in a 1985 article in the Journal of Political Economy. Liebowitz argued that the revenue or profits received by sellers of copies positively affects the willingness-to-pay of these individuals for acquiring new units. In turn, since this positively affects the price that the original works producer can charge for new units, we have that, although the original works producer is not able to directly charge consumers of copies, there is indirect appropriability through the higher willingness-to-pay of new unit consumers. In conclusion, Liebowitz argues that copying can actually help original work producers as opposed to the standard argument in which copying must hurt such producers.[4]

After presenting the basic argument, Liebowitz extends the argument to consider the implications when there are two types of consumers of new units such as in the case of journal publishing: i) individuals who rarely have their units copied; and ii) libraries for whom copying is common. Since it is only libraries for whom copying is important, Liebowitz argues that the indirect appropriability argument only applies to the demand for new units by libraries. After extending the argument in this way, Liebowitz develops a number of predictions concerning how libraries should operate and the journal publishing industry more generally. These include that: i) there should be larger price differences between prices charged to libraries and individual subscribers for more heavily copied journals; ii) the introduction of photocopying should have caused a larger price increase for libraries than individual subscribers; and iii) the introduction of photocopying should have caused libraries to move away from purchasing books which are rarely copied towards purchasing journals which are frequently copied. He presents evidence that supports all three predictions.

[4]Although Liebowitz does not directly refer to Swan's work, he does draw an analogy with the way in which durable goods markets operate.

Besen and Kirby (1989) formally consider the issue of indirect appropriability in markets for copiable goods (Liebowitz's paper discusses the idea but does not contain any formal analysis). The first analysis in Besen and Kirby's paper shows a set of circumstances in which indirect appropriability is not operative. In this analysis new units and copies are imperfect substitutes and each new unit can be used to produce an unlimited number of copies. As found earlier in the analysis of Novos and Waldman (1984), they show that the competition between new unit purchasers on the copy market drives the price for copies down to marginal cost and thus indirect appropriability does not hold. Our analysis in Section 3 is closely related, where one difference is that we show that the assumption that a single unit can be used to make unlimited copies is not crucial.

Besen and Kirby then consider a second model in which marginal costs are increasing and consumers can form clubs which purchase a single unit and then copies are produced for all club members other than the original purchaser. They first show that, if new units and copies are perfect substitutes, club size is at the value that minimizes the average cost of acquiring a unit (where a unit in this specification is defined as either a new unit or a copy). On the other hand, if copies are lower quality, equilibrium club size is more complicated because smaller sized clubs increase the number of individuals who consume the higher quality units. In each case Besen and Kirby find that copying can either help or hurt profitability, where profitability tends to rise when copies can be made significantly more cheaply than originals.

Bakos, Brynjolfsson, and Lichtman (1999) extend Besen and Kirby's second analysis concerning sharing in teams. They consider a model in which the original work producer has a zero marginal cost of production and copies can also be made at zero cost given a new unit. This assumption of zero marginal costs seems reasonable for numerous information goods that take digital form and that can be copied at very low cost. The other key assumption is that groups are determined exogenously rather than endogenously – think of a group as a family or a circle of friends. Given this basic set-up, they consider three specifications: (i) new units and copies are perfect substitutes, groups are of equal size, and valuations across team members are uncorrelated; (ii) everything is as in the first specification except either team size varies or valuations are correlated; and (iii) the same basic set-up but copies are lower quality than new units.

By focusing on settings in which there is no cost difference between producing another new unit by the original work producer and another copy by consumers, Bakos, Brynjolfsson, and Lichtman move away from Besen and Kirby's focus of minimizing the cost of providing consumers with the good. Rather, their focus is on how teams affect the nature of demand and, in particular, that the effect of copying and teams on demand can, but does not in all cases, improve monopoly profitability. The basic argument here is similar to one of the basic arguments in the literature on bundling. That is, having teams will frequently decrease heterogeneity in demand and decreased heterogeneity can result in higher producer profits.[5] They find that, given new units and copies are perfect substitutes, higher producer profits is always the case in their analysis of equal sized teams. When teams vary in size,

[5]See Stigler (1963), Adams and Yellen (1976), and Schmalensee (1984) for analyses of bundling that focus on this point. See Johnson and Myatt (2004) for a general analysis of the impact of consumer heterogeneity on a seller's profit.

profits tend to rise when variation in team size is small relative to variation in individual valuations. Finally, in their analysis in which copies are inferior to new units, they find that the monopolist can sometimes increase profitability by further decreasing the quality of copies (this result is related to the analysis that appears in Section 4).

So the literature concerning indirect appropriability in markets for copiable goods makes two related arguments. On the one hand, as initially put forth by Liebowitz, one reason that the ability of consumers to make copies may help producer profitability is through a logic analogous to that put forth by Swan for the case of secondhand markets. That is, producer profitability may rise because the new unit price reflects the price that copies will sell for in the future. On the other hand, as initially put forth by Besen and Kirby and later extended by Bakos, Brynjolfsson, and Lichtman, profitability can be positively related to the ability to copy in settings in which teams of consumers share new units and copies amongst themselves.

3. Limitation 1: "Flooding" in the Market for Copies

In this section we discuss the first major limitation of the indirect appropriability argument. The first limitation is that, as discussed in Liebowitz (1981) and Besen and Kirby (1989) and as underlies the analysis in Novos and Waldman (1984), there is "flooding" in the market for copies. That is, so many copies become available that, rather than the price for copies reflecting the value that consumers of copies place on copies, this price is driven down to the marginal cost for copies. We begin by showing the similar point in the operation of secondhand markets and then show the argument in the case of copying.

3.1. Flooding in Secondhand Markets.

We consider a simple durable goods monopoly setting which is purposely constructed to clearly illustrate the argument. In this setting there are two groups of consumers who live for two periods and the monopolist's product deteriorates with age. Group 1 consists of n_1 identical consumers who derive a gross benefit of v_1 from consuming a new unit in a period and a value of zero from consuming a used unit in a period. Group 2 consists of n_2 identical consumers who derive a gross benefit of v_2 from consuming either a new unit or a used unit in a period. Further, the monopolist has a constant marginal cost of production equal to c, where $v_1 > c > 2v_2$, there is no discounting, and the scrap value of a used unit equals zero. In this set-up group 1 consumers are the potential buyers of new units while group 2 consumers, because $2v_2 < c$, will never purchase new units but are rather the potential buyers on the secondhand market.[6]

There are two cases. Suppose first that $n_1 < n_2$, i.e., there are more potential secondhand market buyers than new unit buyers. What happens in this case is that in period 1 group 1 individuals buy new units from the monopolist at a price P_1, while in period 2 group 1 individuals sell used units to group 2 consumers at a price v_2 and then purchase new units from the monopolist at a price P_2. Because there are no later periods and thus no future secondhand market sales for new units purchased in period 2, the monopolist sets P_2 equal to v_1. In contrast, because new units sold in the first period are sold at a price of v_2 in the second period on the

[6]Because group 2 consumers never purchase new units, the time inconsistency problem explored, for example, by Coase (1972) and Bulow (1982) does not come into play in our analysis.

secondhand market, the monopolist sets P_1 equal to $v_1 + v_2$. Monopoly profits are therefore equal to $n_1 (2v_1 + v_2 - 2c)$.

This case illustrates Swan's argument concerning the effects of secondhand markets on the profitability of durable goods sellers. Because $n_1 < n_2$, i.e., there are more secondhand market buyers than sellers, the price that used units trade for on the secondhand market in the second period reflects the value that the secondhand market buyers place on the used units. In turn, the anticipation of this by group 1 buyers in the first period increases the group 1 individuals' willingness-to-pay for new units in the first period, so the presence of this secondhand market trade increases firm profits. In other words, the firm earns $n_1 (2v_1 + v_2 - 2c)$ rather than $n_1 (2v_1 - 2c)$ which is what the firm would earn if either the secondhand market was not allowed to operate or the monopolist produced nondurable rather than durable units.

Now suppose that $n_1 > n_2$, i.e., there are more new unit buyers than potential secondhand market buyers. What happens in this case is that in period 1 group 1 individuals buy new units from the monopolist at a price P_1, while in period 2 n_2 group 1 individuals sell used units to group 2 consumers at a price of zero, the remaining used units are scrapped, and all group 1 consumers purchase new units from the monopolist at a price P_2. As before, because there are no later periods and thus no future secondhand market sales for new units purchased in period 2, the monopolist sets P_2 equal to v_1. However, differently than before, because new units sold in the first period are either sold at a price of zero in the second period or scrapped, the monopolist sets P_1 equal to v_1. Monopoly profits in this case are equal to $n_1 (2v_1 - 2c)$.

This case shows that Swan's logic breaks down when used units "flood" the secondhand market. By flooding the secondhand market we mean that there are more used units available for purchase on the secondhand market than potential used unit buyers, so the secondhand market price falls to the scrap value which in this setting equals zero. In other words, rather than the secondhand market price equaling the benefit from consumption of used unit buyers as in Swan's argument, the secondhand market price falls to the scrap value. In turn, what this means is that the presence of the secondhand market has no effect on the willingness-to-pay of new unit buyers in the first period and so, in contrast to Swan's argument, the presence of the secondhand market has no effect on the profitability of the durable goods monopolist.

In the setting we just considered, when the secondhand market is flooded, monopoly profits are not hurt by the existence of the secondhand market. That is, as indicated profits in this case are equal to $n_1 (2v_1 - 2c)$ while, if the secondhand market were eliminated or the monopolist were able to make the units nondurable, profits would again by given by $n_1 (2v_1 - 2c)$. But it would not be hard to change the analysis slightly so that when flooding occurs the monopolist is, in fact, hurt by the secondhand market. For example, suppose we introduced a group 3 set of individuals who enter the market in period 2, where this group consists of n_3 identical individuals who derive a gross benefit of v_3, where $v_3 = v_1$, from consuming either a new unit or a used unit in a period. Further, suppose that similar to the second case $n_1 > n_2 + n_3$.

Analysis of this setting yields that, if the secondhand market is allowed to operate, then the outcome is similar to what happened when there was no group 3 and $n_1 > n_2$. That is, in period 1 group 1 individuals buy new units from the monopolist at a price v_1, while in period 2 $n_2 + n_3$ group 1 individuals sell used units to group 2 and group 3 consumers at a price of zero, the remaining used units are scrapped, and all group 1 consumers purchase new units from the monopolist at a price of v_1. In turn, monopoly profits are the same as when there was no group 3 and $n_2 > n_1$, i.e., profits are equal to $n_1 (2v_1 - 2c)$.

But there is something different about this case. Specifically, now monopoly profits are, in fact, higher if the monopolist has the option of either stopping the secondhand market from operating or similarly producing nondurable units. To see this, suppose the monopolist could stop the secondhand market from operating and decided to do so. Then in period 1 group 1 individuals would buy new units from the monopolist at a price v_1, while in period 2 all used units would be scrapped and all group 1 and group 3 consumers would purchase new units from the monopolist at a price v_1 (remember $v_3 = v_1$). Monopoly profits in this case are equal to $n_1 (2v_1 - 2c) + n_3 (v_1 - c)$, i.e., as indicated monopoly profits here are higher than if the secondhand market were allowed to operate.

In summary, we have considered a simple two-period durable-goods monopoly setting that illustrates that Swan's logic is correct some of the time but not all of the time. When there are more potential used unit buyers than new unit buyers, then the secondhand market price reflects the value that the used unit buyers place on the used units. The result is that, consistent with Swan's argument, new unit buyers in anticipation of the future high price on the secondhand market are willing to pay more for new units with the result that the presence of the secondhand market improves monopoly profitability. In contrast, when there are more new unit buyers than potential used unit buyers, then the secondhand market price falls to the scrap value which in our analysis was zero. In this case, in contrast to Swan's argument, the presence of the secondhand market does not increase the willingness-to-pay of new unit buyers, and so does not improve monopoly profitability. In fact, we showed through the introduction of a third group of consumers that, when the secondhand market price is equal to the scrap value of the good, the presence of the secondhand market can actually hurt monopoly profitability.

3.2. **Flooding in the Market for Copies.** In this subsection we show that the argument of the previous subsection concerning secondhand markets also limits the applicability of the indirect appropriability argument concerning the effects of copying. Consider a one period setting with two groups of consumers and assume that the monopolist's product deteriorates when it is copied. Group 1 consists of n_1 identical consumers who derive a gross benefit of v_1 from consuming a new unit and a value of zero from consuming a copy. Group 2 consists of n_2 identical consumers who derive a gross benefit of v_2 from consuming either a used unit or a copy. Further, the monopolist has a constant marginal cost of production equal to c, where $v_1 > c > v_2$, and $x > 0$ copies can be made from a new unit at costant marginal cost d, where $v_2 > d$.[7] In this set-up group 1 consumers are the potential buyers of new units while group 2 consumers, because $d < v_2 < c$, will never purchase new units but are rather the potential consumers of copies.

As in the secondhand market analysis above, there are two cases. Suppose first that $xn_1 < n_2$, i.e., even if all group 1 consumers purchase new units, there are still

[7] To keep the argument straightforward, we assume a copy cannot be used to produce another copy.

more potential buyers of copies than there are potential copies. What happens is that group 1 individuals buy new units from the monopolist at a price P and then each group 1 buyer turns around and sells x copies to group 2 consumers at a price v_2. Because each new unit purchased allows a group 1 consumer to sell x copies at a price v_2 apiece and the consumer has a constant marginal cost of d for producing copies, the new unit price is given by $P = v_1 + x(v_2 - d)$. Monopoly profits are therefore equal to $n_1 [v_1 - c + x(v_2 - d)]$.

This case illustrates Liebowitz's argument concerning the effects of copying on the profitability of original work producers. Because $xn_1 < n_2$, i.e., there are more potential buyers of copies than the maximum potential number of copies, the price of copies reflects the value that the buyers of copies place on the copies. In turn, the anticipation of this by group 1 buyers at the beginning of the game increases group 1 individuals' willingness-to-pay for new units in the first period so the possibility of copying increases firm profits. In other words, the firm earns $n_1 [v_1 - c + x(v_2 - d)]$ rather than $n_1 [v_1 - c]$ which is what the firm would earn if copying for one reason or another were not a possibility.

Now suppose that $xn_1 > n_2$, i.e., there are more potential copies than potential purchasers of copies. What happens in this case is that group 1 individuals buy new units from the monopolist at price P, and then group 1 consumers sell copies to all group 2 consumers at a price of d. That is, given there are more potential copies than potential purchasers of copies, the competition between the sellers of copies drives the price for a copy down to its marginal cost. This means there is no profit associated with selling copies, so the monopolist sets the price for a new unit at v_1 and monopoly profits are equal to $n_1 [v_1 - c]$.

This case shows that Liebowitz's logic breaks down when copies "flood" the market. Flooding here means there are more potential copies for sale than there are potential buyers of the copies, so the price for a copy falls to the marginal cost of producing a copy which is d. In other words, rather than the price for a copy equaling the benefit from consumption of the consumers of copies as in Liebowitz's argument, the price for a copy falls to the marginal cost of producing copies. In turn, what this means is that the ability to produce copies has no effect on the willingness-to-pay of new unit buyers so, in contrast to Liebowitz's argument, the ability to produce copies has no effect on the profitability of the monopolist.

So far, the flooding of the market for copies does not hurt the profitability of the monopolist. That is, as indicated profits in this case are equal to $n_1 [v_1 - c]$, while if copying were not possible profits would again by given by $n_1 [v_1 - c]$. But, as was also the case with our secondhand market analysis, it would not be hard to change the analysis slightly so that when flooding occurs the monopolist is, in fact, hurt by the possibility of copying. For example, suppose we introduced a group 3, where this group consists of n_3 identical individuals who derive a gross benefit of v_3, where $v_3 = v_1$, from consuming either a new unit or a copy. Further, suppose that similar to the second case $xn_1 > n_2 + n_3$.

Analysis of this setting yields that, if copying is allowed, then the outcome is similar to what happened when there was no group 3 and $xn_1 > n_2$. That is, group 1 individuals buy new units from the monopolist at a price v_1, while $n_2 + n_3$ copies are sold to group 2 and group 3 consumers at a price of d. In turn, monopoly profits are the same as when there was no group 3 and $xn_1 > n_2$, i.e., profits are equal to $n_1 [v_1 - c]$.

But notice there is something different about this case. Specifically, now monopoly profits are, in fact, higher if it has the option of producing units that cannot be copied. To see this, suppose the monopolist can produce noncopiable units. Then the monopolist would sell new units to all group 1 and group 3 consumers at a price of v_1 (remember $v_3 = v_1$). Monopoly profits in this case are equal to $n_1 [v_1 - c] + n_3 [v_1 - c]$, i.e., as indicated monopoly profits here are higher than if copying were allowed.

Comparing this analysis to the previous analysis we see that in each case "flooding" causes indirect appropriability to become nonoperative. In turn, depending on the specifics of the model, the avenue through which indirect appropriability is supposed to operate, i.e., secondhand market sales in the earlier analysis and sales of copies here, can actually hurt rather than help monopoly profitability. The other interesting point to note is that the analyses suggest that flooding is more likely in the copying case than in the case of secondhand markets. In the basic analysis of secondhand markets, flooding occurs when the high valuation group is larger than the low valuation group. In the basic analysis of copying, flooding occurs when the number of high valuation consumers multiplied by the maximum number of copies that can be produced from a single new unit is larger than the number of low valuation consumers. Since for many goods a single new unit can be used to produce many copies, the flooding outcome in the copying case is likely to be quite common.

In related analyses of this issue such as Liebowitz (1981) and Besen and Kirby (1989), one issue that has been discussed is the importance of whether the owner of a new unit faces constant or increasing marginal costs of producing copies. As in the analysis of Novos and Waldman (1984), in the above we have assumed that the marginal cost of copying is constant. We feel that for many real world situations this is a quite reasonable approach. If making a copy means using a copy machine or a professional copying service such as Kinkos, then marginal cost is likely to be constant or possibly even decreasing (the decreasing case follows from the possibility of volume discounts). Similarly, if what is being copied is a digital or electronic document that can be copied through standard computer operation and transmitted over the web, then again the assumption of a constant marginal cost of copying seems realistic.

Although we believe the constant marginal cost case is realistic, we will briefly discuss what would happen in our analysis if the marginal cost of producing copies were increasing but there was still a maximum of x copies that could be made from a single copy.[8] Consider the two group analysis and suppose that were the case. If $xn_1 < n_2$, then the analysis is roughly unchanged, i.e., the only change is that the profitability of selling copies decreases because the price minus marginal cost difference falls as the number of copies made from a single unit increases. Second, if $n_1 > n_2$, then there is no change at all because a single copy produced from each new unit would be sufficient to flood the market for copies. Third, if $n_1 < n_2 < xn_1$, then the analysis changes in the sense that there will be some indirect appropriability due to profits earned on the inframarginal copies. In other words, introducing

[8]One can now think of x as the largest number of copies from a single unit such that the marginal cost of producing the last copy is less than or equal to v_2.

increasing marginal costs of copying does not negate our qualitative conclusions, but it does make the indirect appropriability case more likely.[9]

In summary, we have considered a simple model of copying that illustrates that the indirect appropriability argument is correct some of the time but far from all of the time. When there are more potential buyers of copies than copies, then the price for copies reflects the value that the buyers of copies place on the copies. The result is that, consistent with the indirect appropriability argument, new unit buyers in anticipation of the high copy price are willing to pay more for new units with the result that the possibility of copying improves monopoly profitability. In contrast, when there are more potential copies than buyers of copies, then the copy price falls to the marginal cost of copying. In this case, in contrast to the indirect appropriability argument, the possibility of copying does not increase the willingness-to-pay of new unit buyers, and so does not improve monopoly profitability. In fact, we showed through the introduction of a third group of consumers that, when the copy price equals marginal cost, the possibility of copying can actually hurt monopoly profitability. We also discussed how the analysis changes when the marginal cost of copying is increasing rather than constant.

4. Limitation 2: Imperfect substitutability

In this section we discuss the second major limitation of the indirect appropriability argument. The second limitation is that there is imperfect substitutability between new units and copies. In this argument copies are perceived to be of lower quality than new units with the result that the presence of copies lowers the new unit price and, if this effect is significant enough, also lowers monopoly profitability.

4.1. Imperfect Substitutability in Durable-Goods Markets. The analysis in this section is closely related to earlier analyses that appear in Waldman (1996) and Hendel and Lizzeri (1999).[10] The model we consider is also related to the durable goods model considered in the previous section. There are two important differences. First, in the previous model new unit buyers placed a zero value on consuming used units. This eliminated possible effects on the new unit price due to the substitutability between new and used units. In contrast, here new unit buyers do place a positive value on the consumption of used units. Second, we now abstract away from the flooding issue which was the focus of the previous analysis by assuming there are more used unit buyers than new unit buyers.

As before, we consider a durable goods setting in which there are two groups of consumers who live for two periods and the monopolist's product deteriorates with age. Group 1 consists of n_1 identical consumers who derive a gross benefit of v_1^N from consuming a new unit in a period and a value of v_1^U from consuming a used

[9]Given that as argued above, it is arguably realistic for some situations to assume that the marginal cost of copying is decreasing, one might feel it is worthwhile to consider how the analysis changes with that assumption. However, incorporating that assumption dramatically complicates the analysis because it eliminates the competitive nature of the copy market. Introducing decreasing marginal costs of copying is thus beyond the scope of the current paper.

[10]Related analyses appear in Benjamin and Kormendi (1974), Miller (1974), and Liebowitz (1982). Those earlier papers start by specifying demand functions, while the more recent papers cited above derive results by starting with utility functions and assuming utility maximization. Note also that the argument of this section is closely related to the literature on the monopoly pricing of a product line in a static setting. See Mussa and Rosen (1978) and Maskin and Riley (1984) for analyses. Waldman (1996) discusses the relationship between the two literatures.

unit in a period, $v_1^N > v_1^U$. Group 2 consists of n_2 identical consumers who derive a gross benefit of v_2^N from consuming a new unit in a period and a value of v_2^U from consuming a used unit in a period, $v_2^N > v_2^U$. Further, the monopolist has a constant marginal cost of production equal to c, where $v_1^N - v_1^U > c > 2v_2^N$. We also assume $n_2 > n_1$ (which ensures that there is no flooding), there is no discounting, and that the scrap value equals zero. In this set-up group 1 consumers will want to buy new units in each period, while group 2 consumers never purchase new units but are rather the potential buyers on the secondhand market.[11]

To analyze this case, we start with the second period under the assumption that in the first period all group 1 consumers purchased new units. Because $v_1^N - v_1^U > c$ and $n_2 > n_1$, in the second period group 1 consumers sell used units to group 2 consumers at a price v_2^U and then the monopolist sells new units to group 1 consumers at a price $v_2^U + (v_1^N - v_1^U)$. That is, group 1 consumers sell their used units to group 2 consumers at the valuation group 2 consumers place on the units and then buy new units at a price equal to the used unit price plus the incremental valuation group 1 consumers place on the added quality associated with new units. We now have that second period monopoly profitability is given by $n_1\left[v_2^U + (v_1^N - v_1^U) - c\right]$.

Now consider the first period given this is what happens in the second period if group 1 consumers purchase new units in the first. Because v_2^N is sufficiently small that group 2 consumers never purchase new units, in the first period the monopolist sells new units to group 1 consumers at a price $v_1^N + v_2^U$. The first term here is the valuation that group 1 consumers place on consuming the new unit in the first period, while the second is the price that a group 1 consumer is able to sell a used unit for in the second period. The logic for the value of the first period price for a new unit, denoted P_1, is that this price equates the net benefit a group 1 consumer derives from purchasing a new unit in the first period, i.e., $2v_1^N + v_2^U - P_1 - (v_2^U + v_1^N - v_1^U)$ with the net benefit a group 1 consumer receives from waiting and then buying a used unit in the second period, i.e. $v_1^U - v_2^U$. We now have that first period profitability is given by $n_1\left[v_1^N + v_2^U - c\right]$ and overall profitability is given by $n_1\left[2v_1^N + 2v_2^U - v_1^U - 2c\right]$.

In order to focus on what this analysis tells us concerning Swan's argument about secondhand markets, let us quickly consider what would happen in this model if we made the single change that the monopolist's output was nondurable rather than durable (this is equivalent to assuming $v_1^U = v_2^U = 0$). Given this assumption, the monopolist would simply sell new units to group 1 consumers in each period at a price of v_1^N and overall monopoly profitability would be $n_1\left[2v_1^N - 2c\right]$.[12]

We can now consider what this model tells us concerning the incentives for durable goods producers to eliminate secondhand markets (as mentioned earlier in footnote 2, we now use the term eliminate the secondhand market to refer to an action that makes used units unavailable for consumption such as producing nondurable units). There are two cases. The first case is that $2v_2^U > v_1^U$. In this case the monopolist has no incentive to eliminate the secondhand

[11]As was true in the durable goods analysis of the previous section, because group 2 consumers never purchase new units, the Coase time inconsistency problem does not come into play in our analysis.

[12]An alternative approach would be to assume units are durable but secondhand market trade is not possible. This would yield the same value for overall monopoly profitability given the assumption that in the second period the monopolist can price discriminate between those who own used units and those who do not.

market because indirect appropriability is causing monopoly profitability to be higher rather than lower due to the ability of consumers to trade on the secondhand market. That is, with the secondhand market the monopolist earns $n_1\left[2v_1^N+2v_2^U-v_1^U-2c\right]$ while without it the monopolist earns $n_1\left[2v_1^N-2c\right]$, and if $2v_2^U>v_1^U$ then $n_1\left[2v_1^N+2v_2^U-v_1^U-2c\right]>n_1\left[2v_1^N-2c\right]$.

The other case is that $2v_2^U<v_1^U$. In this case the monopolist has an incentive to eliminate the secondhand market or more generally make used units unavailable for consumption, where the reason is that the negative effects on profitability due to the substitutability between new and used units trumps the positive effects due to indirect appropriability. That is, we again have that with the secondhand market the monopolist earns $n_1\left[2v_1^N+2v_2^U-v_1^U-2c\right]$ while without it the monopolist earns $n_1\left[2v_1^N-2c\right]$, but now since $2v_2^U<v_1^U$ we have $n_1\left[2v_1^N+2v_2^U-v_1^U-2c\right]<n_1\left[2v_1^N-2c\right]$.

To be completely clear, we now describe the logic in a bit more detail. In this model the presence of the secondhand market has two effects on monopoly profitability that work in opposite directions. On the one hand, as emphasized by Swan, the new unit price in the first period reflects the price that used units will sell for on the secondhand market in the second period. That is, the first-period new-unit price is $v_1^N+v_2^U$, so from this standpoint monopoly profitability is $n_1v_2^U$ higher than monopoly profitability in the case with no secondhand market. On the other hand, the new unit price in the second period is lower due to the substitutability between new and used units. That is, the second-period new-unit price is $v_2^U+(v_1^N-v_1^U)$, so from this standpoint monopoly profitability is $n_1(v_1^U-v_2^U)$ lower than monopoly profitability in the case with no secondhand market. When $2v_2^U>v_1^U$ the first effect dominates and the monopolist is helped by the secondhand market, but if $2v_2^U<v_1^U$ the second effect dominates and the monopolist is hurt by the secondhand market.

Note that what this analysis says is that, if secondhand market buyers have sufficiently low valuations for the used product, i.e., v_2^U is sufficiently small, then the monopolist benefits by eliminating the secondhand market. This is very intuitive. First, if the secondhand market buyers have low valuations, then the secondhand market price is low and the extra profitability due to indirect appropriability is small. Second, if the secondhand market buyers have low valuations, then the resulting low secondhand market price in the second period also causes a low second period price for new units. Both effects work in the direction of increasing the profitability associated with the monopolist eliminating the secondhand market.

As a final point, we have focused on making the product nondurable and stopping secondhand market trade as the tactics a durable goods seller with market power might use to increase profits in this type of setting. But as discussed in the literature on this topic, e.g., Waldman (1996, 1997) and Hendel and Lizzeri (1999), there are actually various other tactics a firm might employ to achieve this outcome. For example, a firm might decide to lease rather than sell its output and then make used units unavailable for consumption by retiring the used units when they are returned. Or, alternatively, consistent with what seems to occur in the textbook market, the producer or publisher can introduce new editions which achieves the goal by making old copies of the book obsolete.

In summary, in this subsection we have shown that, even if the secondhand market is not flooded with used units, Swan's argument can still break down because of the substitutability between new and used units and the resulting constraint that used unit availability has on the new unit price. In particular, this leads to a reason for the durable goods producer to eliminate the secondhand market when used unit buyers have low valuations for used units.

4.2. **Imperfect Substitutability in Markets for Copiable Goods.** In this subsection we show that the argument of the previous subsection concerning imperfect substitutability in durable goods markets also applies when copying is an issue. That is, if copies are lower quality than originals, then the price at which copies sell constrains the price that the original works producer can charge for new units. In turn, if the valuation that the buyers of copies have for copies is low, then this constraint lowers the profitability of the original works producer below profitability in the absence of copies which means the firm would prefer if copying was not a possibility.[13]

Note that there are two differences between the model we consider here and the model of copying we considered in the previous section. First, in the previous model new unit buyers placed a zero value on consuming a copy. This eliminated possible effects on the new unit price due to the substitutability between new units and copies. In contrast, here new unit buyers do place a positive value on the consumption of copies. Second, we now abstract away from the flooding issue which was the focus of the previous analysis of copying by assuming there are more potential buyers of copies than new unit buyers and each new unit can only be used to produce a single copy (and a copy cannot be used to produce another copy).

As in our previous analysis of copying, we consider a one period setting with two groups of consumers and assume that the monopolist's product deteriorates when it is copied. Group 1 consists of n_1 identical consumers who derive a gross benefit of v_1^N from consuming a new unit and a value of v_1^C from consuming a copy, $v_1^N > v_1^C$. Group 2 consists of n_2 identical consumers who derive a gross benefit of v_2^N from consuming a new unit and a value of v_2^C from consuming a copy, $v_2^N > v_2^C$. Further, the monopolist has a constant marginal cost of production equal to c, where $v_1^N - v_1^C > c > v_2^N$, and each new unit can be used to produce a single copy at cost d, where $v_2^C > d$. In this set-up group 1 consumers are the potential buyers of new units while group 2 consumers, because $d < v_2^N < c$, will never purchase new units but are rather the potential consumers of copies. We also assume $n_2 > n_1$ and no discounting.

Let us start by considering the price in the market for copies. Suppose that all group 1 consumers purchase new units from the monopolist. Because $n_2 > n_1$ and each new unit can only be used to produce a single copy, each group 1 consumer sells a copy to a group 2 consumer at a price v_2^C. In turn, since when purchasing new units group 1 consumers will correctly anticipate that this will be the price at which copies can be purchased or sold, the monopolist will only be able to charge $(v_1^N - v_1^C) + 2v_2^C - d$ for new units. That is, one equates the net benefit a group 1 consumer derives from purchasing a copy at a price v_2^C, i.e., $v_1^C - v_2^C$, with the net benefit derived from purchasing a new unit at P, i.e., $v_1^N - P + (v_2^C - d)$. This means monopoly profitability is given by $n_1\left[(v_1^N - v_1^C) + 2v_2^C - c - d\right]$.

In order to focus on what this analysis tells us concerning the indirect appropriability argument, let us quickly consider what would happen in this model if we

[13]Analyses related to the one considered here appear in Takeyama (1997), Belleflamme (2003), and Bae and Choi (2003).

made the single change that new units could not be copied (this is equivalent to assuming $v_1^C = v_2^C = 0$). Given this assumption, the monopolist would simply sell new units to group 1 consumers at a price of v_1^N and overall monopoly profitability would be $n_1 \left[v_1^N - c\right]$.

We can now see what this model tells us concerning the effect of copying on monopoly profitability. There are two cases. The first case is that $2v_2^C > v_1^C + d$. In this case the ability of consumers to make copies helps monopoly profitability, where the increased profitability stems from the ability of the monopolist to appropriate the values consumers of copies place on the copies through the new unit price. That is, when copying is possible the monopolist earns $n_1 \left[(v_1^N - v_1^C) + 2v_2^C - c - d\right]$ while, if it is not, the monopolist earns $n_1 \left[v_1^N - c\right]$, and if $2v_2^C > v_1^C + d$, then $n_1 \left[(v_1^N - v_1^C) + 2v_2^C - c - d\right] > n_1 \left[v_1^N - c\right]$.

The other case is that $2v_2^C < v_1^C + d$. In this case monopoly profitability is hurt by the ability of consumers to make copies, where the decreased profitability stems from the negative effect on the new unit price due to the substitutability between new units and copies. That is, we again have that when copying is possible the monopolist earns $n_1 \left[(v_1^N - v_1^C) + 2v_2^C - c - d\right]$ while, if it is not, the monopolist earns $n_1 \left[v_1^N - c\right]$, but now $2v_2^C < v_1^C + d$ so $n_1 \left[(v_1^N - v_1^C) + 2v_2^C - c - d\right] < n_1 \left[v_1^N - c\right]$.

The logic here is basically the same as in the analysis of the previous subsection. In this model the ability of consumers to copy has two effects on monopoly profitability that work in opposite directions. On the one hand, as emphasized by Liebowitz, the new unit price reflects the profits that new unit buyers derive from selling copies. That is, the price for new units is higher by an amount $v_2^C - d$ because of the ability of consumers to copy. On the other hand, the new unit price is lower because of the substitutability between new units and copies. That is, the substitution possibility decreases the new unit price by an amount $v_1^C - v_2^C$. When $2v_2^C > v_1^C + d$ the first effect dominates and the monopolist is helped by the ability of consumers to copy, but if $2v_2^C < v_1^C + d$ the second effect dominates and the monopolist is hurt by copying.

Note that the conclusion of this subsection concerning when the indirect appropriability argument breaks down is similar to the previous subsection's conclusion concerning when Swan's argument breaks down. That is, it is when the consumers of copies have low valuations for copies, i.e., when v_2^C is low, that copying hurts monopoly profitability and thus the firm would prefer to make copying impossible. As was true for the similar result in the previous subsection, there are two factors that contribute to this result. First, when the consumers of copies have low valuations on the copies, the price of a copy is low so the direct increase in the new unit price due to indirect appropriability is small. Second, because the copy price is low, the substitutability between new units and copies also causes a low new unit price.

In summary, we have now identified two reasons why the indirect appropriability argument concerning copying can break down. First, if the number of copies available for purchase is sufficiently large, i.e., copies flood the market, then the price of a copy falls to marginal cost. This means there is no profit associated with selling copies and thus no indirect appropriability component of the new unit price. Second, because of the potential substitutability between new units and copies, the price at which copies are available limits the price the monopolist can charge for new units. In turn, if consumer valuation for copies is low so this constraint causes a low new unit price, then the ability of consumers to copy hurts rather than helps monopoly profitability.

5. Discussion

In the previous two sections we analyzed and discussed two limitations of the indirect appropriability argument for copiable goods. In this section we discuss what we believe are the implications of those analyses for real world markets. Our first focus is on which types of real world markets the indirect appropriability argument is likely to be important. We then briefly discuss optimal copyright policy.

In Section 2 we discussed the literature on indirect appropriability in markets for copiable goods and pointed out that there are two distinct ideas in that literature. The first, due initially to Liebowitz, is that there is an analogy between markets for copiable goods and markets for durable goods. In each case the price for new units should include a component that reflects the profits that a new unit buyer derives from selling either used units or copies in later periods. In turn, this added component in the new unit price can cause profits to rise as a result of either the presence of secondhand markets or of copying being possible.

The second, due initially to Besen and Kirby, is that the ability of consumers to form groups and share new units and copies within a group can also cause profits to rise as a result of copying being possible. One reason is that such copying can be efficient from the standpoint of providing consumers access to the good, while a second reason is that such sharing can reduce heterogeneity of demand.

Our interpretation of the analyses of Sections 2 and 3 is that the first avenue through which consumer copying can improve producer profitability is probably of limited relevance in most real world markets. Our analyses show that there are two important limitations associated with this type of indirect appropriability. First, the market for copies can be flooded in which case the copy price falls to marginal cost and the new unit price contains no added component due to profits associated with copying. Since in many real world markets a single new unit can be used to produce an almost unlimited number of copies and sometimes copies can be used to produce more copies, this seems like a significant drawback of the first indirect appropriability argument. Second, even in the minority of cases in which flooding does not occur, the substitutability between new units and copies constrains the new unit price. If this constraint is sufficiently limiting as would likely be the case if the consumers of copies place a low valuation on copies, then again the ability of consumers to copy will hurt rather than help producer profitability.

On the other hand, the limitations discussed in Sections 3 and 4 are not relevant for the sharing version of the indirect appropriability argument. In fact, our interpretation of Liebowitz's empirical findings concerning libraries is exactly the sharing story. Libraries typically do not charge on a per unit basis for access to their collections. Rather, libraries represent the interests of a set of individuals who share the collection. As copying becomes easier, the collection becomes more valuable to the library's patrons and thus willingness-to-pay of libraries rises. It is in this way, we believe, that the introduction of copying helps original work producers in terms of sales to libraries.

We are not sure, however, how far the sharing argument extends beyond the case of libraries. Both the Besen and Kirby analysis and the analysis of Bakos,

Brynjolfsson, and Lichtman make a strong and to some extent ad hoc assumption. This assumption is that there is no selling or sharing of copies across groups. This assumption seems reasonable for the case of libraries where it would be unusual for a library's collection to consist in any significant way of copies of books and journals that were made by copying parts of other library's collections. But this assumption seems less reasonable for many other applications.

If a small circle of friends share copies of an original recording there is little to stop one of the friends from either selling a copy to or sharing a copy with someone outside of the group. But this type of cross-group sharing potentially has significantly different ramifications than the two sharing analyses discussed in Section 2. That is, our conjecture is that relative to the results found in those two earlier studies, when there is sharing across groups, the introduction of copying is much less likely to result in increases in original work producer profitability. Given that this has not been formally studied as far as we know, however, we believe this is one area of study in which additional theoretical work is important.

As a final point, let us very briefly discuss the ramifications for optimal copyright policy of the assumption that the indirect appropriability argument is important. One might at first think that the correct conclusion is that copyright protection should be weakened. But this is not so clear cut to us. To the extent that copying improves producer profitability in some cases, the producer would have an incentive to allow that type of copying. So, to the extent feasible, it may be optimal to give producers more discretion over which type of copying is allowed and which type is not. Given such discretion, producers would allow copying when copying improves profitability and likely therefore also social welfare, while copying would not be allowed when it hurts producer profitability and possibly also social welfare.

6. Conclusion

In an influential paper, Liebowitz (1985) argued that the traditional argument concerning the effects of copying or piracy is incomplete because it ignores the possibility of indirect appropriability. In this paper we have discussed two important limitations of the indirect appropriability argument. First, if there is a sufficient number of copies available, then indirect appropriability goes to zero because the price on the secondhand market falls to marginal cost. Second, because of potential substitutability between new units and copies, copying does not help original work producer profitability if consumers of copies place a sufficiently low valuation on the copies. We also argued that these limitations are important in real world markets with the result that the traditional argument is closer to reality than one might have thought when the indirect appropriability argument was first put forth.

In this paper we considered simple models characterized by two or three groups and two periods that allowed us to illustrate our main points in an easy to follow manner. However, this approach obviously abstracts from the real world in important ways. One possible avenue for future research would be to investigate some of the same issues that we focus on in richer and more realistic models. Although, as indicated above, we believe our current analysis indicates that indirect appropriability is likely to be of limited significance in most real world markets, analysis of such richer models might give us a clearer picture of the real world role of indirect appropriability.

Note further that, although we conclude that the indirect appropriability argument based on an analogy with durable goods production is of limited importance in many if not most real world markets, we feel that the related idea that copying can have positive effects on profitability when sharing is important is an important and in some settings quite realistic argument. When sharing is important as in the case of libraries, then the ability to copy makes sharing more efficient and also potentially reduces demand heterogeneity. Both factors can increase the profitability of original work producers. There have been some studies of sharing when copying is a possibility. But we feel this is an important but underresearched idea, and that further investigation of this topic would be worthwhile.

To sum up, we believe that Liebowitz (1985) is an important contribution because it points out that the ability of consumers to make copies can in certain circumstances help rather than hurt the profitability of original work producers. In thinking about when this is important, however, we would move away from Liebowitz's original focus which was on drawing an analogy to durable goods production where the new unit price reflects the price the good will sell for in future periods on the secondhand market. We believe that in many cases this avenue for raising the new unit price does not result in the ability of consumers to make copies increasing the profitability of original work producers. Rather, it is settings in which sharing is important in which the ability of consumers to make copies may help producer profitability.

References

Adams, W. and J. Yellen (1976), "Commodity Bundling and the Burden of Monopoly", *Quarterly Journal of Economics*, 90; 475-498.

Arrow, K. (1962), "Economic Welfare and the Allocation of Resources for Invention", in *The Rate and Direction of Inventive Activity: Economic and Social Factors*, Princeton, NJ, Princeton University Press.

Bae, S. and J. Choi (2003), "A Model of Piracy", Mimeo, Department of Economics, Michigan State University.

Bakos, Y., E. Brynjolfsson and D. Lichtman (1999), "Shared Information Goods", *Journal of Law and Economics*, 42; 117-155.

Belleflamme, P. (2003), "Pricing Information Goods in the Presence of Copying", in Gordon, W. and R. Watt (eds.), *The Economics of Copyright: Developments in Research and Analysis*, Cheltenham UK and Northampton MA, Edward Elgar Publishers Ltd.

Benjamin, D. and R. Kormendi (1974), "The Interrelationship Between the Markets for New and Used Durable Goods", *Journal of Law and Economics*, 17; 381-401.

Besen, S. and S. Kirby (1989), "Private Copying, Appropriability, and Optimal Copyright Royalties", *Journal of Law and Economics*, 32; 255-280.

Bulow, J. (1982), "Durable Good Monopolists", *Journal of Political Economy*, 90; 314-332.

Coase, R. (1972), "Durability and Monopoly", *Journal of Law and Economics*, 15; 143-149.

Hendel, I. and A. Lizzeri (1999), "Interfering with Secondary Markets", *Rand Journal of Economics*, 30; 1-21.

Hirshleifer, J. and J. Riley (1979), "The Analytics of Uncertainty and Information – an Expository Survey", *Journal of Economic Literature*, 17; 1375-1421.

Johnson, J. and D. Myatt (2004), "On the Simple Economics of Advertising, Marketing, and Product Design", Mimeo, Johnson Graduate School of Management, Cornell University.

Liebowitz, S. (1981), "The Impact of Reprography on the Copyright System", Copyright Revision Studies, Consumer and Corporate Affairs Canada.

Liebowitz, S. (1982), "Durability, Market Structure, and New-Used Goods Models", *American Economic Review*, 72; 816-824.

Liebowitz, S. (1985), "Copying and Indirect Appropriability: Photocopying of Journals", *Journal of Political Economy*, 93; 945-957.

Maskin, E. and J. Riley (1984), "Monopoly with Incomplete Information", *Rand Journal of Economics*, 15; 171-196.

Miller, H.L. (1974), "On Killing off the Market for Used Textbooks and the Relationship Between Markets for New and Used Secondhand Goods", *Journal of Political Economy*, 82; 612-619.

Mussa, M. and S. Rosen (1978), "Monopoly and Product Quality", *Journal of Economic Theory*, 18; 301-317.

Novos, I. and M. Waldman (1984), "The Effects of Increased Copyright Protection: An Analytic Approach", *Journal of Political Economy*, 92; 236-246.

Rust, J. (1986), "When is it Optimal to Kill off the Market for Used Durable Goods?", *Econometrica*, 54; 65-86.

Schmalensee, R. (1984), "Gaussian Demand and Commodity Bundling", *Journal of Business*, 8; S211-S224.

Stigler, G. (1963), "United States v. Loew's Inc.: A Note on Block Booking", *The Supreme Court Review*, 1; 152-157.

Swan, P. (1980), "Alcoa: The Influence of Recycling on Monopoly Power", *Journal of Political Economy*, 88; 76-99.

Takeyama, L. (1997), "The Intertemporal Consequences of Unauthorized Reproduction of Intellectual Property", *Journal of Law and Economics*, 40; 511-522.

Waldman, M. (1996), "Durable Goods Pricing When Quality Matters", *Journal of Business*, 69; 489-510.

Waldman, M. (1997), "Eliminating the Market for Secondhand Goods", *Journal of Law and Economics*, 40; 61-92.

Waldman, M. (2003), "Durable Goods Theory for Real World Markets", *Journal of Economic Perspectives*, 17; 131-154.

JUSTIN P. JOHNSON AND MICHAEL WALDMAN; JOHNSON GRADUATE SCHOOL OF MANAGEMENT, CORNELL UNIVERSITY, SAGE HALL, ITHACA, NY 14853. JOHNSON; JPJ25@CORNELL.EDU, WALDMAN; MW46@CORNELL.EDU. THE AUTHORS WOULD LIKE TO THANK IAN NOVOS FOR HELPFUL CONVERSATIONS AND KAMESHWARI SHANKAR FOR RESEARCH ASSISTANCE.

[5]

Available online at www.sciencedirect.com

ScienceDirect

Information Economics and Policy 18 (2006) 449–476

INFORMATION ECONOMICS AND POLICY

www.elsevier.com/locate/iep

Piracy of digital products: A critical review of the theoretical literature

Martin Peitz [a,*], Patrick Waelbroeck [b]

[a] *International University in Germany, Campus 3, 76646 Bruchsal, Germany*
[b] *EGSH/ENST, 46 rue Barrault, 75013 Paris, France*

Received 6 July 2005; received in revised form 21 June 2006; accepted 21 June 2006
Available online 14 September 2006

Abstract

Digital products can be copied at almost no cost and are subject to non-commercial copying by final consumers. Because the copy of a copy typically does not deteriorate in quality, copies can become available on a large scale basis – this can be illustrated by the surge of file-sharing networks. In this paper we provide a critical overview of the theoretical literature that addresses the economic consequences of end-user copying. We analyze basic models of piracy, models with indirect appropriation, models with network effects, and models with asymmetric information. We discuss the applicability of the different modeling strategies to a number of industries such as software, video and computer games, music, and movies.

JEL classification: L11; L82; L86

Keywords: Information good; Piracy; Copyright; IP protection; Internet; Peer-to-peer; Software; Music

1. Introduction

With the rise of the computer and the internet, an increasing number of digital products and services have been copied and distributed most of the time without the authorization

* Corresponding author.
E-mail addresses: martin.peitz@i-u.de, Martin_Peitz@hotmail.com (M. Peitz), waelbroe@enst.fr (P. Waelbroeck).

0167-6245/$ - see front matter © 2006 Published by Elsevier B.V.
doi:10.1016/j.infoecopol.2006.06.005

of legal owners. Books, software, music and video files are the main target of internet piracy. This trend has become a concern for both product manufacturers and policy makers. Legal actions in the US by the RIAA against file-sharing technologies and their users, backed up by the reinforcement of the copyright law stated in the Digital Millennium Copyright Act, translate these concerns. The main claim of the record companies is the huge revenue losses due to internet piracy.[1] But in which economic environments can such a claim be substantiated? Are there other strategies that copyright owners can use to counter this new form of piracy? And, from a public policy perspective, to which extent are the social interests aligned with the interests of copyright owners?

Before presenting the various arguments and results that can be found in the theoretical literature, it is useful to analyze the characteristics of digital products and how piracy works. Digital products can be compressed without losing much information or quality. Thus, digital copies have a technical quality similar to the original. However, the original digital product is often bundled with other non-digital components such as a printed manual for software and printed booklet (with lyrics, pictures, song and artist information) and CD case for music CDs. This suggests that the original gives some additional value compared to the copy.

In addition, there may be complementary products for which access can be controlled (examples are live concerts as complements to recorded music and customer support as a complement to software). Complementarities may allow firms to indirectly appropriate some of the rents generated through end-user copying.

In most cases, digital products also involve interactions. These interactions can be of two different natures: formal interaction for software that requires to exchange standardized/formatted information, and social interaction for music and video files about which people like to talk about with their friends. These formal and social interactions imply that there possibly exist network effects in the use of a digital product.

Also, many digital products are complex in the sense that the amount of information required to describe them is large. As a consequence, consumers need to test them in order to correctly value them. In other words, some digital products are experience goods and a copy can be useful in providing information on their characteristics. This feature applies not only to digital products such as music CDs but also to software with a large number of commands and a large potential number of interactions with other computer components and software, etc.

Non-authorized copying of digital products can be done in two different ways: by borrowing originals from friends and family members or by downloading from the internet.

In the former case, networks of friends share the good on a small-scale basis. Then it is possible in some cases to indirectly appropriate revenue from sharing activities as we will argue later on. The copying process only requires a storage device such as a hard-drive or a CD Recorder or any portable media device. Information on the characteristics of the copied product is easy and cheap to obtain by word-of-mouth.

[1] In this paper we do not discuss the empirical evidence on whether file-sharing has hurt the record industry. Starting with Peitz and Waelbroeck (2004a) and Zentner (forthcoming), there is now a large number of empirical studies available on this issue. A good analysis and discussion of the empirical methodologies is provided by Liebowitz (2006). For a detailed analysis of digital music see Peitz and Waelbroeck (2005). Other empirical work has looked at the software industry.

In the latter case, monitoring copies from copies is arduous. However, copying using file-sharing technologies often provides a lower value than copying directly from friends for several reasons. First, users are spending time looking for and downloading files. Secondly, the digital copy lacks valuable information such as instructions on how to install the software or song lyrics. Finally, the file can be badly compressed or incomplete. Therefore, we can expect consumers to be heterogeneous with respect to the value of the original relative to the copy.

Some theoretical efforts have been made by economists to better understand the consequences of copying and piracy on profits and welfare. This survey exclusively considers end-user copying.[2] It is organized according to different modeling features. In general, it is assumed that there exist differences between the original and its copy and that consumers are heterogeneous (in a way to be defined) between their willingness to pay for the original compared to the copy. In a first set of articles, (1) there are no means of indirect appropriation of rents, (2) the value that consumers put on the product is independent of the decision of other consumers for any given price, and (3) consumers are perfectly informed about the characteristics of the digital product. In a second set we elaborate on the possibility to indirectly appropriate rents, this indirect appropriation may occur across consumers and across products. In a third set of articles, the product's value depends on the decision of other consumers. In other words, there are network effects. In a fourth set of articles consumers are not perfectly informed about the characteristics of the product and copying provides information on the value of the product, which facilitates the purchasing decision.[3]

In the four setups the following two questions are raised[4]:

- Do firms suffer from the existence of copies?
- Does the availability of digital copies increase or decrease welfare?

The answer to the first question is an unambiguous "yes" in the first setup. In the second, third and fourth setup, firms may gain when digital copies are available.

The answer to the second question is even more ambiguous. When firms suffer and consumers gain from copies, the second question has to be studied in detail. In the short-term, the set of products is given and we analyze the welfare implications of copying for given market structures and product choice decisions. In a long-term perspective, the set of product is determined by the legal and economic environment, and we analyze the incentives of a firm to enter the market and launch new products. The question becomes: what is the welfare effect of copying on the creation process? Additional public policy questions come to mind: what is the socially optimal level of copyright protection? Are there mechanisms (for example taxes on copying) that improve profits and welfare? While these latter two questions are certainly important, little research has been devoted to them.

The remainder of the review is organized as follows. Section 2 analyzes copying in terms of product differentiation. Section 3 discusses indirect appropriability, Section 4 network

[2] We do not address for-profit piracy. Recent contributions on this topic include Slive and Bernhardt (1998), Banerjee (2003), and Poddar (2005a).

[3] As we will discuss in the Section 5, the third set of articles mainly addresses software piracy whereas the fourth set of articles mainly addresses music piracy.

[4] An early, informal exploration of these questions concerning the copying of books and periodicals can be found in Hurt and Schuchman (1966).

effects and Section 5 information acquisition and sampling. In Section 6 we then discuss the relevance of some of the model features for the analysis of software applications, video and computer games, recorded music and movies. Section 7 concludes.

2. Basic analysis of end-user copying

We consider pirated goods as digital copies of original files. The original has quality q, the copy may be of lower quality, $q^c \leqslant q$. This means that the market offers two versions of the product: the original and a lower quality product that can be obtained at a given price, which possibly varies across consumers. This price may be zero; it is positive if the pirated good is costly to acquire or if there is an expected cost from being detected. The non-authorized copy therefore limits the monopoly power of the supplier of the original. We would therefore expect as a quite general result (without other effects) that the availability of a pirated good either leaves the firm's profits unchanged (this means that piracy is not a real threat) or that it reduces the firm's profits. This is indeed confirmed in a variety of models (see, for instance, Novos and Waldman, 1984; Johnson, 1985 and Belleflamme, 2003). A firm can react to piracy in three different ways: if piracy is not a real threat the firm may not react at all; if it is a threat worth fighting, the firm reduces its price such that all active consumers prefer the original (call this strategy "deter"); otherwise, the firm responds in such a way that some consumers obtain only the pirated good ("accommodate"). Both the deterrence and the accommodation strategy lead to reduced profits.

Changes in profits typically modify incentives to provide quality. In a model in which original and copy have the same quality but in which consumers have heterogeneous copying costs, Novos and Waldman (1984) have shown how lower profits reduce under some assumptions the ex ante incentives to provide quality. Hence, one has the classic trade-off between underprovision and underutilization already pointed out by Arrow (1962). This result is confirmed by Bae and Choi (forthcoming) in a vertical product differentiation model with quality degradation for copies. In a multi-product framework, Johnson (1985) shows how lower profits also reduce the incentives to provide variety. This implies that although a short-term welfare analysis may see piracy in a favorable light, the long-term effects are more likely to be negative.

2.1. Strategies in a single-product scenario

We will now look at this argument in more detail. Following Novos and Waldman (1984), a consumer can either purchase the original or she can copy at a cost $c+z(1+x)$, where c is the marginal cost of production, x is the extent of copyright protection and z is the additional marginal cost of making a copy, which is heterogeneous for consumers. The value that consumers attach to the product depends on its quality. Because of the heterogeneity in the copying costs, for moderate prices, some consumers prefer the original while others the copy. Clearly, if the firm's price is sufficiently low, copying is unattractive to all consumers. While Novos and Waldman clearly had physical copies in mind, this specification also fits digital products such as software for which users who illegally copy have to spend effort and time downloading, copying, and installing files and incur an additional disutility if they are detected. The monopolist produces a single quality and copies have the same quality as the original. However, the model can be interpreted as if the value of the original relative to the copy is heterogeneous but that the associated disutility of copying is the same for all consumers. That is, the original gives a value which is the same across consumers, while the copy gives the same value minus $z(1+x)$. In words, the perceived quality degradation of the copy is heterogeneous.

In this model, the monopolist chooses a quality which is too low compared to the social optimum because the monopolist cannot appropriate all rents from quality improvements. Novos and Waldman then show that an increase in copyright protection leads to an increase in the quality offered by the monopolist provided that the density of z is increasing, i.e., there are relatively more consumers with higher than with lower copying costs. This means that the effect of underprovision favors a strict copyright enforcement. In their model, a stricter copyright protection does not increase the social loss due to underutilization: as the copyright protection increases, some consumers switch from the copy to the original, thus saving the copying cost that is wasteful from a social point of view. See also Bae and Choi (forthcoming).

As Chen and Png (2003) point out, social costs arise if firms spend resources on detection. In their simple setting, there are two groups of consumers: one group never copies (infinite copy costs) and another group has finite copying costs. In each group, consumers have heterogeneous valuations for the good although originals and copies are identical. The expected utility from illegal copying depends on the detection probability. A firm has two possibilities to eliminate copies: it can lower its price or it can spend additional resources in a technology that increases the detection probability. Clearly, from a social point of view, these two strategies have different implications. On the one hand, a lower price unambiguously improves short-run welfare because less effort in copying is needed. On the other hand, increasing the detection probability is wasteful from a social point of view and the surplus of copiers is also reduced.[5]

Another similar set-up is the Mussa–Rosen model of vertical product differentiation (Mussa and Rosen, 1978). In this framework, the heterogeneity with respect to the copying costs is replaced by heterogeneity with respect to the utility derived from the quality difference between the original and the copy. Consumers have unit demand and make a discrete choice between the original and the copy. Consumers differ in their willingness to pay for the products (the original and the copy). A consumer with a larger taste parameter $\theta > \theta'$ has a higher willingness to pay than consumer θ'. She is also willing to pay more for the original if the alternative is to obtain a copy. Two specifications of the heterogeneity of consumers' valuations dominate the literature: (i) discrete types; namely two types (high-valuation and low-valuation consumers). (ii) a continuum of types; the distribution is then typically assumed to be uniform on an interval.

Belleflamme (2003), Yoon (2002) and Bae and Choi (forthcoming) consider a single-product monopolist selling to a continuum of heterogeneous consumers. A consumer derives utility $\theta q - p$ for the original, where θ is the consumer's taste parameter, distributed uniformly on the unit interval, q is the quality of the original (which is exogenously given in Yoon, 2002), and p its price. She derives utility $\alpha\theta q - c$ for the copy, where $1-\alpha$ is the factor of quality depreciation and c the copying cost. (We may set the marginal cost of production equal to zero.) Then pricing in the presence of piracy is the same as pricing

[5] Chen and Png then analyze the socially optimal government policy consisting of a tax on copies and recording equipment, subsidies to originals, and penalties in case of copyright violations.

against a firm pricing at c a product of quality αq. Obviously, in this setup the firm's profits decrease with the availability of digital copies.[6]

The total effect of piracy on welfare is positive because the loss in profits (from deterring or accommodating piracy) is overcompensated by an increase in consumer surplus. Lower profits, however, reduce the ex ante incentives to provide the good. Bae and Choi (forthcoming) also show that more originals are sold if copies are available, albeit at a much lower price. In the example of a uniform distribution this can be explained by the fact that the monopolist faces a flatter linear demand function if copies are available (see Bae and Choi, forthcoming, for details). They also show that piracy leads to an inefficiently low quality of the original.

2.2. *Designing IP law to fight piracy*

Yoon (2002) considers the more elaborate problem in which copyright (or IP) protection leads to a private cost to consumers. Formally, a consumer's utility takes the form $\alpha\theta q - c - x$, where x denotes the consumers' additional cost due to copyright protection (which also constitutes a social cost). Then the monopolist's profits are increasing in x, while consumer surplus is decreasing. Total surplus is initially decreasing in x and then, after reaching its minimum, inversely U-shaped. Yoon then shows that the socially optimal copyright protection should be set such that the monopolist optimally reacts by deterring copying. The copyrighted product is then fully protected in the sense that copies are driven out of the market. However, the monopolist has to lower its price compared to a situation of "blockaded entry", which occurs if copying is not feasible. Thus profits generated by the copyrighted product are reduced under the social optimum.

Bae and Choi (forthcoming) extend the analysis to the situation in which consumers face a type-dependent cost $\beta\theta q$ due to copyright protection. A higher degree of copyright protection reduces the demand for originals. Note that this finding is in contrast to what happens in the previous situation when copyright protection gives rise to a uniform cost x because, with a uniform cost, enacting copyright protection increases the demand for originals. Total surplus unambiguously decreases with the degree of copyright protection.

In a related paper, Alvisi et al. (2002) analyze the incentives of a firm facing piracy to offer a downgraded version.[7] Without piracy, the set-up is a Mussa–Rosen model, which is specified such that only a single quality is offered by the monopolist. Consider now the introduction of copies. Copies are assumed to have the same quality as originals. To make a consumer buy the original, its price has to be less or equal to the copying cost of the consumer, c. Clearly, if these copying costs only represent physical reproduction costs a firm can only make positive profits if there are increasing returns to scale in production. How-

[6] Although profits are reduced in the monopoly setting, committing not to enforce copyright protection may be a profitable strategy in a market with potential entry as it may serve as an entry deterrent. The reason is that an entrant suffers if the incumbent does not enforce copyright protection.

[7] Note that the argument is similar to the decision by a monopolist to introduce a low-quality variant in response to the introduction of a generic drug in the pharmaceutical industry (see Valletti and Szymanski, forthcoming). More generally, recent work has considered conditions under which it is profit-maximizing for a monopolist to introduce a low-quality variant (see e.g. Johnson and Myatt, 2003). In our piracy context, the argument also relates to King and Lampe (2003), see the section on network effects below. In addition, a number of articles have looked at the incentives to provide downgraded goods without piracy but with network effects. These include Hahn (2001, 2004), Csorba (2002), and Csorba and Hahn (2006).

ever, including heterogeneous opportunity costs for the consumers (as discussed above) allow for positive profits even without increasing returns in production. Consumers belong to two different classes: one class of consumers below a certain parameter value θ are assumed to have low copying costs, c_L, and the other class above that value are assumed to have a high copying costs, c_H (for instance because it includes the costs of copyright protection x). This means that a high quality product can be offered at a higher price to consumers with a high valuation of quality. The authors then show that the optimal response of the monopolist to piracy may be to offer two qualities: the lower quality attracts low-value consumers and the high quality attracts high-value consumers. This means that the monopolist effectively discriminates between those consumers with a high copying cost and those with a low copying cost. The optimal strategy is characterized by the fact that prices are below copying costs for each consumer class and that consumers with low copying costs also do not have an incentive to copy the high-quality good.

Cremer and Pestieau (2005) consider a population with high-valuation ($j = 1$) and low-valuation consumers ($j = 2$), the consumer type j is only known to the respective consumer. A firm offers price–quality pairs (p_L, q_L) and (p_H, q_H). Consumers derive utility $u_j(q_i) - p_i$, $i = L, H$. Low-valuation consumers may also make a copy and achieve some quality $q < q_H$. The quality of the copy and the corresponding utility level is obtained by solving the problem $\max_q \theta u_2(q) - x(q, e)$, where x is the individual cost from copying. This cost increases in the chosen quality q and the level of copyright protection e. If e is set by the firm, it corresponds to private attempts of technical protection (e.g. in software or for DVDs). If e is set by the government it corresponds to public measures of IP protection (e.g. those established in the Digital Millennium Copyright Act).

Suppose the government (or a regulator appointed by the government) was in charge of the pricing policy as well as the level of copyright protection. Then it can be socially optimal (in a second-best sense, i.e., respecting the incentive constraints of consumers) to sell only to high-valuation consumers, while all low-valuation consumers copy the product. In this case the product if fully financed by high-valuation consumers. Such a strategy can be replicated by a private firm. However, it may be privately optimal in such a situation to implement a positive level of copyright protection and to sell to both types of consumers. We obtain that the private firm implements a higher level of copyright protection than the government.

Consider now the alternative interpretation of e according to which e is a government policy determining the strength of intellectual property protection. Suppose that we are in a situation in which the socially optimal government policy (again in a second-best sense) requires to sell to both consumer groups and to choose a positive level of IP protection. If the firm controls the pricing the best government policy may be not to provide any IP protection at all. Thus, although IP protection is too low compared to the socially optimal government policy when the government also controls the pricing policy, it is the best not to provide IP protection given that the product is sold by a profit-maximizing firm.

Sundararajan (2004) provides an extended analysis of the impact of end-user copying on profit-maximizing pricing when consumers have variable demand. He shows that the profit-maximizing price schedule is shifted by the level of piracy: the monopolist will use a combination of the profit-maximizing zero-piracy pricing schedule and a pricing schedule that makes all consumers indifferent between the legal and the illegal version of the product. If the firm can use digital rights management (DRM) to fight piracy it has to balance the negative effect of DRM due to value reduction with the positive effect of DRM due to increased piracy deterrence. Consequently, the firm chooses an intermediate protection level.

Takeyama (1997) argues that the loss in profits due to copying may be greater if dynamic effects are taken into account.[8] Consider a two-period model in which there are two types of consumers, one with a high valuation for the good and no propensity to copy (high type) and another type with a low valuation for the good and a strong propensity to copy (low type). Consumers buy up to one unit in the two periods. Takeyama assumes that the monopolist cannot commit to prices, that is, the monopolist suffers from a Coasian commitment problem. Without copying, high type consumers anticipate a lower price in the second period, which is set to make the low type consumers indifferent between buying and not buying. Therefore, the monopolist has to offer a price strictly below the valuation of the high type consumers in the first period so as to satisfy their incentive constraint. When copying is possible, the monopolist has to lower the second period price to make the low type indifferent between buying and copying. The associated reduction in profits is equivalent to profit reduction in an atemporal model. However, the lower second-period price affects the incentive constraint of the high type consumers so that the monopolist also has to lower the first-period price. This also reduces first-period profits.[9]

While the dynamic problem typically amplifies the negative effect of piracy on profits due to copying, Takeyama also notes that copying can increase profits in some cases. Indeed, if the monopolist cannot avoid copying in the second period without making losses in that period, that is, if the marginal costs of production and selling of the good are above the private copying cost of low-type consumers, then, the availability of copies in the second period serves as a commitment not to offer the good in the second period. As a consequence, in the first period, the participation constraint and not the incentive constraint of the high type becomes binding. In other words, the monopolist can extract the full surplus from high-type consumers.

2.3. Multi-product scenario

Following Johnson (1985), Belleflamme and Picard (2004a,b) consider a multi-product framework in which demands are independent without copies. However, when copies are available, demands become interdependent because a consumer's copying technology exhibits increasing returns to scale.[10] This is typically the case if a consumer incurs a high

[8] In related papers on versioning by a durable goods monopolist, Inderst (2003) and Hahn (forthcoming) consider an environment with two consumer types and discrete time in which a firm can sell different versions of a product over time. Here, the firm faces a commitment problem in price and quality. They show that a firm may optimally decide to sell a low- and a high-quality version in the first period (and trade only occurs in this period). The firm may optimally sell the low-quality version below marginal cost in the first period. By serving low-valuation consumers in the first period, it avoids price concessions in later periods to high-valuation consumers. This result can be interpreted in terms of piracy as follows: illegal copying (which resembles a low-quality version) may mitigate the Coasian commitment problem so that copies that are distributed for free actually increase the firm's profit. Hahn (forthcoming) also provides detailed conditions for the monopolist to introduce a low-quality version simultaneously or with a delay.

[9] However, in many markets for information goods we would question whether firms actually lack a commitment power and thus suffer a Coasian commitment problem. Indeed, since most firms offer multiple products, they may not give steep mark-downs over time for reputation reasons. As is well-known in the literature on the durable goods monopoly, reputation concerns may give the firm commitment power.

[10] Grgeta (2004) provides a dynamic analysis based on Johnson (1985), in which products can be horizontally and vertically differentiated and in which there is habit formation. Under strong habit formation legal and pirated products can be substitutes in the short run but complements in the long run.

initial fixed cost to be able to copy, for example by buying a CD burner or by breaking the "moral barrier" to illegal copying. This is formalized by assuming that there is a fixed cost that consumers incur when installing the copying technology. Then, a firm benefits from low prices of the other firms because this makes consumers less prone to install the copying technology. Therefore, prices are strategic substitutes in this setting (for some set of prices).

If the average cost of copying the chosen set of goods is sufficiently high, a multi-product monopolist will either set the unconstrained monopoly price or lower its price so as to avoid copying. In contrast, if each single information good is provided by one firm, these firms might have to accept copying as an industry phenomenon. Namely, for certain configuration each firm tolerates copying and sets a high price to extract a high margin from those consumers who have a strong preference for originals (Belleflamme and Picard, 2004a).[11]

2.4. Broad-based versus targeted copyright enforcement

The copying cost c plays an important role in determining whether original and pirated good are good or bad substitutes. This cost is partly determined by the copyright enforcement policy of the copyright owner (as seen in Novos and Waldman (1984) and Yoon (2002)). A broad-based enforcement policy affects all consumers in the same way. As an alternative, a targeted enforcement policy concentrates on high-value consumers. Harbaugh and Khemka (2001) have analyzed the effects of such a targeted enforcement policy in a model of vertical differentiation with a continuum of consumer types. Compared to the same level of broad-based enforcements, a targeted enforcement policy makes copying relatively more costly for high-value buyers than for low-value buyers. There is thus a wedge between those two groups – the group sizes are determined by the scope of the enforcement policy. The main result of Harbaugh and Khemka (2001) is that the optimal monopoly price with targeted enforcement may be above the monopoly price without piracy, p^{M}. The reason is that with targeted enforcement and positive enforcement costs the monopolist may not want to apply enforcement up to the level of the demand that would be served by the monopolist without piracy but may want to choose a more limited scope. Then, if enforcement is sufficiently effective to deter the targeted consumer segment from copying, prices are above p^{M}. This implies that profits and the surplus of targeted consumers are reduced compared to a world without piracy. At the profit-maximizing scope of enforcement policy, consumer surplus may increase with enforcement. Then the private incentives to enforce copyright may be insufficient from a social perspective with targeted enforcement.

We note that targeted enforcement can be viewed as a costly device to create two types of consumers: those who are willing to pay a high premium on originals and those who are essentially not willing to pay for originals. This means that a model with a continuum of types and targeted enforcement becomes a model with essentially two types.

In summary, basic models of end-user copying postulate product differentiation between original and copy and consumer heterogeneity. In these models copies are viewed as variants of the original product with a lower quality. Consumers with a low willingness

[11] In the model with two firms, Belleflamme and Picard (2004b) provide additional equilibrium characterizations. In particular, they show that independent firms set (on average) higher prices than in monopoly because they do not take the positive externality of a price reduction into account. This price may even be higher than the monopoly price without piracy.

to pay for quality tend to consume the copy, whereas consumers with a high willingness to pay tend to consume the original. The copy competes with the original and the firms have to lower their price (because otherwise the incentive constraint of too many consumers is violated). The presence of the copy leads to a market expansion and thus consumer surplus increases with piracy, at least in the short run (however, some consumers may be worse off).

An important element in the analysis of total welfare is related to the different costs involved in piracy: consumer cost of copying compared to the marginal cost of production, as well as the costs of protecting products and of enforcing rights. If copyright protection is costly, society may want to adopt no or little protection (at least in the short run) since protection policies coupled with the profit-maximizing behavior of firms in the market place perform even worse. While most of the work considers short-term welfare effects, a long-term analysis needs to take into account the incentives for creation. This issue is certainly critical in the context of the design of IP protection. However, due to the fact that often the firms' profits are reduced by piracy under weak IP protection, firms (and creators) have in general lower incentives to improve quality in the market, this hints at negative long-term effects.

Moving beyond the above mentioned basic models, firms' profits may actually increase with piracy. This suggests that in such situations end-user copying appears in a more favorable light with respect to the long-term welfare properties, as will be explained below.

3. Indirect appropriation

3.1. Indirect appropriation across consumers

Although the purchaser of copyrighted work may legally or illegally copy the original, the copyright owner may partially or even fully appropriate the benefits from copying. The issue of indirect appropriation already arises in the case of photocopies of books and other printed material, see Liebowitz (1985). Note, however, that it is difficult to indirectly appropriate revenues from copies when one cannot exactly assess the amount of copying that will be done from a single original. Indirect appropriation requires a homogenous population of buyers of the original or effective price-discrimination devices. Suppose that it is possible to price-discriminate as a function of the potential number of copies that will be made. Then the copyright owner can charge a higher price to those who are expected to copy more. Of course, it must be possible to prevent arbitrage; in the case of a library, this is possible since libraries are easy to identify. Note that indirect appropriation can partially explain the shift from books (weak complement with photocopiers) to journals (strong complements) in the academic profession.[12]

Besen and Kirby (1989) point out that the advantage of direct versus indirect appropriation depends on the technology of copying and the substitutability between originals and their copies. They propose a model with small-scale copying to show that direct appropri-

[12] Liebowitz tests for indirect appropriability by analyzing the change in the relative price of an economic journal charged to institutions and individuals between 1959 and 1982 as a function of its usage (measured by citations). After controlling for journal age and commercial journals, Liebowitz finds a positive relation between the usage and the relative price of copyrighted good. Also, price discrimination increased after the introduction of photocopy machines and demand for material that is easy to copy (such as journal articles) increased compared to other materials (such as books that are more difficult to copy).

ability arises when the marginal cost of copying is constant and indirect appropriability when the marginal cost is increasing in the number of copies. Strong substitutability between originals and copies combined with increasing marginal cost of copying lead to a situation of clubs who share the cost of the original among its members (copiers).[13] Three cases are considered.

Case 1: The marginal cost of copying is constant but greater than the marginal cost of producing the original; copies and originals are imperfect substitutes. In this case, copiers pay the marginal cost of reproduction so that the price of a copy is equal to its marginal cost. In other words, there is direct appropriability: producers can only capture the net surplus from selling the originals.

Case 2: The marginal cost of copying is increasing and originals and copies are perfect substitutes; copies can only be made from the original,[14] and members of the club only consume one unit. Copying leads to an increase of the price of the original and there is indirect appropriation. The analysis is similar to the pricing of a club membership. The fixed cost of the club is the price of the original. Because the marginal cost of copying is increasing, the average cost curve is U-shaped. Competition between clubs drives membership fees down to the minimum average cost. This determines the optimal size of the club. Consider now the difference in profits when copying is possible and when it is not. Besen and Kirby show with numerical methods that this difference is increasing in the marginal cost of producing the original and becomes positive for some values. Thus the firm may increase profits by indirectly appropriating revenues from the copies.

Case 3: The marginal cost of copying is increasing; copies and originals are not perfect substitutes. The club organizer is now the consumer who has the highest surplus from consuming the original rather than the copy. This consumer sells the copy to the other members. Because of the positive surplus of the club organizer and of the copiers, the producer of original work can again indirectly appropriate revenues from the copies.

Bakos et al. (1999) present an argument based on bundling to explain why the existence of clubs may increase the copyright owner's profits. Suppose that consumers belong to clubs that correspond to non-overlapping and exogenous network of friends. The valuation of the club is the sum of valuations of each club member. Bakos et al. highlight two opposing effects of sharing.

The first positive effect of sharing is referred to as the "aggregation effect" and is due to the fact that consumers who team up together reduce the variance of the distribution of consumers' valuation from the point of view of the producer under the strong assumptions that all valuations are independent (and identically distributed) and all teams have the same size. The reason is that as the number of consumers sharing the good increases, the likelihood that the team will value the product at an average value increases — in the limit, this can be seen by applying a Central Limit Theorem. Thus the firm can extract more surplus from larger clubs with a mean (aggregate) valuation. To present the argument in a simple way,

[13] Besen and Kirby (1989) point out that their mechanism is related to the literature about a monopolist facing a second-hand market.

[14] If copies could be made from copies at the same cost (and quality) as from the original then the analysis of case 1 would apply.

suppose that there are two consumers, each with valuation uniformly and independently distributed on the interval (0,1). With two clubs of size 1 with valuation x distributed according to the uniform distribution, $F_1(x)=U(0,1)$, the expected demand at price p is $d_1(p)=2(1-F_1(p))=2(1-p)$ by the definition of the cumulative distribution function of the uniform distribution. The profit is thus $\pi_1=2(1-p)p$ and the profit-maximizing price is $p=1/2$ with corresponding profits $\pi_1=1/2$. When there is one club of size 2, the distribution of valuation of the club is simply the distribution of the sum of the valuation of the team members and has probability distribution $F_2(x)=x^2/2$ if $x\leqslant 1$. Suppose $p\leqslant 1$. The expected demand at price p for the team is $d_2(p)=1-F_2(p)$. Then expected demand is $d_2=1-p^2/2$ and profit is $\pi_2=(1-p^2/2)p$. The first order condition of this concave program yields $p=\sqrt{(2/3)}$ and profits are $\pi_2=(2/3)^{(3/2)}\cong .54>.5=\pi_1$. Thus profit increases with a club of size 2 compared to two clubs of size 1 (regardless of the optimal price set when $p>1$).

There may however exist a second negative effect: introducing positive correlation between valuations of club members and different club sizes leads to a negative "club diversity" effect due to the flattening of the distribution of the club valuations. The net effect of sharing then depends on whether the aggregation or the club diversity effect dominates.

The analysis of Bakos et al. (1999) presumes that clubs are able to extract all surplus from its members. However, unequal contributions by the members of a club may not satisfy the incentive compatibility constraints of some of the members. In contrast, Varian (2000) analyzes the profitability of a monopolist selling to clubs where clubs do not price discriminate among their members. In this case it may be more profitable to sell to clubs rather than to their members directly because of a cost effect. To be precise, suppose that it is cheaper to sell originals to clubs, which have their own system of giving their club members access to the good, than reaching out to the members directly. Then the associated sharing and copying agreements within a club are profit enhancing.

It should be observed that the marginal production costs of a digital product are, by definition, negligible. Therefore, based on production costs only, it cannot be profitable to sell information goods through clubs. However, the definition of costs may be too narrow because marketing and distribution costs should be included, which may well be non-negligible also in the case of information goods. In this case, private copying (done within clubs) may be profit enhancing for the monopoly supplier of an information good. This may, for example, explain the practice of site licenses for software.[15] To the extent that these marketing and distribution costs are due to an asymmetric information problem between firm and consumers, this argument is related to the sampling argument developed in Section 5.

3.2. Indirect appropriation across products

So far, indirect appropriation applied across consumers for a given product. An alternative possibility of indirect appropriation arises in the presence of complementary goods. Here, the possibility of indirect appropriation arises across goods for a given consumer. If illegal copies are consumed together with private goods which cannot be copied, the potential problem of end-user copying for copyright owners is much less pronounced. For example, it has been documented that the popularity of an artist can actually be promoted

[15] Varian (2000) also shows that the use of site licenses and similar agreements may be used as a price discrimination device if there are different types of consumers.

through downloads which then boosts demand for concert tickets. This may explain that artists have a more ambiguous position towards Peer-to-Peer (P2P) networks than big record labels because typically profits from concerts and merchandizing go entirely to the artist (see Gayer and Shy, forthcoming and Curien et al., 2004, for a formal analysis; see also Krueger, 2005 and Connolly and Krueger, forthcoming, who document the increasing importance of concert revenues). Indirect appropriation through complementary goods mitigates the negative of piracy on profits. Note that in the presence of network or sampling effects (that will be analyzed in the following two sections), the firm's profits may actually increase – this is more likely if the firm can charge for complementary products, i.e., if it can indirectly appropriate some rents.

To summarize, indirect appropriation works when it is possible to assess the value of the uses made from a legally purchased product. Producers can indirectly appropriate revenues from homogenous consumers who share its products within a club or community if the marginal cost of copying is increasing. When consumers purchase physical complementary products, producers can also indirectly appropriated revenues from the copies by charging a higher price for the physical good.

4. Network effects

In this section we elaborate on the effect of piracy in the presence of consumption externalities, in particular, in the form of network effects. Hence, the utility derived from consumption depends directly or indirectly on the consumption decision of other consumers. In the presence of positive consumption externalities, not enforcing copyright protection may be privately and socially beneficial.[16] This argument has been made in the case of software piracy but also applies to some extent to other digital products. Network effects for software are likely to be partly direct and partly indirect. The usefulness of a software often directly increases with the number of users because (in case of incompatibility or only partial compatibility with other products) a user can more easily exchange files generated with that software; also, it often indirectly increases with the number of users because more complementary products and services are offered (due to increasing returns).

One can also make the case for network effects for copying books and other written material and music. Copying books and music increases the number of people who are knowledgeable about the product. This may for example increase the social prestige of a legal owner in a social gathering. Direct network effects are also present if copying is done through a file-sharing system such as Kazaa where a larger number of downloads from an upload leads to a better user's priority rating.

4.1. Network effects under monopoly

We first review a number of studies in a monopoly setting. These papers reject the view that without indirect appropriation copying necessarily reduces the monopolist's profits. Conner and Rumelt (1991) propose a model in which a consumer's willingness to pay increases in the number of users. Clearly, piracy can increase the total number of users and therefore under some circumstances indirectly lead to higher private benefits (of the

[16] In this section we focus on the effects on the firm's profit and only make a few remarks on welfare effects.

software developer). Although, a pirated product is "sold" by definition at a price of zero, the willingness to pay for the product increases. This increase can be partially appropriated by the software developer. Conner and Rumelt (1991) present a linear demand model with heterogeneous gains from buying the original instead of using a pirated product (the specification is assumed rather than derived from fundamentals; for a specification which generates such linear demand see Shy and Thisse, 1999). In this specification they show that (i) piracy can increase or decrease the optimal price charged by the software developer and (ii) piracy can increase or decrease profits. Copyright protection may decrease the total number of users. For certain parameter configurations, price and profits move in the same direction, for others they move in opposite directions.

Takeyama (1994) provides a similar analysis in which market demand is explicitly derived from individual behavior. Contrary to the previous model, in her model with full enforcement of copyright protection the optimal strategy of a monopolist may involve selling to all consumers, i.e., also to those consumers who would copy the product without enforcement. The profit-maximizing strategy given no enforcement may then give higher profits than the profit-maximizing strategy given full enforcement.

Taking a closer look at her model, there exist two types of users: high- and low-value users. Each user only receives a share α of the net utility associated with the original when using an illegal copy. This utility depends positively on the number of users. Therefore, her model has two distinctive features. First, the disutility from using the pirated rather than the original version is higher for high-value than for low-value users. In other words, the pirated and the original good are closer substitutes for low-value users than for high-value users – this condition is necessary to separate types. Secondly, the network effect is more pronounced for the original than for the copy.

Under certain conditions the optimal uniform pricing strategy is to set a price such that all users buy the product when piracy is impossible. With this strategy, network effects are fully exploited. However, when the firm faces piracy, low-value users do not purchase when the price is too high but still use the product. This makes it possible to charge a higher price to high-value users because network effects are fully exploited. Under certain parameter configurations, profits without enforcement are higher than profits with full enforcement of copyright protection. The reason is that copying with network externalities is a device which milks high-value consumers without foregoing network effects.

A simple example illustrates this point. Suppose that there is a mass 1 of high-value users and similarly a mass 1 of low-value users. High-value consumers have an indirect utility $N-p$ when purchasing the product and αN when obtaining a pirated copy ($0<\alpha<1$), where N is the consumer mass with a copy or the original. Low-value consumers have an indirect utility $\varepsilon N-p$ when purchasing the product and $\alpha\varepsilon N$ when obtaining a pirated copy ($0<\varepsilon<1$). When copyright protection is fully enforced, the monopolist sets its uniform price either equal to 2ε if all consumers are served or 1 if only high-value consumers are served. Associated profits are 4ε and 1, respectively. Hence if $\varepsilon<1/4$ it is optimal to serve only high-value users, while if $\varepsilon>1/4$ it is optimal to serve all potential users. With piracy it may be optimal to sell the good only to high-value users. The highest price to achieve this is $2(1-\alpha)$. Associated profits are $2(1-\alpha)$. This is optimal if $2(1-\alpha)>4(1-\alpha)\varepsilon$ which is equivalent to $\varepsilon<1/2$. Hence if $1/2>\varepsilon>1/4$ it is optimal to serve high-value users with piracy and all potential users when copyright protection is fully enforced. Profits are higher in the former regime if $(1-\alpha)>2\varepsilon$. This means that the original must be sufficiently superior to the pirated version.

Similarly, Gayer and Shy (2003b) consider a monopoly model in which original and copy are horizontally differentiated and in which the original may give higher fixed utility and stronger network effects. If network effects for the original are sufficiently strong, the monopolist's profits are larger with the availability of copies.[17]

Belleflamme (2003) extends his basic model (see above) to allow for (weak) network effects. Utilities are $(\theta + \mu N)q - p$ for the original and $(\theta + \mu N)\,\alpha q - c$ for the copy. Note the difference to Takeyama (1994) where the type-dependent utility depends on the network size. Here only the fixed utility depends on the network size (as in Conner and Rumelt, 1991). Another difference is the assumption on the heterogeneity of consumers' valuations: Takeyama assumes that there are two types of consumer whereas Belleflamme considers that consumers are uniformly distributed on a certain range. Belleflamme then shows that with limited network effects piracy always reduces profits. This is in contrast to the more striking findings by Takeyama (1994) and Gayer and Shy (2003b).

The result by Takeyama (1994) and Gayer and Shy (2003b) can also be questioned if the monopolist can use versioning strategies himself.[18] In particular, King and Lampe (2003) have shown that a monopolist who offers a downgraded version himself (in order to exploit network effects) suffers from end-used copying because it is often optimal to sell at a low but positive price for the downgraded version. Only if downgrading by the monopolist is sufficiently costly, it is not in the firm's interest to use this strategy.

Takeyama (1994) also obtains some welfare conclusions. She shows that copying can lead to a Pareto improvement compared to the setting in which copying is not possible. This occurs when the monopolist only sells to high-value consumers with and without copyright enforcement and when profits increase with copying.

Gayer and Shy (2003a) analyze the effect of hardware taxation on the demand for software in a model with network effects. They postulate that all active consumers have to buy the hardware. As can be expected, a tax on hardware reduces copying but it reduces demand for the software in general because a higher price for hardware makes the bundle consisting of hardware and software more expensive. Nevertheless, if the software producer receives the proceeds from the hardware tax, its profits may increase if the tax goes up. They show that the profit-maximizing tax-rate is below the tax rate that eliminates piracy.

4.2. Strategic interaction

Shy and Thisse (1999) extend the analysis by Conner and Rumelt (1991) and Takeyama (1994) to a duopoly framework. There are two types of consumers: one type has a strong preference for originals (call them high-value consumers) and another type is indifferent whether the good is an original or a copy (call them low-value consumers). Both types of consumers are distributed in a Hotelling-fashion between the two firms. Parameter restrictions are introduced which ensure that firms never compete for the low-value consumers. The utility of a high-value consumer located at ω from purchasing the good located at 0 is

[17] For each of the two groups of consumers, buyers of originals and "buyers" of copies, Gayer and Shy (2003b) allow in principle for a network effect that depends on the number of buyers of the original and for another network effect that depends on the number of "buyers" of copies. They then assume that there are no intra-group network effects. However, the same result as theirs in Section 4 hold qualitatively if the intra-group and inter-group network effects have the same strength.

[18] For a useful overview on versioning of information goods see Belleflamme (2006).

$\mu N - \omega - p + r$, while the utility of a low-value consumer is $\mu N - \omega - p$ in this case. Copying gives both types a utility $\mu N - \omega$. In this specification, the benefit from purchasing the original, r, is independent of the network effect (contrary to Takeyama, 1994).

Under copy protection, there exist up to two types of symmetric equilibria: one equilibrium in which both firms price low so as to sell the good to some low-value consumers and another equilibrium in which both firms set prices so as to sell only to the high-valuation consumers (the original analysis by Shy and Thisse (1999) contains a mistake, which has been corrected by Peitz, 2004). Selling to high-valuation consumers only, is an equilibrium for sufficiently weak network externalities. Selling also to some low-value consumers is an equilibrium for sufficiently strong network effects. When consumers can copy, firms can exploit network effects without selling to low-value consumers. Suppose that network effects are weak. Then sales are not affected by the copy protection policy. However, there is a price competition effect which leads to a downward pressure on prices. Consequently, profits fall. Suppose, on the contrary, that network effects are strong. To exploit some of these external effects firms have to price low if no copying is available. But if copies are freely available, they can concentrate on high-value consumers and still reap the benefits from network effects. This leads to higher prices and profits. The reason is therefore similar to the one provided by Takeyama (1994), as explained above.

To summarize, the presence of network effects may make end-user copying desirable in the eyes of firms. One of the arguments put forward relies on price discrimination between users of originals and copiers.[19] When profits increase due to network effects there are good reasons to adopt a weak IP protection because consumers and firms gain in the short run and incentives to increase quality are strengthened.

5. Consumer information

Digital products and music in particular require some form of experimentation. Although testing new digital products has always been possible (listening to music in record stores, browsing books on the shelves, using a shareware version of a piece of software), legitimate authors have a hard time trying to monitor unauthorized copies in an interconnected world in which file-sharing technologies are available. Thus we can expect that digital copies will play a positive role for copyright owners (reducing costs to transmit information to consumers) and a negative role, reducing revenues due to copying.[20]

5.1. The sampling effect

Liebowitz (1985) already noted in his photocopying article that books or journals could benefit from photocopies through an exposure or sampling effect. A number of recent arti-

[19] Recall, however, that this implicitly assumes that the firm does not have superior discrimination strategies available.

[20] Interestingly, this may result in a reduced role for record companies, which are intermediaries between artist and consumers. Halonen and Regner (2003) analyze the contractual relationship between artist and label in a Grossman–Hart–Moore setting. They find that the present ownership structure in which the labels own most of the property rights is optimal when digital copies are not available. With new distribution and promotion technologies this may no longer be the case. See also Regner (2002).

cles extend this argument and analyze the informational role of unauthorized copies on firm profits and strategies as well as welfare. Gopal et al. (2006) assume that a single product is sold at a fixed price. Downloading may make the product more attractive (because consumers find out that they like the product). If this is the case consumers with intermediate valuations for the product buy the product if downloading is available whereas they do not buy if downloading is not available. As a consequence, the firm makes a higher profit.

Peitz and Waelbroeck (forthcoming) analyze the informational role of copies in a multi-product environment. They consider digital copies and P2P as a means to obtain information that consumers otherwise lack. In their model a firm sells N products that are horizontally differentiated. Consumers derive some utility from downloading a copy plus an additional utility associated with the purchase of the original of a product that they like, i.e., that is not too different from their ideal product. Consumers can obtain information on the horizontal characteristics of products by using P2P. Without the availability of digital copies, consumers have to choose at random between the N products. P2P allows users to sample. Thus consumers can obtain a very precise signal concerning the location of the products with respect to their own taste. Peitz and Waelbroeck show that for a sufficiently large number of products and a sufficient degree of product differentiation, the firm can benefit from the informational role of digital copies that leads to a higher willingness to pay for the original.

In an extended model, Peitz and Waelbroeck (2004b) analyze P2P as an alternative channel of information transmission to marketing and promotion. They postulate that through marketing and promotion the firm can transmit information on the desirability of its products to consumers with some precision. This gives partial information on the horizontal characteristics of the products, i.e., marketing and promotion reduces the set of preferred varieties to $n < N$ and raises the expected value of the original. Transmitting more precise information is assumed to require higher fixed costs of marketing and promotion. Peitz and Waelbroeck then show that firms can reduce the cost associated with marketing and promotion in the presence of P2P, thus increasing profits. Indeed, P2P can be seen as a substitute to marketing and promotion. They conclude that even if P2P reduces revenues, profits may actually increase because of reduction in the distribution cost.

Duchêne and Waelbroeck (2005) analyze the effect of extended copyright protection on a firm's distribution and protection strategies, when digital copies available on P2P networks play an informational role. To this end they propose a simple model of P2P technologies in which an original provides additional value compared to the copy and where consumers are heterogeneous with respect to the opportunity cost of spending time online searching for files. They model the demand for a new product that is not distributed using the marketing/promotion technology by assuming that consumers can only purchase a good after they have downloaded a digital copy that provide information on the characteristic of the product.[21]

[21] Poddar (2005b) analyzes sampling in a two-period durable good duopoly with a Coasian commitment problem. Sampling in period 1 makes consumers with intermediate types willing to pay a high second-period price if they happen to like the music they experience. Poddar presents a simple parametric example according to which full protection is sometimes not desirable for the monopolist. However, while such an analysis if of some theoretical interest, it is questionable whether firms really suffer from a commitment problem in the markets under consideration. At least, e.g. in the music market we do not often observe steep price decreases of albums after their release – see also Section 2.

They consider a single firm that decides how much costly technological protection to implement in different legal enforcement regimes. Technological protection increases the consumers' disutility of a copy but at the same reduces the fair use value of the original product (although they assume that the first effect dominates the second). A strengthening of legal protection reduces the surplus of copiers through the increase in the expected penalty if caught copying. In this framework, they show that increasing copyright protection has both a direct effect on copiers but also an indirect effect on buyers as technological protection and prices increase with legal protection, unambiguously reducing consumer surplus.

5.2. Stars versus niche performers

Zhang (2002) argues that sticking to the traditional distribution technology is wasteful from a social point of view when P2P technologies are available. His argument is motivated by the observation that the current distribution technology favors artists with a large audience (or stars) preventing marginal artists to be distributed in the market. P2P, by offering a cheaper way (digital copies) to give information to consumers, makes it possible for the marginal artist to enter the market. To make his point, Zhang proposes a model of the music industry with two products that are horizontal differentiated. The product is synonymous with the artist, where a star artist is pushed by a big label and the marginal artist has no backing. Zhang assumes that prices are exogenously fixed and identical for both products. Consumers have different values for each artist described by the unit interval on the Hotelling line. However, without piracy products are asymmetric because the value can be increased by persuasive advertising for one particular artist (the star) but not for the other (the marginal artist). Although the persuasive nature of advertising may be questionable, it is not essential for the argument (although welfare results depend on the particular specification of advertising).

The star artist chooses advertising expenditure to maximize his profits. Although the marginal artist is not prevented from distributing her product, the star artist (or, her label) will choose a positive amount of advertising expenditures to distort demand in its favor. This distortion can be so large that the marginal artist can even be driven out of the market.

With piracy, the marginal artist can distribute his songs using a P2P technology. Zhang assumes that only a portion of consumers have access to P2P, that digital copies provide information on the true characteristics of the products and that a fraction of these consumers (the "honest" downloaders) purchases one of the two songs which provides the highest utility. Then clearly, when P2P exists, marginal artists can gain from the exposure effect, while the star unambiguously loses. This insight is likely to apply to a more general framework in which both artists have a set of strategies available. The basic point would be that in an asymmetric world (with stars and niche performers) the current distribution technology favors the promotion of stars. With digital copies niche performers can more easily access consumers. In effect, the distribution of album sales would be less skewed. The view that digital information transmission leads to a less skewed distribution and that thus niche artists better find their audiences has been popularized by Anderson (2004).

5.3. Copying and adverse selection

Takeyama (2003) analyzes how copies that provide information on the quality of a product can solve an adverse selection in models of asymmetric information. She considers a monopolist selling a durable good that can have two exogenous qualities (high and low) known to the firm, but unknown to the consumers (who, for simplicity, do not value the low quality). There are two periods and all consumers with unit demand are present in both periods. Without copies, Takeyama assumes that a high-quality firm cannot make profits because of the underlying adverse selection problem.

Consider now the situation when copies are available. If a consumer copies the product in the first period, she learns its quality and can decide whether to purchase in the second period. Takeyama assumes that copies give less value than the original. Hence, it may be worthwhile to buy the good after copying.

Furthermore, there are two groups of consumers, who receive different values from the copies (in our previous notation, $\alpha_L\theta q$ and $\alpha_H\theta q$, respectively). A copy can be obtained at price c (that is, there is a disutility from copying). Under some parameter restrictions a fraction of consumers (those consumers with parameter α_L) never copy – call them the captive consumers – regardless of the price and the true high quality (in other words, the reproduction cost is larger than the benefit of the copy for them). The other consumers have the possibility of copying in the first period and then of buying the original if the product turns out to be of high quality. Takeyama shows that there exists a pooling equilibrium in which the monopolist intertemporally price-discriminates, selling to the captive consumers in the first period and charging the price equal to the difference in valuation between the original and the copy to the other consumers in the second period (at a price equal to $(1-\alpha_H)\theta q$). In this equilibrium, a high-quality firm can make profits due to the informational gain brought by copies. Interestingly, consumers with a low value for copies would generate higher price–cost margins in a static discrete choice setting. However, copying provides information and those with a high value for copies are more likely to engage in copying. This solves the adverse selection problem for high quality.

Furthermore, in a separating equilibrium with copies the quality may be revealed to consumers prior to purchase and the low quality original may not be available on the market. Takeyama then makes the availability or non-availability of copies part of the firm's strategy. She shows that the existence of copies (in other words, the lack of enforcement of copyright) is a signal for high quality.

We note that if the firm could choose quality then it may have an incentive to do so when copies are available but not when copies are not available (the model then would become a model of moral hazard). We conjecture that the following situation can then arise: if the copyright enforcement is part of the strategy, a firm has an incentive to provide high quality. If piracy was made impossible no product would be available. Consequently, the possibility of piracy can provide incentives for the provision of high quality in a market which otherwise would not be served. While the aspect of consumer learning is certainly of importance in several markets, Takeyama's intertemporal pricing context is perhaps of limited applicability.

To summarize, complex experience goods, goods for with consumers have heterogeneous tastes and goods for which is there is uncertainty on their existence could strongly benefit from sampling by consumers. Such sampling is facilitated by information-pull technologies such as P2P networks. In particular new or niche firms (and artists) can benefit from this sampling effect. This suggests that there are possibly positive short-term and long-term welfare effects. To the extent that business models are based on traditional information-push technologies, end-user copying (and other forms of decentralized means of information acquisitions) may lead to the emergence of new business models and industry structures.[22]

6. The applicability of the analysis of end-user copying to software, video and computer games, digitally compressed music and films

While digital products share several features (almost zero marginal costs of production, almost perfect copy), problems of piracy are industry specific. While we focus on large-scale end-user copying, some of the industries also face the threat of small-scale end-user copying (which we only briefly discuss) as well as commercial piracy (which we do not discuss at all). The prevalence of piracy in the industries is likely to depend on market characteristics. Recently, we have seen a number of external shocks in some of the industries: in particular, the introduction and adoption of end-user copying technologies and the spread of broadband access. In the light of these shocks we discuss economic aspects of software, video and computer games, music and movie piracy taking into account insights from the literature reviewed above.

6.1. *Software*

We first take a look at the software industry. Here, we observe sophisticated pricing and product bundling strategies. However, it is not clear whether these strategies can be interpreted as instruments to combat piracy or they are simply price discrimination strategies so that different types of consumers self-select.[23] Because of the complexity of the products, end-user copying appears often to be unattractive for consumers: the "true" cost of a piece of software is not only its purchase price, but rather includes the cost to learn how to use the software to its full potential and to make it work with other software (this is sometimes referred to as TCO or Total Cost of Ownership). For this reason, some users place a great value on manuals and online support, which gives a higher value to the original than to the downgraded version or copy. Note that the cost of copying a piece of software can be large. First, because of the complexity of the product the likelihood that one installation file is corrupted or missing is high. Secondly, installing pirated software requires some technical knowledge and can lead to an unstable computing environment; this technical knowledge is costly. If the pirated software is not installed properly, the copy is of inferior quality. Several software companies producing highly complex software also generate a large percentage of their revenues from value-

[22] In the case of the music industry, we refer to Anderson (2004), Peitz and Waelbroeck (2005) for further general discussion, and Dubosson-Torbay et al. (2004) and Duchêne et al. (2005) for specific discussion of alternative business models.

[23] Instead of copying proprietary software, users have in some cases the alternative to adopt open source software. The economics of the provision of open source is a different topic (see e.g. Lerner and Tirole, 2001, 2002, 2005). However, ignoring network effects, the effect of an open source competitor on the profit of a proprietary software provider is qualitatively similar to piracy of that software.

added services. Finally, some software companies offer highly customized software services for which a copy has little value to a person other than the person for which the services were provided. Examples include integration services, centralized information services and software application providers.

It is easy to monitor software copies in large companies and administration or even small businesses because a single threat of the powerful Business Software Alliance of visiting the company for a pirated version of a software is in general enough to trigger purchases of the original. Monitoring leads to direct appropriation. It also worth stressing that Internet product activation is also a means to better monitor the number of copies. Hence, also indirect appropriation in the form of site license agreements that depend on the number of computers using the software survives. Another way to indirectly appropriate surplus from copies is through ad-supported software, where a third-party pays for the free distribution to users. Finally, the internet has enabled software producer to switch from perpetual licenses to (yearly) subscription fees, thus shifting from indirect appropriation to a more direct appropriation scheme.

Direct network effects, although very strong in the past, have been reduced following the development of standards for file formats. Therefore, it seems that the argument of using copies to promote sales of originals is weakening. Important exceptions are online games and applications (see below), online collaboration and instant messaging (including video conferencing), where full compatibility is critical. In addition, some analysts of the software industry have argued that the weak intellectual protection of Microsoft products together with the increasing lobbying of Microsoft for increased future intellectual property in China is based on a strategy that exploits network effects. Finally, producers such as Adobe have exploited cross-network externalities between its PDF reader and writer to generate more revenue from sales of the writer while distributing the reader for free.

Software producers have for a long time used the practice of offering their product for free, either the full featured version or a downgraded version for a limited time only (these copies are often designated as "shareware"). Indeed, a new piece of software is typically an experience good that needs to be used before evaluating all its benefits. Hence, there is potentially a role for digital copies to provide information on the characteristics of the original product.

6.2. *Video and computer games*

Video and computer games are interesting to analyze for two reasons. First, the protection policy has changed over the last decades. While games developed in the 1980s were strongly password as well as technically protected, the quality difference between the original and the copy was low. With the explosive growth of computing power, game developers have changed their protection strategies by dramatically increasing the quality of the original (including sounds, speeches, videos, cinematic effects), making the purchase of the original game a great value compared to the copy. At the same time, the number of games using password protection and technical protection has decreased. Secondly, contrary to what might have been expected, the development of the internet has not had strong negative effects on sales of computer games.[24] A segment that generates increasing revenues is the market for online games that, according to NPD, is set to represent 15% of new generation software dollars. Because games that have an online component require connection to a proprietary site (using a unique identification number), it is easy to monitor connection time and the number of times a game is played, without implementing fancy Digital Rights Management (DRM) technologies that can monitor and limit the number of uses of a digital product. Thus, copies have no value for online players since they do not provide an additional identification number; although they are still valuable to players who only play in single-user mode.

Video game software producers technologically protect their products by bundling them to hardware devices. Indeed, the technology of copying video games is specific. There is a large fixed cost of purchasing a copying device (which does not have alternative uses) and then a very low marginal cost for each additional copy.[25] This is especially true for portable consoles. This deters most end-user piracy in countries with strong IP protection where copying devices are hard to find. However, here the original and the copy have almost the same quality.

In principle, online game developers could fully price discriminate consumers according to their use of the software. In practice, firms do not price discriminate apart from charging a fixed monthly fee to players who play online.[26] Online game subscription could be seen as direct appropriation of gamers willingness to pay.

Although most computer and video games are played alone, there are some games where players can compete against each other or that require some interaction with other people (intranet and internet games). For these reasons, one can expect strong network effects for network games. Some software producers such as Blizzard partly exploit network effects by letting players play on an intranet from a single copy, thus creating an expanding installed base through word-of-mouth that they benefit from when they introduce an expansion pack (or upgrade). Note also that sampling is limited due to the unavailability of free copies.

6.3. Music/P2P

The internet has made it easier for consumers to download Mp3 files and millions of internet users are downloading music without authorization from copyright owners. But searching for files even in a world of broadband connection is still time consuming. There are several reasons. First, file names do not always correspond to the requested file; they can be corrupted and the downloading speed depends on the priority rating of the user in

[24] Over the recent years, sales of computer games have slightly decreased while total sales of video games has exploded. This is the only segment of the entertainment industry to have experienced a sustained growth over the last 5 years, increasing from $6.9 billion in 1999 to $9.9 billion in 2004 in the United States, according to NPD. Decreasing sales in the computer game market are possibly rather due to a substitution to console and portable platforms than to increased piracy.

[25] Some gaming consoles such as Sony's Playstation use standard format such as the DVD and are therefore more subject to piracy. However, copying games still requires technical knowledge to modify the hardware, which is costly because games format evolve and may require further modifications. Copying is also risky because with some probability the console will no longer work after the hacking procedure.

[26] We can only speculate about the reasons. Possibly, the intensity of use and willingness-to-pay are not highly positively correlated. Also, price discrimination may be difficult to sustain when a firm faces fierce competition.

the P2P network. Secondly, song and title information are often poorly documented and getting this information is also costly. Thus, a digital copy (from a P2P system) provides less value than an original but at a lower cost. This cost depends on the user's opportunity cost of spending time online.

In principle, digital rights management (DRM) is a tool to fully appropriate the values of the copies as well as to price discriminate. Thus there is scope for direct appropriation of the digital music user's willingness to pay. However, such technological protection is unlikely to eliminate end-user piracy, since it is always possible to crack software protection (that is included in the music file) and diffusion of these anti-protection devices would be fast in P2P networks.

It would be in theory possible to indirectly appropriate revenues from the "uses" if the file-sharing rating of a user depends positively on the number of uploads and negatively on the number of downloads and if the rating itself makes searching and downloading faster (see Liebowitz, 2003). Indeed, users would be ready to purchase the original at a higher price as they expect many other users to download the file, thus improving their rating. While indirect appropriation may work for members of the P2P community, the fact that an important number of potential buyers do not belong to it, makes it unlikely that labels can profitably increase the price of a CD to indirectly appropriate revenues. Other means to indirectly appropriate consumers' willingness to pay for music were already discussed before: sales of complementary physical products such as MP3 players and revenues from live concerts.

There is a case for positive network effects in music consumption if users derive a value from the number of people listening to the same music. These social network effects can result from the fact that consumers want to belong to a community or be able to talk about music in social gatherings (see the development of Pod Fighting during which owners of portable music players alternately play short samples of their playlists). Recent attempts to exploit these network externalities to increase the value of music include MySpace.com where internet users share their playlists and recommendations. This feature is also available in most legal download sites such as Apple iTunes and Yahoo! Music stores. In principle, network effects could depend on both the number of originals and copies.

When facing new music, consumers like to spend time getting recommendations from music magazines, listening to music on the radio or in record store before making their purchase decision. The traditional way for record companies to provide information to consumers on the existence and the genre of new CDs and artists is to spend large costs on advertising and promotion. However, after the Napster experience, it has become clear that there is a cheaper way for some consumers to obtain this information: by searching, downloading and testing digital music files made available through P2P or other file-swapping technologies. This information transmission technology is rather different from traditional ads/promotions, as consumers not the firms are spending time and resources. In a sense, it is information-pull against information-push technologies. To sum up, digital copies of music files can be expected to have a strong informational role.

6.4. Movie piracy

Another related product is movies on DVDs. So far, movies have not faced serious competition from free illegal copies on the internet although small-scale copying may be relevant in the light of increasing DVD burner penetration and high sales of blank DVDs.[27]

There are a couple of reasons why movie piracy is currently less of a concern than music piracy for content owners. First, movies are much more storage hungry, so that downloading is more cumbersome and time-consuming. Secondly, similar to video games, copying DVDs is hardware protected. (This partly explains the music industry's enthusiasm for music DVDs). Because of these two facts copies that are available for free on the internet are of lower quality than the originals so that they are less of a threat to the original (no choice of format, language and subtitles, no extra material). Clearly, this is a snapshot. As a result of faster internet connections (increasing bandwidth) digital copies distributed through file-sharing systems may become a good substitute to movies sold on DVDs. Note, however, that both downloading and uploading speed have to increase significantly (which will be the case if for instance fiber-to-the-home becomes common). Movie piracy may in principle give rise to social network effects and the sampling effect, similar to the case of movies. However, while many consumers listen to a lot of music frequently they often watch a movie only once. Hence, there is less scope for the sampling effect to be important in the case of movies. Thus movie piracy is potentially more damaging for firms.

Movies that are watched only once or twice by individual consumers – this is the case for the vast majority of movies – may be rented (through DVD rental stores or Netflix distance service). In addition, movie-on-demand may become successful with a high penetration of fast internet connections. These additional income-generating business models may allow firms to directly appropriate rents and effectively deter large scale music piracy.

To summarize, end-user piracy is an important challenge for industries producing digital goods. Several strategies described in this review have been successfully applied to fight such piracy. With respect to product differentiation, customized software services reduce the value of a copy to a pirate. The internet may also allow firms to better appropriate rents directly e.g. by monitoring of software use through internet activation and subscription services and through online accounts with personal identification numbers for online games. Technological protection such as DRM protected music files and protected DVDs also ranks high in the list of anti-piracy tools.

We have, however, argued that in order to exploit for example network effects in music consumption through online communities or network effects among software users, the (limited) distribution of free copies can be a successful way to generate sales of digital products, in particular for new releases. Producers of experience goods such as new music albums and software may decide to (for limited time or to a certain extent) refrain from measures against piracy or even actively encourage end-user copying to foster sampling and word-of-mouth.

7. Conclusion

End-user copying of digital products has received a lot of interest in the popular press and in the courtroom, as exemplified by the recent ruling by the US Supreme Court on the P2P network Grokster (*MGM Studios, Inc. v. Grokster, Ltd.*, 545 US, 125 S. Ct. 2764

[27] With respect to small-scale copying (e.g. sharing among friends) there is in theory some scope for indirect appropriation.

(2005)) according to which Grokster could be sued for inducing copyright infringement. On November 7, 2005, Grokster announced that it would no longer offer its peer-to-peer file-sharing service. The notice on their website says. "The United States Supreme Court unanimously confirmed that using this service to trade copyrighted material is illegal. Copying copyrighted motion picture and music files using unauthorized peer-to-peer services is illegal and is prosecuted by copyright owners. There are legal services for downloading music and movies. This service is not one of them." (checked May 2006). This is the latest major court decision in the history of copying information goods.

Technological innovations such as CD and DVD burning, portable devices for music in digitally compressed formats, and online file-sharing technology have made copying, transferring and using of digital products by end users easier. In a sense the availability of these technologies increase the value of the product (e.g. movies and recorded music). However, since creators are often not remunerated for these additional uses (except when particular DRM is implemented), digital copying is likely to affect industry profits. Such changes not only raise questions about intellectual property rights, but also about incentives to engage in creative activities and about the viability of traditional business models.

In this review paper, we analyzed the theory of end-user copying. We organized our analysis by first considering markets with end-user piracy in which, (1) there are no means of indirect appropriation of rents, (2) the value that consumers put on the product is independent of the decision of other consumers for any given price, and (3) consumers are perfectly informed about the characteristics of the digital product. In such markets end-user copying is profit reducing. However, it may be welfare-increasing, in particular because piracy leads to market expansion. It reduces the incentive to enter the industry and thus tends to reduce product variety.

We then analyzed markets in which there is the possibility of indirect appropriation. Here, we distinguished between indirect appropriation across consumers and indirect appropriation across products. In the case of increasing marginal costs of distribution, small-scale copying may be profit and welfare increasing. Selling physical products that are complements to the information goods mitigates the negative effect of piracy on profits.

Moreover, we analyzed markets in which the value of a product derived by a consumer depends on the decision of other consumers, i.e., markets in which there are network effects. With positive network effects end-user copying may increase profits resulting from price discrimination and market expansion. Network effects tend to make end-user copying welfare-increasing.

Finally, we analyzed markets in which consumers are not perfectly informed about the characteristics of the product and copying provides information on the value of the product, facilitating the purchasing decision. Because sampling is valued by consumers, firms may partially capture the increased demand and end-user copying may be profit increasing. Combined with the positive effect for consumers, sampling tends to make end-user copying welfare-increasing.

While the theoretical literature on illegal copying provides some general insights, positive and normative effects of end-user copying in a particular industry depend on the particular features of that industry. For that purpose we discussed a number of industries in the light of the previous analysis. The analysis revealed that there are important industry differences which can be explained by differences in technology and consumer behavior. We give a number of examples. With respect to technology, copying in the video game industry used to be less of an issue because of proprietary formats. Music piracy became more widespread before movie piracy because copying movies requires more bandwidth. With respect to consumer behavior, movie piracy is arguably more damaging for the movie studios than music piracy for the music labels, because consumers tend not to repeatedly watch the same movie. However, in the movie industry there already exist legal versions for viewing movies at a price which may deter a large amount of movie piracy (traditional movie rental, Netflix, and increasingly video-on-demand). Legal alternatives to downloaded movies have only recently received attention with the success of iTunes.

The effect of piracy on firm profits and investment incentives is often difficult to evaluate given the specific characteristics of an industry. The software industry is a special case. A first observation is that software firms have included in their business model ways to account for the fact that their product is an experience good. In particular, many share-ware versions are offered. In addition, special student versions and similar offers provide low price alternatives to the full price versions for certain groups of consumers. These strategies can be partly explained by the desire to capture the value users place on testing a product before purchasing it as well as to exploit network and intertemporal demand effects. As argued before, it appears that many software developers have already adjusted to the environment they operate in, including the threat of piracy. On the other hand, widespread end-user copying is a more recent phenomenon in the music and movie industries. As a consequence, players in these industries have only recently begun to rethink their business models. While recent changes in profitability can partly be attributed to piracy, the software industry has not been exposed to a recent shock. More theoretical and empirical industry studies are therefore welcomed to shed more light on the effect of piracy and IP protection on firm strategy and industry structure.

In particular in the light of technological changes (broadband, burners, DRM etc.), an important area for future research is to analyze alternative business models that better allow firms to avoid negative effects of end-user copying and public policy with respect to the design and enforcement of IP protection. In this survey we discussed a number of contributions in this direction but, as it has become apparent, many open questions remain.

Acknowledgements

We received helpful comments from three referees.

References

Alvisi, M., Argentesi, E., Carbonara, E., 2002. Piracy and Quality Choice in Monopolistic Markets. University of Bologna, Mimeo.

Anderson, C., 2004. The Long Tail. Wired, October 12, 2004.

Arrow, K., 1962. Economic welfare and the allocation of resources for inventions. In: Nelson, R. (Ed.), The Rate and Direction of Inventive Activity. Princeton University Press.

Bae, S.-H., Choi, J.P., forthcoming. A model of piracy. Information Economics and Policy.

Bakos, J.Y., Brynjolfsson, E., Lichtman, G., 1999. Shared information goods. Journal of Law and Economics 48, 117–156.

Banerjee, D.S., 2003. Software piracy: a strategic analysis and policy instruments. International Journal of Industrial Organization 21, 97–121.

Belleflamme, P., 2003. Pricing information goods in the presence of copying. In: Gordon, W.J., Watt, R. (Eds.), The Economics of Copyright. Developments in Research and Analysis. Edward Elgar.

Belleflamme, P., 2006. Versioning information goods. In: Illing, G., Peitz, M. (Eds.), Industrial Organization and the Digital Economy. MIT Press.
Belleflamme, P., Picard, P., 2004a. Competition over piratable goods. CORE Discussion Paper 2004/55, Université catholique de Louvain.
Belleflamme, P., Picard, P., 2004b. Piracy and Competition. CESifo Discussion Paper #1350.
Besen, S.M., Kirby, S.N., 1989. Private copying, appropriability, and optimal copying royalties. Journal of Law and Economics 32, 255–280.
Chen, Y., Png, I., 2003. Information goods pricing and copyright enforcement: welfare analysis. Information Systems Research 14, 107–123.
Conner, K.R., Rumelt, R.P., 1991. Software piracy – an analysis of protection strategies. Management Science 37, 125–139.
Connolly, M., Krueger, A., forthcoming. Rockonomics – the economics of popular music. In: Ginsburgh, V., Throsby, D. (Eds.), Handbook of the Economics of Arts and Culture, Elsevier Science, Amsterdam.
Cremer, H., Pestieau, P., 2005. Piracy Prevention and the Pricing of Information Goods. University of Toulouse and University of Liége, Mimeo.
Csorba, G., 2002. Read-only Versions for Free and for Profit: Functional Quality Differentiation Strategies of a Software Producing Monopoly. Central European University, Budapest, Mimeo.
Csorba, G., Hahn, J.H., 2006. Functional degradation and asymmetric network effects. Journal of Industrial Economics 54, 253–268.
Curien, N., Laffond, G., Lainé, J., Moreau, F., 2004. Towards a new business model for the music industry: accommodating piracy through ancillary products, Mimeo.
Dubosson-Torbay, M., Pigneur, Y., Usunier, J.-C., 2004. Business models for music distribution after the P2P revolution. In: Proceedings of the Fourth International Conference on Web Delivering of Music, pp. 172–179.
Duchêne, A., Waelbroeck, P., 2005. Peer-to-peer, piracy and the copyright law: implications for consumers and artists. In: Takeyama, L., Gordon, W., Liacos, P., Towse, R. (Eds.), Developments in the Economics of Copyright: Research and Analysis. Edward Elgar.
Duchêne, A., Peitz, M., Waelbroeck, P., 2005. Marketing digital music: the role of DRM. International University in Germany Working Paper 31/2005. Available from: <www.ssrn.com>.
Gayer, A., Shy, O., 2003a. Copyright protection and hardware taxation. Information Economics and Policy 15, 467–483.
Gayer, A., Shy, O., 2003b. Internet and peer-to-peer distributions in markets for digital products. Economics Letters 81, 51–57.
Gayer, A., Shy, O., forthcoming. Publishers, artists, and copyright enforcement. Information Economics and Policy.
Gopal, R., Bhattacharjee, S., Sanders, G.L., 2006. Do artists benefit from online music sharing. Journal of Business 79, 1503–1534.
Grgeta, E., 2004. Copies and Originals in a Horizontally and Vertically Differentiated Market with Habit and Quality Differences. University of Chicago, Mimeo.
Hahn, J.-H., 2001. Functional Quality Degradation with Network Externalities. Keele University, Mimeo.
Hahn, J.-H., 2004. The welfare effects of quality degradation of software with network externalities. Information Economics and Policy 16, 535–552.
Hahn, J.H., forthcoming. Damaged durable goods. Rand Journal of Economics.
Halonen, M., Regner, T., 2003. Technology Change and the Allocation of Ownership: The Music Industry. University of Bristol, Mimeo.
Harbaugh, R., Khemka, R., 2001. Does copyright enforcement encourage piracy? Claremont colleges working paper 2001-14.
Hurt, R.M., Schuchman, R.M., 1966. The economic rationale of copyright. American Economic Review 56, 421–432.
Inderst, R., 2003. Durable Goods with Quality Differentiation. LSE, Mimeo.
Johnson, W., 1985. The economics of copying. Journal of Political Economy 93, 158–174.
Johnson, J., Myatt, D., 2003. Multiproduct quality competition: fighting brands and product line pruning. American Economic Review 93, 748–774.
King, P.S., Lampe, R., 2003. Price discrimination and profitable piracy. Information Economics and Policy 15, 271–290.
Krueger, A., 2005. The economics of real superstars: the market for concerts in the material world. Journal of Labor Economics 23, 1–30.

Lerner, J., Tirole, J., 2001. The open source movement: key research questions. European Economic Review 45, 819–826.
Lerner, J., Tirole, J., 2002. Some simple economics of open source. Journal of Industrial Economics 50, 197–234.
Lerner, J., Tirole, J., 2005. The economics of technology sharing: open source and beyond. Journal of Economic Perspectives 19, 99–120.
Liebowitz, S., 1985. Copying and indirect appropriability: photocopying of journals. Journal of Political Economy 93, 945–957.
Liebowitz, S., 2003. Will MP3 downloads annihilate the record industry? The evidence so far. In: Libecap, G. (Ed.), Advances in the Study of Entrepreneurship, Innovation, and Economic Growth. JAI Press.
Liebowitz, S., 2006. Economists examine file-sharing and music sales. In: Illing, G., Peitz, M. (Eds.), Industrial Organization and the Digital Economy. MIT Press.
Mussa, M., Rosen, S., 1978. Monopoly and product quality. Journal of Economic Theory 18, 301–317.
Novos, I.E., Waldman, M., 1984. The effects of increased copyright protection: an analytic approach. Journal of Political Economy 92, 236–246.
Peitz, M., 2004. A strategic approach to software protection: comment. Journal of Economics and Management Strategy 13, 371–374.
Peitz, M., Waelbroeck, P., 2004a. The effect of internet piracy on CD sales – cross section evidence. Review of Economic Research on Copyright Issues 1, 71–79.
Peitz, M., Waelbroeck, P., 2004b. File sharing, sampling, and music distribution. International University in Germany Working Paper 26/2004. Available from: <www.ssrn.com>.
Peitz, M., Waelbroeck, P., 2005. An economist's guide to digital music. CESifo Economic Studies 51, 359–428.
Peitz, M., Waelbroeck, P., forthcoming. Why the music industry may gain from free downloading – the role of sampling. International Journal of Industrial Organization.
Poddar, S., 2005a. Network Externality and Commercial Software Piracy. National University of Singapore, Mimeo.
Poddar, S., 2005b. Music Product as Durable Good and Online Piracy. National University of Singapore, Mimeo.
Regner, T., 2002. Innovation of music. In: Watt, R. (Ed.), The Economics of Copyright: Developments in Research and Analysis. Edward Elgar.
Shy, O., Thisse, J., 1999. A strategic approach to software protection. Journal of Economics and Management Strategy 8, 163–190.
Slive, J., Bernhardt, D., 1998. Pirated for profit. Canadian Journal of Economics 31, 886–899.
Sundararajan, A., 2004. Managing digital piracy: pricing and protection. Information Systems Research 15, 287–308.
Takeyama, L.N., 1994. The welfare implications of unauthorized reproduction of intellectual property in the presence of network externalities. Journal of Industrial Economics 42, 155–166.
Takeyama, L.N., 1997. The intertemporal consequences of unauthorized reproduction of intellectual property. Journal of Law and Economics 40, 511–522.
Takeyama, L.N., 2003. Piracy, asymmetric information and product quality. In: Gordon, W.J., Watt, R. (Eds.), The Economics of Copyright. Developments in Research and Analysis. Edward Elgar.
Valletti, T., Szymanski, S., forthcoming. Parallel trade, international exhaustion and intellectual property rights: a welfare analysis. Journal of Industrial Economics.
Varian, H.R., 2000. Buying, sharing and renting information goods. Journal of Industrial Economics 48, 473–488.
Yoon, K., 2002. The optimal level of copyright protection. Information Economics and Policy 14, 327–348.
Zentner, A., forthcoming. Measuring the effect of music downloads on music purchases. Journal of Law and Economics.
Zhang, M.X., 2002. Stardom, Peer-to-Peer and the Socially Optimal Distribution of Music. Sloan School of Management, MIT, Mimeo.

[6]

Review of Economic Research on Copyright Issues, 2006, vol. 3(2), pp. 3-13

COPYRIGHT: A PLEA FOR EMPIRICAL RESEARCH

IVAN P.L. PNG

ABSTRACT. I review empirical research into the economic impact of copyright law. A key difficulty is that there is little systematic measurement of creative output and copying: there are only fragmentary statistics for the various industries. Studies of U.S. copyright registrations provide conflicting results: one shows that small changes in fees have large impacts on renewals, while another shows that many movies and books have long lives. All but one studies find that music piracy – whether conventional or digital – has hurt legitimate CD sales. Studies of extensions of copyright duration yield conflicting results: one focusing on U.S. registrations finds no effect, while a multi-country study finds that extensions are associated with substantial increases in movie production. I conclude with directions for future empirical research.

1. INTRODUCTION

Copyright law involves a fundamental trade-off between incentives for creators of new work against the benefits from use of existing work for final consumption and as inputs into further creative activity.

> "Copyright protection ... trades off the costs of limiting access to a work against the benefits of providing incentives to create the work in the first place. Striking the correct balance between access and incentives is the central problem in copyright law." (Landes and Posner 1989).

In this trade-off, the "access" to existing work includes use by consumers as well as use by creators of derivative or incremental works. Both research and development and creative activity may be cumulative in the sense that they build on earlier discoveries and creations.

In assessing the trade-off, it is important to consider that copyright law provides protection on three dimensions (Watt 2004): (i) duration – the length of time for which copyright is in force; (ii) depth – which aspects of the creation are protected (generally, copyright law protects the expression but not the idea); and (iii) breadth – the limits of "fair use", the rights to derivative works, and limits on rental and re-sale. It is also important to consider the costs of tracing and transacting with the copyright owner (Landes and Posner 1989).

This review is based on my keynote address to the Annual Congress of the Society for Economic Research on Copyright Issues (SERCI) in Singapore, June 29-30, 2006. I thank the Executive Committee of SERCI for inviting me to present the lecture, and Congress participants for valuable comments and advice.

There has been a substantial volume of theoretical research into copyright. This has pointed to many empirical issues surrounding the fundamental trade-off.[1] However, there has been relatively little empirical research, hence major questions remain open.

- "In the formation of copyright policy, the lack of empirical data and the inability to quantify important variables ... preclude precise evaluation of the impact of any significant changes in the degree of copyright protection" (Bard and Kurlantzick (1999) page 3).
- "Perhaps the most pressing area in which the economics of copyright is lacking is in serious empirical studies" (Watt 2004).

In this review, I shall first discuss the barriers to empirical research, then the results of the limited empirical research so far published, and finally, directions for future work. The discussion is organized around three issues:

(1) How to measure creative output and copying;
(2) How do changes in copyright law (duration, depth, and breadth) affect the expected earnings of creators of new work?
(3) What is the creators' elasticity of supply of new work?

2. Measurement

The first issue is very basic, viz., the availability of the relevant data, and in particular, data regarding the creation of copyrightable items. The limited availability of such information may well be the single most important reason for the dearth of empirical research into copyright.

The "production" of a copyrightable item has two dimensions – one is the number of different titles, while the other is the volume of each title. The distinction between the two dimensions is important for two reasons. One, production of copyrightable items is subject to a high "first copy cost" relative to the marginal cost of subsequent units. Two, consumers value variety – another copy of the same movie seldom provides as much benefit as a different title. To avoid confusion, I shall use the terms "creation", "publication", and "creative activity" rather than "production".

A subtler issue is that creative activity itself has two dimensions – one is the number of titles, and the other is the quality of each title. Generally, there is no data on the quality of creative activity, so I shall focus on the data available for the number of titles.

Books. The International Publishers Association (IPA) provides annual statistics on titles published in various countries from 1990-1999. The IPA provides complete coverage for only 13 countries, viz., Argentina, Austria, Brazil, Denmark, Finland, France, Germany, Hungary, Latvia, Norway, Sweden, Switzerland, and the U.K. The IPA obtained the data from its national member organizations.

The United Nations Educational, Scientific and Cultural Organization (UNESCO) provides statistics on titles published for a broader set of countries (Canada, Croatia, Cuba, Cyprus, Czech Republic, Denmark, Ecuador, Estonia, Finland, France, Hungary, Iran, Italy, Lithuania, Morocco, Norway, Philippines, Poland, Moldova, Romania, Slovenia, Spain, Switzerland, Macedonia, and Turkey), but for

[1]For research into copyright in general, see Landes and Posner (2003), Watt (2004), Varian (2005). See also Boldrin and Levine (2002), Legros (2005), and Liebowitz and Watt (2006).

a shorter time period, 1995-1999. The UNESCO website does not disclose the primary sources of the data.

The coverage of the IPA and UNESCO statistics overlap for five countries – Denmark, Finland, France, Norway, and Switzerland. For these five countries, the correlation between the IPA and UNESCO numbers over the period 1995-1999 ranged from – 57% (Norway) to 99.5% (Hungary), with an average of 32%.[2]

Recorded Music. The International Federation of the Phonographic Industry (IFPI) provides annual statistics of aggregate sales of recorded music (both unit volume and monetary value) for 70 countries. However, IFPI does not report information on the number of titles. The IFPI information is provided by its national member organizations. Accordingly, the coverage of the IFPI statistics depends on the degree to which the various national member organizations provide representative information. For instance, in the case of the United States, "data is collected from RIAA [Recording Industry Association of America] member companies that distribute approximately 84% of the prerecorded music" (RIAA 2006).

Motion pictures. There are two sources of information about movie creation. One is the Internet Movie Database (IMBb), sponsored by Amazon.com, which proclaims itself to be "Earth's biggest movie database". The other is the Film Index International, published by the British Film Institute.

The IMDb encompasses various categories of audio-visual work, including movies, shorts, TV movies, TV series, and videos. IMDb records vary in detail. Most of the information in the IMDb is volunteered by industry members and website visitors.

The Film Index International provides information only about movies. The correlation in the number of movies created across a panel of OECD countries in the Film Index International and IMDb was 93% (Png and Wang 2006).

Electronic games. The Entertainment Software Association represents publishers of video and computer games that account for more than 90% of the U.S. entertainment software market. It provides annual statistics of aggregate sales of video and computer games (both unit volume and monetary value) for the United States only. However, ESA does not report information on the number of titles. The data is provided by NPD, a commercial information vendor.

The United Kingdom is the world's third largest market for video and computer games after the United States and Japan. The Entertainment & Leisure Software Publishers Association (ELSPA) provides annual statistics for the United Kingdom.

Software. So far as I am aware, there are no publicly available statistics on the creation of software. Indeed, it may well be futile to compile such statistics. The reason is that software differs essentially from the other categories of copyrightable items. First, software is much more heterogeneous – ranging from enterprise systems for thousands of concurrent users to simple single-user online programs. Second, there is relatively more emphasis on new versions of existing titles (eg, Windows, 2.0, 3.0, 98, 2000, ME, XP, etc.) than creation of completely new titles. Moreover,

---

[2]The International Standard Book Number (ISBN) uniquely identifies every book, but does not provide information about number of titles created (see http://www.isbn.org/standards/home/isbn/us/isbnqa.asp; last accessed October 15, 2006). Specifically, the ISBN is a 10-digit number, comprising four parts of variable length, viz., country or region identifier, publisher identifier, title identifier, and a check digit. Each publisher acquires ISBNs from the national ISBN agency in blocks, and uses the numbers in running sequence until exhausted and then applies for a fresh allocation. There is no correspondence between ISBN and year of publication.

as software is continually "fixed", it is difficult to identify what counts as a new version.

Based on the preceding review, I conclude that what is most urgently needed is accurate statistics of the creation of three categories of copyrightable items – books, recorded music, and electronic games – across countries in recent years. Unfortunately, despite its importance, such work is relatively unglamorous. The best hope is that the relevant industry associations and possibly international organizations such as the World Intellectual Property Organization (WIPO) can be persuaded to collect and publish these statistics.

As with creative activity generally, empirical research into copying depends on reliable measures. By contrast with measurement of the creative activity itself, there is much more public attention to measurement of piracy. (For the purposes of this review, any unauthorized copying is considered to be "piracy".) Most prominently, the BSA publishes an annual report on piracy of business software with statistics for 97 countries and territories (see Business Software Alliance, 2006), and the IFPI publishes an annual report on piracy of recorded music with statistics for 73 countries and territories (see International Federation of the Phonographic Industry, 2006).

Owing to the public policy interest, the Organisation for Economic Co-operation and Development (OECD), and also the World Intellectual Property Organization (WIPO) have initiated projects to develop methodologies for measurement of piracy (Olsen 2005). The WIPO project focuses on measurement of copyright piracy (Hui and Png 2005). Hopefully, these efforts will yield internationally-accepted methodologies, that various countries will implement and so produce reliable national statistics on piracy.

3. Expected Earnings

Plant (1934) observed that, for most of the 19th century, U.S. copyright law did not provide any protection to British authors, yet British authors received substantial income from U.S. publishers. Remarkably, following Plant's (1934) seminal contribution, almost 70 years elapsed before any further research into the impact of copyright on creators' earnings.

Under U.S. law, registration of copyright is not mandatory. However, the law provides an incentive for registration, as the owner must register (or, under the 1976 Copyright Act, apply to register) before the infringement (or within three months of first publication) if the owner seeks statutory damages and attorney fees.

A historical study of registrations with the U.S. Copyright Office provides evidence that the expected value of copyright protection is very low (Landes and Posner 2003). During the period 1910-2000, the registration fee increased several times. Although the fee was quite low (an average of \$20.48 in 2000 dollars over the period), the demand for registrations was price sensitive. Specifically, the elasticity of registrations with respect to the fee ranged from –0.20 (± 0.93) to –0.24 (± 1.34). This price sensitivity to even low registration fees suggests that the present value of the future earnings from the copyright item was quite small.

Baker and Cunningham (2006) conducted an event study of changes in U.S. copyright law on the stock-market value of companies in copyright-related industries between 1986-98.[3] They considered both case and statutory law, and found that increases in copyright protection were associated with an average US$4 - 8.4 million increase in the market value of these companies.[4]

Note, however, that the increase in stock-market value tends to over-state the impact of legal changes on the earnings from a given set of creative activity. The reason is that any increase in market value reflects the increased profit from existing creative work and future *infra-marginal* creations, as well as the increase in expected profit arising from marginal future creations stimulated by the increased copyright protection.

Next, I review studies that focused on the impact of particular dimensions of copyright law on creators' earnings.

Duration. Rappaport (1998) studied the commercial value in 1998 of movies first copyrighted in the period 1922-1941. He found two trends. First, more recently created movies were more likely to be still played commercially. Specifically, the commercial survival rates were 11% among movies created in 1926-1928, 40% among movies created in 1929-1932, and 65%, among movies created 1933-1941. Second, more recently created movies were of relatively greater commercial value. Specifically, the average commercial value was $175,000 among movies created in 1926-1930, $250,000 among movies created in 1931-1934, and $400,000 among movies created in 1935-1941.

Landes and Posner (2003) also studied the pattern of renewals of registration with the U.S. Copyright Office during the period 1910-91. Until 1962, renewals were effective for an additional 28 years, while from 1962, the renewal was for 47 years.

Generally, the renewal rate increased from a low of 3% in 1914 to a high of 22% in 1991, and the renewal rate was highest for music, middling for books, and lowest for graphic-arts works. Assuming that works were not renewed because the expected future earnings fell below the cost of renewal ($10 plus the time and effort), Landes and Posner (2003) concluded that almost 80% of copyrighted works had little economic value after the initial term.

By contrast, (Liebowitz and Margolis 2005) studied a sample of 236 titles reviewed by Book Review Digest in the 1920s. Fifty-eight years later, 41% were still in print.

In assessing the value of copyright protection, it is important to note that, at the point in time where the creator incurs the cost of creative effort, she will not know whether her work will turn into a blockbuster. Hence, copyright, copyright registration, and most importantly, renewal of copyright registration should be valued as real options rather than absolute amounts.

Depth. So far as I am aware, there has been no empirical research into the impact of changes in the depth of copyright protection on creator's earnings.[5]

---

[3]Specifically, the industries were SICs 27 (Printing, Publishing and Allied Industries), 73 (Business Services), and 78 (Motion Pictures).

[4]Khong and Khong (2006) conducted a similar study of U.K. companies, and found no significant effect.

[5]In the case of *Baker v. Selden* (101 U.S. 99, 1879), Selden published a book describing a new book-keeping system which included sample forms. Baker modified and sold the forms, and was held not to have infringed Selden's copyright. Landes and Posner (1989) explain that the court was correct to limit the depth of copyright protection, as there are limited ways to express the

Breadth. The overwhelming bulk of empirical research into copyright has focused on the impact of the breadth of copyright on creators' earnings, and specifically, the impact of copying. Illegal copying is also called "piracy". An issue of particular interest is the effect of advances in information and communications technology on copying and the creator's earnings.

In principle, copying could affect creators' earnings positively or negatively. Positive effects include advertising, sampling, and sharing, all of which would stimulate demand for the legitimate item. The obvious negative effect is the direct substitution of pirated for the legitimate item.

A key innovation in the technology of copying was the photocopying machine. How did that affect the earnings of creators? Liebowitz (1985) observed that, following the widespread adoption of photocopying machines, journal publishers raised subscription rates to libraries relative to rates for individuals. Further, the differential was highest for the most frequently copied journals. By charging discriminatory rates, the publishers could "indirectly appropriate" some of the libraries' benefit from copying.

Widdows and McHugh (1984) studied the impact of home copying on sales of recorded music in the United States between 1956-81. In a finding which presaged much of the subsequent literature, they found that the impact of home copying was much smaller than claimed by the recorded music industry.

Hui and Png (2003) studied the impact of piracy on sales of music CDs in 28 countries between 1994-98. The demand for music CDs decreased with piracy, suggesting that "theft" outweighed any positive effects of piracy. Hui and Png (2003) calculated that, in 1998, actual *unit losses* amounted to about 6.6% of sales. The actual *revenue loss* would have been higher as publishers would have raised prices in the absence of piracy.[6]

A relatively recent innovation in the technology of copying is peer-to-peer online file sharing. Owing in part to the landmark *Napster* and *Grokster* cases,[7] online file sharing triggered a veritable cottage industry of empirical research.

The challenge has been to measure the extent of file-sharing and relate it to changes in the sales of music CDs, while taking account of any simultaneity in the relation. Most researchers used various proxies for file-sharing, including the self-reported downloading of music (Peitz and Waelbroeck 2004; Zentner 2006), Internet and broadband penetration (Zentner 2005), Internet penetration (Hong 2004), and Internet usage (Liebowitz 2005). By contrast, Rob and Waldfogel (2006) and Oberholzer-Gee and Strumpf (2005) used direct information on downloading.

While Oberholzer-Gee and Strumpf (2005) found that file-sharing had no impact on music CD sales, all of the other studies concluded that file-sharing caused music CD sales to fall (Liebowitz 2006).[8] See Table 1.

idea of the book-keeping system. Allowing copyright over the forms (an expression) would have essentially provided copyright over the book-keeping system (the idea).

[6]A related question that has drawn substantial academic interest is what determines piracy. The factors identified include culture (Husted 2000; Marron and Steel 2000), income (Marron and Steel 2000; Rodriguez-Andres 2002), the size of the domestic software industry (Gopal and Sanders 1998), and judicial efficiency (Holm 2003).

[7]A&M Records v. Napster, 239 F.3d 1004 (9th Cir. 2001), and Metro-Goldwyn-Mayer Studios Inc. et al. v. Grokster, Ltd., et al., 125 S. Ct. 2764, 2005 respectively.

[8]Stevans and Sessions (2005) also found that file-sharing reduced CD sales, inferring this from a change in the trend of growth of music CD sales without any information on downloading.

Table 1: Peer-to-peer file sharing and music CD sales		
Study	*Period*	*Sales impact*
Hong (2004)	2000	U.S.; -7.8%
Liebowitz (2005)	1998-2003	U.S. cities; -3.2%
Peitz and Waldbroeck (2004)	2000-01	Worldwide; -11%, U.S.; -12%
Rob and Waldfogel (2006)	2003/04	U.S. university students; -9%
Zentner (2005)	1997/98-2000/01	56 countries; -6.6%
Zentner (2006)	2001	7 European countries; -7.8%
Oberholzer-Gee and Strumpf (2005)	Fall 2002	Not significant

Another aspect to the breadth of copyright protection is the extent to which the seller of a copyrighted item can control the buyer's commercial use, and specifically, rental and re-sale. In the United States, by the "first sale doctrine", movie studios cannot restrict buyers of pre-recorded videotapes from renting to others. Accordingly, studios have only two choices of pricing – uniform pricing, or indirect discrimination by initially pricing high to capture surplus from video rental stores and then cutting price for "sell through". In the European Union, however, studios can directly discriminate – charging stores different prices for videotapes for rental and for sell through.

Mortimer (2005) estimated the retail demand for rental vis-a-vis sell through videotapes and DVDs, and calculated that direct discrimination would benefit studios and consumers at the expense of retailers in the case of DVDs, but not necessarily in the case of videotapes.

4. Elasticity of Supply

Given how changes in copyright law affect the expected returns to creative activity, the next question is how creators respond to changes in earnings. Equivalently, what is their elasticity of supply? For a 1% increase in earnings, by how much would creators increase their effort, as measured by the number of titles and the quality of each title?

In 2002, the U.S. Supreme Court heard the Eldred case, which challenged the Sonny Bono Copyright Term Extension Act (CTEA).[9] Seventeen distinguished economists, including five Nobel laureates, filed an amici curiae brief against the CTEA (Akerlof et al. 2002). Based on illustrative calculations, they concluded that, "The CTEA's longer copyright for new works provides at most a very small additional incentive".

In a trenchant criticism, Liebowitz and Margolis (2005) argued that Akerlof et al. had skirted the central issue: "The present value of additional revenues to authors might be heavily discounted (and small), but this need not imply that the impact of these revenues on the creation of works is small ... The change in the number of new titles depends on the additional reward received by authors and on the elasticity of creation with respect to reward" (pp. 443, 445-446).

[9] *Eric Eldred et al., v. John D. Ashcroft*, Attorney General, U.S. Supreme Court, No. 01-618.

So what is this elasticity? Until 1891, U.S. copyright law did not provide any protection to foreign authors. Then, Congress passed the International Copyright Act, which extended copyright protection to foreign authors, and through reciprocal recognition, extended international copyright protection to U.S. authors. However, the Act did not have a substantial impact on the number of full-time authors in the United States (Khan 2004).[10]

Png and Wang (2006) studied the impact of extensions of copyright duration on the creation of movies. With retrospective effect from July 1995, the European Union extended the term of copyright over movies to 70 years following the death of the last among the principal director, the screenplay and dialogue authors, and the music composer to die. The extension applied retroactively to any existing work with copyright still in force.

In a sample of 18 countries, Png and Wang (2006) found that the extensions were associated with a 1.80% (± 1.77%) to 12.7% (± 5.82%) increase in movie production. An especially compelling result was that the increase in production was higher in countries with lower rates of piracy. The findings were robust to various specifications, including controlling for changes in government funding of movie production. These results suggest that even small increases in creators' earnings can induce substantial increases in movie production.

Separately, Baker and Cunningham (2005) studied the impact of changes in copyright law (both statutory and case-law) on applications for copyright registration. They found that increases in copyright protection were associated with a small positive effect on applications.

In future work, it is important to drill deeper into the incentive effect of copyright law. Specifically, how are increases in future earnings divided among the various parties to creation of new work, for instance, in the case of music, song-writer, performer, and recording studio, and what are the respective incentive effects on each of them? Further, what is the link between creation of new work and registration of copyright?

5. Concluding Remarks

I have reviewed various strands of empirical research into copyright law. Clearly, much more work needs to be done. Above, I have pointed to various directions for future work. Here, I will highlight three others.

First, with regard to the fundamental trade-off of intellectual property, there has been no study at all of the "costs of limiting access to a work" (Landes and Posner 1989) – with regard to both end-use and follow-on creation. Isaac Newton famously declared, "If I have seen further [than certain other men] it is by standing upon the shoulders of giants". The same applies to the creation of movies, music, and software as well. A key cost of copyright is the impediment to future creators.

Second, we need research into the costs of tracing, transactions, and enforcement involved in the administration of copyright. The magnitude of these costs is crucial to the question of whether copyright should be for fixed term or indefinite (Landes

[10]Towse (2001) observed that that: "Estimates suggest artists' elasticity of supply to arts work is high and so a relatively small financial reward ... can have a greater than proportionate impact on creativity". From Australian data, Throsby (1996) found that A$1 (Australian dollar) of income from non-artistic activity displaced A$0.14 of creative income and A$0.36 of arts-related income.

and Posner 2003). In particular, it would be interesting to measure the contribution of collecting societies towards reducing the costs of copyright administration. A study of U.K. copyright cases suggests that bigger companies are relatively more involved in copyright litigation (Mazeh and Rogers 2005). However, is this because of fixed costs of copyright litigation or because bigger companies have more copyrights to enforce?

Third, we need empirical research into the different impact of copyright law on the various categories of creative work. For instance, Landes and Posner (1989) observe that the possible range of popular songs is more limited than of other creative work, and so, support stronger copyright protection for song-writers. To support such differentiation in copyright law, it is necessary to have the appropriate empirical justification.

References

Akerlof, George A. et al. (2002), "The Copyright Term Extension Act of 1998: An Economic Analysis", *AEI-Brookings Joint Center for Regulatory Studies*, Washington DC.

Baker, Matthew J. and Brendan M. Cunningham (forthcoming 2006), "Court Decisions and Equity Markets: Estimating the Value of Copyright Protection", *Journal of Law and Economics*.

Baker, Matthew J. and Brendan M. Cunningham (2005), "Law and Innovation in Copyright Industries", U.S. Naval Academy, November 2005.

Bard, Robert L. and Lewis Kurlantzick (1999), *Copyright Duration: Term Extension, the European Union and the Making of Copyright Policy*, San Francisco: Austin & Winfield.

Boldrin, Michele and David K. Levine (2002), "The Case Against Intellectual Property", *American Economic Review*, 92(2); 209-12.

Business Software Alliance (2006), *Third Annual BSA and IDC Global Software Piracy Study*, May 2006. Available on http://www.bsa.org/globalstudy/upload/2005%20Piracy%20Study%20-%20Official%20Version.pdf [Accessed, July 27, 2006].

Gopal, Ram D. and G. Lawrence Sanders (1998), "International Software Piracy: Analysis of Key Issues and Impacts", *Information Systems Research*, 9(4); 380-97.

Holm, Håkan J. (2003), "Can Economic Theory Explain Piracy Behavior?", *Topics in Economic Analysis & Policy*, 3(1); Article 5. Available on http://www.bepress.com/bejeap/topics/vol3/iss1/art5

Hong, Seung-Hyun (2004), "The Effect of Napster on Recorded Music Sales: Evidence from the Consumer Expenditure Survey", Stanford Institute for Economic Policy Research, Paper No. 03-018.

Hui Kai-Lung and Ivan Png (2003), "Piracy and the Legitimate Demand for Recorded Music", *Contributions to Economic Analysis & Policy*, 2(1), Article 11.

Hui Kai-Lung and Ivan Png (2005), "Measuring Piracy of IP-Protected Goods: A Methodology", World Intellectual Property Organization: Working Group of Experts on Developing a Methodology for Measuring Copyright Piracy, November 1-4, 2005. Available on http://www.econaa.com/resources/methodology_piracy_rate_sector.pdf [Accessed, July 27, 2006].

Husted, Bryan W. (2000), "The Impact of National Culture on Software Piracy", *Journal of Business Ethics*, 26(3); 197-211.

International Federation of the Phonographic Industry (2006), *The Recording Industry 2006: Piracy Report*, London: IFPI.

Khan, B. Zorina (2004), "Does Copyright Piracy Pay? The Effects of U.S. International Copyright Laws on the Market for Books, 1790-1920", Working Paper 10271, National Bureau of Economic Research, Cambridge, January 2004.

Khong, W.L. Roy and Dennis Khong (2006), "Does United Kingdom's Stock Market Respond to Copyright Term Extension", Faculty of Business and Law, Multimedia University, Malaysia.

Landes, William M. and Richard A. Posner (1989), "An Economic Analysis of Copyright Law", *Journal of Legal Studies*, 18(2); 325-63.

Landes, William M. and Richard A. Posner (2003), *The Economic Structure of Intellectual Property Law*, Cambridge, MA: Belknap Press.

Legros Patrick (2005), "Art and the Internet: Blessing the Curse?", *NAJ Economics*, 10.

Liebowitz, Stan J. (1985), "Copying and Indirect Appropriability: Photocopying of Journals", *Journal of Political Economy*, 93(5); 945-57.

Liebowitz, Stan J. (2005), "Testing File-Sharing's Impact by Examining Record Sales in Cities", Working Paper, School of Management, University of Texas at Dallas, September 2005.

Liebowitz, Stan J. (2006), "Economists Examine File-Sharing and Music Sales", in Gerhard Illing and Martin Peitz (eds.), *Industrial Organization and the Digital Economy*, Cambridge: MIT Press.

Liebowitz, Stan J. and Stephen Margolis (2005), "Seventeen Famous Economists Weigh in on Copyright: The Role of Theory, Empirics, and Network Effects", *Harvard Journal of Law & Technology*, 18(2); 435-57.

Liebowitz, Stan J. and Richard Watt (2006), "How to Best Ensure Remuneration for Creators in the Market for Music? Copyright and its Alternatives", *Journal of Economic Surveys*, 20(4); 513-45.

Marron, Donald B. and David G. Steel (2000), "Which Countries Protect Intellectual Property? The Case of Software Piracy", *Economic Inquiry*, 38(2); 159-74.

Mazeh, Yoav and Mark Rogers (2005), "The Extent and Significance of Copyright Cases: An Analysis of Large UK Firms", Oxford Intellectual Property Research Centre, December 2005.

Mortimer, Julie Holland (2005), "Price Discrimination, Copyright Law and Technological Innovation: Evidence from the Introduction of DVDs", Working Paper No. W11676, National Bureau of Economic Research, Cambridge, October 2005.

Oberholzer-Gee, Felix and Koleman Strumpf (2005), "The Effect of File Sharing on Record Sales: An Empirical Analysis", Harvard Business School and UNC Chapel Hill, June 2005.

Olsen, Karsten (2005), "Counterfeiting and Piracy: Measurement Issues", WIPO/OECD Expert Meeting on Measurement and Statistical Issues, Geneva, October 17-18, 2005.

Peitz, Martin, and Patrick Waelbroeck (2004), "The Effect Of Internet Piracy On Music Sales: Cross-Section Evidence", *Review of Economic Research on Copyright Issues*, 1(2); 71-9.

Plant, Arnold (1934), "The Economic Aspects of Copyright in Books", *Economica*, 1(2); 167-95.

Png, I.P.L. and Qiu-hong Wang (2006), "Copyright Duration and the Supply of Creative Work", Department of Information Systems, National University of Singapore, April 2006.

Rappaport, Edward (1998), "Copyright Term Extension: Estimating the Economic Values", Washington, DC: Congressional Research Service, May 11, 1998. Available on http://countingcalifornia.cdlib.org/crs/pdf/98-144.pdf

Recording Industry Association of America (2005), *Year End Report*, http://www.riaa.com/news/marketingdata/yearend.asp [Accessed, March 22, 2006].

Rob, Rafael and Joel Waldfogel (2006), "Piracy on the High C's: Music Downloading, Sales Displacement, and Social Welfare in a Sample of College Students", *Journal of Law and Economics*, 49(1); 29-62.

Rodriguez, Andres (2002), "The European Software Piracy: An Empirical Application", Department of Economics, University of Southern Denmark, March 2002.

Stevans, Lonnie K. and David N. Sessions (2005), "An Empirical Investigation Into the Effect of Music Downloading on the Consumer Expenditure of Recorded Music: A Time Series Approach", *Journal of Consumer Policy*, 28; 311-24.

Throsby, David (1996), "Disaggregated Earnings Functions for Artists", Chapter 13 in Victor A. Ginsburgh and Pierre-Michel Menger (eds.), *Essays in the Economics of the Arts*, New York: Elsevier.

Towse, Ruth (2001), "Partly for the Money: Rewards and Incentives to Artists", *Kyklos*, 54(2/3); 473-90.

Varian, Hal (2005), "Copying and Copyright", *Journal of Economic Perspectives*, 19(2); 121-38.

Watt, Richard (2004), "The Past and the Future of the Economics of Copyright", *Review of Economic Research on Copyright Issues*, 1(1); 151-71.

Widdows, Richard and Richard J. McHugh (1984), "Taxing Purchases of Home Tape Recorders and Supplies to Compensate for Copyright Infringements: An Econometric Analysis of the Role of Economic and Demographic Factors", *Journal of Consumer Affairs*, 18(2); 317-25.

Zentner, Alejandro (2005), "File Sharing and International Sales of Copyrighted Music: An Empirical Analysis with a Panel of Countries", *Topics in Economic Analysis & Policy*, 5(1), Article 21.

Zentner, Alejandro (2006), "Measuring the Effect of File Sharing on Music Purchases", *Journal of Law and Economics*, Vol. 49(1); 63-90.

IVAN P.L. PNG, NATIONAL UNIVERSITY OF SINGAPORE AND IP ACADEMY OF SINGAPORE; TEL: +65 6516-6807; HTTP://WWW.COMP.NUS.EDU.SG/~IPNG/.

[7]

The Case Against Intellectual Property

By MICHELE BOLDRIN AND DAVID LEVINE*

According to a common argument, the presence of strong intellectual property rights spurs innovation leading to higher economic growth and increasing benefits for all. The argument seems coherent. No economic agent exercises productive effort without the certainty of controlling its fruits. What is true for physical effort must be true for the intellectual one: if strong property rights provide good incentives for the production of potatoes, they must also provide good incentives for the production of ideas.

Why then do we argue a "case against intellectual property?" Are we arguing that, while stealing potatoes is bad, stealing ideas is good? We are not. Economic efficiency and common sense argue that ideas should be protected and available for sale, just like any other commodity. But "intellectual property" has come to mean not only the right to own and sell ideas, but also the right to regulate their use. This creates a socially inefficient monopoly, and what is commonly called intellectual property might be better called "intellectual monopoly." When you buy a potato you can eat it, throw it away, plant it, or make it into a sculpture. Current law allows producers of CDs and books to take this freedom away from you. When you buy a potato you can use the "idea" of a potato embodied in it to make better potatoes or to invent french fries. Current law allows producers of computer software or medical drugs to take this freedom away from you. It is against this distorted extension of intellectual property rights that we argue.

It is a long jump from the assertion that inventors deserve the fruits of their efforts to the conclusion that current patent and copyright protection are the best way of providing such reward. Statements such as "A patent is *the* way of rewarding somebody for coming up with a worthy commercial idea ..."[1] abound in the business, legal, and economic press. In arguing the case against "intellectual monopoly" we will examine this argument with care.

I. Downstream Licensing

Intellectual property has two components. One is the right to own and sell ideas. The other is the right to control the use of those ideas after sale. The first, sometimes called the right of first sale, we view as essential. The second, which we refer to as downstream licensing, we view as economically dangerous. All producers would impose downstream-licensing agreements if they could: producers prefer not to compete against their customers. But the absence of competition leads to monopoly. That the downstream-licensing provisions of patent, copyright, and other private contracts lead to monopoly is well understood. Among economists, the argument has been that it is only through monopoly that it is possible to reward inventive activity. There is a seemingly compelling logic: the cost of innovation is a fixed cost, and ideas are distributed at zero, or at least constant, marginal cost. Since perfect competition prices at marginal cost, the fixed cost cannot be recouped. Consequently, if producers of intellectual property are forced to compete with their customers, they will not be able to recoup the cost of creation. This point is forcefully made, for example, in Paul Romer (1990).

In other work (Boldrin and Levine, 2001) we have pointed out that creation is not a fixed, but a sunk, cost. Since only ideas embodied in people or products matter, the cost of creation is the cost of producing the first unit. Such a "sunk cost" is very ordinary in economics and poses no particular threat to perfect competition. As far as we know there is no organized movement to provide producers of potatoes, or any other commodity involving sunk costs, with a

* Department of Economics, University of Minnesota, Minneapolis, MN 55455, and Department of Economics, University of California, Los Angeles, CA 90024. Our thanks to the NSF and the University of Minnesota Grants in Aid program for financial support.

[1] *The Economist*, 23 June 2001, p. 42; italics added.

government monopoly. What is different about creative activity is the indivisibility involved in producing the first unit: two half-baked ideas do not equal one fully baked idea.

The theory of competition with indivisibilities is not yet fully worked out. In Boldrin and Levine (2001) we show that competition often yields the first best: that diminishing costs of replication can increase, rather than decrease, the incentive for creative activity; and that downstream licensing may hurt, rather than help, innovation. We illustrate these ideas below by means of a simple example.

Nevertheless, there is an expectation, which we share, that there are cases where ordinary competitive rents will be insufficient reward to induce socially desirable creative activity. In the rest of this essay, we also argue that the monopoly power in downstream licensing has costs that vastly exceed the usual "welfare triangle," and that creative competitive mechanisms can provide the right reward for inventive activity, even where monopoly fails.

II. Collateral Costs

Like all property, intellectual property is expensive to protect. However, downstream-licensing agreements are especially costly to enforce because they require either the producer or the government to tightly supervise the use of ideas. Of course, there are the direct costs of writing laws, catching lawbreakers, and bringing legal action against them. However, there are many other forms of "collateral damage" to economic welfare. Here we focus on ideas that can be embodied in digital form, such as computer programs, music, books, and movies. To supervise usage of these products requires copy-protection technology. Copy protection mandated by law is especially pernicious because the potential economic damage (think of abolishing all computers because they can be used to pirate music) bears no relationship to the underlying value that is being protected.

Unless mandated by law, few people will choose to install software that enforces copy protection instead of software that does not. This was recognized, for example, in the case of digital audiotape, where copy protection was legally mandated. Unfortunately, copy-protection technology often does not work very well. Digital audiotape recorders that do not work very well do not pose much of an economic threat. However, the same computers that play music, also hold financial records, creative work, e-mail records, and much of economic value. A malfunctioning copy-protection system that destroys files, causes computers to crash, or causes other forms of collateral damage can easily have an economic cost far exceeding the value of all recorded music.

The inability to reverse-engineer software that enforces copy protection has other collateral costs. If copy-protection software is secretly phoning home to provide its issuers with private information about users, this flagrant violation of privacy is difficult or even illegal to prevent. There is also an important commitment problem with copy-protected ideas: if the producer goes out of business, the copy-protected products may lose their value. Unfortunately there does not seem to be a credible mechanism by which producers can commit to putting their software into the public domain if they go bankrupt.

Suppression of ideas through the legal system creates other collateral problems through the impact on research and development. Although laws are designed in an effort to minimize this impact, it is a fact that research and development under the watchful eye of a regulatory agent is going to be greatly inhibited. Similar conflicting goals arise in the protection of the freedom of speech and of political discourse. The same technology used to track "music free-loaders" can be used to track individuals who express unpopular opinions, for example.

On the patent front, more time and energy seems to be spent on nuisance and defensive patenting of the obvious than on innovation. Individuals exploit the ignorance of patent examiners by patenting ideas already in wide-spread use in hopes of collecting licensing fees from a few large companies; large corporations patent and cross-license everything imaginable, both to protect themselves against greenmail and to suppress entry into their industry. That cross-licensing and "protection of intellectual property" can be instrumental in promoting collusion within an industry seems transparent. On the empirical side, Joshua S. Gans et al. (2000 p. 29) provide evidence from a 1999 survey of high-tech start-ups that "stronger [intellectual] property protection is associated with higher, rather than lower levels of cooperation between incumbents and start-up innovator entrant."

Ultimately, the case against monopoly rests less upon the welfare triangle from monopoly pricing than upon the rent-seeking activity used to get and keep a monopoly. In the brief example of Section IV we show how, with government enforced monopoly, the incentives for rent-seeking lead to large welfare costs in the production of ideas.

III. Competition Without Downstream Licensing

We provide an example to illustrate the idea in Boldrin and Levine (2001) that innovation can thrive in a competitive economy even in the face of indivisibility. In this economy, individuals live forever. There are many consumers, indexed by $c < 0$. In each period, consumers either consume one unit of the good, or not. The benefit to consumer c of consuming a unit of the good is $c^{-\psi}$ with $\psi > 0$. Consumers also prefer to consume early rather than later: a unit of good consumed today is worth $\delta < 1$ of a unit of the same good consumed next period.

Initially, there is a single prototype of a durable commodity that generates the flow of consumption service. The inventor or producer owns this prototype. Once sold, no downstream licensing is possible. At each moment of time the prototype can either be used to generate a flow of consumption or be reproduced. To make things less abstract, let us imagine that the new good is a recording of a new musical piece that is embodied in an MP3 file. Copying takes one period, and each MP3 that is copied produces $\beta > 1$ additional MP3's. A technology such as Napster increases β.

Under competitive conditions, in the tth period each MP3 sells for a market price p_t or may be rented for one period at a rental rate r_t. Notice that consumers for whom $c^{-\psi} > r_t$ value the song more highly than the rental cost and will choose to listen to an MP3 that period; consumers for whom $c^{-\psi} < r_t$ will choose not to listen to the MP3: if they have a copy, they prefer renting out their copy to someone else. In a competitive environment, everyone is potentially a buyer and a seller.

We are interested in two questions. Is the price of the very first copy enough to compensate the producer for its sunk cost? Does the price of the first copy increase or decrease when new technologies increase β?

According to standard competitive theory the sale price of an MP3 is just the present value of the rental rates. A simple calculation[2] shows that

$$p_0 = \frac{\beta\left(\dfrac{1+\beta}{\beta} - \delta^{1/\psi}\beta^{(1-\psi)/\psi}\right)^{-\psi}}{\beta - 1}.$$

For finite values of β, p_0 is a positive and finite number. Since p_0 is what the producer can earn from the first sale when he has no downstream protection at all (in practice he should be able to do better than this), there is money to be made for producers of intellectual products.

Is this competitive value of intellectual products enough to motivate the producers to spend the effort and time required? We do not know. To answer this question one needs to know the particular opportunity cost of time of the particular creator, which clearly varies from case to case. It seems to us, though, that there is no hard empirical evidence supporting the view that this value would not be enough.

We also want to understand the social impact of a technology that facilitates the reproduction of "idea-goods." Does it increase or decrease the value of intellectual products in a competitive market? Basically, received wisdom argues that cheap copying makes it impossible for innovators to earn back their production costs. If, in a competitive setting, increasing β lowered p_0, received wisdom would be correct: without downstream protection, fewer "idea-goods" would be created as a result of the advent of the new technology.

What does happen to p_0 as β grows larger? The answer depends on ψ. If $\psi < 1$, demand is elastic. This is the empirically interesting case. As β grows larger, it is easy to check from the equation above that the price of the initial copy

[2] Details on this and other calculations in this paper can be found online at ⟨http://levine.sscnet.ucla.edu⟩ or ⟨http://www.econ.umn.edu/~mboldrin⟩.

goes to infinity as more of it is allocated to reproduction. In fact, this happens as β approaches a finite value, but this is a special implication of the analytic forms we are using. Notice that, in all cases, the rate at which the price falls over time is proportional to β. Nevertheless, with elastic demand and large β, the increase in the rate with which price falls over time is associated with a higher initial price and greater rent for the innovator.

In summary, under competition and in the empirically interesting case where demand is elastic, improving the technology for reproduction increases the first sale price without bound. The improved technology makes it much easier for a producer to recover sunk costs in a competitive market. This does not mean that the producer will argue against downstream licensing and in favor of increased competition. She will still be able to earn more revenues with a monopoly than under competition. However, it is a good argument for not giving in to the producers and granting them the monopoly: the social benefit of the monopoly (the ability to cover sunk costs and produce a socially desirable good) is reduced by the new technology.

This establishes competitive markets as a viable institutional setting for fostering innovative activity.[3] We move now to consider the viability of alternative institutional settings.

IV. The Hidden Costs of Imperfect Monopoly

What happens when competitive rent is insufficient to cover the cost of producing the first unit? Let us consider the stark case traditionally considered in economic theory in which there is a fixed cost that must be recovered, and in which the marginal cost of production is zero. With demand that is perfectly elastic up to an upper bound, there is no cost of monopoly, so this would seem the ideal environment to impose downstream-licensing restrictions.

This is correct only if it is not possible to produce similar items. In the case of textbooks, for example, it is easy to produce books that are sufficiently different to be entitled to a separate copyright, but sufficiently similar as to make no difference to consumers. When there are many firms competing for monopoly rents, and market conditions are such that rents can be obtained even with some degree of competition, the rent-seeking behavior of competing monopolists dissipates the social surplus by overproduction of too many similar items. When we allow for creativity in the use of markets by having consumers submit contingent bids, then no copyright is unambiguously better than copyright.

Suppose in particular that firms are identical, face a fixed cost, and produce at zero marginal cost. Suppose also that there are H identical risk-neutral customers with fixed reservation price who may reproduce the good at marginal cost $\xi \geq 0$. When intellectual monopoly is legally enforced through copyright, we assume that the post-entry price lies between the price needed to recover costs (for each firm) and the monopoly price in a way that depends on the number of firms and consumers. This particular form of market arrangement (call it "copyright-induced competition for niches") results in what we describe as the *Pareto worst outcome*.

Without copyright there will be no output and no social surplus only if $\xi H < FN$; otherwise, social surplus will be higher than under copyright. This, however, does not do justice to the competitive instinct: we have excluded the important possibility that consumers may submit contingent bids prior to production. In a symmetric equilibrium of a contingent-bidding model, with copyright, the Pareto worst outcome is still an equilibrium, while without copyright, the first best is obtained.

[3] In Boldrin and Levine (2001) we develop a more general version of this argument.

REFERENCES

Boldrin, Michele and Levine, David K. "Perfectly Competitive Innovation." Mimeo, University of Minnesota, 2001.

Gans, Joshua S.; Hsu, David H. and Stern, Scott. "When Does Start-up Innovation Spur the Gale of Creative Destruction?" National Bureau of Economic Research (Cambridge, MA) Working Paper No. W851, 2000.

Romer, Paul. "Are Nonconvexities Important for Understanding Growth?" *American Economic Review*, May 1990 (*Papers and Proceedings*), *80*(2), pp. 97–103.

Part III
Issues in Copyright Administration

Introduction to Part III

The administration of copyright has been a topic of interest for economists for the last 30 years or so. Peacock and Weir (1975) seem to have done the first economic investigation of a copyright collecting society (CCS), which was a study of the UK's Performing Rights Society (PRS) that administers rights in works by composers and music publishers. Many features of the CCSs (or CMOs, copyright management organisations, as they are called in some circles) have interested economists since then. The CCSs are private membership organisations which provide the service of collective rights management (CRM) thereby enabling authors to effectively administer their rights in secondary markets and at the same time enabling users to obtain the necessary licences at low cost. Secondary markets are those, such as radio plays of sound recordings and photocopying, in which there is no contact or contract between the user and the author. In this section, we reprint papers that cover only three of the several aspects that have been studied: the economic rule for setting the licence fee (Baumol), which is a general problem not just one confined to CCSs; the distribution of the licence fee income (Snow and Watt) and the organisational efficiency of the CCS (Rochelandet). However, several other topics have been studied and in this introduction, we briefly outline what they are and reference work that has been published on them. A survey of the economics of CCSs is Handke and Towse (2007).

One of the points of interest for economists is that many of the national CCSs developed spontaneously as authors' and publishers' cooperative collectives, membership societies that overcame the failure of copyright law to effectively protect authors because the transactions costs of collecting royalties and monitoring use were too high for the individual. CCSs, like copyright law, are national bodies and administer rights mostly (but not only) for copyright holders who reside in their territory as well as administering the use of copyright works owned by foreigners that takes place in that territory. Many national societies collaborate across borders by arrangement with equivalent foreign societies. So, for example, the UK's PRS administers rights for UK copyright holders and for composers from other countries whose work is performed in the UK and it pays the royalties for the latter to their national society. This arrangement allows the UK society to issue licences for foreign repertoire as well as for that of its own members and this system, organised by the rights holders themselves, effectively lowers the costs of using copyright works for licensees as well because without it, anyone wanting to use such material would have huge transaction costs of searching for owners (Towse, 2001; Watt, 2000). This 'unintended effect' of the CCS system was noted by Besen et al., who pioneered analytical work in this area (Besen and Kirby, 1989a and 1989b; Besen, Kirby and Salop, 1992).

Given that copyright is a bundle of rights, a CCS will specialise in a particular bundle and in countries with a well-developed copyright system, there can easily be 20 such societies, dealing with various rights and uses of them – public performance, reproduction in sound recording and film, broadcasting, photocopying, to give some examples. In most countries (the USA is an exception in this with ASCAP and BMI both administering performing rights in music), each CCS has a monopoly over the rights it administers, a feature that has caused them to be the target of antitrust/competition law authorities in several countries. Hollander (1984) was the first paper to analyse the market structure of the CCSs, pointing out that they are natural monopolies. However, due to this monopoly, CCSs are typically regulated by the state and with copyright law being somewhat different in different countries, they have a somewhat different legal status from place to place (for institutional details, see Besen and Kirby, 1989a; Ficsor, 2003; also Crampes et al., 2005). The effect of these differences on efficient administration is analysed empirically in the paper by Rochelandet included here (**III, 10**): he is, to our knowledge, the only author who has endeavoured to test empirically the effect of the structure and governance of CCSs on their administration charges.

The feature of the CCSs that has attracted most interest from economists, however, is their use of the blanket licence fee. This device has the overwhelming advantage that it vastly reduces administration costs by avoiding the need to set a fee for each work in the members' repertoires of works (which would be a very large number in a CCS in a major country); instead, the whole repertoire is licensed to users and the fee that each user pays is geared to the (potential) audience size. So, for example, a restaurant pays a fee according to the number of diners it can accommodate. As MacQueen and Peacock (1995) point out, this is often the result of an agreement between bilateral monopolies; a user might be a monopoly broadcaster or a trade association representing all restaurant owners and the CCS. The disadvantage of the blanket licence is that it bundles together a whole repertoire of copyright works (many going back for decades) and licensees may want only a small part of it; secondly, that the same fee is paid for all works regardless of how valuable they are to the user and this blunts the price signal to the authors of the most popular works (Watt, 2000; Towse, 2001). This also has welfare implications, as the Baumol article reprinted here (**III, 8**) demonstrates. However, this signalling problem is to some extent mitigated by the distribution system used by the CCS, which uses playlist information on the number of times, say, a radio station plays a particular work (data they collect as part of the licensing contract with the CCS) to distribute the fee revenues to members. Watt (2000) and Snow and Watt reprinted here (**III, 9**) argue this distribution system adds to administration costs somewhat negating the value of the reduction in transaction costs the blanket licence promotes.

That introduces a topic that is currently under discussion: the impact of digital rights management (DRM) and the introduction of new legal protection for them on the ability of copyright holders to administer their own rights in digital works (Einhorn, 2002; Graber et al., 2005; Katz, 2006; Liebowitz, 2005; Oksanen and Välimäki; Towse, 2005). Several aspects of this still new situation have been considered: the problem of individual bargaining (Towse, 2007) and the destruction of the 'solidarity' principle of the CCS (Kretschmer, 2002). These authors have also pointed out the already relatively low earnings from copyright (Kretschmer, 2006; Towse, 2001. See also Matsumoto, 2002).

References

Besen, Stanley M. and Sheila N. Kirby (1989a), *Compensating Creators of Intellectual Property – Collectives That Collect*, Santa Monica, CA: The RAND Corporation.

Besen, Stanley M. and Sheila N. Kirby (1989b), 'Private Copying, Appropriability, and Optimal Copying Royalties', *Journal of Law and Economics*, **32** (2), 255–80.

Besen, Stanley M., Sheila N. Kirby and Steven C. Salop (1992), 'An Economic Analysis of Copyright Collectives', *Virginia Law Review*, **78** (1), 383–411.

Crampes, Claude, David Encaoua and Abraham Hollander (2005), 'Competition and Intellectual Property in the European Union', Unpublished paper, Université de Toulouse http://www.inomics.com/cgi/repec, handle=RePEc:ide:wpaper:416.

Einhorn, Michael A. (2002), 'Music Licensing in the Digital Age', in Ruth Towse (ed.), *Copyright in the Cultural Industries*, Cheltenham, UK and Northampton, MA, USA: Edward Elgar, pp. 165–77.

Ficsor, Mihaly (2003), *Collective Management of Copyright and Related Rights*, Geneva: World Intellectual Property Organisation.

Graber, Christoph Beat, Carlo Govoni, Michael Girsberger and Mira Nenova (eds) (2005), *Digital Rights Management – The End of Collecting Societies?*, Berne: Stämpfli.

Handke, C. and R. Towse (2007), *Economics of Copyright Collecting Societies, International Review of Intellectual Property and Competition Law*, 8/2007 (38), 937–57. Also available at www.serci.org.

Hollander, Abraham (1984), 'Market Structure and Performance in Intellectual Property: The Case of Copyright Collectives', *International Journal of Industrial Organization*, **2**, 199–216.

Katz, Ariel (2006), 'The Potential Demise of Another Natural Monopoly: New Technologies and the Future of Collective Administration of Copyrights', *Journal of Competition Law and Economics*, **2** (2), 245–84.

Kretschmer, Martin (2002), 'Copyright Societies Do Not Administer Individual Rights: The Incoherence of Institutional Traditions in Germany and the UK', in Ruth Towse (ed.), *Copyright in the Cultural Industries*, Cheltenham, UK and Northampton, MA, USA: Edward Elgar, pp. 140–64.

Kretschmer, Martin (2006), 'Artists' Earnings and Copyright: A Review of British and German Music Industry Data in the Context of Digital Technologies', in F. Macmillan (ed.), *New Directions in Copyright Law. Vol. 2*, Cheltenham, UK and Northampton, MA, USA: Edward Elgar, pp. 61–78.

Liebowitz, Stan (2005), 'MP3s and Copyright Collectives: A Curse Worse than the Disease?', in Lisa N. Takeyama, Wendy J. Gordon and Ruth Towse (eds), *Developments in the Economics of Copyright: Research and Analysis*, Cheltenham, UK and Northampton, MA, USA: Edward Elgar, pp. 37–59.

MacQueen, Hector L. and Alan Peacock (1995), 'Implementing Performing Rights', *Journal of Cultural Economics*, **19** (2), pp. 157–75.

Matsumoto, Shinji (2002), 'Performers in the Digital Era: Evidence from Japan', in Ruth Towse (ed.), *Copyright in the Cultural Industries*, Cheltenham, UK and Northampton, MA, USA: Edward Elgar, pp. 196–209.

Oksanen, Ville and Mikko Välimäki, 'Music Collecting Societies and Webcasting', Unpublished paper, Society for Economic Research on Copyright Issues (SERCI) Annual Conference, Northampton (MA), USA, 19–20 June 2003. Online: http://www.valimaki.com/org/serci_2003.pdf.

Peacock, Alan and Ronald Weir (1975), *The Composer in the Marketplace*, London: Faber.

Towse, Ruth (2001), *Creativity, Incentive and Reward: an Economic Analysis of Copyright and Culture in the Information Age*, Cheltenham, UK and Northampton, MA, USA: Edward Elgar.

Towse, Ruth (ed.) (2002), *Copyright in the Cultural Industries*, Cheltenham, UK and Northampton, MA, USA: Edward Elgar.

Towse, Ruth (2005), 'Economics and Copyright Reform: Aspects of the EC Directive', *Telematics and Informatics*, **22** (1–2), 11–24.

Towse, Ruth (2007), 'The Singer or the Song? Developments in Performers' Rights from the Perspective of a Cultural Economist', *Review of Law and Economics*, **3** (6). Available at: http://www.bepress.com/rle/vol3/iss3/art6.

Watt, Richard (2000), *Copyright and Economic Theory – Friends or Foes?*, Cheltenham, UK and Northampton, MA, USA: Edward Elgar.

[8]

Review of Economic Research on Copyright Issues, 2004, vol. 1(1), pp. 83-92

THE SOCIALLY DESIRABLE SIZE OF COPYRIGHT FEES

WILLIAM J. BAUMOL

ABSTRACT. Licensing of copyrighted material can contribute to welfare. But what fee is socially desirable fee? The owner's marginal cost of licensing is often near zero, but $P = MC = 0$ is arguably neither equitable nor an efficient incentive for further creative activity. Here two fee-setting approaches are described, assuming copyright rules are pre-established and determine the holder's earnings, absent licensing. One approach is Ramsey pricing, theoretically second best and able to preserve the copyholder's earnings. The second is 'parity pricing', as derived in the price-regulation literature, which can ensure effective free entry into commercial use of the licensed material.

1. INTRODUCTION

It is generally agreed that it is quite appropriate for the use of material covered by copyright to require payment of a fee by the user to the holder of the intellectual property. But that is virtually an empty statement if it entails no guidance on the magnitude of the fee. A minuscule copyright fee is tantamount to a gift of access to the material, while an extremely high price is effectively equivalent to outright refusal to license. The issue is whether there is some defensible procedure or standard for determination of some intermediate level of copyright fee for which one can lay some claim of superiority or even optimality. The purpose of this paper is to suggest one way in which such a socially desirable fee can be determined. I shall focus on the important set of cases in which the material covered by copyright is used as an input to another product sold in a downstream market, and in which the copyright proprietor competes with the licensees in that market. An example is a compact disc producer/distributor firm that owns copyrights to a large portfolio of music, some of which other such firms want to license for inclusion in their own competing CDs. The rule described below is designed to ensure that the copyright fees do not constitute an exclusionary handicap or an unjustified subsidy to rival firms. I will note, however, that a somewhat broader interpretation of the rule proposed here is also possible. But it should also be recognized that other approaches to license fee analysis are also possible, as via Ramsey theory or bargaining-model analysis.

Copyright fee determination is complicated by the propensity to consider it to be a matter of equity: What is the "just price" for, say, a composer to charge for performance of his or her work, and should that depend on the performer's ability to pay? Since we do not know how to answer these questions, the conclusion that such considerations should constitute the foundation for the price determination process is evidently a counsel of despair. Happily, there are other implications of

I am extremely grateful to Ruth Towse for suggesting the topic of this note, which takes off from a comment in my article in her volume (2003).

the choice of license fee that provide a firmer handle on the process. For that price does affect the allocation of the intellectual property as a productive resource, that is, as an input to the final product that is supplied with the aid of the intellectual property in question. The choice of fee can also facilitate or impede competitiveness in the affected markets. Both of these implications can offer us guidance for the price-setting process. In particular, as economists, we can be expected to consider the consequences for efficiency of resource allocation as a valuable guide to determination of what we may consider to constitute an "efficient" or "optimal" fee.

To see how the resource allocation issue arises, consider the following parable (which is perhaps somewhat reminiscent of the movie, Citizen Kane). Suppose a noted playwright offers to permit performance of his latest play in the commercial theater, but insists on a high license fee unless his female companion is cast in the romantic lead. Suppose a much more capable actress covets the role, but the prospective producer feels that the fee demanded precludes her from the role. Clearly, the high fee is apt to lead to resource misallocation. It may be said that, while this is true, the problem has its roots in the discriminatory character of the pricing. But a similar problem arises if the playwright offers the script to others for a fee that he can be sure no one can afford, and then decides to put the play on himself, casting himself in the lead. Of course, the second scenario entails price discrimination in that the playwright is implicitly charging himself zero for use of the script, and hence pays himself much less than the fee he proposes to others. But what fee is he really charging himself? What fee to others would eliminate the price discrimination and permit the play to be performed with the lead actor who is best suited to the role? Since there is no visible act of payment of the owner of the property to himself in exchange for its use, and it is not even obvious how such a payment can be defined, the difficulty raised by the issue here is evident. Note that what is entailed is not only the possibility of misallocation of resources, but also the creation of an impediment to competition, with a candidate lead actress or actor protected from rivalry by the fee.

Moreover, the story can be generalized to the case where others want permission to perform a piece of music under copyright protection or want to play at a school performance a song that has been recorded on a CD, or the case in which a music distributor wants to include the song in a compendium of similar music to be issued on another CD. Yet, as will be indicated next, not only is the problem amenable to solution-the solution is, in fact, known. I will describe it, and then turn to two objections that have been raised against it in other arenas where exactly the same sort of problem arises.

2. ECPR: The Pro-Competitive License Fee and The Level-Playing-Field Theorem

The solution to the problem is a form of pricing that, in a significant sense, can be said to be nondiscriminatory as between licensor and licensee, even though there is no direct way of observing what the licensor can be said to be "paying itself" when it uses the item covered by copyright for itself. This price is referred to in the regulatory literature as the parity price, or as the price that follows the efficient component-pricing rule (ECPR). To understand the logic of what follows, it is convenient to think of the material covered by copyright as an input to some final product, for instance, a script for a play whose performance is the final product, or a song to be included in a final-product CD. Then the license fee that is derived from the parity pricing formula can be shown to have the following three relevant features, two of which are no more than corollaries of the third:

Feature 1. Defining superior efficiency in the supply of a final product of a given quality as the ability to do so at a lower cost than a rival supplier, the parity license fee permits a supplier who can make more efficient use of the copyrighted material to provide the final product at a lower price than is financially feasible for a less efficient rival.

Feature 2. This parity price thereby ensures that an inefficient supplier of the final product cannot take the market away from the more efficient rival. This also means that the price does not exclude any efficient entrants whose activities require use of the material covered by copyright.

Feature 3. Feature 1 also means that the parity price is not discriminatory, in the following sense. Suppose the copyright owner uses the copyrighted material in a final product. Then the owner cannot underprice a rival final-product supplier who is also a licensee unless the owner is the more efficient supplier.

The parity-price solution to the problem of determining an efficient price for access to material covered by copyright is based on a result that has been called the "level-playing-field theorem".[1] This theorem has a very simple proof, given below. It asserts that only by using the following formulas [in equivalent equations (1) or (2) below] can we neutrally price a monopoly-owned input that is required by both the owner of the input and its final-product competitors, giving neither a market or pricing advantage in the market aside from any differential made possible by superior efficiency.

All of this can be described formally, giving explicit formulas for an efficient license fee. For brevity, we will refer to the owner of the copyright in question as "the IP (intellectual property) owner." We use the following notation:

$P_{f,i}$ = the IP owner, I's, given price per unit of final product;

$\min P_{f,c}$ = tthe competitor, C's, minimum viable price of final product;

P_i = the price charged for a license to use the IP, per unit of final product;

$IC_{r,i}$ = the incremental cost to the owner of the remaining final-product inputs, per unit of final product;

$IC_{r,c}$ = the corresponding figure for the competitor;

IC_i = the incremental cost to the IP owner of use of the IP by itself or by others.

As will be demonstrated presently, the efficient component-pricing rule requires that the licensing price satisfy either (and, hence, both) of two equivalent rules. The first is expressed in the formula:

$$P_i = P_{f,i} - IC_{r,i} \qquad (1)$$

In words, license price = I's final-product price - I's incremental cost of remaining inputs.

Alternatively, and equivalently (as will be shown), the ECPR price of the bottleneck input must satisfy:

$$P_i = IC_i + \text{ the IP owner's profit per unit of final-product output.} \qquad (2)$$

[1]This result was originally contributed by Robert D. Willig, with the current author participating in dissemination and adaptation of the result to particular regulatory and analytic issues. For an early description of the analysis, see Willig (1979).

Equation (1) tells us that the ECPR establishes a tight link between the price, $P_{f,i}$, that the IP owner charges for its final product and the price, P_i, it charges its rivals for the license to use the IP. If incremental production costs do not change, efficiency requires that a rise in one of these prices must be matched dollar for dollar by a rise in the other. Equation (2) tells us that the efficient price of the license is the direct incremental cost to the owner of the IP resulting from use of the invention by others, plus the associated incremental opportunity cost. This opportunity cost is the loss of profit made possible because the IP has been licensed to the rival, which can then take final-product business away from the licensor. Thus, the second form of the ECPR asserts that the price of the license should equal any direct incremental cost incurred in supplying it to a competitor, plus any incremental opportunity cost incurred as a result of that transaction.[2] Standard economic analysis tells us that this is a proper way to price-that is, the price should equal marginal (incremental) cost including marginal (incremental) opportunity cost-so that, at least at first, this result should not be surprising.

Then the task is to prove the following:

Proposition 1. *The "Level-Playing-Field" Theorem. The parity price, as given by (1) or (2), for use of a bottleneck input such as a legally protected innovation is both necessary and sufficient in order for the "playing field" to be level. This term is defined to mean that, at the selected license fee, the maximum difference between the remunerative prices of the perfect-substitute final-products of the two firms, the IP owner (I) and its final product competitor (C), will be exactly equal to the difference in the firms' remaining incremental costs (other than the license fees), that is, any pricing advantage must equal the cost-saving made possible by any superior efficiency of the firm in question.*

Proof. The level playing field is defined by

$$\min P_{f,c} - P_{f,i} = IC_{r,c} - IC_{r,i} \tag{3}$$

That is, the lowest compensatory price the competitor can afford to charge should differ from the IP owner's price exactly by the amount (positive or negative) that the competitor's remaining costs are below the IP owner's. But the lowest price that is financially viable for the competitor clearly is given by:

$$\min P_{f,c} = P_i + IC_{r,c} \tag{4}$$

That is, the price must cover the IP licensing cost plus the remaining cost of supplying the final product (of course, including the cost of the required capital, made up of depreciation and normal competitive profit).

Comparing the two equations, we see at once that the level-playing-field condition (3) will be satisfied if and only if:

$$P_i = P_{f,i} - IC_{r,i} \tag{5}$$

But this is the parity-pricing formula (1). Thus, parity pricing is both necessary and sufficient for a level playing field. ∎

[2]Notice that the relevant opportunity cost here is average profit forgone-the total profit forgone by the IP holder as a result of the transaction, per unit of final product sold. It is not the marginal opportunity cost, which is likely to be zero, because a profit-maximizing IP holder that produces the final product in which the innovation in question is used will produce the quantity of final product at which marginal profit falls to zero.

The parity-pricing formula (5) is also identical to the opportunity-cost variant of the rule, (2), since, by definition,

$$P_{f,i} = IC_i + IC_{r,i} + \text{I's profit per unit of final-product output,} \quad (6)$$

or, by (5),

$$P_i = P_{f,i} - IC_{r,i} = IC_i + \text{I's profit per unit of final-product output.} \quad (7)$$

This is the parity-pricing formula (2).

This completes the proof that parity pricing of an IP license is a necessary and sufficient condition for a competitively neutral license fee. It also follows that ECPR is necessary for economic efficiency in the provision of a final product by competing suppliers. If this rule is violated, a less-efficient supplier of the remaining inputs can win the competition for the business of supplying those inputs, instead of the task going to a more efficient rival. That is, violation of (1) or (2) permits a less-efficient supplier of the inputs other than the required IP to underprice its more efficient competitors.

One can add to this that ECPR mimics the prices of inputs such as intellectual property that would emerge in a fully competitive market where, as we know, the license fee would be set to cover the direct marginal cost of providing the input plus any marginal opportunity cost that is entailed in its provision by the owner to the licensee. This is clearly the same, for all practical purposes, as the parity pricing formula.[3] Hence, it can be asserted, that since the public interest is served by competitive market pricing, this can be presumed true of parity pricing as well. There are also arguments suggesting that these prices, ultimately, are consistent with the interests of all the immediately affected parties. Specifically, (3) tells us that if the licensee of the copyright-protected material prices final product at a level close to the price for that product charged by the copyright proprietor, then the former will retain any and all of the rent that derives from whatever superior efficiency it may possess, so that the ECPR price in that sense serves the interest of the licensee. But it also serves the licensor who is protected from loss as a result of the licensing, since the fee covers the opportunity cost. Moreover, in the process the copyright owner, in effect, reaches a make-or-buy decision on the final-product inputs other than those covered by copyright, because, as usual, it pays the copyright owner to buy rather than make those inputs if and only if their seller is the more efficient supplier and so provides them at lower cost than the copyright holder can provide them for itself. But that is exactly what ECPR accomplishes, giving the task of supplying those remaining inputs to the licensee if and only if it is the more-efficient provider.

3. Two Criticisms of Parity Pricing

Still, it is important to make clear, parity pricing of access to inputs hardly commands general approval. It has elicited considerable disagreement in the courts, the regulatory agencies and in political arenas, as well as in the economic literature.[4]

[3] The only difference is the substitution in ECPR of incremental cost (the cost of the pertinent increment of output) for marginal cost.

[4] Among the most directly critical pieces are Economides and White (1995) and Tye and Lapuerta (1996). Laffont and Tirole (2000) are more sympathetic to ECPR, but nevertheless express reservations and propose what are at least theoretical alternatives. The discussions in the courts and before regulatory agencies are profuse and an assembly of references is beyond the scope of this article.

Much of the opposition to ECPR can be dismissed as mere pursuit of self-interest by those who hope to obtain prices more favorable than parity prices to themselves, even though the last argument of the previous section may suggest that such attempts are misguided, resting on misunderstanding of where the parties' true interests lie. Yet there remain two more-persuasive grounds for opposition. The first asserts that the public interest requires prices to be set at the levels required by the Ramsey theorem, and that those prices will generally differ from the ECPR levels. Second, the opportunity-cost element of the ECPR result is a major focus of current debate over use of a parity pricing standard in the regulation of firms deemed to possess monopoly power. The problem is that the bottleneck owner is a monopolist, and its final-product price may therefore be set at a level that yields monopoly profits. These monopoly profits are among the profits forgone as a result of sale of final product lost to a licensee who might have been unable to supply that product without the license. Consequently, these forgone monopoly profits constitute a part of the opportunity cost for which, according to (2) (at least without further modification of the ECPR regime), the bottleneck owner will be compensated when it sells the bottleneck input to a rival. In other words, the argument here is that ECPR is an instrument for the protection of any monopoly profit of the input supplier. Let us examine each of these arguments in turn.

3.1. **Ramsey Pricing Versus ECPR Pricing.** Ramsey pricing is defined at the second-best pricing for quasi-optimal resource allocation where scale economies prevent marginal-cost pricing from being feasible financially, or where it is deemed desirable to provide the supplier with some pre-selected level of economic profits other than zero. A vastly oversimplified derivation of the Ramsey theorem for the easiest relevant case will suffice to indicate how the problem arises.[5] Consider a vector of outputs whose quantities are $y = (Y^1, ..., Y^n)$; assume that the cross elasticities of the demands for these products are all zero; and that there is a well-defined social utility function $u(y)$. Then optimality requires maximization of the net utility:

$$\max u(y) - c(y), \tag{8}$$

where $c(y)$ is the total social cost of y (the opportunity cost of the resources needed to produce it) and the maximization is subject to the constraint:

$$\sum_{i=1}^{n} P^i Y^i - c(y) = k, \tag{9}$$

that is, the prices, P^i, are determined as to permit the supplier to obtain the fixed and pre-selected amount of economic profit k (where k may be zero).

Then the Lagrangian obviously is

$$L = u(y) - c(y) - v\left[\sum_{i=1}^{n} P^i Y^i - c(y) - k\right], \tag{10}$$

[5]The oversimplifications here are numerous, and the mathematical argument is offered only to suggest the character of the logic. Among the oversimplifications are the implied direct comparability of social welfare and consumer expenditure, the failure to deal with the regularity conditions needed to guarantee the existence of a unique maximum, and avoidance of an inequality form of the revenue requirement.

with the first-order maximum conditions

$$u_j - c_j - v\left(P^j - c_j + Y^j \frac{\partial P^j}{\partial Y^j}\right) = 0 \quad \text{all } j, \tag{11}$$

in which the subscripts denote partial differentiation with respect to Y^j and by assumption, the derivative of any P^i with respect to Y^j is equal to zero whenever j and i are not the same. Taking consumer demand to obey the "price equals marginal utility" rule, this can be rewritten directly as

$$\left[P^j - c_j\right](1 - v) = vY^j \frac{\partial P^j}{\partial Y^j},$$

or dividing both sides by P^j and writing $-w = v/(1-v)$ we obtain at once

$$\frac{P^j - c_j}{P^j} = -w\left(\frac{Y^j}{P^j}\right)\left(\frac{\partial P^j}{\partial Y^j}\right) = \frac{w}{E_j}, \tag{12}$$

where E_j is the price elasticity of demand of output j. In this simple case, we have obtained what is known, for obvious reasons, as the inverse-elasticity form of the Ramsey theorem, meaning that the second-best price of product j subject to a profit constraint is inversely proportionate to the elasticity of demand of that product. The intuitive explanation of the result is straightforward. It starts from the very well-known proposition that adoption of prices each of which is equal to the corresponding marginal cost is a necessary condition for "first-best" optimality in resource allocation. But from there the investigation goes on to ask, for the case where it is for some reason necessary to obtain revenues different from those that marginal cost prices would yield, what modifications from the first-best prices can yield the required revenues with minimum damage to consumer welfare? And the answer (where, for expository simplicity, I take the required revenue to be larger than that of MC prices) is to increase most the prices of the items whose demands are inelastic, since that will cause the least contraction in quantities demanded and hence yield the largest contributions to revenue from a given rise in price. In other words, Ramsey pricing can be said to yield the needed revenue via the smallest overall distortion of prices from their marginal-cost levels.

It should be clear from direct comparison that the Ramsey rule (12) and the ECPR, as contained in (1) or (2) that they do not generally yield the same price figures and are, consequently, not consistent. The Ramsey approach assigns a primary role to the configuration of demands, while it takes the cost function to be given. Thus, it pays no attention to the requirements of efficiency in production. The reverse is true of ECPR, in which demand plays no explicit role, and where the focus is upon ensuring that the task of product supply is allocated to those firms that can carry out the task most efficiently. Even the data the two approaches take into consideration are not the same, so it is clear that they will generally yield different results.

Since both of these rules are second-best, it may not even be possible to offer a general ranking of their relative preferability. One can argue that the Ramsey principle is far more difficult to put into practice, because it requires up-to-date estimates of all the pertinent demand elasticities and cross-elasticities, clearly a requirement that it is virtually impossible to satisfy in practice. Not that utilization of ECPR is a trivial and easy process. But it can be done and it has in fact been carried out and presented to courts and regulatory agencies, at least to a reasonable degree of approximation (though not without strong criticism by those on the opposite side in the litigations).

More to the analytical point, one can argue that the Ramsey rule is not clearly superior, since by itself it patently is consistent with inefficiency in the supply process. Indeed, it has been contended that legitimate use of the Ramsey rule should confine its application to the prices of final products and that input prices should be affected only by those consequences of the Ramsey rule for the prices of the associated final products. Since input demands are derived demands, the preferences of final consumers should enter the determination of input prices through that derivation process. Or put another way, once a Ramsey calculation has determined what modifications in final-product prices should be adopted in order to meet the revenue requirement, it would damage welfare to add contributions to the revenue requirement by extracting further contributions from the purchasers of inputs. I am not prepared to argue that these observations settle the issue, but it suggests that the ideal solution to the problem of copyright fees for the use of the protected material as input is to use the Ramsey rule as the standard for the final-product prices and to use ECPR for the fees to the input users.

3.2. **ECPR as Protector of Monopoly Profits.** A far-more frequent criticism of ECPR is the claim-and it is one that has considerable validity-that parity pricing preserves any monopoly profits that may be present, and extends their reach from the exploited final consumer to the licensee user of the pertinent input. Once again, the argument is straightforward. The ECPR requires input pricing to include any opportunity cost that the licensor incurs if the licensee is enabled by the licensing transaction to take business away from the input owner. But if the owner has any monopoly power, and uses it to extract a monopoly profits from its own sales of final product, then any loss of such a sale must entail giving up the monopoly profit on that sale. Since the parity price "makes the input owner whole," by restoring any profits forgone in the transaction, the parity price will clearly restore any monopoly profit component of final-product price that the competition of the licensee might otherwise have eliminated.

The defenders of ECPR, including Willig and the present author, have long recognized the justice of this criticism in general. They have stated repeatedly that legitimate use of ECPR must take it into account. However, they have taken the position that modification of input license fees is not the proper way to deal with the problem. Indeed, that follows from the level-playing-field theorem, which tells us that any deviation from the parity price is an invitation to inefficiency in supply, that is, in the choice of supplier that the market will thereupon select for the role of final-product supplier. The problem is a real one, but its source is to be found in the prices of the final products, not in the prices of the input-use licenses. It is concluded that for ECPR to serve the public interest it must be included in a package that also contains measures that eliminate the monopoly profits on the final product by means such as appropriate price ceilings or other rules constraining the setting of final-product prices. Only with the aid of such a package can one really protect consumers from exploitation, prevent the allocative inefficiencies that monopoly prices introduce and ensure efficiency in the roles assigned to licensors and licensees. The conclusion here is that ECPR is, indeed, an instrument that is ineffective as a means to eliminate monopoly profits. But this is surely not the purpose for which the instrument was designed. The rule could just as easily be criticized for inability to cure venereal disease or eliminate pollution of rivers.

But the answer to the criticism that ECPR preserves monopoly profits is even more direct in the case of copyrights and patents. After all, a central purpose of these instruments is to ensure the opportunity to earn appropriate incentive payments to creative individuals such as composers and inventors, via payments presumably legally permitted to exceed what is required for restitution of costs incurred in the creative process. It is true that in the United States the courts have held that the earnings generated by patents or copyrights cannot automatically be deemed to entail monopoly earnings. What constitutes monopoly profit in the analogous case of bottleneck industrial inputs can be interpreted simply as a socially desirable incentive for innovation protected by the intellectual property laws in the case where the bottleneck is an IP that is constituted by an innovation.

Still, a Schumpeterian point of view would lead most economists to agree that excesses of prices over some pertinent cost levels that are obtained by restriction of competition via copyright or patent protection constitutes a temporary monopoly earning, albeit one that is justified by the requirements of the public interest. If these be monopoly earnings they surely can be deemed to constitute virtue, rather than vice. Then if ECPR serves to preserve those earnings when the protected materials are used as inputs, there is no reason to deplore this result.

One last observation is pertinent here. Licensees in other arenas often complain that ECPR fees are higher than seems justified. After all, as we have seen, ECPR fees ensure that a final-product producer for whom access to the protected inputs is essential, and who is no more efficient than the licensor, will earn zero economic profit, while the licensor may earn more, and possibly considerably more, without sharing any of this surplus with the licensee. Of course, in the circumstances, it is not clear on what grounds the licensee, with its lack of superior efficiency, can lay claim to any share in those earnings. But here it may also not be irrelevant to point out that if Ramsey pricing rules for the license fees were substituted for the ECPR, the price whose magnitude is complained about is likely to become still higher. For under the inverse-elasticity rule, as we have seen, the less elastic the demand for any affected product, the larger the Ramsey adjustment will be, other things being equal. In particular, in a Ramsey regime, if there is a product whose elasticity of demand is zero, it will be assigned the entire burden of meeting the revenue requirement. But where material covered by copyright is indeed essential for the activities of the supplier of final product, then, at least within the relevant range, the demand can be expected to be extremely inelastic, and therefore is apt to lead to a license fee well above that under ECPR.

Finally, another word must be said about the special scenario upon which the ECPR solution focuses. The underlying story is that of a copyright owner who competes with licensees in a downstream market. But, in the arts, the item covered by copyright does not always serve as an input in any final product market, and holders of such copyrights often have no intention of competing in such a market (e.g., the songwriter who cannot sing). The last case still fits directly into the analysis if the composer forms a partnership with a singer, but that still is surely not the general case. Instead, we can perhaps interpret the scenario hypothetically, as dealing with the prices that would be appropriate if, contrary to fact, the composer were to sing. But perhaps, in such cases in which our scenario does not hold, one must return to Ramsey pricing as the second-best solution.

REFERENCES

Baumol, William J., Janusz A. Ordover and Robert D. Willig (1997), "Parity Pricing and its Critics: A Necessary Condition for Efficiency in the Provision of Bottleneck Services to Competitors," *Yale Journal on Regulation*, Vol. 14, Winter; 149-163.

Baumol, William J. (2003), "Applied Welfare Economics," in Ruth Towse, ed., *An Handbook of Cultural Economics*, Cheltenham, United Kingdom and Northampton, Massachusetts: Edward Elgar Publishers; 20-31.

Economides, Nicholas, and Laurence J. White (1995), "Access and Interconnection Pricing: How Efficient is the 'Efficient Component Pricing Rule'?," *The Antitrust Bulletin*, Vol. XL, No. 3; 557-579.

Laffont, Jean-Jacques, and Jean Tirole (2000), *Competition in Telecommunications*, Cambridge, Massachusetts: MIT Press.

Tye, William B., and Carlos Lapuerta (1996), "The Economics of Pricing Network Interconnection: Theory and Application in the Market for Telecommunications in New Zealand," *Yale Journal on Regulation*, Vol. 13, No. 2; 419-500.

Willig, Robert D. (1979), "The Theory of Network Access Pricing," in H.M. Trebbing, ed., *Issues in Public Utility Regulation*, Vol. 109; 109-152.

WILLIAM J. BAUMOL, PROFESSOR OF ECONOMICS, NEW YORK UNIVERSITY, AND SENIOR RESEARCH ECONOMIST AND PROFESSOR EMERITUS, PRINCETON UNIVERSITY.

[9]

Risk sharing and the distribution of copyright collective income

Arthur Snow and Richard Watt

1 INTRODUCTION

Hollander (1984, p. 200) sums up the basic functions of copyright collectives as follows:

> Copyright collectives are associations to whom authors transfer copyrights for purposes of exploitation. In general, collectives are concerned with the following functions: (1) they grant licenses for the use of works in their repertory, (2) they negotiate and collect royalties, and distribute them to their members, (3) they take legal action against those who infringe the copyrights to which they hold title.

Each of these three aspects of collective administration of copyrights (as well as the monopoly position that such collectives enjoy) has been subject to the analysis of economic theory. In particular, the literature asserts that the underlying reason for copyright collectives to form naturally is that by joining together and marketing a blanket license to the entire repertory, each individual member can achieve a better utility position than by acting alone. In this chapter, we shall consider the possible ways in which collective administration improves the welfare of its members.

In the above quote from Hollander, it is clear that the principal idea is to share certain transactions costs over collective members (costs of negotiating, receiving payment for, and protecting license agreements). Clearly, then, the most obvious reason for collective administration is the welfare gains that the members can enjoy as transactions costs are diminished.

The Coase theorem implies that final resource allocations may, in general, be socially inefficient whenever transactions costs exist. When it comes to intellectual property markets, in which access to intellectual products between individuals is traded, transactions costs not only exist, but they may even be more significant than the final value of the object of the transaction. The reason for this is the fact that intellectual products are typically of a public good nature, and so there is a very low cost of free-riding associated with them. Once access has been granted to one user, it becomes very costly to then exclude access being taken by the entire set of potential users.

This problem is often overcome, at least partially, by collective administration. The example of copyright is perhaps the most prevalent case. When a copyrightable product is created, along with it is created an entire set of access rights, some of which can be transacted with low transactions costs, but others of which can only be transacted at a very high transactions cost. For example, consider the case of a musical composition. Once the composition has been fixed onto a physical support, say a CD Rom, it can easily be listened to by whoever has that CD Rom. When a consumer purchases the CD Rom from a recognized retailer, the right to a limited set of access privileges is automatically purchased as well. These include the right to listen to the music at any time and the right to sell the CD Rom to a third party. In most countries, the consumer has the right to make a copy of the CD Rom for personal use as well. However, with the purchase price of the CD Rom, the consumer will not acquire the right to make copies of the music for resale, or the right to play the music to an audience, especially for economic gain. The problem for the owner of the copyright in the music is how to monitor the use that the consumer makes of the CD Rom at a reasonable cost. One partial method lies in collective administration of the copyright.

Whenever the set of users of a particular type of intellectual product is common to many (say, n) copyright holders, in principle they can, by joining together and selling a license to the entire repertory, save on the transactions costs implied by $n-1$ individual rounds of negotiation, and likewise they can also save on both the monitoring costs and the costs of litigation whenever such recourse is needed.[1] In this way, the option of collective administration can make feasible a set of transactions that is unprofitable when carried out individually. In economic terms, copyright collectives enjoy the benefits of a natural monopoly.

However, saving on transactions costs is not the only manner in which collective administration can be of value to individual copyright holders. If we assume, as is indeed very natural, that the final market value of each copyright is a random variable (that is, there is uncertainty as to its final value), then a copyright collective is able to alleviate the risk-bearing situation of its members. If the members are risk-averse (again, a very natural assumption), then an improved risk situation provides for expected utility gains which are just as important as the gains that the transactions costs savings provide for. It is curious to note that this aspect of collective administration seems to have been entirely ignored, both in theoretical contributions and in real-life cases.

Given the diversity in the market value of each composition in a copyright collective's repertory, it is quite common for copyright collectives to take great pains in analysing the markets in which their repertories are used in order to determine how much use is made of each particular composition in the repertory. This is puzzling since it goes quite against the idea that the songs are bundled in the first place, in a blanket license, in order to save on such transactions costs.[2] The reason why this is done is simply to be able to base the final distribution of net income on the use made of each individual copyright. In this way, the copyright holders of the songs that are most played can be given a proportionately greater share of the collective's surplus. Abstracting from the fact that monitoring the market use of individual songs increases the transactions costs of running the collective, there are important reasons strongly rooted in the economic theory of risk bearing that suggest that doing this is inconsistent with the best interests of the pool of members, thereby making current copyright collective activity inefficient.

In this chapter, we think of a copyright collective as a simple coalition, in the sense of traditional game theory. Each potential individual member has the opportunity to join the coalition, or to act alone. In such a setting, it is very clear that the decision on whether or not to join the coalition is affected both by how much of the coalition's income is distributed among the members, and by exactly how that income is distributed. Therefore, the distribution rule will affect the number of members that the coalition has (in equilibrium) as well as the welfare of each individual. We shall impose two basic requirements of the distribution mechanism of a coalition's net income. First, we will require that the distribution method be such that individual copyright holders prefer to become members of the coalition rather than acting alone (we refer to this as the 'participation condition'). Second, we will require that existing members of the coalition prefer new members to join (we refer to this as the 'incentive compatibility condition'). Given these two requisites, we first ask if a distribution method that consists of learning the true market value of each composition and then paying each individual member accordingly satisfies these requirements. We then propose alternative distribution mechanisms that satisfy the two requirements and are preferred by all individuals to the 'learn-then-distribute' option.

2 A SIMPLE MODEL OF A COPYRIGHT COLLECTIVE

Let us assume that there is a set of n individuals, each of whom can create a composition that has strictly non-negative market value, but where the market value of the composition is a random variable. Here, we make the simplest possible assumption, namely that all composition lotteries are identical. Indeed, the assumption that all compositions are identical, albeit deterministic, is common in the literature (see, for example, Besen et al. 1992).

Moreover, we will assume that the composition lotteries are not only identically distributed, but that they are also statistically independent with a probability of success that is common knowledge.[3] Concretely, we assume that each composition can be either a 'success', in which case its market value is $x = 1$, or a 'flop', in which case its market value is $x = 0$. We assume that the probability of success is p, which is assumed strictly between 0 and 1, and we denote the true outcome of composition i by x_i.

Now, assume that the (monetary equivalent) costs of creation of each composition are constant and equal to c, and that if the composition is indeed marketed by the copyright holder (acting alone), then there exist transactions costs (costs of negotiation, monitoring, and litigation), denoted by t.

All copyright holders are assumed to be strictly wealth-loving and strictly risk-averse. In order to avoid the need for formally considering utility, instead we take the approach of mean-variance analysis. Concretely, we shall assume that all copyright holders have a strict preference for greater expected wealth, and a strict preference for lower variance of wealth. If copyright holder i goes ahead with the creation and marketing of the composition on an individual basis, then the expected value of his final wealth (assuming that he has no wealth outside of what the composition generates) is given by

$$E(x - c - t) = p(1 - c - t) + (1 - p)(0 - c - t) = p - (c + t). \qquad (2.1)$$

On the other hand, the variance of his wealth is given by

$$E(E(x - c - t) - (x - c - t))^2 = E(p - x)^2 = p(1 - p), \qquad (2.2)$$

which depends only on the probability of success.

Now, consider the situation of the coalition. Assuming that the coalition has $m \leq n$ members, the final market value of the blanket license follows a binomial distribution. It can take on any of the discrete values 0, 1, 2, 3, . . ., m, depending on exactly how many of the m member compositions are successes. Using the well-known formula for the binomial distribution, the probability that exactly h of the m compositions will be successful is given by

$$\frac{m!}{(m - h)!h!} p^h (1 - p)^{m-h}.$$

Given this, the expected final market value of the coalition's repertory is

$$X(m) = \sum_{h=0}^{m} \frac{m!}{(m-h)!h!} p^h (1-p)^{m-h} h.$$

True to the public good assumption of the compositions in question, and to the fact that each composition has the same user set, we assume that the total cost of marketing the blanket license to all the compositions in its repertory is the same as for any particular individual; that is, the entire repertory can be marketed at a (transactions) cost of t.[4] Given this, the coalition (with m members) earns a net income of $X(m) - t$ for distribution to the members.

Now assume that the collective can learn the true outcome of each individual composition lottery at some cost, which we fix at k, and then give individual member i a payment of

$$x_i - \frac{t+k}{m}.$$

Under this 'learn-then-distribute' system, a member's expected wealth is

$$E\left(x - c - \frac{t+k}{m}\right) = p\left(1 - c - \frac{t+k}{m}\right) + (1-p)\left(0 - c - \frac{t+k}{m}\right) \quad (2.3)$$

$$= p - c - \frac{t+k}{m}$$

with a variance of

$$E\left(E\left(x - c - \frac{t+k}{m}\right) - \left(x - c - \frac{t+k}{m}\right)\right)^2 = E(p-x)^2 = p(1-p). \quad (2.4)$$

Clearly, under this distribution rule, all members get a final wealth lottery with the same variance as acting alone. It is also clear from (2.3) that the expected wealth of each collective member is strictly increasing in m, so that all collective members will welcome new members to the coalition, implying that the incentive compatibility condition is satisfied. However, it is not clear that the participation condition is satisfied. Comparing the expected wealth in (2.3) with that in (2.1), participation (that is, all individuals prefer to become members of the coalition) can be guaranteed if and only if

$$\frac{t+k}{m} < t.$$

Clearly, this requirement is more easily satisfied when k is small, when t is large, or when m is large, each of which is intuitively understandable.

In short, for any given values of t and k, we have:

Proposition 2.1 A distribution rule under which a collective learns (at a cost of k) the final result of each independent composition in its repertory, and distributes final income accordingly, is incentive compatible. There is a minimum membership, given by $m^* = (t+k)/t$, beyond which the distribution rule also satisfies the participation condition.[5]

Assuming that the coalition has sufficient members, the fact that the learn-then-distribute system satisfies both incentive compatibility and participation is due entirely to the transactions costs savings that the coalition offers. However, the risk-bearing situation of each coalition member has not changed, since the coalition offers the same variance of the final wealth lottery as acting alone. Hence, while the coalition increases the expected value of income (by saving on transactions costs) it does nothing at all to alleviate the risk situation of the members. Given that the creators are risk-averse, it would be welfare enhancing if the coalition could offer a better risk situation as well as transactions costs savings. We now go on to consider if this is indeed possible.

3 RISK SHARING DISTRIBUTION MECHANISMS

Consider first the opportunity that the copyright collective has of offering full and fair insurance to all members. Since no learning is done as far as the final result of each individual lottery, the only costs of administering the set of copyrights is t. Now, assume that the collective pays each member the expected value of his composition less his share of the transactions costs with certainty. In this case, each creator receives an expected wealth of

$$p - c - \frac{t}{m} \tag{2.5}$$

with zero variance. Clearly, this distribution rule satisfies both participation and incentive compatibility. Moreover, it also Pareto dominates the learn-then-distribute rule, since all members get a lower variance of wealth and a higher expected final wealth. Thus, we have:

Proposition 2.2 A sharing rule stipulating that each individual copyright holder receives the expected value of his composition with certainty satisfies both participation by all individuals and incentive compatibility. It also strongly Pareto dominates the learn-then-distribute rule.

The fact that the welfare benefits of the full insurance mechanism are so obvious begs the question of why this system is not typically used. Perhaps the answer lies in the fact that, if the collective pays each member his expected value, then there is a strictly positive probability that the final market value of the repertory will either exceed or fall short of the total outlay paid to the members as royalties. Unless the collective has access to a perfect reinsurance market, the members of the collective would still bear some risk with respect to their final wealth positions, although this risk becomes smaller as the membership increases. Clearly though, the full and fair insurance option may not be feasible. However, there are intermediate options that have full insurance, although not fair insurance, that satisfy both participation and incentive compatibility, and that still Pareto dominate the learn-then-distribute rule.

Consider the following simple option. The collective distributes a fixed sum to each individual member such that the expected value of each member's income is the same as if the distribution rule had been learn-then-distribute. That is, each member is given a fixed payment of

$$p-\frac{t+k}{m}=p-\frac{t}{m}-\frac{k}{m}.$$

Once again, this rule clearly satisfies incentive compatibility, and satisfies participation under the same proviso as in Proposition 2.1.[6] Moreover, this system is strictly preferred by all copyright holders to the learn-then-distribute rule since it offers the same expected wealth with a lower variance. Since no learning is done, this rule implies that total royalty payments are $mp-t-k$, while the total net income of the collective is $X(m)-t$. Under this system, the probability that the collective runs into a bankruptcy problem can be significantly reduced (although, naturally, the reduction depends on the size of k). For example, if we assume that $m=100$, and if we assume that $k=10$, then the probability of bankruptcy is under 3 per cent.[7] Naturally, the accumulated but not distributed net income of the collective would, at certain times, be distributed to the members as profit (as opposed to strict royalty payments). Whether or not such a system is indeed feasible depends on the true values of the parameters m, p and k, and on the access that the collective has to other financial products (short-term loans, third party insurance, etc.), but at least in principle it would seem to be feasible in most modern societies.

Proposition 2.3 A sharing rule stipulating that each member of the collective receives with certainty a payment equal to the expected value of the payment under the learn-then-distribute rule, satisfies incentive compatibility always, and satisfies participation under the same restriction on total collective membership as in Proposition 2.1. Moreover, this rule Pareto dominates the learn-then-distribute rule, since it sets the variance of each copyright owner's final wealth to 0. The probability of bankruptcy under this distribution rule becomes negligible as k increases.

Even if the full but not fair insurance option were not feasible, there are other options that also Pareto dominate the learn-then-distribute rule and that never run into bankruptcy problems. To see some of these options, note that the expected value of the repertory is[8]

$$EX(m) = mp \tag{2.6}$$

and the variance of the market value of the repertory is

$$E(mp - X(m))^2 = mp(1-p). \tag{2.7}$$

Now assume that the collective's net income is distributed according to pre-agreed shares, such that member i receives a proportion λ_i of the final net income of the collective, where

$$\sum_{i=1}^{m} \lambda_i = 1$$

in order to avoid all bankruptcy issues (that is, the collective will distribute exactly all of its net income, whatever that turns out to be). Using this rule, the expected final wealth of member i is

$$\begin{aligned} E\left(\lambda_i\left(X(m) - \frac{t}{m}\right) - c\right) &= E\lambda_i X(m) - c - \frac{t}{m} \\ &= \lambda_i EX(m) - c - \frac{t}{m} \\ &= \lambda_i mp - c - \frac{t}{m} \end{aligned} \tag{2.8}$$

with variance

$$\begin{aligned} E\left(\lambda_i mp - c - \frac{t}{m} - \left(\lambda_i X(m) - c - \frac{t}{m}\right)\right)^2 &= E(\lambda_i(mp - X(m)))^2 \\ &= \lambda_i^2 E(mp - X(m))^2. \end{aligned}$$

Using (2.7), we find that the variance of final wealth under this distribution rule is

$$\lambda_i^2 mp(1-p). \tag{2.9}$$

Now, since each composition is, ex ante, identical, let us simply assume that $\lambda_i = 1/m \,\forall\, i$. In this case the expected value of final wealth for each member of the collective is

$$p - c - \frac{t}{m}, \tag{2.10}$$

which is the same as under the full and fair insurance mechanism, and greater than under the learn-then-distribute rule. On the other hand, the variance of the final wealth of each of the collective members is

$$\frac{p(1-p)}{m}, \tag{2.11}$$

which is greater than any full insurance mechanism (under which variance is 0), but less than what the learn-then-distribute rule offers (which from (2.4) is $p(1-p)$).

Finally, note that this sharing rule satisfies both incentive compatibility (expected value is increasing in m and variance is decreasing in m) and participation (expected value of being a collective member is strictly greater than acting alone because of the transactions costs savings, and the variance that being a member offers is strictly less than that corresponding to acting alone), and that it Pareto dominates the learn-then-distribute rule (since it offers both a greater expected value, as the learning costs are saved, and a lower variance). Thus, we have:

Proposition 2.4 A sharing rule stipulating that each collective member is paid an equal share of the final net income of the collective is both incentive compatible and satisfies participation. It also strictly Pareto dominates the learn-then-distribute rule.

Although we have found a manner in which the net income of a copyright collective can be distributed that strictly Pareto dominates the currently used method, and that will not imply any bankruptcy issues, one wonders if this method can be improved upon. This type of question has been analysed extensively in the literature on efficient risk sharing. Two main results of that literature are worth mentioning here. First, the so-called 'mutuality principle' of Karl Borch (see Borch 1960) implies that if a group of risk-averse agents each contribute a random variable to a common pool (known as a mutual), then a Pareto-efficient risk-sharing rule must make the final wealth of each individual member independent of the particular contribution that he made. In other words, the final wealth of each member of a copyright collective should depend only on the final value of $X(m)$, and not on the individual composition lotteries. This has been achieved in our proposal, where each individual receives an equal share of $X(m)$, but is clearly not achieved in the learn-then-distribute rule.

Second, the question naturally arises: can the equal-share rule also be improved upon. In particular, since it satisfies the mutuality principle, the equal-share rule fully diversifies all diversifiable risk, but it leaves the final wealth of each individual dependent upon the aggregate, or social, risk as determined by the random variable $X(m)$. The question is exactly how this aggregate risk should be shared. This question was solved by Wilson (1968), who proves that full risk sharing efficiency will require that each member of a mutual should receive a fraction of the total pooled wealth (here $X(m)$) that is equal to his individual risk tolerance divided by the sum of the risk tolerances of all members.

The sharing rule based on risk tolerances would, almost certainly, imply that members who supply identically valued compositions to the repertory receive different shares of the final pooled wealth. Besen et al. (1992, pp. 395–7) note that discriminatory practices in the distribution of collective income are often frowned upon by regulatory authorities.[9] Given this, it remains to be seen if the fully efficient sharing rule offered by Wilson is indeed feasible in the regulatory scenario of most copyright collectives.

4 HETEROGENEOUS AND CORRELATED COMPOSITION LOTTERIES

Our simple model of a copyright collective assumes that the composition lotteries are identical and independent. In this section we briefly examine the implications of relaxing these assumptions.

When different compositions have different probabilities of success, an additional condition comes into play that is satisfied vacuously when probabilities are identical, namely, the distribution rule must satisfy the requirement of 'group rationality.' That is, it must not be the case that a subset of the members prefers to defect to an alternative collective. As an example, suppose that half of the compositions in the repertory have a high probability of success while the others have a low probability. Clearly, the equal sharing rule introduced in the preceding section will not be viable if the difference in probabilities is so large that those more likely to succeed prefer defecting to a collective of their own, even though transactions costs are then spread over half as many members as in the original collective. However, group rationality can be restored by appropriately increasing the share allotted to those with a high probability of success. As long as the collective can categorize copyright holders according to their probabilities, the benefits of risk pooling described in the previous section can be realized by viable copyright collectives.

Although we have focused on the case of independent composition lotteries, correlated lotteries would yield the same qualitative results, except in the unrealistic case of perfect positive correlation where all compositions either succeed or fail together and there are no insurance possibilities. Negative correlation introduces hedging opportunities that improve the collective's own risk situation. Indeed, with perfect negative correlation, the collective can attain a riskless position, just as it can whenever it has access to a perfect reinsurance market. In these cases the collective can offer its members full and fair insurance for their composition lotteries. As correlation among the lotteries and reinsurance opportunities become imperfect, the insurance benefits a collective can offer become less valuable, but nonetheless dominate the learn-then-distribute rule.

5 ASYMMETRIC INFORMATION

Thus far we have abstracted from the informational asymmetries associated with moral hazard and adverse selection. The learn-then-distribute rule provides the strongest incentive to create a profitable copyrightable work, since the author is rewarded for the effort to produce a successful composition precisely in proportion to the success actually realized. In this manner the rule addresses the problem of moral hazard, whereby a composer's costly effort to produce a successful piece cannot be monitored and rewarded directly. However, the rule is an inefficient response to the problem, since it leaves the risk-averse composer bearing all the risk of failure when, as we have seen, insurance opportunities are available. If moral hazard poses a significant problem for the membership of a collective, then it would be inefficient to take full advantage of the available insurance opportunities, since the members would then have the least incentive to be productive. As a general matter, an efficient response to moral hazard entails balancing the benefits of enhanced incentives to put forth productive effort against the risk-bearing costs that this necessarily entails. An optimal balance would call for a distribution rule that ties royalty payments partially to a composition's realized success, offering some incentive for productive effort, and partially to the realized success of the entire repertory, offering some insurance against failure. Thus, moral hazard would mitigate, but not eliminate the advantage we have identified for distribution rules that incorporate risk pooling.

Adverse selection, whereby individual composers and the collective have different perceptions of the likelihood of success, poses a different problem. In a heterogeneous population, when individual composers are better informed about the probability of success than the collective, risk classification through categorization and screening, as commonly practiced in insurance markets, would allow the collective to provide insurance to its members, although not as effectively as when information is symmetric.[10] For those more likely to be successful, screening mechanisms would pay a higher proportion of royalties based on actual performance and a smaller proportion through insurance. Thus, while all of the benefits of risk pooling could not be realized, it would still be possible for members of the collective to enjoy some of those benefits through a distribution mechanism that does not rely exclusively on the learn-then-distribute rule.

It is also possible for the collective to be better informed about the likelihood of success than overly optimistic copyright holders.[11] Indeed, it is possible for the divergence in beliefs to be so great that the insurance terms offered by the collective are unacceptable to the members. In this case the learn-then-distribute rule would be the only viable system available to a copyright collective.

6 CONCLUSIONS

In this chapter we have proposed that copyright collectives may not be offering their members as great a welfare benefit as they could. By focusing all of their attention on the transactions costs savings of their services, they have ignored the opportunity to offer their members important risk-sharing benefits. We have described several methods under which the net income of copyright collectives is distributed to members in a manner that takes advantage of risk-sharing opportunities and that Pareto dominates exclusive reliance on a distribution rule that calls for first learning the outcome of each composition lottery and then paying out royalties accordingly.

Two explanations may be offered for the failure of copyright collectives to depart from complete reliance on the learn-then-distribute rule. First, a partial explication can be found in the existence of asymmetric information – adverse selection and/or moral hazard. In these cases, it is well known that the agent (the informed party, here, the creator) must retain risk in order to satisfy incentive compatibility. Secondly, copyright holders may be unrealistically optimistic about their chances of success and therefore unwilling to accept financially viable alternatives to the learn-then-distribute rule.[12]

Both of these explanations imply that the full potential of copyright collectives to provide benefits for their members could be realized if their members were better informed about the value of the risk pooling services available through the collectives.

NOTES

1. We note that in some instances, some of the monitoring costs are borne by the purchasing entity which is required to report usage rates to the collective. In any case, the collective still needs to suffer some costs in processing and administering this information.
2. Blanket licensing may also serve to eliminate competition among composers and allow them to act as a cartel. However, in many jurisdictions, tariffs are regulated, limiting the opportunity to exercise monopoly power.
3. In sections 2.4 and 2.5 we consider the implications of relaxing these assumptions.
4. Really we only require that the collective has a transactions cost of $t' < mt$; that is, the collective is more efficient than the sum of its members. Setting $t' = qt$, the requirement is that $q < m$, and in the chapter we have assumed $q = 1$. In fact, the more the underlying product (here compositions) resembles a pure public good, the lower is the value of q, and q goes to 1 in the extreme case of a pure public good. It seems likely that for the case at hand, we will typically have a very low value of q, and so our assumption of $q = 1$ is only meant to be a rough approximation that facilitates the argument significantly.
5. Clearly the condition can be expressed equivalently as $k < mt - t$; that is, the cost of learning is less than the total transactions cost savings.
6. Indeed, participation can be achieved with a lower membership than under the learn-then-distribute rule, since each member gets a better risk-bearing situation. Exactly how the limit value of m is affected is impossible to determine unless we introduce an analysis based on utility functions.
7. Concretely, the probability is 1.76 per cent if $p = 0.5$. This compares to the figure of 46.02 per cent when fair insurance is offered.
8. These results are not so easy to prove. See, for example, Chapter 4 of Canavos (1989) for proofs.
9. In spite of this, the American Society of Composers, Authors and Publishers (ASCAP) in particular does discriminate. They distribute income in a way that discriminates according to how long an individual has been a member (see Besen and Kirby, 1989 p. 21). Also, these authors (p. 10), note that, when comparing copyright collectives over the world 'a very wide range of methods are employed to distribute the proceeds of blanket licences'.
10. See Crocker and Snow (2000) for a theoretical analysis of risk classification in the insurance industry.
11. The possibility that authors may be overly optimistic about the chances of success of their work was discussed by Watt (2000, p. 89), and also by Besen (1987).
12. We note that in some instances the creator is paid a fixed fee by a third party who then holds the copyright. Risk pooling offers no benefits to these third parties when they are sufficiently diversified to be risk neutral.

REFERENCES

Besen, S. (1987), 'New technology and intellectual property: An economic analysis', *RAND Report N° N-2601-NSF.*

Besen, S. and S. Kirby (1989), 'Compensating creators of intellectual property: Collectives that collect', *RAND Report Nº R-3751-MF.*

Besen, S., S. Kirby and S. Salop (1992), 'An economic analysis of copyright collectives', *Virginia Law Review*, **78**, 383–411.

Borch, K. (1960), 'The safety loading of reinsurance premiums', *Skandinavisk Aktuarietskrift*, 153–84.

Canavos, G. (1989), *Applied Probability and Statistical Methods*, New York: McGraw-Hill.

Crocker, K.J. and A. Snow (2000), 'The theory of risk classification,' in G. Dionne (ed.), *Handbook of Insurance*, Boston, MA: Kluwer Academic Publishers, pp. 245–76.

Hollander, A. (1984), 'Market structure and performance in intellectual property: The case of copyright collectives', *International Journal of Industrial Organization*, **2**, 199–216.

Watt, R. (2000), *Copyright and Economic Theory: Friends or Foes?*, Cheltenham, UK and Northampton MA, USA: Edward Elgar.

Wilson, R. (1968), 'The theory of syndicates', *Econometrica*, **36**, 113–32.

[10]

Are Copyright Collecting Societies Efficient Organisations? An Evaluation of Collective Administration of Copyright in Europe

Fabrice Rochelandet[1]

1 INTRODUCTION

This contribution examines the performances of copyright collecting societies (CCS), which play a key role in the field of copyright management. They are non-governmental non-profit organisations, which administer some of the rights of copyright holders. They negotiate licences with users and receive payments they distribute among their members.[2] CCS historically act as private institutions that minimise search and contracting costs between and among intermediary users and copyright holders (Merges, 1996). Nowadays, the question is, whether this idea still prevails with the dissemination of information and communication technologies. On the one hand, given the emergence of self-help systems, opponents of collective administration argue that ICTs permit to reduce transaction costs in such a manner that these private institutions turn out to be unnecessary.[3] On the other hand, even though ICTs permit some components of transaction costs to be reduced – for instance, by facilitating identification or by tightening up enclosure – they do not reduce them all.[4] So, by playing the role of intermediaries and representatives of their members, CCS can figure among the main private institutions that enable effective governance of transaction in the digital economy (Rochelandet, 2000).

Beyond this important current debate, it should be noted that CCS are also specific organisations. Thus, before drawing some general conclusions about the (in)effectiveness of the collective administration in the digital age, it is necessary to evaluate their performance as organisations. One possible method would be to measure and compare the performances of each kind of organisation likely to manage copyright, i.e. for-profit, public and non-profit organisations. Economic theory would then determine the efficient copyright arrangement according to a given criterion such as Pareto-optimal allocation of copyrights[5] and transaction costs minimisation. This study, however, is based on another perspective. It attempts to compare *existing* organisations with similar features by isolating the respective impact of ownership structure and legal supervision on their performance.

I elsewhere highlight performance dispersions between French CCS (Rochelandet, 2001). Among the main factors to explain these results are ownership concentration and copyright administration complexity.[6] However, these results have been established with no possibility of isolating the very impact of legal supervision on CCS performance. Drawing on meaningful data on three major European CCS, the current study tries to fill this gap. It addresses thereby three questions: (1) Which organisations are characterised by the best performance? (2) What relationship is there to be found between ownership structure, legal control and performances in the case of CCS? (3) Under what legal system will we observe better results for collecting societies? At the time of important discussions about copyright management methods, this study could help European regulators to specify what kind of regulation should be implemented in European countries.

2 THE COLLECTIVE ADMINISTRATION OF COPYRIGHT: AN AGENCY PROBLEM

Collective administration of copyright figures among the different methods to administrate copyright, that is primarily individual administration, for-profit private management by publishers (who link this function with their business), collective administration and non-voluntary licences. Factors to explain the implementation of such methods are of economic nature (searching and contracting costs minimisation, respective bargaining power of authors, publishers and commercial users) as well as of historical nature (institutional path dependencies).[7] Each method displays some drawbacks, in particular in terms of monopolistic pricing and risk of abuse of dominant position through hold-up strategies. That explains in the case of CCS why legal supervision plays a key role in order to control their behaviour. In this section, these organisations are analysed through the lens of positive agency theory.

Hypotheses

The nature and running of CCS can be characterised by some hypotheses.

(H1) Divergence of interests between members and managers.

A general assumption underlying this study is that the interests of managers and members of CCS diverge. The former are supposed to maximise an objective function grounded on their remuneration, power, job security and status. Two complementary strategies make it possible for managers to achieve these goals: *boosting management costs* in such a way that copyright distributions are reduced in proportion and *maximising copyright collection* so that administration costs are automatically increased. As for the members, they are wealth maximisers in the sense that they expect their individual share in collected sums to be as great as possible.

(H2) Informational asymmetries and lack of significant market pressure.

However, large informational asymmetries make it generally impossible for the members of any CCS at zero cost to ensure that the managers will make optimal decisions from their viewpoint. Relinquishing controls would be favourable to opportunistic behaviour of managers. They would be all the more important if no effective market pressure such as product market competition and potential hostile takeovers forced CCS towards higher performances. The monopolistic position of CCS makes it very difficult to compare the results of each CCS with similar organisations. So managers have room for discretionary allocation of collected copyrights. In this case,[8] the more dispersed the membership is, the more managers are incited to raise their remunerations of all kinds far beyond their actual productivity and results.

How do members convince managers to minimise administration expenses and so maximise copyright distribution? How do they make sure that the managers do not boost the running costs and squander collected copyrights in acts and projects unrelated to the main objectives of the CCS? In short, how to solve this agency problem?[9] In fact, some governance mechanisms are likely to reduce these organisational rents by leading managers to act in the interest of members: on the one hand, ownership concentration and especially existence of large members; on the other hand, legal controls.

(H3) Divergence of interests between large and less important members.

As for large members, their market power gives them not only greater incentives to monitor managers but also the power to control managerial behaviour and, if necessary, to replace managers. In other words, many large members make it possible to reduce significantly managerial rents. Nonetheless, beyond their common goal of individual revenue maximisation, all members have not the same interest. From the large members' viewpoint, CCS have to specialise on the collection of the most valuable rights, i.e. those that are the less costly to administrate in comparison to their amount. By contrast, less important members expect their organisation to collect any right, even if it would be costly for a CCS to adopt such a development strategy.[10] In fact, this conflict is centred on the existence of cross-subsidies between highly valuable copyrights and costly-to-collect copyrights.

Although the presence of many large members could be effective in solving the agency problem, they may also inefficiently redistribute collected sums from members without any significant power to themselves. In this case as well as in the case of dispersed membership, an effective governance system supposes at first glance that legal supervision should be established. This legal supervision is all the more needed as in the spirit of law, copyright is not aimed to favour some copyright holders to the detriment of others. So copyrights should tend to their social value for all kinds of copyrighted uses and CCS should maximise the sums they collect *and* distribute. But the question then is, to what extent their intensity should be established.

(H4) A diversity of legal supervision national systems.[11]

The purpose of this study is to determine the impact of institutional supervision systems on the results of CCS. It is therefore necessary to highlight their nature. The extent of legal control of CCS differs among countries and especially among the European member states.[12] Two opposite cases are to be found. On the one hand, the less restricting national regulation is characterised by the absence of specific control: only competition and contract laws apply to CCS. Greece is a significant example. It looks like the American legal system, which mainly consists in supervising the pricing and licensing practices of CCS.[13] On the other hand, the most restricting system takes the form of a public administration of copyrights. The Italian system illustrates this case. Since the 1941 copyright law, the Italian CCS – the SIAE – has enjoyed a legal monopoly. In return, any statutory changes must be approved by a presidential decree in accordance with the main government ministries. The running of this public law association is subject to a permanent control of the prime minister. This control is strengthened by an auditors' division and some government officials sit on the SIAE board.

Between these two opposite cases are intermediary systems, which combine a control on the establishment of any CCS and a control of their activities. All of these systems take into account the interests of users (pricing and licensing contracts) and those of individual members (quality of the management, equitable distribution, etc.). Therefore, controls differ according to their intensity: no control, control at the request of users, founding control, permanent control and intense control.

The following table classifies European countries according to the control intensity.

Table 10.1 Legal supervision systems in European countries

Countries	Lack of control	Control at request	Setting up control	Permanent control	Extreme control
Germany			+++	+++	
Austria			++	++	
Belgium	+++*				
Denmark			+		
Spain			+++	++	
France		+	++	++	
Greece	+++				
Luxembourg			++	++	
Ireland		+++			
Italy					+++
Netherlands			++	++	
Portugal			+		
United		+++			
Kingdom			++		
Switzerland					

* Since 1994, the Belgium system has been significantly strengthened.
Sources: Hilty (1995), Sénat Français (1997)

Note that supervision is very intense in Germany, somewhat low in the UK and intermediary in France. In the German case, the establishment of any CCS requires to be jointly authorised by the German Patent Office and the Kartellamt. Their activities are placed under the control of these institutions. Not only can the Patent Office demand any information and attend board meetings, but they can also require the CCS to replace their manager or even forbid them to carry out their activity. Furthermore, any CCS can be legally bound to enter into contract with any user and to conclude blanket contracts with representative association of commercial users on their request. Finally, the Patent Office plays a role of arbitrator when CCS and users are in conflict. Only in case of failure, the dispute takes the form of a trial. By contrast, the British legal system is much less restrictive. It applies to the price setting by CCS and proceedings are undertaken only at the request of users when they litigate a claim towards the copyright tribunal. No specific control applies to their establishment and running. Finally, they are placed under the regime of competition law as anywhere in Europe. The French legal system is a go-between institutional environment, which consists mainly in heavy control of establishment and a moderate control of activity.[14]

Propositions

On the basis of the previous hypothesis, it is possible to make the following propositions.

(P1) Many large members can lead managers to minimise administration expenses.

Not only large members with market power have greater incentives to monitor managers but also they have the power to control their behaviour and, if necessary, to replace them. Therefore, many large members make it possible to reduce significantly managerial rents.

(P2) By contrast, dispersed membership can lead managers to boost their declared costs to the detriment of distributions to members.

In this case, managers have much more room for discretionary allocation of collected copyrights, for instance, by raising the running costs of the organisation in order to improve their own status.

(P3) The stronger the legal supervision is, the smaller managerial rents are likely to be.

This external governance is supposed to be all the more effective when internal control proves to be low (dispersed membership or informational asymmetries). I have tested propositions P1 and P2 in a previous study about French collecting societies by suggesting that the bargaining power of members – more or less concentrated ownership – affects sharply the performance of these organisations (Rochelandet, 2001). So internal governance appears to be a strong constraint in managerial behaviour. For instance, it explains the better results of producers' collecting societies in comparison to performers' ones. However, it doesn't highlight proposition P3. The impact of legal supervision obviously is impossible to determine because comparisons are made in the same legal system. So this study aims to analyse the impact of legal supervision systems on the results of CCS.

3 THE PERFORMANCES OF CCS AS ORGANISATIONS: AN EVALUATION

Data

In order to compare CCS, it is necessary to highlight the common features of the services they produce. Among the data generally available on a relevant period are the total copyright royalties they collect from content users P, the total revenues they distribute to their members R, the licensing and administration expenses C, their membership size M, the number of their employees E, and the amount of their cultural and social funds F. Then, a collecting society is characterised by

$$R = P - C - F + e_t\,,$$

where e_t is a parameter that approximates the various sums collected – or distributed – by the CCS and added to – or deducted from – the collected sums during period t: financial revenues from invested non-distributable sums; collected sums during previous periods t–1, t–2... that are effectively distributed during period t; and non-distributable sums from periods t, t–1, t–2, ... This parameter could be of positive or negative sign and its components prove to be very difficult to get from CCS.

The present study focuses on copyright collecting societies that carry out their activities in radically different legal control systems. The data set includes organisations that manage the same kind of rights (musical rights) and benefit from a dominant position relative to the other national collecting societies. Most of the data have been obtained from the 1992-1999 annual yearbooks of the studied CCS and supplemented by official reports (BPLA, 1995, 1997; Sénat Français, 1997) as well as personal inquiries. The study is limited to the three largest European organisations, i.e. PRS, GEMA and SACEM. Indeed, analysing the other important international organisations raises specific problems that prevent any relevant comparison. For instance, the SIAE, which manages copyright in Italy, is a public law organisation and its repertoire covers musical rights as well as audiovisual, literary rights, and the like. As for the American ASCAP and BMI – which administrate more than 90 percent of collectively managed copyrights in the USA – their competition proves to impact positively their results (Sénat Français, 1997).

Two complementary methods: performance criteria and data envelopment analysis

Two methods are used in order to evaluate the performance of CCS. The first one is based on the elaboration and comparison of specific performance criteria and the second is a complementary dynamic evaluation through the data envelopment analysis.

Performance criteria analysis: advantages and limits

Several specific criteria can be built from the aggregates P, R, C, F, E and M. The first one, *OPTIC* (the 'optimisation criterion') assesses the ability of a CCS to maximise its collected sums at the lowest cost. It is given by

$$OPTIC = \frac{P}{C}$$

At first glance, this ratio estimates the performance of a given CCS regarding its collecting activity. It implicitly assumes that the higher the management costs in comparison with collections, the less effective the organisation. Thus, this criterion proves to relate more to cost optimisation than merely to cost minimisation.

Among its main drawbacks, however, figures the fact that the administration expenses C include costs incurred in the collection of rights – i.e., contract concluding, licensed users supervision, etc. – as well as costs relating to their distribution among members such as the determination of effective beneficiaries, right measurement and effective payments. One solution would be to identify these two components of C and therefore, to calculate two criteria: one would apply to the effectiveness of collection and the other would assess distribution activities. However, this task turns out to be extremely difficult for two main reasons: the lack of detailed accounts for all societies and the existence of joint costs. Thus, in the absence of relevant data, the criterion *OPTIC* proves a good approximation of the ability of a CCS to manage its members' rights at the lowest cost.

The growth rates of collections ΔP_t and of distribution ΔR_t allow the variation of collected and distributed sums from one year to another to be measured. For a year t, they are respectively given by

$$\Delta P_t = \frac{P_t}{P_{t-1}} - 1 \text{ and } \Delta R_t = \frac{R_t}{R_{t-1}} - 1$$

These dynamic ratios evaluate the productivity gains due to rationalisation strategies. But both have the same flaw: they depend too heavily upon specific growth of cultural markets where collectively managed copyrights are exchanged. Thus, it turns out to be very difficult to distinguish what is due to the effective efforts of CCS and what is explained by the fluctuations of content markets. A better criterion would incorporate a weighting according to the relative share of each market contributing to the collections made by CCS. Given the tangle of their repertoires, it would not be, however, an easy task to do.

Nevertheless, these two indicators make it possible to build a more interesting ratio, even though it has the same drawbacks as ΔP_t and ΔR_t. As an elasticity, it measures the additional amount of distributions when copyright collection increases by 1 percent. It is given by

$$ELRP_t = \frac{\Delta R_t}{\Delta P_t}$$

Another criterion, *GDRAT*, measures the gross proportion of distributed revenues over a given period in comparison with the effective collected sums. For a given CCS, it is given by

$$GDRAT = \frac{R}{P}$$

It evaluates the effectiveness of the distribution activity of a given CCS, i.e. its ability to distribute the maximum of the collected rights. It is based on the preferences of its members: the greater the proportion of collected sums they get, the greater their satisfaction. This ratio compares the final result (actual distributions) to the initially available sums (the collected sums from users).

But it raises two problems. On the one hand, it implicitly incorporates the dynamic factor e_t which relates to the distributable sums from one period to another. It can therefore be greater than 100 percent, in which case collected sums from previous years are distributed only the year this ratio is calculated. The calculation of an average ratio over the tested period reduces significantly this problem.[15] On the other hand, before being distributed, some proportion of the collected sums is allocated in professional, social and cultural actions (subsidies to festivals, pension funds, etc.). To overcome this difficulty, the net distribution ratio *NDRAT* takes into account these various funds, whether or not they are legally imposed to the CCS. For a given CCS

$$NDRAT = \frac{R+F}{P}$$

Symmetrically, the difference 1–*NDRAT* is the proportion of collected sums that are not allocated to the distribution or to the cultural and social funds. The greater the *NDRAT* ratio is, the more efficient is the CCS regarding its activity of distribution.

The proportion of undistributed copyrights *NONR* compares the distributable sums to the effectively distributed sums for a given year. Its evolution permits to assess the ability of a CCS to distribute the most part of the copyrights it has collected. It is given by

$$NONR = \frac{R_{pot}}{R_{eff}} - 1$$

where R_{pot} is the distributable sums and R_{eff} is the actual distributions. Unfortunately, the amount of R_{eff} is not available in all cases and over the whole period. It would be possible to approximate it through the amount of financial revenues – the invested sums correspond partly to the non-distributed copyrights – but this calculation requires the exact composition of the financial portfolios of the CCS and the respective share of financial interests yielded by the other components of their private assets.

The average productivity per employee *COPE* measures the collected sums per employee. In a similar way, it is possible to elaborate *DIPE*, i.e. the distributions per employee.

$$COPE = \frac{P}{E} \text{ and } DIPE = \frac{P}{E}$$

The higher are these ratios the more productive are the employees. However, it is difficult to infer systematically a greater performance from an increase of these ratios and vice versa. The collected sums could decrease more slowly than the number of employees and that could reveal a decreasing quality of services.

The average cost per employee *ACE* is a counter-performance criterion.

$$ACE = \frac{C}{E}$$

The higher is the cost of an employee, the higher is the *ACE* ratio. Nevertheless, explaining this criterion is problematical when comparing the various CCS. For instance, the impact of any technological change is not similar on every CCS, but it depends upon the structure of their respective repertoire. Moreover, the increase of this ratio could mean a higher quality of their services or the need for lawyers more and more qualified. Because of the heterogeneous competences and needs of CCS, this criterion was not adopted in the comparisons between French CCS (Rochelandet, 2000). By contrast, it proves to be more relevant in the current study based on CCS managing similar repertoires.[16]

The collected sums per member *COPM* and the distributions per member *DIPM* are respectively given by

$$COPM = \frac{P}{M} \text{ and } DIPM = \frac{R}{M}$$

The higher these indicators are, the more efficient is the CCS. They are much more 'profitability-orientated' since they take account of the average member viewpoint. From a dynamic perspective, they allow the improvement of production methods implemented by CCS to be evaluated. But their main limit is that they do not incorporate revenue dispersion. So if a CCS regroups only 'wealthy' – or more exactly 'valuable' – members, it would seem more efficient than a CCS regrouping all the copyright holders of a given repertoire.[17] This drawback raises many problems regarding comparisons between the CCS with many large members and the ones with dispersed membership.

Finally, variation indicators are made from *C*, *COPE* and *COPM* in order to retrace their trend, that is respectively ΔC, $\Delta COPE$ and $\Delta COPM$.

This comparison does not take into account either productivity measures such as capital intensity and R&D expenditure per employee – which appear to be difficult to obtain and somewhat irrelevant – or the traditional profitability ratios – which make no sense in the case of non-profit organisations. Table 10.2 shows the different tested criteria.

Data envelopment analysis: a more dynamic perspective

The basic problems with expressing the economic performance in separate single indicators like the previous method are manifold. First, it is impossible to aggregate and compare a number of non-commensurate performance indicators (for example, collections and membership) to one single performance measure and secondly, to establish a benchmark for comparing the performance of CCS. An alternative is data envelopment analysis (DEA),

Table 10.2 Summary of the performance criteria used in the study

Criteria	Formula	Relevance
OPTIC: management ratio	$OPTIC = \frac{P}{C}$	+++
ΔP_t: annual variation of collected sums	$\Delta P_t = \frac{P_t}{P_{t-1}} - 1$	+
ΔR_t: annual variation of distributable sums	$\Delta R_t = \frac{R_t}{R_{t-1}} - 1$	+
$ELRP_t$: elasticity of distributions compared to collections	$ELRP_t = \frac{\Delta R_t}{\Delta P_t}$	++
ΔC_t: annual variation of administration expenses	$\Delta C_t = \frac{C_t}{C_{t-1}} - 1$	++
GDRAT: gross distribution ratio	$GDRAT = \frac{R}{P}$	++
NDRAT: net distribution ratio	$NDRAT = \frac{R + F}{P}$	+++
COPE: collected sums per employee	$COPE = \frac{P}{E}$	+++
DIPE: distributed sums per employee	$DIPE = \frac{R}{E}$	++
ACE: average cost of an employee	$ACE = \frac{C}{E}$	++
$\Delta COPE_t$: annual variation of COPE	$\Delta COPE_t = \frac{COPE_t}{COPE_{t-1}} - 1$	++
COPM: collected sums per member	$COPM = \frac{P}{M}$	+++
DIPM: distributable sums per member	$DIPM = \frac{R}{M}$	+++
$\Delta COPM_t$: annual variation of COPM	$\Delta COPM_t = \frac{COPM_t}{COPM_{t-1}} - 1$	++
NONR: non-distributed copyrights	$NONR = \frac{R_{pot}}{R_{eff}} - 1$	+++

which is a non-parametric non-stochastic approach that uses a linear programming technique. It defines the best production frontier which serves as a benchmark and minimises the relative distance to this benchmark. The relative performance of any CCS is measured as the relative distance to the productive frontier. The DEA method is a multiple-input/multiple-output optimisation method that generalises the Farrell (1957) technical efficiency measure. Originally developed by Charnes, Cooper and Rhodes (1978) and extended by Banker, Charnes and Cooper (1984) to include variable returns to scale, this non-parametric non-stochastic approach is frequently applied in the field of non-profit organisations such as hospitals and schools.[18]

Applied to collecting societies, the DEA method makes it possible to consider many various cases. This study explores three complementary options according to an output maximisation/input minimisation test and the number of inputs to be considered in the analysis.

According to the first option, collections *P* and costs *C* are considered as inputs and distributions *R* as output. This case focuses only on the distribution activity. The underlying idea is that a CCS combines its collected sums with various factors, evaluated by *C*, to distribute them among its members. What is entering into the organisation is its collected copyright and its administration expenses and what is coming out of the organisation are the copyrights.

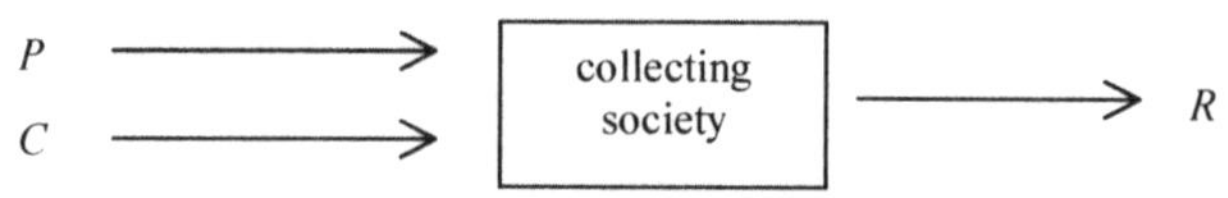

According to the second option, the number of employees *E* and members *M* (as an estimation of the repertoire size of each CCS) are added to inputs. The membership and employment levels are supposed to impact the output. Here, what is analysed is the joint impact of, on the one side, *P* and *C* and on the other side, the essential production factors of collective administration: labour and copyrights.

The third case considers two inputs (*E*, *C*) and two outputs (collected sums per member *COPM* and *R*). It corresponds to a more productivity-orientated test.

In each case, efficiencies are tested under two complementary hypotheses: output maximisation and input minimisation. In each case, variable returns to scale are supposed to prevail and the production frontier is fixed at 100 percent.

Results and recommendations

The average criteria for the 1991-1998 period figure in Table 10.3 (in the appendix) and the results from the DEA method appear in Table 10.4 (in the appendix). As for the DEA results, the figures can be read as follows: for a given year, the more the indicators depart from 100 percent (indicating the production frontier), the less efficient is the CCS relative to the others. For instance, in the first table, '100.00 GEM96' means that by being on the production frontier (100%), the GEMA is more efficient than the SACEM in 1996 ('85.90 SAC96', i.e. 85.9%) and as efficient as the SACEM in 1992 ('100.00 SAC92'). According to both methods, the most efficient organisation is the GEMA, PRS comes second and SACEM is classified third.

Several conclusions can be drawn from these data. Given the fact that the most efficient organisation is the GEMA which carries out its activities in the most binding legal supervision system, a first conclusion is the following:

(C1) The most restrictive legal control gives rise to the lowest rents.

Accordingly, a first general recommendation could be made according to which it is in the interests of members to claim a large reinforcement of institutional controls. However, a second result qualifies such a recommendation. For the same period, the results of the PRS, which runs in the less restrictive legal system, are better than those of the SACEM and, above all, not so far from those of GEMA as Tables 10.3 and 10.4 show. In other words, implementing low supervision (UK) is better than setting up intermediary control (France). Therefore, a second conclusion could be that:

(C2) No general positive correlation can be made between the intensity of legal supervision and the results of CCS.

Should we therefore recommend a large reduction in the intensity of legal control? Indeed, lightening supervision could generate social savings in terms of reduced regulation costs, though the interests of members would be less respected. So, in a social welfare perspective, the gains from a reduction in supervision overcome the social loss of CCS' members due to lower revenues.

However, such a recommendation is difficult to defend. As a matter of fact, the PRS differs from the two other CCS by the greater power of its members. Publishers play a key role in the UK system of copyright. Accordingly, their internal governance proves to be sufficient to compensate a low legal control.

A third conclusion is that:

(C3) Intermediary levels of supervision appear to be imperfect and a source of inefficiencies.

The managers of SACEM are supposed to benefit from monopolistic rents due to an easing of external and internal control relatively to the GEMA and PRS. So two general recommendations can be made:

1. supervision reinforcement should be implemented only for CCS with dispersed membership.
2. correlatively, competition law is supposed to be sufficient to compel CCS with large members to act in the interest of their members.

Further comments

All these conclusions and recommendations are based on the SACEM results relative to the two other CCS. However, these results can be challenged by two facts: on the one hand, a CCS could strategically limit the scope of its repertoire in order to focus on its more valuable rights, i.e. those for which the management costs are significantly lower than the collected fees. For instance, these strategies can consist in only controlling and collecting copyrights from the biggest, easy-to-identify users. Limiting the scope of copyright management in such a manner can certainly imply better performance. In fact, it could also be interpreted as a socially inefficient specialisation to the detriment of copyright law spirit.

On the other hand, by offering its members the most equitable and diversified services, a CCS can incur higher costs of collection and distribution. In my point of view, this idea is essential but it requires a more meticulous study through, for instance, specific audits. It would consist in determining such things as homogeneous classes of members according to their revenues, management costs by specific piece of repertoire, and the number of members who actually perceive copyrights relative to the total membership. By definition, a CCS would be efficient if and only if it collects more copyrights and distributes them 'better' than its members. Of course, it could be costly to allocate equitably, but in this case, evaluating a given CCS would necessitate to include the criterion of quality of service in its objectives. Providing members with more equitable and diversified services can be costly and imply lower performance. In fact, there is a trade-off between costs and quality, especially in the case of collecting societies for which members are both owners and customers.

Beyond a purely productive efficiency analysis, it would thus be necessary to introduce some qualitative factors to compare collecting societies: quality of services to members as well as to users; equity of distributions among members; and correlation between development strategies of CCS and copyright law purposes.

Furthermore, testing this hypothesis would require to take into account the features of each cultural market in which CCS operate. Indeed, for a similar national market, PRS collects much less copyrights than SACEM (its collected sums are about 60 percent of those of PRS for the period 1990–1998). PRS is then likely to be more selective regarding the copyrights it administrates. In this perspective, a significant proof is the greater number of employees of the SACEM. At first glance, this greater number could be perceived as a bureaucratic bias or a strategic objective of managers in order to entrench themselves into their organisation. However, another viewpoint is to consider this greater number as an indicator of the quality of the services the SACEM supplies for its whole membership. A more detailed investigation would therefore be necessary to evaluate the relation between quality and costs in these non-profit organisations.

Finally, the sole criteria of costs minimisation and productivity turn out to be insufficient to evaluate the performance of a given CCS. No definitive conclusion could be made if the quality of provided services – assessed by the collection of *any* copyright and the improvement of their distribution – is not integrated into the analysis. There is a very delicate balance between the purpose of cost minimisation and the provision of valuable services in terms of quality and equity. Nevertheless, the impossibility of comparisons with similar for-profit organisations requires a more detailed investigation of the CCS as non-profit organisations. Thereby, members are not confined to their role of owners, but they are also considered as consumers of the whole production of CCS (Rochelandet, 2000).

4 CONCLUSION

Among the key factors to explain the performance of copyright collecting societies are the concentration of ownership and the intensity of institutional control. First of all, the bargaining power of their members and hence the more or less concentrated structure of ownership are proposed to affect sharply their performances. A previous comparison between French collecting societies suggests that internal governance appears to be the stronger constraint in all cases (Rochelandet, 2001). This explains the better results of societies that represent producers in comparison to performers' societies. By contrast, the impact of legal supervision is much more problematical to determine. Although the current study is still an exploratory paper, with more data to analyse in futures studies, initial results are very encouraging. The measure of the performance of three collecting societies with all the same repertoire in contrasted but complementary legal systems suggests several conclusions. First, the stronger control in Germany explains the best results of the GEMA. On the contrary, the worse results of the SACEM are certainly due to the intermediary level of supervision in France. Compared to the intermediary results of the PRS, this suggests that a strong internal control is sufficient to overcome the potential failure inherent in limited institutional constraints. But in the case of failure of this internal governance mechanism, the strengthening of legal supervision should be recommended.

However, all these results are essentially grounded on productive efficiency. Further investigations are needed to take into account the quality of delivered services and the non-profit nature of CCS. In addition, one must isolate the key institutional factors to determine which one affects the most CCS performance. Moreover, another question is whether ICTs do not challenge these results nowadays. At a first glance, these technologies reinforce the various controls on collecting societies by enabling better information, which benefits their members as well as the authorities. ICTs will enable the CCS to improve their performance by reducing management costs and allowing members to receive their remuneration more rapidly. In addition, they represent a new form of market governance through an extension and a renewal of competition in the field of copyright management (Rochelandet, 2000). Another objective drawn from this research is therefore to study in which way these technologies are adopted by the CCS and to determine their impact on the effectiveness of collective administration of copyright.

APPENDIX

Acronyms and abbreviations

ASCAP: American Society of Composers, Authors and Publishers
BMI: Broadcast Music, Inc.
BPLA: Bureau de la Propriété Littéraire et Artistique [*Copyright division of the French ministry of culture*]
CCS: Copyright Collecting Societies
GEMA: Gesellschaft für musikalische aufführungs-und vervielfatigungsrechte

PRS: Performing Rights Society
SACEM: Société des auteurs, compositeurs et éditeurs de musique
SIAE: Società italiana degli autori ed editori

TABLES

Table 10.3 Average Ratios for the period 1991–1998

M$ and %	relevance	GEMA	SACEM	PRS	most efficient
OPTIC	+++	738%	446%	594%	GEMA
GDRAT	++	86.4%	73.7%	83.5%	GEMA
NDRAT	+++	89.1%	79.9%	83.5%	GEMA
ELRP	++	0.98	0.43	1.28	PRS
ACE	++	0.089	0.084	0.068	PRS
ΔACE	+++	8.7%	3.6%	5.2%	SACEM
ΔC	++	5.9%	4.1%	2.2%	PRS
COPE	+++	0.651	0.374	0.408	GEMA
DIPE	++	0.563	0.277	0.343	GEMA
ΔCOPE	+++	8.6%	3.5%	10.3%	PRS
COPM	+++	0.020	0.008	0.010	GEMA
ΔCOPM	++	-2.2%	0.4%	2.4%	PRS
DIPM	+++	0.017	0.006	0.008	GEMA

Table 10.4 Efficiencies from DEA method (1991-1998 period, variable returns to scale used)

Input minimisation radial model			Output maximisation radial model		
Inputs: P, C / Output : R			Inputs: P, C / Output : R		
85.90	86.13	87.12	78.32	83.36	85.16
SAC96	SAC95	SAC97	SAC91	SAC93	SAC96
87.20	88.27	91.62	85.37	86.44	86.47
SAC98	SAC94	PRS93	SAC95	SAC97	SAC94
92.89	93.03	93.37	86.58	91.15	91.56
PRS92	PRS94	SAC93	SAC98	PRS93	PRS92
94.49	96.27	98.49	92.67	94.24	94.98
PRS96	PRS95	GEM98	PRS94	PRS96	PRS91
98.71	98.73	99.35	96.08	98.48	98.70
GEM93	GEM94	SAC91	PRS95	GEM98	GEM93
99.66	99.74	99.75	98.73	99.66	99.75
GEM92	GEM97	GEM95	GEM94	GEM92	GEM95
99.76	99.98	100.00	99.80	99.98	100.00
PRS91	PRS97	GEM91	GEM97	PRS97	GEM91
100.00	100.00	100.00	100.00	100.00	100.00
GEM96	PRS98	SAC92	GEM96	PRS98	SAC92

(continued overleaf)

Table 10.4 (cont.)

Input minimisation radial model			Output maximisation radial model		
Inputs: P, C, E, M / Output: R			Inputs: P, C, E, M / Output: R		
87.20	88.31	90.32	78.32	83.36	85.16
SAC98	SAC97	SAC96	SAC91	SAC93	SAC96
91.60	93.25	94.14	85.37	86.44	86.47
SAC95	SAC94	PRS92	SAC95	SAC97	SAC94
94.43	94.80	95.93	86.58	91.15	91.56
SAC93	PRS93	PRS94	SAC98	PRS93	PRS92
97.72	98.71	98.73	92.67	94.98	96.08
PRS95	GEM93	GEM94	PRS94	PRS91	PRS95
99.85	100.00	100.00	96.63	98.70	98.73
PRS96	GEM91	GEM92	PRS96	GEM93	GEM94
100.00	100.00	100.00	100.00	100.00	100.00
GEM95	GEM96	GEM97	GEM91	GEM92	GEM95
100.00	100.00	100.00	100.00	100.00	100.00
GEM98	PRS91	PRS97	GEM96	GEM97	GEM98
100.00	100.00	100.00	100.00	100.00	100.00
PRS98	SAC91	SAC92	PRS97	PRS98	SAC92
Inputs: C, E / Outputs: R, COPM			Inputs: C, E / Outputs: R, COPM		
73.50	74.23	76.11	81.19	84.22	84.82
SAC98	SAC97	SAC95	SAC92	SAC97	SAC93
76.45	78.50	79.03	86.91	86.94	87.11
SAC96	SAC94	SAC93	SAC91	SAC95	SAC98
80.26	83.31	86.14	87.19	87.28	87.94
SAC92	PRS92	PRS93	SAC96	SAC94	PRS92
86.16	87.89	88.08	88.53	91.32	93.33
SAC91	PRS94	PRS91	PRS91	PRS93	PRS94
91.60	97.12	97.56	94.81	97.72	97.82
PRS95	PRS96	GEM94	PRS95	GEM93	GEM94
97.68	100.00	100.00	99.17	100.00	100.00
GEM93	GEM91	GEM92	PRS96	GEM91	GEM92
100.00	100.00	100.00	100.00	100.00	100.00
GEM95	GEM96	GEM97	GEM95	GEM96	GEM97
100.00	100.00	100.00	100.00	100.00	100.00
GEM98	PRS97	PRS98	GEM98	PRS97	PRS98

NOTES

1. Helpful suggestions by Didier Lebert (University of Paris 1 Panthéon-Sorbonne) are gratefully acknowledged.
2. Further, their activities extend to copyright claims, litigation, measurement, enforcement, defence of the moral interest of their members and sometimes social and cultural action.
3. And, according to the *contract law paradigm*, copyright law itself must vanish (Dam, 1999).
4. This is particularly true the greater the number of economic partners and the larger the informational asymmetries.

5. For instance, see Hollander (1984).
6. For instance, neighbouring rights are less costly to manage than author's rights. In the same way, collecting copyrights from national radios or through legal devices such as private copying levies is easier to run than collecting copyrights from nightclubs or in country festivals.
7. For example, in France, the initial domination of the SACEM regarding the administration of musical rights in the cafés-concerts has permitted its expansion in musical activities (Rochelandet, 2000). The implementation of non-voluntary licences in the USA – which are frequently adopted in this country – is undoubtedly explained by the political power of consumers and intermediary users' lobbies.
8. I assume that the very reputation of managers turns out to be an insufficient mechanism to solve this problem.
9. See Jensen and Meckling (1976, 1979), Fama and Jensen (1983), Schleifer and Vishny (1986).
10. Some of them – the less rich – prefer to earn something rather than nothing.
11. See Dietz (1978), Hilty (1995) and Sénat Français (1997). Since then, changes have occurred in some countries, for example Belgium.
12. In fact, Katzenberger (1995) emphasises the lack of harmonisation in Europe.
13. For instance, the 'ASCAP consent decree' prohibits the ASCAP to supply users with exclusive licences. However, no particular legal control is applied to the running of the CCS.
14. However, some reforms have recently been adopted in order to strengthen control. But they are not taken into account in the present study because they occurred after the analysed period.
15. Of course, the amount of undistributed sums is a relative indicator of the efficiency of a CCS over a given year. The delays of copyright distributions could be the sign of inefficient information processing and distribution schedule. An interesting fact here is that before announcing their results to their members, some CCS deduct from their administration expenses the financial incomes derived from the investments of undistributed sums. However, the importance of these investments and their incomes does not necessarily result from economies due to efficient rationalisation or from a fine portfolio management.
16. It assumes, however, that the cost of hiring a lawyer is more or less the same from one country to another.
17. It is possible to integrate this dispersion but this kind of data is not homogeneous amongst CCS and therefore does not allow a general comparison.
18. An introduction to the DEA model can be found at http://www.deazone.com/index.htm.

REFERENCES

Banker, R.D., A. Charnes and W.W. Cooper (1984), 'Some Models for the Estimation of Technical and Scale Inefficiencies in Data Envelopment Analysis', *Management Science*, **30**, 1078–1092.

Bureau de la Propriété Littéraire et Artistique (1997), *La Gestion Collective du Droit d'Auteur et des Droits Voisins en 1995 et 1996 par les Sociétés de Perception et de Répartition des Droits*, Paris: Ministère de la Culture.

Bureau de la Propriété Littéraire et Artistique (1995), *La Gestion Collective du Droit d'Auteur et des Droits Voisins*, Paris: Ministère de la Culture.

Charnes A., W.W. Cooper and E. Rhodes (1978), 'Measuring the Efficiency of Decision Making Units', *European Journal of Operational Research*, **2**, 429–444.

Dam, K.W. (1999), 'Self-help in the Digital Jungle', *Journal of Legal Studies*, **28(2)**, 393–412.

Dietz, A. (1978), *Das Urheberrecht in der Europäischen Gemeinschaft*, Baden-Baden.

Fama, E. and M. Jensen (1983), 'Separation of Ownership and Control', *Journal of Law and Economics*, **26**, 301–325.

Farrell, M.J. (1957), 'The Measurement of Productive Efficiency', *Journal of the Royal Statistical Society*, **120(3)**, 253–290.

Gesellschaft für musikalische aufführungs-und vervielfatigungsrechte, *Jahrbuch* (1993-1999), Berlin: Nomos.

Hilty, R.M. (ed.) (1995), *Die Verwertung von Urheberrechten in Europa – La Gestion Collective de Droit d'auteur en Europe*, Bale: Helting & Lichtenhahn, Bruylan, Carl Heymanns Verlag.

Hollander, A. (1984), 'Market Structure and Performance in Intellectual Property. The Case of Copyright Collectives', *International Journal of Industrial Organisation*, **2**, 199–216.

Jensen, M. and W. Meckling (1976), 'Theory of the Firm: Management Behavior, Agency Costs and Ownership Structure', *Journal of Financial Economics*, **3**, 305–360.

Jensen, M. and W. Meckling (1979), 'Rights and Production Functions: An Application to Labor-Managed Firms and Codetermination', *Journal of Business*, **52(4)**, 469–506.

Katzenberger, P. (1995), 'Les Divers Systèmes du Droit de Contrôle de la Gestion Collective des Droits d'Auteur dans les Etats Européens', in R. M. Hilty (dir.), *La Gestion Collective du Droit d'Auteur en Europe*, Bale: Helting & Lichtenhahn Verlag AG, 17–31.

Merger and Monopoly Commission (1996), *Performing Rights: A Report on the Supply in the UK of the Services of Administering Performing Rights and Film Synchronisation Rights*, London: MCC.

Merges, R.P. (1996), 'Contracting into Liability Rules: Intellectual Property Rights and Collective Rights Organisations', *California Law Review*, **84(5)**, 1293–1393.

Performing Rights Society, *Yearbook* (1992-1999), London: PRS Corporate Communications Department.

Rochelandet, F. (2001), 'La Mise en Œuvre Collective des Droits d'Auteur: Une Évaluation", *Réseaux*, **19**, **n°110**, 93–130.

Rochelandet, F. (2000), *Changement Technologique et Propriété Intellectuelle: La Mise en Œuvre du Droit d'Auteur dans les Industries Culturelles*, PhD thesis, University of Paris I.

Société des Auteurs, Compositeurs et Éditeurs de Musique, *Rapport d'Activité* (1992-1999), Paris.

Sénat Français (1997), *La Gestion Collective des Droits d'Auteur et des Droits Voisins*, Service des Affaires Européennes, Novembre.
Shleifer, A. and R. W. Vishny (1986), 'Large Shareholders and Corporate Control', *Journal of Political Economy*, **94(3)**, 461–488.

Part IV
Copyright and Incentives to Artists

Introduction to Part IV

This part of the book purposefully refers to copyright as an incentive to 'artists' rather than to 'authors' to highlight the fact that one of the main purposes of this law is to stimulate artistic activity. Copyright law, or authors' rights in the civil law tradition, applies to a range of 'authors' – composers, choreographers, film directors, literary authors of all kinds (novelists, poets, journalists and the rest), visual artists and sculptors and so on as authors. However, copyright law also includes rights related to copyright or neighbouring rights for performers as well as for broadcasters, phonogram makers and other 'publishers' in the creative or cultural industries. The two articles reprinted here emphasise the latter aspect of copyright law: the Towse article (**IV, 12**) is a survey of the economic literature on aspects of copyright that are often ignored – moral rights, *droit de suite* or artists' resale rights and performers' rights; and Gayer and Shy (**IV, 11**) provide a formal model of the differential incentives copyright and its enforcement have for artists and publisher (the archetype being a musical performer and a record label).

The 'mainstream' literature in the economics of copyright has mostly considered copyright in a generic sense and there has been little concern with the details of the bundle of different rights that constitute copyright, such as publication and distribution rights, all of which, however, have different values to the parties concerned. Moreover, though Plant (1934) long ago pointed out the differing interests of author and publisher, the literature implicitly (and sometimes explicitly) assumes that author and publisher share a common interest (though this has been questioned by Towse (1999, 2003) in the case of performers). In the article by Gayer and Shy they present a model in which it is assumed that performer and record label have different interests and they formalise this with reference to the issue of enforcing copyright: given that performers, unlike record companies, have the option of performing in concerts as well as making recordings, they have an interest in maximising their exposure even if this happens through illegal downloads of their recordings. Using a network externalities model of the type introduced by Takeyama (1994), Gayer and Shy reach the conclusion that the performer may well not benefit from the strict enforcement of copyright anyway, not to the extent that the record label does. They point out that their model is a static one and that the dynamic effects should also be taken into account (and the same could be said of Watt and Towse (2006) who attempt to model the choice of time allocation between royalty-earning recording activity and the 'spot' fee earning activity in live performance that an artist makes).

The 'mainstream' literature in economics of copyright has also ignored other aspects of copyright law; however, it can be seen from the Towse survey (**IV, 12**) that there is a substantial and varied body of work on the economic analysis of features of copyright that are important to artists rather than to commercial copyright owners. Moral rights – the rights of attribution, integrity, disclosure and withdrawal – that protect artists from misuse of their work are usually contrasted to economic rights that protect their financial incentive, though to many artists, moral rights are important as an incentive. Moral rights fit more comfortably with the authors' rights tradition from which they arose more than with copyright and that may explain why they have received little attention. It is worth noting in passing that in the USA, the Visual Artists' Rights Act (VARA) was passed in 1990 as a separate law according rights to artists during their lifetimes, unlike moral rights in authors' rights law that have the same term as economic rights – see Landes and Levine (2006). *Droit de suite* or artists' resale rights are designed to obtain for visual artists a share of the profits made by owners of their work when they are sold on (usually at auction); almost all economists think they defeat the purpose of offering an incentive to create works of art and harm the market for the first sale. Finally, the economic analysis of performers' rights has received very little attention at all in the literature, as the Towse survey shows.

Together, therefore, the two articles in Part IV offer a perspective on different aspects of copyright from the standard literature and these articles take the discussion of copyright into its economic effects on artists' labour markets.

References

Landes, W. and D. Levine (2006), 'The Economic Analysis of Art Law', in Victor Ginsburgh and David Throsby, *Handbook of the Economics of the Arts and Culture*, Amsterdam: North Holland Elsevier, pp. 232–50.

Plant, A. (1934), 'The Economic Aspects of Copyright in Books', *Economica*, **1**, 167–95.

Takeyama, Lisa (1994), 'The Welfare Implications of Unauthorised Reproduction of Intellectual Property in the Presence of Network Effects', *Journal of Industrial Economics*, **62**, 155–66.

Towse, R. (1999), 'Copyright, Incentives and Performers' Earnings', *KYKLOS*, **52** (3), 369–90.

Towse, R. (2003), 'Copyright Policy, Cultural Policy and Support for Artists', in R. Watt and W. Gordon (eds), *The Economics of Copyright Developments in Research and Analysis*, Cheltenham, UK and Northampton, MA, USA: Edward Elgar, pp. 63–74.

Watt, R. and R. Towse (2006), 'Copyright Protection Standards and Authors' Time Allocation', *Industrial and Corporate Change*, published online 31 October 2006.

[11]

Available online at www.sciencedirect.com
ScienceDirect

ELSEVIER

Information Economics and Policy 18 (2006) 374–384

INFORMATION ECONOMICS AND POLICY

www.elsevier.com/locate/iep

Publishers, artists, and copyright enforcement

Amit Gayer [a], Oz Shy [a,b,*]

[a] *Department of Economics, University of Haifa, Haifa 31905, Israel*
[b] *WZB – Social Science Research Center Berlin, Reichpietschufer 50, D-10785 Berlin, Germany*

Received 27 January 2005; received in revised form 13 March 2006; accepted 16 March 2006
Available online 2 May 2006

Abstract

This paper investigates whether and to what extent there is a conflict of interest between artists and their publishers, regarding to whether and to what degree illegal distributions of their copyrighted recordings should be prevented. This conflict arises because artists also earn their profit from other market activities such as giving live performances, in addition to their share of profits from sales of their copyrighted recordings via the publishers.

JEL classification: L82; K42

Keywords: Piracy; Copyright enforcement; Artists; Publishers; Music industry

1. Introduction

The massive number of highly publicized law suits in the past two years initiated by the Recording Industry Association of America (RIAA) against individuals who downloaded music files via the Internet, and the recent declaration by the Motion Picture Association of America (MPAA) to follow the RIAA massive law suits, raise the question who really benefits and who loses from these litigations. An interesting clue to answer this question, hinting that these law suits may damage artists, comes from a recent survey by the Pew

* Corresponding author.
E-mail addresses: amit_gayer@yahoo.com (A. Gayer), ozshyMail@gmail.com (O. Shy).

0167-6245/$ - see front matter © 2006 Published by Elsevier B.V.
doi:10.1016/j.infoecopol.2006.03.003

Internet & American Life Project[1] that finds that 43% of paid artists agree that, "file-sharing services are not really bad for artists, since they help to promote and distribute an artist's work to a broad audience". The same survey also found that 37% of all artists and 35% of paid Artists say that file sharing of music and movies should be legal. The purpose of this paper is to investigate whether artists gain or lose from music file sharing and compare it with their publishers' incentives to reduce or eliminate file sharing activities over the Internet.

The economics literature has already characterized situations under which sellers of copyrighted material benefit from some infringement on their intellectual property. In theoretical papers, Conner and Rumelt (1991), Shy and Thisse (1999), and Peitz (2004) demonstrated that strong network externalities imply that a firm's earnings need not be reduced as a result of piracy as long as the demand for legal copies is enhanced with the actual distribution of illegal copies. Other theoretical contributions include Takeyama (1994, 1997), Slive and Bernhardt (1998), Gayer and Shy (2003), and a critical review by Peitz and Waelbroeck (2003). Peitz and Waelbroeck (in press) demonstrate an environment where publishers can enhance their profit by allowing free downloading of digital products, because sampling enhances willingness to pay when it informs the consumers on which product corresponds to their most preferred one. There is also an empirical investigation by Givon et al. (1995) which estimates how the degree in which an increase in illegal usage of software boosts the demand for buying legal copies. Finally, Rob and Waldfogel (2004) and Oberholzer-Gee and Strumpf (2004) empirically demonstrate that a free download does not imply a lost sale.

Caves (2003) analyzes the contractual arrangements in the music industry in terms of the efficient division of risk, incentives, and rewards. Krueger (2005) presents data showing that from 1996 to 2003, concert ticket prices grew much faster than inflation while ticket sales and the number of concerts by star performers have declined. He then provides several theoretical explanations. One explanation attributes this observation to the erosion of complementarities between concerts and album sales because of file sharing and CD copying, and the [somewhat disputed, as he remarks] decline in CD sales due to file sharing.

In all of the above theoretical literature, sellers and copyright owners were *modeled as a single entity*. Whereas this assumption may be appropriate for the software industry, it does not capture the music industry where artists and publishers are different agents. More interestingly, artists and publishers may benefit differently from the network effects generated by the number of those who buy legal copies and those who obtain illegal recordings.

This short paper fills in this gap by explicitly modeling how network effects affect artists and publishers separately. We identify the conditions under which artists and publishers have different incentives regarding to whether to pursue an enforcement of their copyrighted recordings, or whether to allow for piracy. This is captured by assuming that artists earn profit not only from their share in the publishers' profit from sales of recorded media, but also from other market activities such as selling tickets for live performances, getting hired to perform on television and on radio advertising, and even selling ringtones for mobile phones. Now, if the demand for, say, live performances is enhanced by the "popularity" of the artists generated from the number of distributed recordings (legal

[1] See, http://www.pewinternet.org/press_release.asp?r=94, or a New York Times article entitled "Pew File-Sharing Survey Gives a Voice to Artists" by Tom Zeller dated December 6, 2004.

and illegal copies combined), then we obtain the conditions under which publishers of recorded media may lose from piracy, whereas artists may gain from piracy.[2]

Section 2 develops a simple model of an artist and her publisher. Section 3 solves for the equilibrium distribution of legal and illegal recordings and prices when piracy prevails. Section 4 solves for the equilibrium when copyrights are enforced so that piracy is eliminated. Section 5 compares artist's profit and the publisher's profit under piracy to a regime when piracy is prevented. Section 6 discusses our results.

2. A model of musicians and publishers

Consider a market for certain musical recordings marketed on various magnetic and optical media. The products that we have in mind include music performances marketed on compact discs, video cassettes and DVDs showing live performances, all of which consumers can buy and repeatedly play at home. The unit production cost of each unit sold in store, borne by the publisher, is denoted by $c > 0$.

To demonstrate our thesis, we focus on a single musician artist who also sells other services such as live performances in addition to selling her recorded music.

2.1. Consumers: The demand for recorded media

Consumers who wish to obtain these recording have three options: They can buy the recorded medium at a store for the price of p_r. Alternatively, they can make an illegal copy without having to pay for it. Finally, they can choose not to obtain any copy (nonusers in what follows).

Whether or not consumers hold legal or illegal copies, the consumers (users in what follows) benefit from network externalities stemming from the popularity of the artist's recording. More precisely, let N denote the total number of users (legal and illegal combined). Then, each user's utility is enhanced by γN, where $\gamma > 0$ measures the marginal benefit from the network size, N. In other words, consumers gain when more people play the recorded medium due to the common social and other "fashion" popularity effects.

Suppose that all potential users are indexed on the nonnegative real line by $x \in [0, +\infty)$ according to a declining preference for obtaining this recording. The utility function of a consumer indexed by x is given by[3]

$$U_x \stackrel{\text{def}}{=} \begin{cases} \alpha(1-x) + \gamma N - p_r & \text{if buys a legal recording,} \\ \beta(1-x) + \gamma N & \text{if uses a pirated recording,} \\ 0 & \text{does not use this recording.} \end{cases} \tag{1}$$

Observe that for users indexed by $x > 1$, the first part of the utility function (1) is negative reflecting a situation that consumers may be dissatisfied from having to find and to obtain the product, but are still better off obtaining it one way or another to "enjoy" the

[2] We shall be using the example of "live performances" to mean any income generating activity to artists in addition to artists' share in publishers' profits or royalties from the sales of recorded media.

[3] Treating all music records as being subjected to the same bandwagon effect is clearly a limitation of the present model. One possible extension would be to separate the network effects into those generated by pirated copies, $\gamma_{NL}N_{NL}$, and those generated by legal copies, $\gamma_L N_L$, where N_{NL} and N_L are the number of illegal and legal users, respectively.

popularity of this recording. We now make the following assumption regarding the preferences described by (1).

Assumption 1.

(a) Legally- and illegally-obtained recordings are vertically differentiated. Formally, $\alpha > \beta > \gamma > 0$.
(b) The publisher's cost of producing a copy sold to consumers is lower than consumers' additional utility gain associated with buying a legal copy instead of obtaining a pirated copy. Formally, $c < \alpha - \beta$.

Assumption 1(b) is naturally needed as otherwise there cannot be any private or social incentives to justify the production and sale of legal copies. To see why Assumption 1(a) implies vertical differentiation, note that when $p_r = 0$, $\alpha > \beta$ implies that any consumer x would prefer the legal copy over a pirated recording. The intuition behind this assumption is that legal copies are generally both easier to obtain and easier to use. In addition, legal copies could be bundled with some extra features such as lyrics, pictures, and manuals, that cannot be easily copied. The extra benefits from buying a legal copy also include discounts on similar products, and avoiding a punishment and the embarrassment associated with being caught using an illegal copy. Finally, the above restriction on γ to be bounded below the basic utility parameters α and β is always needed in network models to avoid having the number of users approaching $N = \infty$.

2.2. Consumers: The demand for live performances

We assume that consumers' demand for live performances is heavily influenced by the magnitude of distributed recordings, as measured by the combined number of legal and illegal users, N. Denote by p_p the ticket price of a live performance, and by q_p the demand for tickets. We assume that the demand for live performances is linear and takes the form of[4]

$$q_p \stackrel{\text{def}}{=} \max\{\delta N - p_p, 0\}, \tag{2}$$

where the parameter $\delta > 0$ measures the intensity in which the legally- and illegally-distributed recordings affect the popularity of the artist and hence the demand for her live performances. The demand for live performances specification (2) rests on our assumption that live performances and recorded music are complements, due to reputation and advertising effects. Clearly, our argument falls apart if consumers view recorded media as perfect substitutes to live performances. However, the very fact that sales of CDs and DVDs are commonly observed during live performances implies recorded media and live performances are complements for some consumers. In fact, most modern operas and concert halls have stores selling CDs and DVDs of the performing artists and orchestras during the intermissions.

[4] Note that for the sake of simplicity we choose a demand which is linear with respect to the network size. However, one should not rule out some alternative specifications, such as $q_p = \delta N^{\lambda} - p_p$, for $0 < \lambda \leqslant 1$, reflecting diminishing (or constant) network size effects on the part of consumers. This demand specification is analyzed in Appendix A.

Suppose that the artist acts as a monopoly when selling tickets for live performances and bears no production costs. Then, given N, the artist chooses a performance price p_p to maximize $\pi_p = p_p q_p = p_p(\delta N - p_p)$ yielding the price and the profit generated from performances given by

$$p_p = \frac{\delta N}{2} \quad \text{and} \quad \pi_p = (p_p)^2 = \frac{\delta^2 N^2}{4}. \tag{3}$$

Therefore, an increase in the number of distributed recordings, N, increases linearly the ticket price of a live performance, and increases quadratically the artist's profit from performances.

3. Equilibrium sales with piracy

If piracy prevails, the number of users N (the network size) clearly exceeds the number of buyers which we denote by $\hat{x}$. Therefore, these two endogenously-determined variables must be distinguished when used for evaluating utility levels. First note that the second and third rows in (1) imply the utility of a consumer who is indifferent between making an illegal copy and becoming a nonuser is affected only by the total number of users N. Therefore, the number of users is equal to this consumer's indexed variable, so substituting $x = N$ into the second line of (1) implies that the total number of users is uniquely determined by $\beta(1 - N) + \gamma N = 0$. Hence, $N = \beta/(\beta - \gamma)$.

We now turn to buyers. The consumer who is indifferent between buying and making an illegal copy, indexed by $\hat{x}$, is determined by $\alpha(1 - \hat{x}) + \gamma N - p_r = \beta(1 - \hat{x}) + \gamma N$. Substituting for N from the above expression we have it that

$$N = \frac{\beta}{\beta - \gamma} \text{ implies that } \hat{x} = \frac{\alpha - \beta - p_r}{\alpha - \beta}. \tag{4}$$

The top part of Fig. 1 illustrates how consumers are divided among buyers, illegal users, and nonusers, when piracy prevails.

Suppose that the agreement between the publisher and the artist is that the artist is entitled to a share of s $(0 < s < 1)$ of the profit generated from the sales of the recorded medium. Denoting the total profit made from the sales of the recorded medium by π_r, under this agreement $s\pi_r$ is given to the artist, and $(1 - s)\pi_r$ is left for the publisher. Recall that each recorded medium sold in stores costs c to produce. Then, the recording firm (publisher) sets the price of the recorded medium p_r to solve

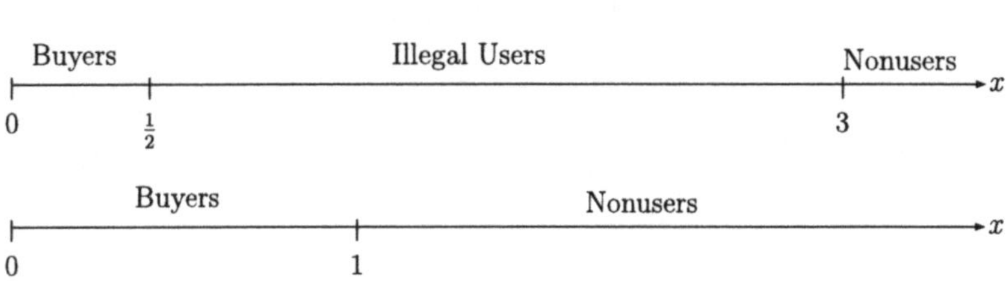

Fig. 1. Top: Consumer allocation in the presence of piracy. Bottom: Consumer allocation in the absence of piracy. *Note.* Exact numbers should be ignored at this stage since they correspond to a numerical example given in Table 1 below.

$$\max_{p_r}(1-s)\pi_r \stackrel{\text{def}}{=} (1-s)(p_r-c)\hat{x} = (1-s)(p_r-c)\frac{\alpha-\beta-p_r}{\alpha-\beta}, \tag{5}$$

yielding a price, sales of legal copies, and total profit given by

$$p_r = \frac{\alpha-\beta+c}{2}, \quad \hat{x} = \frac{\alpha-\beta-c}{2(\alpha-\beta)}, \quad \text{and} \quad \pi_r = \frac{(\alpha-\beta-c)^2}{4(\alpha-\beta)}. \tag{6}$$

Clearly, in view of the utility function (1), an increase in the difference $\alpha-\beta$ enhances the recording publisher's monopoly power. That is, (6) shows that both the price of a legal recording and the associated profit level rise with an increase in this difference, which is interpreted as the degree of vertical differentiation between legal and illegal copies.

We now turn to the artist whose recordings are sold by the recording publisher. The artist earns profit from two sources: First, from selling tickets for her live performances, as summarized by (3). Second, she earns royalties from the publisher's sales of the recorded medium. Recall that s $(0 < s < 1)$ denotes the artist's share (royalties) from the profit generated from the sales of the recorded medium, given in (6). Substituting the network size N from (4) into (3), the artist's profit is given by

$$\pi_a = \pi_p + s\pi_r = \frac{\beta^2\delta^2}{4(\beta-\gamma)^2} + s\frac{(\alpha-\beta-c)^2}{4(\alpha-\beta)}. \tag{7}$$

The artist's total profit (7) stems from our assumption that the artist's share in profit from sales of recorded media is proportional to π_r, thus assuming away fixed sums of money which are sometimes transferred from publishers to artists. The reason for this omission follows from the observation that often these fixed sums are used as advances against future royalties.[5]

4. Equilibrium when there is no piracy

Suppose that the publisher is able to completely eliminate piracy of the recorded medium. In this case, all users are legal buyers, as illustrated on the bottom part of Fig. 1. That is, when piracy becomes infeasible, the number of users equals the number of buyers, N. In this case, the utility function (1) implies that N is determined by

$$\alpha(1-N) + \gamma N - p_r = 0, \text{ hence } N = \frac{\alpha-p_r}{\alpha-\gamma}. \tag{8}$$

The publisher then chooses a price p_r to solve

$$\max_{p_r}(1-s)\pi_r = (1-s)(p_r-c)N = (1-s)(p_r-c)\frac{\alpha-p_r}{\alpha-\gamma} \tag{9}$$

yielding

$$p_r = \frac{\alpha+c}{2}, \quad N = \frac{\alpha-c}{2(\alpha-\gamma)}, \quad \text{and} \quad \pi_r = \frac{(\alpha-c)^2}{4(\alpha-\gamma)}. \tag{10}$$

[5] Quoting from Caves (2003, p. 79), "The label advances the musician a sum to cover the cost of recording... If one record's royalties fail to cover its advance, the shortfall becomes a charge against records issued subsequently."

Finally, substituting the network size N from (10) into (3), the artist's profit when there is no piracy is given by

$$\pi_a = \pi_p + s\pi_r = \frac{\delta^2(\alpha - c)^2}{16(\alpha - \gamma)^2} + s\frac{(\alpha - c)^2}{4(\alpha - \gamma)}. \tag{11}$$

5. Who gains and who loses from copyright enforcement?

We now turn to our main investigation which is finding the conditions under which the artist and the publisher will have conflicting incentives whether to enforce copyright protection for the purpose of preventing piracy.

5.1. The recording publisher

Comparing the publisher's profit under no-piracy (full copyright enforcement) given in (10), to the profit level when piracy prevails (6), implies that enforcement is profitable to the publisher if and only if

$$(1 - s)\frac{(\alpha - c)^2}{4(\alpha - \gamma)} \geqslant (1 - s)\frac{(\alpha - \beta - c)^2}{4(\alpha - \beta)}. \tag{12}$$

It is important to note that if condition (12) is reversed, piracy enhances the publisher's profit for the same reason as in Conner and Rumelt (1991) and Givon et al. (1995) since piracy enhances the value of the recording via network effects thereby enhancing the demand for legal recordings. Finally, notice that condition (12) must hold when $c = 0$, that is, when recordable media are costless to produce.

5.2. The artist

Turning now to the artist, comparing (11) with (7) implies that piracy enforcement is profitable to the artist if and only if

$$\frac{\delta^2(\alpha - c)^2}{16(\alpha - \gamma)^2} + s\frac{(\alpha - c)^2}{4(\alpha - \gamma)} \geqslant \frac{\beta^2\delta^2}{4(\beta - \gamma)^2} + s\frac{(\alpha - \beta - c)^2}{4(\alpha - \beta)}. \tag{13}$$

We are now ready to state our main result, which is proved in Appendix B.

Result 1. Copyright protection is profitable to the artist as long as the number of distributed recordings does not have a significant impact on the demand for live performances [δ, first used in (2), is small], and/or when the artist's share in profit s is sufficiently large. Formally, this happens if

$$s \geqslant \phi\delta^2, \tag{14}$$

where ϕ satisfies

$$\phi \stackrel{\text{def}}{=} \frac{(\alpha - \beta)[c(c - 2\alpha)(\beta - \gamma)^2 - \alpha^2(3\beta^2 + 2\beta\gamma - \gamma^2) + 8\alpha\beta^2\gamma - 4\beta^2\gamma^2]}{4(\alpha - \gamma)(\beta - \gamma)^2\{c^2(\beta - \gamma) + 2c\gamma(\alpha - \beta) + (\beta - \alpha)[\alpha(\beta + \gamma) - \beta\gamma]\}}.$$

In contrast, if the network spill-over effect from the recorded medium market onto the market for live performances, measured by the parameter δ, is significant, then the artist should "utilize" the legal and illegal distribution of the recorded medium in order to enhance the sales and profits from live performances. In this case, the artist benefits from piracy.

Fig. 2 illustrates condition (14) in the $\langle s, \delta \rangle$ space. Fig. 2 is drawn under the assumption that piracy is not profitable to the publisher, that is condition (12) applies. Therefore, the figure shows that high values of the artist's profit share parameter "s" make the artist better off if piracy is prevented. However, larger values of δ would increase the artist's profit from live performances and this profit is higher when piracy prevails in the market for the recorded medium. Thus, Fig. 2 demonstrates that the artists face a tradeoff between higher spill-over network effects and a higher share in the profit from selling the recorded medium.

The implications of Result 1 are summarized as follows.

Result 2. Suppose that the publisher earns a higher profit when copyrights are enforced and piracy is prevented, that is (12) holds. Then, if $s < \phi\delta^2$ the artist and the publisher have conflicting interests in pursuing enforcement of the recorded copyrighted material.

5.3. Numerical examples

Fig. 1 displays the equilibrium allocation under piracy and when piracy is prevented for parameter values given by $c = 0$, $\alpha = 400$, $\beta = 300$, and $\gamma = 200$. In this case, (12) implies that the publisher will prevent piracy. However, (14) implies that the artist is better off under piracy as long as $s < (2/175)\delta^2$.

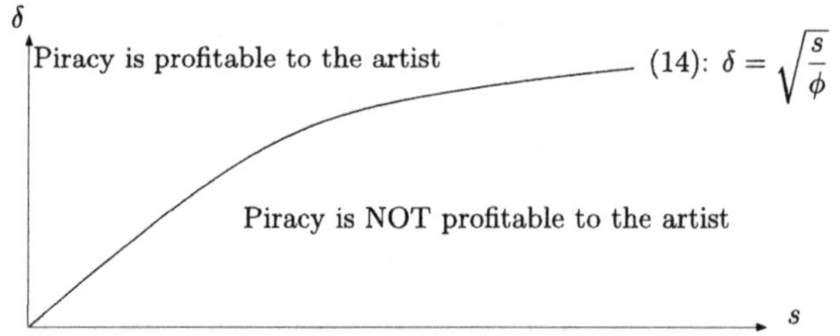

Fig. 2. Artist's profit from copyright enforcement: spill-over network effect versus artist's share in publisher's profit.

Table 1
Profits under piracy and no piracy

	Piracy prevails		Piracy prevented
Publisher's profit	$25(1-s)$	<	$200(1-s)$
Artist's profit from performances	$\frac{9\delta^2}{4}$	>	$\frac{\delta^2}{4}$
Artist's total profit	$25s + \frac{9\delta^2}{4}$	Depends	$200s + \frac{\delta^2}{4}$
$\hat{x}$ = Buyers (legal copies)	$\frac{1}{2}$	<	1
N = Users (legally and illegally)	3	>	1

For the sake of completeness, the various profit levels for this numerical example are given in Table 1 which is further discussed in the concluding section below. Some values are also drawn in Fig. 1.

6. Discussions and concluding comments

Table 1 demonstrates that even when the publisher's profit is lower when piracy prevails, the profit generated from live performances is higher when piracy prevails, compared with an equilibrium when piracy is eliminated. The reason for this is that illegal copies directly compete with the monopoly publisher, thereby forcing the publisher to reduce prices. The elimination of piracy enables the publisher to exercise full monopoly power.

As for the artist, the demand for live performances is substantially reduced when piracy is prevented since, as shown in Table 1, the number of users falls from $N = 3$ to $N = 1$. That is, the elimination of piracy increases the number of legal buyers to $\hat{x} = 1$, but also eliminates all illegal users. Thus, the total network size shrinks to one-third of the network size when piracy is eliminated. This reduction makes the artist significantly less popular thereby reducing the demand for the artist's live performances.

The present model is static. However, if we look at some dynamic considerations which are not addressed in the present model, it becomes clear that many artists may want to have as many records as possible listened to, even if pirated, because of prestige, status seeking, and for the sake of enhancing future reputation. To capture this effect, one can define artists' utility as a function of the extra utility generated from having N recordings listened to by N users, in addition to the combined profits earned from artists' share of profits from selling recorded media and the profit from live performances, given by (7) and (11).

We do not explicitly discuss or analyze policy issues in this short paper. We merely want to point out that massive anti-piracy campaigns, and the large number of ongoing and pending law suits that we now observe in many countries, may eventually hurt artists and authors. Clearly, these massive campaigns are heavily pushed by the private legal sector. Thus, this short paper highlights the fact that the recent wave of litigations against individuals who illegally use copyrighted material may not be to the best interest of the artists whose recordings are being pirated. Alternatively, artists should reconsider whether to surrender their copyrights to publishers when signing a recording contract. In view of the present model, artists may be better off by signing an exclusive recording contract with one publisher while not surrendering their copyrights. Under this arrangement, the artists themselves will make the decision whether and to what extend enforcement of their intellectual property should be pursued.

Acknowledgements

We thank three anonymous referees for most valuable comments on an earlier draft.

Appendix A. Demand for performances: An extension

We now show that our results continue to hold for a more general class of demand functions for live performances. Formally, we now replace the demand for live performances (2) with $q_p = \delta N^{\lambda} - p_p$, for $0 < \lambda \leqslant 1$, which exhibits positive and can also capture diminishing marginal benefit from users' network size. Maximizing profit from live performances yields the equivalent of (3) given by

$$p_p = \frac{\delta N^{\lambda}}{2} \quad \text{and} \quad \pi_p = \frac{\delta^2 N^{2\lambda}}{4}, \text{ hence } \pi_p = \frac{\delta^2}{4}\left(\frac{\beta}{\beta-\gamma}\right)^{2\lambda}, \tag{15}$$

where the value of the network size N when piracy prevails is substituted from (4). Hence, the artist's total profit, that is the equivalent of (7), is now given by

$$\pi_a = \pi_p + s\pi_r = \frac{\delta^2}{4}\left(\frac{\beta}{\beta-\gamma}\right)^{2\lambda} + s\frac{(\alpha-\beta-c)^2}{4(\alpha-\beta)}. \tag{16}$$

We now proceed to analyzing the no-piracy case. Substituting N from (10) into the middle term in (15) yields the profit from live performances. Adding this profit to the artist's share in profit from record sales also given in (10) yields the artist's profit when there is not piracy. Thus, the equivalent of (11) is given by

$$\pi_a = \pi_p + s\pi_r = 2^{-2(1+\lambda)}\delta^2\left(\frac{\alpha-c}{\alpha-\gamma}\right)^{2\lambda} + s\frac{(\alpha-c)^2}{4(\alpha-\gamma)}. \tag{17}$$

Comparing the artist's total profit under piracy (16) to the profit when piracy is eliminated (17) yields the equivalent of (14) where

$$\phi = \frac{2^{-2\lambda}\delta^2(\alpha-\beta)(\alpha-\gamma)\left[\left(\frac{\alpha-c}{\alpha-\gamma}\right)^{2\lambda} - \left(\frac{2\beta}{\beta-\gamma}\right)^{2\lambda}\right]}{c^2(\beta-\gamma)+2c\gamma(\alpha-\beta)+(\beta-\alpha)[\alpha(\beta+\gamma)-\beta\gamma]}. \tag{18}$$

Observe that (18) is identical to (14) for the special case where $\lambda = 1$ (linear demand for live performances).

In order to confirm the validity of the extended condition (18), we utilize the same numerical example as in Section 5.3. The profit of the publisher is unaffected by the change in the demand for live performances and therefore maintains the same level as in the first row of Table 1. However, the total profit made by the artist is affected by this change since artists make profit from live performances. Setting, for example, $\lambda = 0.5$, the artists total profit when piracy prevails, and when eliminated, that is the equivalent of the third row in Table 1, are now given by

$$\pi_a^{\text{piracy}} = 25\text{ s} + \frac{3\delta^2}{4} \text{ and } \pi_a^{\text{no}} = 200\text{ s} + \frac{\delta^2}{4}. \tag{19}$$

Therefore, the artist earns a higher profit under piracy compared with no piracy, that is $\pi_a^{\text{piracy}} > \pi_a^{\text{no}}$, if her share in the profit from record sales is sufficiently small, formally if $s < \delta^2/350$.

Appendix B

Proof of Result 1. The parameter ratio listed in (14) follows directly from (13) as long as the sum of the coefficients of "s" in (13) is positive (meaning that we do not divide by a negative number when solving for s). Straightforward computations reveal that the sum of these coefficients is positive if

$$\frac{(\alpha - \gamma)\{c^2(\beta - \gamma) + 2c\gamma(\alpha - \beta) + (\beta - \alpha)[\alpha(\beta + \gamma) - \beta\gamma]\}}{\alpha - \beta} < 0. \tag{20}$$

To prove that (20) holds for all values of c satisfying Assumption 1, we first substitute $c = 0$ into the LHS(20) to obtain $(\gamma - \alpha)[\alpha(\beta + \gamma) - \beta\gamma]$ which is negative. Next we substitute $c = \alpha - \beta$ (the largest permissible value under Assumption 1) again into the LHS(20) we obtain $\beta^2(\gamma - \alpha)$ which is also negative. Finally, we differentiate LHS(20) with respect to c to obtain $(\alpha - \beta)\mathrm{d}\mathrm{LHS}(20)/\mathrm{d}c = 2(\alpha - \gamma)[c(\beta - \gamma) + \gamma(\alpha - \beta)] > 0$ for $c \geqslant 0$. Hence, LHS(20) does not flip signs when c varies on the interval defined by Assumption 1. □

References

Caves, R., 2003. Contracts between art and commerce. Journal of Economic Perspectives 17, 73–83.

Conner, K., Rumelt, R., 1991. Software piracy: an analysis of protection strategies. Management Science 37, 125–139.

Gayer, A., Shy, O., 2003. Copyright protection and hardware taxation. Information Economics & Policy 15, 467–483.

Givon, M., Mahajan, V., Muller, E., 1995. Software piracy: estimation of lost sales and the impact on software diffusion. Journal of Marketing 59, 29–37.

Krueger, A., 2005. The economics of real superstars: the market for rock concerts in the material world. Journal of Labor Economics 23, 1–30.

Oberholzer-Gee, F., Strumpf, K., 2004. The Effect of File Sharing on Record Sales: An Empirical Analysis. Harvard Business School.

Peitz, M., 2004. A strategic approach to software protection: comment. Journal of Economics & Management Strategy 13, 371–374.

Peitz, M., Waelbroeck, P., 2003. Piracy of Digital Products: A Critical Review of the Economics Literature. CESifo Working Paper #1071. Electronic document available at: <www.ssrn.com>.

Peitz, M., Waelbroeck, P., in press. Why the music industry may gain from free downloading – the role of sampling. International Journal of Industrial Organization.

Rob, R., Waldfogel, J., 2004. Piracy on the High C's: Music Downloading, Sales Displacement, and Social Welfare in a Sample of College Students. NBER Working Paper No. W10874.

Shy, O., Thisse, J., 1999. A strategic approach to software protection. Journal of Economics & Management Strategy 8, 163–190.

Slive, J., Bernhardt, D., 1998. Pirated for profit. Canadian Journal of Economics 31, 886–899.

Takeyama, L., 1994. The welfare implications of unauthorized reproduction of intellectual property in the presence of network externalities. Journal of Industrial Economics 62, 155–166.

Takeyama, L., 1997. The intertemporal consequences of unauthorized reproduction of intellectual property. Journal of Law and Economics 40, 511–522.

[12]

COPYRIGHT AND ARTISTS: A VIEW FROM CULTURAL ECONOMICS

Ruth Towse

Erasmus University Rotterdam

Abstract. Most of the standard economic literature on copyright ignores a number of aspects that have considerable significance for cultural production and for artists, the primary creators of copyright works, the supply of which copyright is supposed to stimulate. Specifically, there is little mention in that literature of moral rights, no distinction is made between copyright for authors and neighbouring rights for performers, the distributional effects of copyright are barely referred to, and the question of how much artists earn from copyright is ignored. In this article, I survey work that relates copyright and cultural economics showing that cultural economics offers another view to the 'standard' economics of copyright. Moreover, the case for government intervention in the arts and heritage made by cultural economists has resonance for the economic rationale of copyright.

Keywords. Artists' labour markets; Cultural economics; Economic and moral rights; Economics of copyright

1. Introduction

In this paper, I survey work that relates copyright and cultural economics and I shall show that cultural economics offers another view to the 'standard' economics of copyright. The literature is not large but it throws an interesting light on the economic role of copyright in relation to artists (using that term in a broad way to mean creators and performers in all the various art forms).

Cultural economics[1] is the application of economics to the arts, heritage and the cultural industries and one of the subjects that it deals with is the supply of works of art, music, literature, etc. Copyright is supposed to influence the supply of artistic work in a positive way by providing an incentive through statutory protection but it may also raise the cost of creating new works and so reduce their supply; it also influences the demand for works of art, in part by raising prices; this is considered undesirable for goods like the arts, which are held to offer public good benefits (see Throsby, 2001).[2] It has also been argued that copyright's effects are asymmetric and that it benefits the distributor rather than the content creator. As cultural policy is concerned with stimulating creativity and with the provision of and access to the arts and culture, it follows that copyright law is important for cultural policy, as well

0950-0804/06/04 0567–19 JOURNAL OF ECONOMIC SURVEYS Vol. 20, No. 4

as for cultural economics. These matters are all grist for the cultural economists' mill and they have a particular contribution to make to the study of the economics of copyright.

Cultural economics can also contribute to the discussion about alternatives to copyright law as a stimulus to creating works of art. One area of cultural economics, the study of artists' labour markets, specifically tries to understand artistic motivation and the likely impact of copyright on the supply of creative work. Moreover, the case for government intervention in the arts and heritage made by cultural economists has resonance for the economic rationale of copyright. As we shall see, copyright sceptics have often advocated a policy of giving grants and awards to artists as an alternative to copyright as the incentive to create works of art.

Most of the standard economic literature on copyright (as reviewed, e.g. by Liebowitz and Watt in this issue) ignores a number of aspects that have considerable significance for cultural production in general and for artists in particular. Specifically, there is little mention in that literature of moral rights, although artists set great store by them and they may also have economic effects; no distinction is made between copyright for authors and neighbouring rights for performers; the distributional effects of copyright are barely referred to and the question of how much artists earn from copyright is ignored. Moreover, most writers assume that the interests of creators and performers are in perfect harmony with those of publishers, sound recording makers, broadcasters and all the other businesses that process and distribute their work as if there were no contractual problems between them over property rights. Caves (2000) has shown that there are economic explanations for the problems of contracting between artists and 'humdrum' enterprises dealing with the commercial side of the arts and culture. There are therefore good reasons to view copyright through the lens of cultural economics.

2. Comparing Cultural Subsidies and Copyright Law as Government Policy

Subsidies or grants to artists are one of the ways to stimulate creativity that have been proposed as an alternative to copyright law. Both are seen as overcoming market failure in cultural production. They were seriously considered by Macaulay in the 1840s (see Hadfield, 1992), by Plant (1934) and again by Hurt and Schuchmann (1966); Macaulay grudgingly found copyright law to be preferable; the other authors opted for subsidies or a system of grants, prizes and awards.[3] Subsidy to the arts is one of the topics that have been thoroughly investigated by cultural economics, and much has been written on its benefits and costs. Accordingly, that research forms a basis from which to compare these government policies for the cultural sector.

In the 'high' arts, it is common to find state subsidy, and in some sectors and in some countries, there is also direct state provision. Subsidies typically take the form of direct grants of monetary aid to arts and cultural organizations (theatre and opera companies, orchestras, museums, etc.). In many European countries, museums and heritage buildings are mostly owned and operated by the state.[4]

Subsidies also extend beyond the high arts to broadcasting, film, the press and even pop music as countries seek to maintain their language and national cultural identity. Public finance contributes a very high proportion of total income for the 'high arts' cultural organizations – in the Netherlands, for example, around 85% comes from government grants. Despite these high outlays, however, only a small proportion is typically spent on grants to individual artists, as government bodies tend to prefer to channel funds through cultural organizations, on the one hand, because transaction costs are high and, on the other, because there are moral hazard problems of supporting individuals.

The advantage of a reward system that directly targets the artist is that it can discriminate quality and the type of art that is perceived to be under-produced. By contrast, copyright is indiscriminate with respect to these features – any work within the scope of copyright attracts its protection and the threshold for originality is pretty low. It is worth noting that one of Plant's very perceptive (and frequently ignored) objections to copyright was that it encourages *over*-production of literary works (by contrast to the usual argument of under-production) and that it enables lower quality work to survive on the market because of the protection of the copyright monopoly than would otherwise be possible: too many artists and not good enough art. That is also the conclusion, however, of Abbing's (2002) review of the Dutch subsidy scheme of a minimum income for visual artists. The snags of public subsidies are that there is a danger of some concept of official state art developing if grants are administered by civil servants or cronyism if the job is delegated to artists themselves. This may also be a problem for prizes and other such awards (Wijnberg, 1994).

In some countries there are long-term grants or stipends to artists as incentives to creativity: in Finland stipends of up to 15 years' duration are awarded by a board of senior 'peer' artists to a select few creative artists, usually writers, visual artists and composers, and in the Netherlands visual artists receive grants under a general government funding scheme. Heikinnen (1995) and Rengers and Ploeg (2001) have studied these schemes and concluded that they display a 'winner-takes-all' character, that is, artists who are anyway successful on the open market tend to receive these awards. Thus, such grants are unlikely to provide an incentive to supply more or better quality work and may be mostly economic rent. Indeed, they may even be a disincentive owing to moral hazard (the composer Sibelius is often cited as an example; he is said to have composed less after receiving a lifetime stipend from the state). The possibility of a backward-bending supply curve always has to be considered as a response to higher rewards from whatever source.

The public finance of these two alternative systems is interesting to contrast. As Macaulay famously pointed out in 1841: 'Copyright is a tax on readers for the purposes of a bounty for writers.'[5] With copyright, it is the consumer who finances the incentive to create works of art (in the broadest sense), whereas with subsidies, taxpayers, who may well not be 'readers', do so. Cultural economists have shown that, at least for 'high arts', which absorb the lion's share of cultural subsidies, subsidy out of general taxation is regressive since arts consumers, who are only a small proportion of the population, generally have above-average incomes. While that is not the case for popular music or television programmes, it is something that should be taken into consideration in comparing the copyright law and subsidies as an incentive to create works of art. There are other differences: the subsidy or grant is an *ex ante* reward, while prizes and copyright are *ex post*. It may be that these have different incentive effects: the artist may have to satisfy certain criteria to obtain the grant, which could influence the work she plans to produce, and the success of that work (however it is evaluated) may influence her chances of a subsequent award. With copyright, the work gets automatic protection whatever the quality and there is no incentive to produce high quality work.[6] Subsidy, though, usually involves some evaluation of quality. Another point is that there is a significant difference in the timing of the outcomes: a copyright work involves a considerable inter-generational transfer before it is available in the public domain, depending upon the duration of the copyright term (if an artist creates a work aged 25 and lives to 75, the work is in copyright for 120 years with a term of 70 years *post mortem autoris*). Of course, most copyright works do not survive on the market for the duration and that raises the costs of access. Without copyright, a subsidized work would be in the public domain from its publication. This discussion is reminiscent of that about the public finance of cultural heritage – how much should we spend on it now for future generations, who will be wealthier and have different tastes? Finally, the copyright system relies heavily upon the market to make works available, thus leaving the choice of which works and which artists to promote in the hands of the commercial enterprises in the cultural industries. These industries are dominated by oligopolistic international corporations that are run in share-holders' interests, not those of the cultural policy of any given country. The Disney Corporation's interests do not necessarily coincide with those of Dutch television audiences! That brings into the discussion the public choice aspects of copyright, which take us too far from the one in hand but they should not be ignored.

In most developed countries, copyright and subsidies to the arts, along with prizes and other such awards, co-exist and are usually complementary. The popular arts rely more on copyright as an incentive while subsidies are used as well to stimulate creativity in the 'high' arts. It might be considered whether some version of works for hire should not be used for works of art that have been financed by taxpayers with the copyright belonging to the government or put in the public domain; such arrangements could be made by contracts between the funding body and the artist. Another variation could be a loan fund for artists established along the lines of a student loan system and artists required to pay a percentage of any royalties into it to pay off the loan (Towse, 2001a). These are details, however; the main point here is to show that there are contrasts and connections between copyright as an incentive system and subsidy to the arts, systems which have been considered in the literature as alternatives.

3. Variations on a Theme: Moral Rights, *Droit de Suite* and Performers' Rights

In this section, aspects of copyright law not usually dealt with in surveys by economists are considered: moral rights, *droit de suite* and performers' rights.

3.1 *Moral Rights*[7]

The economic analysis of copyright, being strongly influenced by American authors, is almost exclusively concerned with what are called 'economic' rights, as contrasted to the 'moral' right. The European tradition of authors' rights (*droit d'auteur*) stresses what have come to be called in English moral rights (*droit moral*) – rights of attribution, integrity, disclosure and withdrawal. In the European Union, the moral right is inalienable and unwaivable. With the globalization of the cultural industries and increasing standardization of copyright worldwide, the distinction between the civil law countries' emphasis on moral rights and copyright in the common law tradition is eroding. As part of this trend, a form of moral rights has been incorporated in both UK and US law, in the former as part of the 1988 Copyright Act and in the latter in the 1990 Visual Arts Rights Act (VARA).[8]

The moral right may also have been ignored because it was thought to have no economic value and to exist for equity reasons without efficiency implications. The literature in cultural economics on moral rights shows this is not the case. Rushton (1998) argues that there is pecuniary benefit from the moral right and therefore they must be regarded as having efficiency effects: the moral right has an incentive effect for artistic production because it encourages artistic recognition of status and professionalism. It can also have significant hold-up power and so be used in bargaining situations. Hansmann and Santilli (1997) consider both equity and efficiency arguments for artists' moral rights. As an example, they present an economic perspective on the right of integrity; knowing who the artist is, and therefore the stock of works on which her reputation is based, is important market information. Landes (2001) and Landes and Posner (2003), though, are dismissive of this argument in the light of VARA. It would be interesting to see an economic analysis of moral rights in a country, such as France, where the rights are stronger and fully established and the moral rights may not be waived as they can be in the USA.

It seems likely that there are relatively high transaction costs in connection with moral rights, for while it is a fairly simple matter to identify the creator of a work of visual art, such as a painting or sculpture, it will be more difficult or even impossible to do so in other areas of the cultural industries, such as multimedia and sound recording. This is also an issue with performers' rights, where costly arrangements have to be made to identify their contribution to works. The World Intellectual Property Organisation (WIPO), the UN agency responsible for IP treaties, in 1996 negotiated the WIPO Performers and Phonograms Treaty (WPPT), which required the recognition of performers' moral rights for the first time (this treaty has now been translated into national law by most European countries, in the USA through the Digital Millennium Copyright Act, and by a considerable number of other countries). This is discussed in relation to performers' rights in Section 3.3 below.

3.2 *Droit de Suite or Artists' Resale Right*

Although not part of the copyright proper, *droit de suite* (known in English as the artist's resale right) is linked closely to it. It is an *ad valorem* levy on the resale of paintings over a certain price in public sales which has existed for many years in most European countries[9] and in the state of California; more often than not, it is not exercised by artists, as predicted when it was introduced (Rottenberg, 1975). In Europe, it is an inalienable and unwaivable right designed, with the best will in the world, to assist artists in obtaining their share of any increase in the price of their work once it has passed out of their hands, but is generally believed by economists to reduce prices for the work of young artists and thus have unintended adverse incentive effects. As with other incomes of artists, it seems that *droit de suite* royalties, where they are collected, for example in France, are a significant source of income for the top artists but pay little to, or even harm, young artists by depressing prices (Perloff, 1998; Ginsburgh, forthcoming). Moreover, *droit de suite* is likely to act as a disincentive to dealers etc. to promote artists' work (Perloff, 1998). The effect of *droit de suite* on the art market should be testable empirically. Although there is now a considerable literature of econometric work on art as an investment, almost no one has tested the impact of *droit de suite* on art prices.

However, Solow (1998) introduces a new approach that challenges the negative view of *droit de suite*. He analyzes its dynamic external effect on an artist's work over her lifetime. By having a claim on resale prices of past works, the artist has an interest in the future value of her early work, creating an incentive to maintain her reputation. Thus resale prices are 'endogenized'. The question of complementarity and substitutability between early and late works of a still-producing artist is an interesting one in other areas too, such as in sound recordings and literature where the value of back catalogue can be enhanced by present activities, such as going on tour, being interviewed by the media and so on. Cheung (1986) is relevant to this question; he has argued that unless both parties, licensor and licensee (e.g. author and publisher), share revenues, the licensee will obtain market information on the value of the invention, which is not signalled directly to the licensor (and authors have the incentive to overstate the value of their work and publishers to understate it).

An alternative to *droit de suite* that has been suggested is to give artists an exhibition payment right, a share of the entrance charge to public exhibitions of their work (Santagata, 1995). An interesting question that could be analyzed in this context is the different values of the bundle of rights that are sold with a painting or the work of art; although the buyer acquires the painting, the copyright remains with the artist, who then has reproduction and other secondary use rights. An objection to a scheme for exhibition payments, however, is that it would have high costs of tracing artists; any royalty scheme necessitates keeping in touch with copyright owners and that is also the case to a lesser extent for *droit de suite*. A similar proposal for a display right is discussed in Hansmann and Santilli (2001).

3.3 *Performers' Rights*[10]

Performers did not become vulnerable to having their performances copied until the advent of home-taping and later CD burning and downloading. However, in the first half of the 20th century, they suffered considerable loss of work owing to the substitution of records and radio play for live performance. Performers do not have copyright proper but property rights related to copyright or neighbouring rights. The conventional justification given in law books and the like is that copyright and authors' rights are the reward and stimulus for creativity but performers do not create works, they just 'execute' the performance of existing works and that does not merit the grant of the exclusive right as for the author. I have argued (Towse, forthcoming) that this does not make economic sense, as explained below. There has been no other economic analysis of performers' rights of which I am aware.

The recognition of the case for performers' rights began with the onset of commercial sound recording and early on performers acquired some rights; to give the example of the UK, in 1925 performers acquired the right to control the fixation and use of their performances (mainly in sound recordings). The full establishment of performers' rights really began with the 1961 Rome Convention on neighbouring rights, which forms the basis of national laws and also forms the basis for the WPPT. In 1992, the so-called EC Rental Directive[11] was drawn up, which basically enforced the Rome Convention for all European Union countries. Musical performers[12] acquired the right to control the recording of live performances, fully assignable property rights and individual rights to equitable remuneration for public performances of sound recordings, for which protection lasts 50 years from the date of fixation. Rights to remuneration are essentially compensation for compulsory licences that override the general copyright principle that the author/creator has the exclusive right to control exploitation of his or her work (Gallagher, 2002). In the case of sound recordings, what this means in practice is that once a performer has contracted with a record label to make a sound recording, she has no further control over its exploitation (e.g. by public performance) but she receives payment for these uses. (The same applies in this case to composers as well.)[13]

The apparent intention of the Rental Directive was to correct the weaker bargaining position of non-featured performers, and that was done by laying down the requirement that equitable remuneration could only be administered by a collecting society set up for that purpose. This is one of perhaps many examples where the law has been used in the attempt to 'correct' a perceived market failure for equity rather than efficiency reasons.[14] Non-featured performers were targeted in this way because they do not have a royalty contract with, in the case of the music industry, a record label, and are typically paid a standard fee, for example, for a studio recording.

As mentioned earlier, the WIPO Performances and Phonograms Treaty (WPPT) has made important changes to performers' rights introducing a new exclusive right in favour of performers, who make their works available on-line to the public (known as the 'making available right'). It also mandates the prohibition of the circumvention of copyright protection (TPMs – technological protection measures) and of tampering with rights management information (DRM – digital rights management). Thus, with the WPPT, performers now have an individual exclusive right (though not a full copyright) more or less equivalent to that of authors. The USA has not signed the Rome Convention and performers there have rights only in digital works.

Turning to the economics of performers' rights, we note that as the economic aim of copyright law is to offer an incentive to create works of art, literature, music and so on, we may reasonably assume that this aim applies to the creation of performances by performers. Performers are identified in UK copyright law as persons who have rights in their performances. A performance is formed by talent, years of training and investment in human capital and involves considerable risk of how it will be received by audiences. A performance is a work in the sense of copyright law and so the same economic logic should apply to it as it does to the work of an author. However, the difference is that the performance, while a work in its own right, cannot be separated from the work being performed. The received view is that when performers perform a work created by an author – say an existing song already written by a composer – their performance is already 'propertized' by copyright law so there is no need to intervene further by granting other property rights on the same work: the performer is only able to produce her performance on licence from the composer. Thus the law favours the creator over the performer. I dispute this rationale, however, because it fails to take into account how value is added to the author's work by the performer. When a singer makes a song famous, thus adding value to the song due to her talent, the singer should be awarded the value added but, instead, the benefit accrues to the composer, who cannot have anticipated (in most cases) that the singer would perform the work. The composer therefore 'free-rides' on the singer's performance. Coasean logic would suggest that well-known singers should commission songs from a lesser known composer and therefore own the song and, indeed, that did happen historically (Towse, forthcoming).

Until the introduction of legislation following the WPPT, non-featured performers, such as backing singers and instrumentalists, received only collective remuneration but now they also have individual exclusive rights. It is frequently argued that these performers have already been paid for their work and therefore a royalty on top of that would just be paying them twice for the same thing. However, even if the performer were already on salary with an orchestra or chorus, economic efficiency requires that their pay reflect the revenues received by the organization employing them; if they receive payment through other means, for example, royalties, then economists would expect that the 'spot' pay for work (fees or salary) would be reduced to take into account the future royalty or remuneration payment. That principle raises an issue that has only been touched on (Towse, 2001a) – 'Who pays' for extended rights for performers (or any other claimant, in fact)? And when a new claimant is introduced, where is the money to come from – higher consumer prices, less for authors or lower profits for (in the case of music) sound recording makers?

One argument against royalties for non-featured performers is that the transaction costs of tracing, contracting and maintaining contact with many performers would be high for the sound recording maker; however, a composers' collecting society incurs similar costs. Apparently, this objection to performers' rights is now deemed to be outdated by the possibility of DRM as the WPPT has caused individual exclusive rights to be introduced. It remains to be seen how effectively 'ordinary' non-star performers are able to exercise these rights. So far, DRM is not standardized and it is not clear who will bear the associated costs. There is scope for a great deal more work on the economics of performers' rights, both analytical and empirical, the more so as the European Commission is currently pursuing collecting societies for anticompetitive behaviour.

4. Distributional Aspects of Copyright for Artists

Economists' concentration on the efficiency aspects of copyright has meant that its distributional effects have received little attention. Several topics are considered under this heading: analysis of contracting between 'art and commerce', the economic analysis of copyright collectives and empirical studies of artists' earnings from royalties and other copyright remuneration.

4.1 *Contracting Between 'Art and Commerce'*

Caves (2000) analyzes the economic organization of creative industries by applying the insights of contract theory to deals between artists and the firm in the cultural industry over the control of rights. He shows that the firm always has the incentive to acquire control over the creator's copyrights when it has to incur an outlay on sunk costs, the typical situation, say, with an advance to an author or the costs of publication or marketing. It does so in part to avoid hold-up problems, which may arise in the creative industries because of the author's or artist's particular concern over her reputation and care for artistic content, and in part because of the inherent radical uncertainty (Caves' 'nobody knows') surrounding the fruition and reception of creative work. A royalty contract is a typical incentive contract that forces the creator or performer to share with the publisher in the success or failure of the final product and the associated risk. Caves' focus is on industrial organization in the creative industries rather than on the distribution of the share of rewards for the artist, although, along the way, he demonstrates very well the weak bargaining position in which most artists find themselves. Alonso and Watt (2003) provide a formal model of the contract for sharing revenues, showing that the barrier to an efficient contract lies in the differing attitudes to risk on the part of the parties involved – the creator likely being more risk averse than the publishing firm that markets the product.

Artists are typically at a disadvantage in relation to firms in the cultural industries for several reasons: as individuals, artists have poor access to the capital market and therefore need to contract with a firm to get their work distributed, whereas the firm, often a multinational giant corporation in an oligopolized industry, has easy access to capital. With little capital reserves, artists have to sell their work within a short time of its creation; thus their time preference rate is much shorter than a firm's; and artists have a relatively small portfolio of work and cannot pool risks, unlike a large firm with a huge portfolio of copyrighted work, which it can exploit when market conditions are favourable. Another source of asymmetry is in relation to market information; artists have considerably less experience of market conditions than do firms. Moreover, individual artists cannot afford the legal costs of defending their rights in court, whereas firms can.

Transaction costs of contracting often lead to standardization of contracts as a means of reducing the costs. Standard contracts, of course, are not tailored to the specific work of its creator and therefore do not provide an individual incentive. Towse (1999) observes that different combinations of the incentive to produce high quality work, willingness to share risk and transaction costs that are to be found in different types of contracts and payment methods. The incentive to do high quality work depends on whether the payment is a flat-rate single-spot payment or a royalty on sales. The former offers little incentive to improve quality and therefore is more likely to result in, or be more commonly associated with, routine work and a standard contract. However, with a flat-rate fee the artist bears no risk. Under the royalty system, the contract ties author and publisher in a longer term relationship and the artist shares risk with entrepreneur. That gives the artist the motive to do good quality work now and in the future since it provides a feedback for the present work to increase the sales of earlier work. A pure royalty deal has a stronger incentive than if an advance on the royalty is paid because it is a combination of spot and future payments.[15] The outcome turns on the response of the artist not only to the amount and type of the payment but also to her attitude to risk-taking and ability to sustain risk.

4.2 *Economic Analysis of Copyright Collectives*

The above, of course, assumes that contracting is possible between the artist and the user of her work; that is the case in the primary market for copyright works – the author contracts with the publisher, the song writer and the performer with the record company and so on. That is not feasible with secondary users of their work, such as photocopying of books and public performance of sound recordings. The same type of contracting problems is faced by copyright-collecting societies, which act collectively on behalf of authors and performers with secondary users. The need to economize on transaction costs of contracting and monitoring usage leads to 'blanket licensing' of the whole repertoire of the society (Hollander, 1984; Besen *et al.*, 1992; Watt, 2000; Liebowitz, 2005). This minimizes transaction costs but has the disadvantage from the economic point of view that the individual creator's contribution to the demand for the licence is not distinguished. Transaction costs are further reduced by the natural monopoly of collecting societies, which often specialize in administering one or a closely related bundle of rights. Kretschmer (2003), however, finds fault with the economic explanation of transaction cost minimization and argues instead that collective rights management is a form of unionization or 'solidarity'. In a paper whose title says it all, 'Copyright Societies Do Not Administer Individual Property Rights: the Incoherence of Institutional Traditions in Germany and the UK' (Kretschmer, 2003), he argues that the joint membership of publishers with authors or performers in collecting societies reduces their ability to concentrate on the interests of the creator members because the economically stronger publishers dominate the societies.

The first work on the economics of copyright collectives was by Peacock and Weir (1975) on the UK Performing Rights Society (PRS). The PRS was formed in 1914 as a private co-operative society to administer musical copyrights and it is a monopoly because it requires the exclusive assignment of copyrights in order to license use. For the distribution of income to members, it holds a large database of information about its members and their works, as well as lists of music users and work-by-work use and it is this database that makes it a natural monopoly. There are economies of scale in royalty administration and duplication of this information would increase costs. The PRS had several concerns at the time of Peacock's research: one was the low earnings of many of their composer members and the unequal distribution of distributed income; a second was the increasing use of home taping devices; and the third was the fact that their biggest single customer was the BBC (British Broadcasting Corporation) with its monopoly on music broadcasts of live concerts and recorded music. Peacock and Weir therefore undertook a three-pronged research into composers' earnings (from all sources, not just from royalties), ways of compensating copyright holders for private home-taping (for which they recommended the introduction of a 'blank tape' levy) and analysis of the de facto bilateral monopoly between the PRS and the BBC (Peacock, 1993). This analysis has proved to be prototypical of the problems facing collecting societies.

This was pioneering work and it established the basic economic analysis of copyright collectives as natural monopolies operating blanket licensing and dealing with other monopolies in the form of trade associations that collectively negotiate licence fees for their members, thus reducing the transaction costs for the composer and for the user. Other work on the economics of collecting societies is by Hollander (1984), Besen *et al.* (1992), MacQueen and Peacock (1995), Watt (2000), Einhorn (2002), Liebowitz (2005) and Snow and Watt (2005). These authors have all investigated a range of efficiency questions about the optimal size of the membership, the effect of competition on the natural monopoly, blanket licensing, setting the tariff and, lately, the effect of digital delivery on the collective administration of copyrights. Watt (2000) points out, in addition to these questions, that collecting societies' practice of distributing the revenues from blanket licensing on an individual basis according to use increases the costs of administration that the blanket licence saves. Snow and Watt (2005) add another dimension by arguing that collecting societies could pool risks and thus reduce the risk bearing of their members.

4.3 *Empirical Studies of Artists' Earnings from Royalties and Other Copyright Remuneration*

The points discussed above are efficiency questions and they ignore both equity matters and the actual distribution of revenues to individual artists. For that, we have to look at empirical evidence on the distribution of earnings of collecting society members. It is important to stress that such data do not show what artists earn from all their copyright works, just what they earn from one right or a limited number of rights that the collecting society exercises on their behalf. Towse (1999) found evidence of the value of remuneration for the public performance of sound recordings resulting from performers' rights that were newly introduced in the UK following the EU Rental Directive and compared the figures for those of similar Swedish and Danish societies, which had been in existence for some 20 years (the figures and distributions were all similar). Kretschmer (2005) uses figures submitted by the PRS in its evidence to the Monopolies and Mergers Commission enquiry into its operation and in addition provides data for the German performing rights society GEMA and the Künstlersozialkasse (social insurance fund for artists) on the distribution of remuneration. Matsumoto (2002) presents detailed figures on performers' remuneration earnings for sound recordings in Japan. These figures all follow what has come to be seen as a familiar pattern in artists' labour markets – the so-called winner-takes-all phenomenon, whereby by the top earners, the few superstar singers, bands, authors, film directors and suchlike who dominate the markets in the cultural industries, also earn the highest royalties. The available evidence (and there is very little of it made public) shows that the top few receive highly disproportionate shares of the total revenues, while many members (sometimes 50% or so) earn less than the minimum that is distributed.

Another issue that has not been deeply investigated is the distribution of the costs of administering the copyright system. While there has been some interest on the part of regulatory bodies (and now by the European Competition authorities) in the often-considerable charges made by collecting societies for the services of administering their members' rights, these are not the only costs of administration. Maintaining databases of the use of copyright material is costly and there is a strong incentive to push the costs onto others. As mentioned above in relation to performers, it is not yet clear who will pay the costs of DRM administration or how much it will cost. In some countries, collecting societies are state or quasi-official bodies and the state bears some of the costs. The state usually bears the cost of protection and also for conflict resolution through a copyright board or tribunal.

To sum up on this section, then: there is more than a strong suspicion to be found in these economic studies that the main benefits of copyright are enjoyed by the 'humdrum' side of the cultural industries rather than the creators and, while it may well be the case that collecting societies have considerable revenues, the distributions of royalties to artists other than the top few stars show how relatively little they get through the copyright system.

5. Artists' Labour Markets and Artists' Motivation

The economics of artists' labour markets is a well-researched area of cultural economics. It has established some by now stylized facts about the economic life of the artist through empirical evidence in a number of countries. These are as follows: artists' median annual earnings are below the national average, given their age and level of education; there is a highly skewed distribution of income within artistic professions, with many earning very little, while the few superstars have very high earnings; most artists have frequent and prolonged periods of unemployment and experience high search costs as they frequently change jobs; most artists are multiple-job-holders because they earn insufficient income from their chosen arts occupation and so must do other sorts of work to make ends meet; and most artists work on standard contracts and at standard fees. Even so, there is an excess supply of artistic services at all levels of payment, something that is exacerbated by subsidy to training and grants to artists. It is believed by most cultural economists that this excess supply is the main reason not only for low earnings but also for their weak bargaining position leading to poor contracts, frequent spells of unemployment and no set career structure (Towse, 2001a).

These disadvantages raise questions about the motivation of artists, whether they are rational maximizers and if so what is it they seek? Research has shown that artists' labour supply is responsive to the (imputed) wage rate: the higher the rate of payment for arts work, the more hours artists spend on art work. There is also positive cross elasticity – when they earn more from *non-arts* work, they devote more time to *arts* work (Throsby, 1997, 2001). Abbing (2002) argues that when artists obtain an increase in earnings, whether from arts work, non-arts work or a grant, they reinvest it in equipment, etc. in order to improve their production of art, rather than raise their material standard of living. Other writers have pointed to the risky nature of work in the arts and, given the absence of information on the artist's chances of success, the only way to find out one's chances are to 'have a go' (MacDonald, 1988). Caves (2000) sees this as applicable to all markets in the cultural sector, dubbing it the 'nobody knows' characteristic of the creative industries.

Bruno Frey, in his book *Not Just for the Money* (Frey, 1997), has developed an economic analysis of intrinsic and extrinsic motivation, applying the study of artistic motivation developed in social psychology. Creative artists are said to have 'intrinsic' motivation, inner drive, which is motivated by intrinsic reward – inner satisfaction, fame, recognition, etc. Extrinsic motivation and reward refers to the 'normal' assumption in economics that financial reward is a motivation to effort. The particular contribution of Frey is his 'crowding out' theory – that an inappropriate type of reward could have the opposite of the desired effect. In particular, intrinsic motivation may be crowded out by extrinsic reward.[16] Moreover, financial payment (extrinsic reward) could even inhibit intrinsically motivated people by stifling their inner drive. This led Frey to distinguish two kinds of creativity, institutional and personal. Arts organizations of necessity have to be institutionally motivated to be creative by extrinsic reward in the form of financial grants; personal creativity, however, is only motivated by intrinsic reward (Frey, 2000). Frey believes that cultural policy, with its reliance on financial payments, may all too easily crowd out true artistic creation. In Towse (2001b), I argue that the combination of the economic and moral rights in copyright/authors' rights satisfies Frey's requirement for intrinsic as well as extrinsic reward for creativity. Over and above its role as establishing property rights so that authors can obtain their economic reward, copyright intrinsically rewards creativity through moral rights. It is therefore an instrument of cultural policy that may be more significant to artists than the extrinsic financial incentive of a subsidy.

As a final observation on this topic, it should be said that the dearth of empirical studies on artists' response to copyright and their motivation to supply works of art in general is a real criticism not only of cultural economics but of all those international and national bodies as well that so strongly advocate copyright as a stimulus to creativity. We have to stop simply assuming that stronger copyright means higher earnings for artists and that this therefore leads to greater and better creative output. It is not an easy task to test these relationships – indeed, cultural economists who have worked in this area know how difficult it is to research artists' labour markets – but lack of information on the subject does not strengthen the case for copyright; it weakens it.

6. New Technologies and New Arts

The effect of digitalization on the music industry has by now been well researched by economists and well documented by Liebowitz and Watt in this volume. Digitalization has its effects on other of the cultural industries too, especially broadcasting, the press and journalism, publishing and film production (although the full effect of movie downloading has yet to impact on the industry). Media economists, whom one could call close cousins of cultural economists, have a significant research programme in this area, particularly looking at the impact of the Internet on these industries and the new business models it calls for (Küng, 2004; Picard, 2004). However, there is little that specifically deals with copyright. In cultural economics, there has been some interest in the effect of digitalization on artists' work and on new types of art and the implications this has for copyright. Farchy and Rochelandet (2002) discuss the protection of copyright holders with private copying using digital technologies, Einhorn (2002) discusses the effect of digitalization on licensing musical copyrights in different platforms and Liebowitz (2005) deals with different ways of collecting licence fees with music downloads. Farchy (2003) deals with a question that has been on many people's lips – does digitalization enable the artist (creator or performer) to break loose from the intermediaries (the 'publishers') in the cultural industries and go it alone using the Internet for publicity and marketing? So far, there is little evidence of this and Farchy suggests that it is unlikely to develop to any great extent. This is another topic that calls for detailed empirical research.

Lastly, a topic that has begun to be analyzed is the copyright implications of new art forms, specifically, borrowed images and appropriation art (Landes, 2002) and musical sampling (Thèberge, 2004). Rushton (2001) discusses the economic aspect of artists' rights and moral rights in similar contexts. Not unrelated is the question of copyright and the digitalization of museum images (Aalberts and Beunen, 2002) and archives; here the concern is about the power of digital rights management to cut off works in the public domain or for 'fair use' reasons (for a general discussion, see Schneider and Henten, 2005). These are very specialized subjects, however, even within cultural economics.

7. Conclusion

The purpose of this survey paper has been to show that economists have been concerned with a wider aspect of copyright than with just economic rights. Moreover, economists working specifically in the field of culture tend to look at the economics of copyright from a rather different standpoint than the general welfare economics or property rights approach adopted by economists and law and economists. In this paper, I have put the focus on the artist and selected the issues for review on that basis. I do not think that all of the people whose work is cited here would regard themselves as cultural economists but I hope they would acknowledge that it adds up to a distinct body of work. Cultural economics' main distinction is that it applies economics to the production and consumption of the arts and culture, areas in which copyright supposedly has a strong influence. The insights of cultural economics about cultural policy seem to throw some additional light on the more general questions about the economic and cultural role of copyright in a world that increasingly emphasizes creativity and the creative industries as the source of economic growth in the post-industrial world.[17]

'Do artists need copyright?' is a question that many people have asked since its introduction in England in 1710. What this survey shows is that the answer is a complex one. There has been some interesting work in economic history on creation without copyright and on artists' earnings, especially in the case of composers (Scherer, 2001; Tschmuck, 2002) and it is obvious that a great deal of the canon of great Western art (and no doubt of Eastern art too) was created without the intervention of copyright or state subsidy.

There is good reason to believe that copyright is asymmetric in its effects and favours the industry side of the creative industries rather than the creators and performers whose work they exploit. If we are to believe that copyright, or more precisely authors' and performers' rights, are fundamental to cultural production, we need far more evidence than at present exists to demonstrate the case. Moreover, it may be that artistic motivation and the incentive to produce works of art are not just due to financial rewards and economic rights but also to moral rights. Economists may have to venture out of their usual eeries to investigate these things. If they do not, they should be far more careful in following the line that what is good for Sony is good for the world of art.

Acknowledgements

I am grateful to Michael Rushton and Richard Watt for reading and commenting on this paper.

Notes

1. For a comprehensive survey of cultural economics, see Blaug (2001). For a general introduction and short chapters on many of the topics mentioned below, see Towse (2003). Towse (2005) traces the development of cultural economics over the last 35 years.

2. The economic arguments for copyright are not rehearsed here – see Liebowitz and Watt in this volume or for a fuller treatment, Landes and Posner (2003).
3. Shavell and van Ypserle's (2003) suggestion for a reward system for innovation does not discuss its application to copyright.
4. In some European countries, there has recently been a programme of deétatization, that is, turning the management over to self-managing non-profit organizations.
5. Cited in Hadfield (1992, pp. 29–31).
6. That is not true of *droit de suite*, the artists' resale right, which does give the incentive to maintain quality and reputation (see Section 3.2).
7. This section draws on Towse (2001a).
8. Boylan (2005) makes it clear that the US version differs considerably from its European origins.
9. The right did not exist in the UK, Ireland or the Netherlands until the recent EU Directive that harmonized its provision throughout Europe.
10. This section draws on Towse (2006).
11. The European Council Directive 'on rental and lending rights and on certain rights related to copyright in the field of intellectual property' (EC Directive, 1992).
12. Audio visual performers, such as film actors, were not included in this legislation. There is now talk of their acquiring copyright protection.
13. Rushton (2003) discusses criticisms of compulsory licensing in the arts.
14. However, in so doing, it risked creating a situation in which the increased transaction costs to users threaten to swamp any benefits (see Towse, 2001a). Burrows (1994) has argued that all copyright is based on equity arguments alone.
15. In practice in the cultural industries there are many different ways of rewarding artists that include prizes, wages, wages plus a bonus and profit-sharing deals besides spot fees and royalties (see Towse, 2004).
16. The 'classic' case is that of blood donorship, where voluntary donation is displaced or 'crowded out' if financial payment is made. Not only that – there is also a moral hazard problem because people who sell blood (i.e. they are extrinsincally motivated) are likely to be less healthy that those who are intrinsically motivated to donate.
17. A topic that has not been discussed in this article is the attempt to measure the effect of copyright in these industries. For a recent review of this topic, see the articles in the Symposium on the Empirical Measurement of the Contribution of Copyright to National Economies, *Review of Economics of Copyright Issues* volume 1, number 1, June 2004.

References

Aalberts, B. and Beunen, A. (2002) Exploiting museum images. In R. Towse (ed.), *Copyright in the Cultural Industries* (pp. 178–194). Cheltenham: Edward Elgar Publishing.

Abbing, H. (2002) *Why Are Artists Poor? The Exceptional Economy of the Arts*. Amsterdam: Amsterdam University Press.

Alonso, J. and Watt, R. (2003) Efficient distribution of copyright income. In W. Gordon and R. Watt (eds.), *The Economics of Copyright* (pp. 81–103). Cheltenham: Edward Elgar Publishing.

Besen, S., Kirkby, S. and Salop, S. (1992) An economic analysis of copyright collectives. *Virginia Law Review* 78: 383–441.

Blaug, M. (2001) Where are we now in cultural economics? *Journal of Economic Surveys* 15(2): 123–143.

Boylan, P. N. (2005) Reconciling artist's moral rights with economic principles and the problem of parody: Some modest proposals. *Journal of Law and Communications* 1(1) Spring 2005 (no page numbers).

Burrows, P. (1994) Justice, efficiency and copyright in cultural goods. In A. Peacock and I. Rizzo (eds.), *Cultural Economics and Cultural Policies* (pp. 99–110). Dordrecht: Kluwer.

Caves, R. (2000) *Creative Industries: Contracts Between Art and Commerce*. Cambridge, MA and London: Harvard University Press.

Cheung, S. (1986) Property rights and invention. In J. Palmer (ed.), *The Economics of Patents and Copyrights* (pp. 5–18). Greenwich, CN, and London: Research in Law and Economics Series 8. JAI Press.

EC Directive (1992) *On Rental Right and Lending Right and on Certain Rights Related to Copyright in the Field of Intellectual Property*. 92/100/EEC. Luxembourg.

Einhorn, M. (2002) Music licensing in the digital age. In R. Towse (ed.), *Copyright in the Cultural Industries* (pp. 165–177). Cheltenham: Edward Elgar Publishing.

Farchy, J. (2003) Internet: culture. In R. Towse (ed.), *A Handbook of Cultural Economics* (pp. 276–280). Cheltenham: Edward Elgar Publishing.

Farchy, J. and Rochelandet, F. (2002) Copyright protection, appropriability and new cultural behaviour. In R. Towse (ed.), *Copyright in the Cultural Industries* (pp. 178–194). Cheltenham: Edward Elgar Publishing.

Frey, B. (1997) *Not Just for the Money*. Cheltenham: Edward Elgar Publishing.

Frey, B. (2000) *Arts and Economics, Analysis and Cultural Policy*. Berlin, Heidelberg, New York: Springer.

Gallagher, T. (2002) Copyright compulsory licensing and incentives. In R. Towse (ed.), *Copyright in the Cultural Industries* (pp. 85–98). Cheltenham: Edward Elgar Publishing.

Ginsburgh, V. (forthcoming) The economic consequences of *droit de suite* in the European Union. www.ecare.ulb.ac.be/ecare/people/members/ginsburgh/papers/134.droit%20de%20suite.pdf.

Hadfield, G. (1992) The economics of copyright: an historical perspective. *Copyright Law Symposium* 38: 1–46. Reprinted in R. Towse (ed.), (1997) *Cultural Economics: The Arts, the Heritage and the Media Industries I*, pp. 129–174.

Hansmann, H. and Santilli, M. (1997) Authors' and artists' moral rights. *Journal of Legal Studies*, 95–143.

Hansmann, H. and Santilli, M. (2001) Royalties for artists versus royalties for authors and composers. *Journal of Cultural Economics* 25(4): 259–281.

Heikinnen, M. (1995) Evaluating the effects of direct support on the economic situation of artists. *Journal of Cultural Economics* 19(3): 261–272.

Hollander, A. (1984) Market structure and performance in intellectual property. *International Journal of Industrial Organisation* 2: 199–216.

Hurt, R. and Schuchman, R. (1966) The economic rationale of copyright. *American Economic Review* 56: 421–432.

Kretschmer, M. (2003) Copyright societies do not administer individual property rights: the incoherence of institutional traditions in Germany and the UK. In R. Towse (ed.), *Copyright in the Creative Industries* (pp. 140–164).

Kretschmer, M. (2005) Artists' earnings and copyright: a review of British and German music industry data in the context of digital technologies. In www.firstmonday.org/issue10_1/kretschmer.

Küng, L. (2004) What makes media firms tick? Exploring the underlying drivers for firm performance. In R. Picard (ed.), *Strategic Responses to Media Market Changes*. Jönköping: Jönköping International Business School.

Landes, W. (2001) What has the Visual Artist's Rights Act of 1990 accomplished? *Journal of Cultural Economics* 24(4): 283–306.

Landes, W. (2002) Copyright, borrowed images and appropriation art: an economic approach. In R. Towse (ed.), *Copyright in the Cultural Industries* (pp. 9–31). Cheltenham: Edward Elgar Publishing.

Landes, W. and Posner, R. (2003) *The Economic Structure of Intellectual Property Law*. Cambridge, MA: The Belknap Press of Harvard University Press.

Liebowitz, S. (2005) MP3s and copyright collectives: A curse worse than the disease? In L. N. Takeyama, W. J. Gordon and R. Towse (eds.), *Developments in the Economics of Copyright: Research and Analysis* (pp. 37–59). Cheltenham, UK and Northampton, MA: Edward Elgar.

MacDonald, G. (1988) The economics of rising stars. *American Economic Review* 78: 155–166.

MacQueen, H. and Peacock, A. (1995) Implementing performing rights. *Journal of Cultural Economics* 19(2): 157–175.

Matsumoto, S. (2002) Performers in the digital era: empirical evidence from Japan. In R. Towse (ed.), *Copyright in the Cultural Industries* (pp. 196–209). Cheltenham: Edward Elgar Publishing.

Peacock, A. (1993) *Paying the Piper: Culture, Music and Money*. Edinburgh: Edinburgh University Press.

Peacock, A. and Weir, R. (1975) *The Composer in the Marketplace*. London: Faber.

Perloff, J. (1998) Droit de Suite. In *New Palgrave Dictionary of Law and Economics*, pp. 645–648. London: Macmillan.

Picard, R. (2004) (ed.) *Strategic Responses to Media Market Changes*. Jönköping: Jönköping International Business School.

Plant, A. (1934) The economic aspects of copyright in books. *Economica*, May, 1: 167–195.

Rengers, M. and Ploeg, E. (2001) Private or public? *Journal of Cultural Economics* 25(1): 1–20.

Rottenberg, S. (1975) The remuneration of artists. Reprinted in R. Towse (ed.), (1997) *Cultural Economics: The Arts, the Heritage and the Media Industries, I*, pp. 590–594.

Rushton, M. (1998) The moral rights of artists: droit moral or droit pecunaire? *Journal of Cultural Economics* 22(1): 1–13.

Rushton, M. (2001) The law and economics of artists' inalienable rights. *Journal of Cultural Economics* 25(4): 243–257.

Rushton, M. (2003) Artists' rights. In R. Towse (ed.), *A Handbook of Cultural Economics* (pp. 76–80). Cheltenham: Edward Elgar Publishing.

Santagata, W. (1995) Institutional anomalies in the contemporary art market. *Journal of Cultural Economics* 19(2): 187–197.

Scherer, F. M. (2001) The evolution of free-lance music composition, 1650–1900. *Journal of Cultural Economics* 25(4): 307–319.

Schneider, M. and Henten, A. (2005) In 'DRMS, TCP and the EUCD: technology and law'. *Telematics and Informatics* 22(1–2): 25–39.

Snow, A. and Watt, R. (2005) Risk sharing and the distribution of copyright collective income. In L. N. Takeyama, W. J. Gordon and R. Towse (eds.), *Developments in the Economics of Copyright: Research and Analysis* (pp. 23–36). Cheltenham, UK and Northampton, MA: Edward Elgar.

Solow, J. (1998) Economic analysis of *droit de suite*. *Journal of Cultural Economics* 22(3): 209–226.

Théberge, P. (2004) Technology, creative practice and copyright. In S. Frith and L. Marshall (eds.), *Music and Copyright*, 2nd edition (pp. 139–156). University of Edinburgh Press.

Throsby, D. (1997) Artists as workers. Reprinted in R. Towse (ed.), *Cultural Economics* (pp. 261–268). Aldershot: Edward Elgar.

Throsby, D. (2001) *Economics and Culture*. Cambridge, UK and New York: Cambridge University Press.

Towse, R. (1999) Copyright, incentives and performers' earnings. *Kyklos* 52(3): 369–390.

Towse, R. (2001a) *Creativity, Incentive and Reward*. Cheltenham, UK: Edward Elgar Publishing.

Towse, R. (2001b) Partly for the money: rewards and incentives to artists. *Kyklos* 54(2/3): 473–490.

Towse, R. (ed.) (2003) *A Handbook of Cultural Economics*. Cheltenham, UK and Northampton, MA: Edward Elgar Publishing.

Towse, R. (2004) Copyright and cultural policy for the creative industries. In O. Granstrand (ed.), *Economics, Law and Intellectual Property* (pp. 419–438). Boston/Dordrecht/London: Kluwer Academic Publishers.

Towse, R. (2005) Alan Peacock and cultural economics. *The Economic Journal* 115: F262–F276.

Towse, R. (2006) The singer or the song? Developments in performers' rights from the perspective of a cultural economist. Mimeo.

Tschmuck, P. (2002) Creativity without a copyright: music production in Vienna. In R. Towse (ed.), *Copyright in the Cultural Industries* (pp. 210–220). Cheltenham, UK: Edward Elgar Publishing.

Watt, R. (2000) *Copyright and Economic Theory: Friends or Foes?* Cheltenham, UK: Edward Elgar Publishing.

Wijnberg, N. (2003) Awards. In R. Towse (ed.), *A Handbook of Cultural Economics* (pp. 81–84). Cheltenham, UK: Edward Elgar Publishing.

Part V
Copyright and Open Source

Introduction to Part V

Ever since the seminal contribution by Arnold Plant (Plant, 1934), copyright academics have long debated whether or not copyright is a necessary condition for the juggernaut of creativity to continue in a manner that in any way resembles what is best for society. Indeed, a handful of articles, few in number but certainly influential, have put forward convincing reasons why copyright might not even be in the best interests of authors and the distributors of works of authorship (see section 5 of Liebowitz and Watt, 2006, for a survey of some of the more salient papers that offer reasons why copying can be of benefit to copyright holders). However, until very recently, nothing of any real substance appears to have been done in regard to alternative mechanisms for generating appropriability for authors in the markets for their works, who continued to rely almost exclusively on copyright.

The change seems to have taken place together with the so-called 'digital revolution' that made a virtual mockery of copyright law as a device for guaranteeing the true legal reward for authors of such products as music and software. While the music industry continues to grapple with the problem, using a variety of solutions ranging from systems of digital rights management to taxes imposed on blank supports, the software industry has added a more novel mechanism – open source – based paradoxically upon not demanding royalty payments at all!

In a nutshell, proprietary software is delivered to users in such a way that the source code (the computer language instructions that make the program function) is hidden. In that way, the copyright holders in proprietary software hope to protect their products from competition based on the use by other software developers of all or part of the code involved. In fact, this is quite similar to a digital rights management (DRM) system protecting the source code from misuse via copying. However, it should also be clear that software development is very much a collaborative enterprise, with bugs being fixed as they appear, and better, more streamlined versions of programs substituting for obsolete ones at an alarmingly rapid rate. This process is clearly hampered by the hidden nature of the source code on proprietary software, a fact that has led to the development of the open source movement, under which the source code for a program is made available along with the program itself.

Although there are a great many different open source licenses (a good legal analysis of open source licenses can be found in Rosen, 2004; and a brief overview of them is available in Kennedy, 2001; the interested reader can also consult the Open Source Initiative website for details), with very few exceptions, they are based upon the principle that if you take code from the 'commons', then you cannot use it in proprietary commercial versions of software. Developer 1 writes code (which could be an entire program, or simply specific subroutines or parts of programs), releases it to the commons for free use by any other developer who finds it useful. Then, say, Developer 2 uses this code for improving or developing another program. Under the open source conditions the resulting program must be used privately only, or delivered to the commons under the same conditions as the original code. The curious aspect of this, above all for economists, is that it is hard to see why software developers would ever participate in an activity that by its very nature cannot generate a direct financial remuneration for them.

The challenge to the economics profession has been twofold; firstly the incentive mechanisms for participating in open source projects needed to be satisfactorily explained, and secondly, the effects of the open source movement upon the general market for proprietary software needed to be examined, and whether the two business models can co-exist side-by-side, or if one will eventually lead to the demise of the other. Aside from those questions, it is also interesting to consider whether or not open source software is more successful in achieving an efficient outcome – are the right individuals producing the right software for the right users?

The first of these challenges seems to have been surmounted, and the explanations as to why developers would participate, seemingly gratuitously, in open source projects are now generally accepted to include such things as the ability to bundle good software with other complementary products (for example, with hardware), the reputation effects that can be garnered for individual software writers that are of direct benefit in the labour market, and the fact that a good deal of open source software is written not by firms whose primary product is software, but whose primary activities depend upon software (see, for example, Lerner and Tirole, 2002, and Maurer and Scotchmer, 2007, for a good analysis of these things). So the incentive to participate in open source projects is largely indirect, and reliant upon the linkages and spillovers between the software and other appropriable aspects of software business.

The other issues seem to be still largely unresolved, at least to any reasonably high degree of certainty. And, since a full analysis of the final effects of the open source movement on the market for proprietary software will certainly benefit from empirical observations of real-world data, it may still take some time before any general consensus is reached on this particular issue. Nevertheless, Mustonen (2003) provides a theoretical model that suggests that whether or not proprietary and open source software can co-exist will depend upon the implementation costs of software.

In this volume, given our logistical restrictions on the space allocated to any one topical area, we have elected to include only two papers on the economics of open source; Lerner and Tirole (**V, 13**) and Johnson (**V, 14**). The first of these two papers, written by two of the most well-known authors on the topic of the economics of open source, provides a brief survey and commentary of the literature thus far, as well as offering some very interesting thoughts on the prospects of the open source model spreading to other industries. In contrast to the very literary styled paper by Lerner and Tirole, which was written with a very wide audience in mind, the other paper that we include here, by Johnson, provides an excellent example of the use of formal economic modelling for the case of open source. Johnson addresses the issue of the relative efficiencies of the open source model and the proprietary software model. Proprietary software firms have access to a far more restricted set of developers than an open source project, that can access developers from anywhere in the world on the Internet; but on the other hand open source also faces a free-riding problem in that developers' efforts end up becoming a public good. So it seems likely that not all potentially valuable projects will be undertaken in an open source model, but those that do are likely to enjoy a greater talent pool of programmers. Although, not surprisingly, no consensus as to which model is the better can be arrived at, along the way Johnson provides a great many modelling tools and theorems that are of much interest in their own right.

References

Kennedy, D.M. (2001), 'A Primer on Open Source Licensing Legal Issues: Copyright, Copyleft, and Copyfuture', *Saint Louis University Public Law Review*, **20**, 345–76.

Lerner, J. and J. Tirole (2002), 'Some Simple Economics of Open Source', *Journal of Industrial Economics*, **52**, 197–234.

Liebowitz, S. and R. Watt (2006), 'How Best to Remunerate Creators in the Market for Music: Copyright and its Alternatives', *Journal of Economic Surveys*, **20** (4), 513–45.

Maurer, S. and S. Scotchmer (2007), 'Open Source Software: The New Intellectual Property Paradigm', in T. Hendershott (ed.), *Handbook of Economics and Information Systems*, Amsterdam: Elsevier.

Mustonen, M. (2003), 'Copyleft – The Economics of Linux and Other Open Source Software', *Information Economics and Policy*, **15**, 99–121.

Open Source Initiative Website, http://www.opensource.org/licenses/

Plant, A. (1934), 'The Economic Aspects of Copyright in Books', *Economica*, **1**, 167–95.

Rosen, L. (2004), *Open Source Licensing – Software Freedom and Intellectual Property*, Upper Saddle River, NJ: Prentice Hall.

[13]

Journal of Economic Perspectives—Volume 19, Number 2—Spring 2005—Pages 99–120

The Economics of Technology Sharing: Open Source and Beyond

Josh Lerner and Jean Tirole

The open source process of production and innovation seems very unlike what most economists expect. Private firms usually pay their workers, direct and manage their efforts, and control the output and intellectual property thus created. In an open source project, however, a body of original material is made publicly available for others to use, under certain conditions. In many cases, anyone who makes use of the material must agree to make all enhancements to the original material available under these same conditions. This rule distinguishes open source production from, say, material in the public domain and "shareware." Many of the contributors to open source projects are unpaid. Indeed, contributions are made under licenses that often restrict the ability of contributors to make money on their own contributions. Open source projects are often loosely structured, with contributors free to pursue whatever area they feel most interesting. Despite these unusual features, recent years have seen a rise of major corporate investments into open source projects; for instance, IBM is reported to have spent over $1 billion in 2001 alone on such projects.[1]

The most prominent example of open source production is software, which involves developers at many different locations and organizations sharing code to

[1] See ⟨http://news.com.com/2100-1001-825723.html⟩ (accessed March 21, 2004).

■ *Josh Lerner is Jacob H. Schiff Professor of Investment Banking, Harvard Business School, Boston, Massachusetts, and Research Associate, National Bureau of Economic Research, Cambridge, Massachusetts. Jean Tirole is Research Director, Institut d'Economie Industrielle, University of Social Sciences of Toulouse, Toulouse, France, and Visiting Professor, Massachusetts Institute of Technology, Cambridge, Massachusetts.*

develop and refine computer programs. The importance of open source software can be illustrated by considering a few examples. The market for server software, which is used by the computers that make web pages available to users through the Internet, has been dominated by the open source Apache project since the inception of systematic tracking by Netcraft in 1995. As of March 2004, more than two-thirds of servers employed this or other open source products, rather than commercial alternatives from Microsoft, Sun and other firms. The open source operating system called Linux accounts for 23 percent of the operating systems of all servers; moreover, Linux has rapidly outstripped Microsoft's Windows program as the operating system most frequently embedded into products ranging from mobile phones to video recording devices.[2] Open source software is dominant in a number of other areas as well; for example, PERL and PHP are the dominant scripting languages.

Open source software seems poised for rapid growth in the future. A recent survey of chief information officers suggests that Linux will play an increasingly important role as the operating system for web servers. Linux also has plenty of room to grow in the market for desktop operating systems; at the end of 2003, only 1.4 percent of the queries to Google came from machines running Linux, although that share was rising.[3] The dissemination of open source databases remains in its infancy, but these are projected to become by 2006 significant challengers to commercial systems sold by firms such as IBM and Oracle.[4] As of March 2004, the website SourceForge.net, which provides free services to open source software developers, listed over 78,000 open source projects.

The article reviews the intriguing and rapidly growing phenomenon of open source production. After describing briefly the origins of open source software, we examine the incentives and roles of the various actors in the open source process. We end by highlighting how exploring open source can help us understand other economic problems, as well as considering the prospects of the open source model spreading to other industries and the parallels between open source and academia.

[2] On web server software and Apache, see ⟨http://news.netcraft.com/archives/web_server_survey.html⟩ (accessed March 21, 2004). On the use of Linux in web server operating systems, see ⟨http://www.pcworld.com/news/article/0,aid,112840,00.asp⟩ (accessed March 31, 2004). On the use of Linux for embedded software, see ⟨http://www.linuxdevices.com/articles/AT8693703925.html⟩ (accessed March 21, 2004).

[3] For the survey of chief information officers, see ⟨http://www.morganstanley.com/institutional/techresearch/pdfs/ciosurvey1203.pdf⟩ (accessed March, 21, 2004). On Linux software used for Google searches, see ⟨http://www.internetnews.com/dev-news/article.php/3302941⟩ (accessed March 31, 2004).

[4] The challenge is expected to be led by MySQL, which received a $16 million financing from the venture capital organizations Accel and Benchmark in 2003. MySQL provides its program for free under an open source license and for a substantial fee under a commercial license. See ⟨http://www.informationweek.com/story/showArticle.jhtml?articleID=18312009⟩ (accessed August 8, 2004).

A Brief History of Open Source Software

Software development has a tradition of sharing and cooperation. But in recent years, both the scale and formalization of the activity have expanded dramatically with the widespread diffusion of the Internet. We will highlight three distinct eras of cooperative software development.[5]

During the first era, the 1960s and 1970s, many of the key features of computer operating systems and the Internet were developed in academic settings such as Berkeley and MIT, as well as in central corporate research facilities where researchers had a great deal of autonomy, such as Bell Labs and Xerox's Palo Alto Research Center. Software can be transmitted in either "source code" or "object (or binary) code." Source code is the code using languages such as Basic, C and Java. Object, or binary, code is the sequence of 0s and 1s that directly communicates with the computer, but which is difficult for programmers to interpret or modify. Most commercial software vendors today provide users only with object or binary code; when the source code is made available to other firms by commercial developers, it is typically licensed under very restrictive conditions. However, in this first era, the sharing by programmers in different organizations of the source code for computer operating systems and for widely used transmission protocols was commonplace. These cooperative software development projects were undertaken on a highly informal basis. Typically, no efforts to delineate property rights or to restrict reuse of the software were made. This informality proved to be problematic in the early 1980s, when AT&T began enforcing its (purported) intellectual property rights related to the operating system software UNIX, to which many academics and corporate researchers at other firms had made contributions.

In response to the threats of litigation over UNIX, efforts to formalize the ground rules behind the cooperative software development process emerged, which ushered in the second era. The critical institution during this period was the Free Software Foundation, begun by Richard Stallman of the MIT Artificial Intelligence Laboratory in 1983. The foundation sought to develop and disseminate a wide variety of software without cost. The Free Software Foundation introduced a formal licensing procedure, called a General Public License, for a computer operating system called GNU. (The name GNU is a recursive acronym which stands for "GNU's Not UNIX.") In keeping with the philosophy of the organization that this software should be free to use, free to modify and free to redistribute, the license aimed to preclude the assertion of copyright or patent rights concerning cooperatively developed software. Also, in exchange for being able to modify and distribute the GNU software, software developers had to agree to a) make the source code freely available (or at a nominal cost) to whomever the program is

[5] This history is highly abbreviated. See Lerner and Tirole (2002) and the sources cited therein for a longer account.

distributed; and b) insist that others who use the source code agree to do likewise. Furthermore, all enhancements to the code—and even in many cases code that intermingled the cooperatively developed software with that developed separately—had to be licensed on the same terms. This kind of license is sometimes called "copyleft," because if copyright seeks to keep intellectual property private, copyleft seeks to keep intellectual property free and available. These contractual terms are distinct from "shareware," where the binary files, but not the underlying source code, are made freely available, possibly for a trial period only. The terms are also distinct from public domain software, where no restrictions are placed on subsequent users of the source code: those who add to material in the public domain do not commit to put the new product in the public domain. Some projects, such as the Berkeley Software Distribution (BSD) effort, took alternative approaches during the 1980s. The BSD license also allows anyone to copy freely and modify the source code, but it is much less constraining than the General Public License: anyone can modify the program and redistribute it for a fee without making the source code freely available as long as they acknowledge the original source.

The widespread diffusion of Internet access in the early 1990s led to the third era, which saw a dramatic acceleration of open source activity. The volume of contributions and diversity of contributors expanded sharply, and numerous new open source projects emerged, most notably Linux, an operating system related to UNIX, developed by Linus Torvalds in 1991. Another innovation during this period was the proliferation of alternative approaches to licensing cooperatively developed software. In 1997, a number of individuals involved in cooperative software development adopted the "Open Source Definition." These guidelines took an ecumenical approach to licenses: for instance, they did not require that proprietary code compiled with the open source software become open source software as well.

The Actors' Strategies in Open Source

The key actors in an open source product are the individual contributors and for-profit companies. Both sets of actors respond to the legal incentives embodied in open source production. We will take up the individual contributors, for-profit firms and legal incentives in turn.

What Motivates Open Source Contributors?

The decision to contribute without pay to freely available software may seem mysterious to economists. However, the standard framework of labor economics can be adapted to capture activity in the open source environment (Lerner and Tirole, 2002).

The unpaid programmer working on an open source software development project faces a variety of benefits and costs. The programmer incurs an opportunity cost of time, which can manifest itself in different ways. For example, a programmer who works as an independent on open source projects forgoes the monetary compensation that could otherwise be earned by working for a commercial firm or a university. For a programmer with a commercial company, university or research lab affiliation, the opportunity cost of working on open source software comes from not focusing on other tasks. For example, the academic's research output may sag and the student's progress toward a degree slow down.

Several short- or long-run benefits may counter these costs. First, open source programmers may improve rather than reduce their performance in paid work. This outcome is particularly relevant for system administrators looking for specific solutions for their company. Second, the programmer may find intrinsic pleasure if choosing a "cool" open source is more fun than a routine task set by an employer. Third, in the long run, open source contributions may lead to future job offers, shares in commercial open source-based companies, or future access to the venture capital market, and last (but not least) ego gratification from peer recognition. Of course, different programmers may put different values on monetary or personal payoffs and on short-term or long-term payoffs.

Economic theory suggests that long-term incentives for working on an open source project are stronger under three conditions: 1) the more visible the performance to the relevant audience (peers, labor market and venture capital community); 2) the higher the impact of effort on performance; and 3) the more informative the performance about talent (for example, Holmström, 1999).[6] The first condition gives rise to what economists call "strategic complementarities." To have an "audience," programmers will want to work on software projects that will attract a large number of other programmers. This argument suggests the possibility of multiple equilibria. The same project may attract few programmers because programmers expect that other programmers will not be interested; or it may flourish as programmers (rationally) have faith in the project.

To compare programmers' incentives in the open source and proprietary settings, we need to examine how the features of the two environments shape incentives. From the standpoint of the individual, commercial projects typically offer better current compensation than open source projects, because employers are willing to offer salaries to software programmers in the expectation that they will capture a return from a proprietary project. Yet even commercial firms that compensate programmers may want their employees to work on open source projects. Besides the strategic reasons described below, we already noted that the impossibility of appropriating one's contribution to an open source project can be offset if the activity brings private benefits like the ability to fix bugs and customize the product to one's own ends for the programmer. (Commercial software vendors—like Microsoft in its shared source initiative—have sometimes tried to

[6] For a discussion as to how firms might otherwise have superior information about employees and how this might deter job offers from outsiders—a problem that open source programming can address—see Greenwald (1986) and Waldman (1984).

emulate this benefit by opening their code to selected users under a confidentiality arrangement.) Also, open source code may already be familiar to programmers: because it is freely available to all, it can be used in schools and universities for learning purposes, thus creating an "alumni effect." (Again, commercial software vendors are trying to emulate this benefit through university licenses to, say, Windows code.)

When we consider the delayed rewards of working on an open source project, the ability to signal a high level of competence may be stronger in the open source mode for three reasons. First, in an open source project, outsiders can see the contribution of each individual, whether that component "worked," whether the task was hard, if the problem was addressed in a clever way, whether the code can be useful for other programming tasks in the future, and so forth. Second, the open source programmer takes full responsibility for the success of a subproject, with little interference from a superior, which generates information about ability to follow through with a task. Finally, since many elements of the source code are shared across open source projects, more of the knowledge they have accumulated can be transferred to new environments, which makes programmers more valuable to future employers.

These incentives are likely to be stronger and the project more successful if there is an effective leader. While the leader of an open source project has no formal authority—that is, he cannot direct any one to do anything—the leadership often has considerable "real authority," in the terminology of Aghion and Tirole (1997). Leaders play a key role in formulating the initial agenda, setting goals as the project evolves and resolving disputes that might lead to the splintering or outright cessation of the project.

The empirical evidence is largely consistent with the belief that individual contributors to open source projects do benefit directly. The sole econometric study we are aware of, by Hann, Roberts, Slaughter and Fielding (2004), examines contributors to the Apache project, drawing on a wide variety of project records. The authors complement these data with a survey on employment, which yield useable data for multiple years for 147 contributors to the project. The authors then estimate a series of regressions, in which they use the logarithm of earnings in a given year as the dependent variable, and information on the respondents' background, work experience and contributions to and current position in the Apache project in the previous year as independent variables. While in a number of projects such as Linux there is an undisputed central leader, in Apache and many other projects a series of committees at different levels resolves open issues. As a result, there are five observable levels of recognition or rank within the Apache Software Foundation (ASF), which runs the project: in order of increasing status, the titles are developer, committer, project management committee member, ASF member and ASF board member. Advancement is made in recognition of an individual's commitment and contributions to an Apache project. To control for unobserved individual characteristics, individual fixed effects are employed. The results suggest that the sheer volume of contributions to the Apache project have little impact on salary. But individuals who attain high rank in the Apache organization enjoy wages that are 14 to 29 percent higher, whether or not their work directly involves the Apache program. The results appear to be robust to controls for the possible alternative explanations: for instance, the authors address the possibility that Apache promotions may be driven by commercial success by using lags of the key independent variables.

Academics have also attempted to understand motivations of those who work on open source projects through surveys. Given the inherent subjectivity of these assessments and the self-serving biases in reporting, the low response rates that many of these surveys have obtained, and the sensitivity of some of these questions, it is perhaps not surprising that self-reported motivations vary considerably across studies. For instance, Haruvy, Wu and Chakravarty (2003) find that commercial objectives—particularly, the promise of higher future earnings—are an important driver of contributions to open source projects. However, Lakhani and von Hippel (2003) suggest that the overwhelming driver of open source contributors is the need to solve their own specific programming needs, while a Boston Consulting Group (2003) survey implies that intellectual curiosity is the most important determinant.

How Do Commercial Firms Work and Compete with Open Source?

Commercial companies may interact with an open source project in a number of ways. While improvements in the open source software are not appropriable, commercial companies can benefit if they also offer expertise in some proprietary segment of the market that is complementary to the open source program. Also, firms may temporarily encourage their programmers to participate in open source projects to learn about the strengths and weaknesses of this development approach. For-profit firms may compete directly with open source providers in the same market. Finally, commercial companies may interface with the open source world because it generates good public relations with programmers and customers.

A for-profit firm that seeks to provide services and products that are complementary to the open source product, but are not supplied efficiently by the open source community, can be referred to as "living symbiotically." IBM, which has made open source software into a major focus for its consulting business, exemplifies this approach. A commercial company in this situation will want to have extensive knowledge about the open source movement, and may even want to encourage and subsidize open source contributions, both of which may cause it to allocate some programmers to the open source project. Because firms do not capture all the benefits of the investments in the open source project, however, the free-rider problem often discussed in the economics of innovation should apply here as well. Subsidies by commercial companies for open source projects should remain somewhat limited.

The *code release* strategy arises when companies release some existing proprietary code and then create a governance structure for the resulting open source development process. For example, IBM released half-a-million lines of its Cloudscape program, a simple database that resides inside a software application instead of as a full-fledged database program, to the Apache Software Foundation. Hewlett-Packard released its Spectrum Object Model-Linker to the open source community to help the Linux community write software to connect Linux with Hewlett Packard's RISC computer architecture. This strategy is to give away the razor (the released code) to sell more razor blades (the related consulting services that IBM and Hewlett Packard hope to provide).[7]

When can it be advantageous for a commercial company to release proprietary code under an open source license? In general, it will make sense if the increase in profit in the proprietary complementary segment offsets any profit that would have been made in the primary segment, had it not been converted to open source. Thus, the temptation to go open source is particularly strong when the product is lagging behind the leader and making few profits, but the firm sees a possibility that if the released code becomes the center of an open source project and is utilized more widely, the profitability of the complementary segment will increase. (An example may be Netscape's 1998 decision to make "Mozilla," a portion of its browser source code, freely available.) If network effects and switching costs are very strong, the second-best commercial package might have a tiny market share. In these cases, the cost to corporations of releasing code may be very small. Moreover, such a strategy may reassure potential users that the released software will never be withdrawn—and thus that the user will always be able to maintain the product itself.

This motivation can also depend on the evolution of vertical relationships between small and large firms in the software industry in commercial software environments, a subject that would reward further study. Indeed, many small developers are uncomfortable doing business with leading software firms. They fear that the commercial platform owner has an incentive to introduce substitutes in the developers' segment to force prices down in that segment and to raise the demand for licenses to the broad software platform (Farrell and Katz, 2000). By contrast, when a large firm makes its platform available on an open source basis through (say) a General Public License-style license, the small firm need no longer fear being squeezed in this way.

Numerous challenges appear, though, when a for-profit firm seeks to become the center of an open source development project. Leadership by a commercial entity may not internalize enough of the objectives of the open source community. In particular, a corporation may not be able to make a credible commitment to keeping all source code in the public domain and to highlighting important contributions adequately. These difficulties help to explain why Hewlett-Packard

[7] For more details, see ⟨http://www.infoworld.com/article/04/08/03/HNclouscape_1.html⟩ (accessed August 3, 2004), ⟨http://www.collab.net/customers/cdp_solutions_at_work.html⟩ (accessed March 31, 2004) and the associated links.

released its code through Collab.Net, a venture by leading open source programmers, which organizes open source projects for corporations who wish to open up part of their software. In effect, Collab.Net offers a kind of certification that the firm is committed to the open source project. (The Apache Software Foundation plays a similar role in Cloudscape case mentioned above.) In a theoretical model, Dessein (2002) shows that a principal with formal control rights over an agent's activity in general gains by delegating control rights to an intermediary with preferences or incentives that are intermediate between the principal's and the agent's. The partial alignment of the intermediary's preferences with the agent's fosters trust and boosts the agent's initiative, ultimately offsetting the partial loss of control for the principal. In the case of Collab.Net, the congruence with the open source developers is obtained through the employment of visible open source developers and the involvement of O'Reilly, a technical book publisher with strong ties to the open source community.

While the relative merits of open source and proprietary software are discussed in a number of contributions, direct competition between the two paradigms has received little attention. An exception is Gaudeul (2004), who builds a duopoly model with one open source and one proprietary software project.[8] In his model, open source software has both costs and benefits relative to proprietary software. Open source software suffers from some lack of coordination: the same code may be written twice or not at all. Another cost of open source software in Gaudeul's model is that its designers, the developers, may not bother developing interfaces that appeal to unsophisticated users. By contrast, the profit-maximizing proprietary software firm in his model is keener to develop such an interface. However, the proprietary model must pay its developers and, despite good project coordination, may choose to develop a limited set of features. In this model, the proprietary software is sold to users at a positive price that excludes some possible users. In equilibrium, the open source software, if it survives, is used either by low-demand or low-income consumers, who cannot afford buying the proprietary software, or by developers who like the potentially larger set of features and do not care about the missing or insufficient user interface. Furthermore, the presence of open source software raises welfare, at least if it does not discourage the development of proprietary software with a good interface.

How Does the Legal System Affect Open Source?

Open source software is shaped by the legal rules under which it operates. In each case, the product originator gives users the right to employ the copyrighted code through a license. But the licenses differ tremendously in the extent to which they enable licensors and contributors to profit from the code that is contributed.

In Lerner and Tirole (2005), we explore what drives firms to choose particular

[8] See also the discussion below of Casadesus-Masanell and Ghemawat (2003).

licenses. We begin with a model of license choice. We suppose that an entity, either an individual or a firm, is deciding a) whether to make some software available under an open source license; and b) if so, what type of license to employ. We depict the interactions between the licensor and the community of programmers. The programmers' benefits from working on the project may depend on the choice of license. The licensor must assess how its choice of license, together with project characteristics—such as the environment, the nature of the project and the intended audience—impacts the project's likely success.

The model suggests that permissive licenses such as the Berkeley Software Distribution model, where users retain the ability to use the code as they see fit, will be more common in cases where projects have strong appeal to the community of open source contributors—for instance, when contributors stand to benefit considerably from signaling incentives or when the licensors are well-trusted. Conversely, restrictive licenses such as the General Public License will be commonplace when such appeals are more fragile. Examples of cases where we would expect a restrictive license are projects geared for end users who are unlikely to appreciate the coding, such as computer games, or those sponsored by corporations, who potential contributors might fear would "hijack" the project and use the code for commercial ends.

One of the most visible of the disputes over licensing was the Mozilla case alluded to above. This effort initially encountered severe difficulties because of the license choice. Netscape initially proposed the "Netscape Public License," which would have allowed Netscape to take pieces of the open source code and turn them back into a proprietary project again (Hamerly, Paquin and Walton, 1999). Ultimately, the firm announced the "Mozilla Public License," under which Netscape cannot regain proprietary rights to modifications of the code: in fact, the terms of the final license are even stricter than those of the General Public License.

In Lerner and Tirole (2005), we also present an empirical analysis of the prevalence of different types of open source licenses. The analysis employs nearly 40,000 open source projects in the SourceForge database. Since all of the projects in this database are open source, we focus on whether the license requires that when modified versions of the program are distributed, the source code must be made generally available and/or whether the license restricts modified versions of the program from mingling their source code with other software that does not employ such a license. We term such licenses "restrictive." We find that restrictive licenses are more common for applications geared toward end-users and system administrators—like desktop tools and games. However, restrictive licenses are significantly less common for those applications aimed toward software developers. Restrictive licenses are also less common for projects operating in commercial environments or that run on proprietary operating systems. Projects whose natural language is not English, whose community appeal may be presumed to be much smaller, are more likely to employ restrictive licenses. Projects with less restrictive licenses tend to attract more contributors.

Further Issues about Open Source

This section will highlight three other particularly interesting and challenging areas about open source projects: the quality of their output; whether open source projects should be encouraged by public policy; and how open source projects may be affected by software patents.

What is the Relative Quality of Open Source Software?

One of the most contentious issues in the literature has been the relative virtues of the open source and proprietary development process. Advocates of open source software have long claimed that the open source development process leads to superior software (for example, Raymond, 1999). A number of studies have sought to explore these claims, but consensus remains elusive.

Kuan (2001) was the first to offer a formal model of some of the advantages of open source software for users. She focused on the consumer's choice between employing "off-the-shelf" commercial software and adapting open source code to the consumer's own use. While the proprietary software can (and indeed must) be used "as is," open source code can be enhanced in quality through the user's efforts. Such refinements, however, require effort, with more effort leading to higher quality code. If consumers differ in type, commercial companies may either offer different quality levels of programs, or else may offer a single product to all users. She shows that under certain circumstances, some consumers will prefer the open source option and invest in producing software that is of superior quality to commercial alternatives. The paper tests this model by comparing dates at which program errors or "bugs" were reported and fixed in three open source programs—Apache, FreeBSD and Gnome—with three commercial projects matched by subject matter and age. For two of the three pairs that she examines, the rate at which bugs are fixed is significantly faster in the open source project, and there is little difference in the third case.

Bessen (2002), in a related paper, emphasizes another dimension along which open source software may have an advantage: the ability of heterogeneous users to customize it to meet their own particular needs. Proprietary software manufacturers cannot anticipate all manifestations of consumer demand, and thus cannot offer every conceivable variation that consumers might desire. Again, consumers face a "make versus buy" choice, where the complexity and idiosyncrasy of the project, as well as the cost of modifications, will drive the choice. While Bessen does not test this model, he cites Franke and von Hippel's (2003) finding that one-fifth of Apache users adapted security features to meet their particular needs as consistent with his model.

While these two authors attribute the superiority of open source projects to the ability of end-users to adapt an initial code base, Johnson (2004) focuses on a different rationale: that open source programs are developed through a superior process that may avoid pathologies that affect commercial projects. In particular, he argues that workers in commercial firms may collude not to report programming errors of fellow employees, lest their own reputation and future earnings be damaged. He hypothesizes that because programmers do not receive wages in open source projects, they will have fewer incentives to engage in such collusion. (Note, though, that the ego gratification and career incentives may also motivate collusion.) It may be argued that the large number of potential eyeballs in open source software makes collusion difficult to sustain. Johnson argues that reduced collusion will lead to open source projects undergoing more peer review and having higher quality.[9]

Another issue that may differentiate proprietary and open source software is security. Open source advocates have argued that when source code is open and freely visible, programmers can readily identify security flaws and other problems: as Eric Raymond (1999) has argued, "to many eyes, all bugs are shallow." Proponents of proprietary software, on the other hand, argue that the openness of the source code allows malicious hackers to figure out its weaknesses. Anderson (2002) argues that under certain plausible assumptions, the openness of the system should have no impact on its security. Making bugs harder for hackers to find by keeping the source code hidden will also mean that software companies have a more difficult time identifying errors through "beta" testing, where lead users experiment with the product, also without access to the underlying source code. (While software firms will also do internal testing by employees with access to the source code, the effort devoted to these "alpha" tests is usually many times smaller than that in later-stage tests.) Thus, he concludes, "other things being equal, we expect that open and closed systems will exhibit similar growth in reliability and in security assurance." However, Anderson does not attempt to assess this claim empirically. Any such effort is difficult because hackers may attack a software program for reasons unrelated to the intrinsic security of the program; for instance, some hackers may derive more gratification from an attack on a leading public company, even though hackers have targeted both commercial and open source programs at various occasions.[10]

Open source and commercial software could be compared as well along numerous other dimensions. For instance, we argue in our 2002 work that it is likely that the incentive structure for open source programmers will lead to poorer documentation and user interfaces in these projects. These claims, and numerous others in the literature, deserve careful scrutiny.

[9] Also in this paper, Johnson (2004) suggests that individuals in commercial software companies may be reluctant to report programming problems to superiors, because the firm's management may be unable to commit not to demand that they then address these issues. In open source projects, programmers can never be compelled to work on fixing a bug that they identify. He predicts that while the speed of the bug fixing process may be slower in open source projects, more problems will ultimately be identified.
[10] For a discussion of a hacker attack on Apache, see ⟨http://thewhir.com/marketwatch/hac062102.cfm⟩ (accessed March 31, 2004).

What are Appropriate Public Policies Toward Open Source?

Government commissions and agencies have proposed—and in some cases implemented—a variety of measures to encourage open source developers. For example, in the United States, the President's Information Technology Advisory Committee (2000) recommended direct federal subsidies for open source projects to advance high-end computing, and a report from the European Commission (2001) also discussed support for open developers and standards. Many European governments have policies to encourage the use and purchase of open source software for government use ("Microsoft at the Power Point," 2003). Governments may even mandate the development of localized open source projects, as has occurred in China (Open Source Development Labs, 2004).

Economists have sought to understand the consequences of a vibrant open source sector for social welfare. Perhaps not surprisingly, definitive or sweeping answers have been difficult to come by; instead, the policy conclusions focus on specific instruments in specific contexts. We will first discuss two papers that consider the impact of open source on social welfare more generally and then discuss a number of works that address public policies.

Most analyses have suggested that government support for open source projects is likely to have an ambiguous effect on social welfare. For example, Johnson (2002) presents a model where programmers decide whether to devote effort to a project, in which their contributions become a public good once they are developed. Users thus face a decision whether to enhance an existing open source program or to wait in the hope that another programmer will undertake the development process. Johnson then compares this process to a stylized depiction of the development of proprietary software in a corporate setting. Open source projects have the advantage of being able to access the entire pool of developer talent, not just employees in a single firm. Given the larger talent pool, they can aggregate and exploit more private information. But because of the free riding problem, some potentially valuable projects will not be developed under an open source system. Johnson concludes that a comparison of the social welfare consequences of these two systems is ambiguous.

Casadesus-Masanell and Ghemawat (2003) depict competition between an open source operating system available at no cost and a proprietary commercial product. The crucial feature of their model is on the demand side: the larger the market share of a given operating system, the more valuable that system to users. This effect could be due to better learning about the program's features (if users contribute comments and suggestions to improve the product) or to the presence of complementary software developed by other firms. In this setting, the presence of an open source operating system leads the commercial firm to set lower prices, which in turn means that the overall use of operating systems is higher. However, the value of the commercial system for users is lower: for instance, the presence of a competing product may lead third-party developers to develop fewer complementary products for the commercial operating system. Thus, the presence of open source projects may either make society better or worse off. This model also suggests that in some cases, the proprietary operating system may be able to drive the market share of the open source alternative to zero, and also that the parameter ranges where this will occur need not correspond to those where such an action is socially desirable.

Schmidt and Schnitzer (2002) highlight similarly that open source software has social costs and benefits. Building on a line of economic reasoning that extends back to Arrow (1962) and even earlier, they highlight two countervailing effects. From a static point of view, free or nearly free open source will insure greater social welfare, as virtually any potential user will be able to access software. But from a dynamic perspective, with so few profits to be gleaned, developers may lack incentives to introduce new products. While career concerns and other incentives may motivate developers to identify bugs in open source programs and undertake certain modest adaptations to meet their own needs, they are unlikely to be sufficient to encourage major breakthroughs. The authors argue that while open source programs will enhance social welfare in some settings, this outcome will be far from universal. They caution against subsidies that may lead to an undesirably high level of open source activity.

Saint-Paul (2003) reaches an even bleaker conclusion about the open source phenomenon. He employs a Romer-style endogenous growth model, in which both commercial firms and "philanthropists"—individuals who are willing to give their contributions away for free—innovate. He shows that the free contributions will lead to economic growth, but also reduce the profits, and hence the incentives to innovate, among commercial firms. Unless the proprietary sector is quite profitable, then the second effect will dominate, and innovation and growth be harmed by the presence of open source software. He argues that the negative effect is likely to be even stronger than his model shows, because he neglects, for instance, the possibility that philanthropic products do not meet users' needs as well as commercial products (though see the previous section for a counter-argument) and can also divert programming talent that could have been devoted to commercial products.

In a more informal piece, Shapiro and Varian (2004) suggest another consideration that formal models have not so far discussed: the impact on human capital and entrepreneurship. They suggest that an open system will facilitate learning by students as to how to program and will provide opportunities for third-party developers to introduce complementary products. They argue that all else being equal, these considerations should lead public policymakers in nations that seek to encourage the development of their software industries to boost the development of open source activity.

How Will Software Patents Affect Open Source?

Software patents will interact with open source activity.[11] This issue is clearly a timely one, in light of the litigation launched by the SCO Group, which holds to (at

[11] In this section, we will avoid discussing the highly contentious and unsettled question of the economic impact of software patents more generally: for more on this topic, see, for instance, Bessen and Hunt (2003), Caillaud (2003), Graham and Mowery (2003) and Hahn and Wallsten (2003).

least partial) rights to UNIX (acquired from Novell, who in turn had purchased them from AT&T). Beginning in 2003, the firm initiated a series of lawsuits against, among others, AutoZone, DaimlerChrysler, IBM and Novell, alleging that they were violating SCO's intellectual property by contributing to or using Linux.[12] The allegedly detrimental impact of software patents on open source was also a frequently invoked reason for opposing software patents in the September 2003 debate in the European Parliament on this question.[13]

Software patents create the possibility of holding up software producers. In the case of commercial software, individuals and companies that do not produce software themselves (like hardware manufacturers and software users), but hold a software patent, can try to obtain royalty payments from major software vendors. Large software vendors are less likely to engage in such behaviors against each other, as they have accumulated patent portfolios that they can use for retaliatory purposes against other vendors that would try to hold them up.

Open source software is vulnerable in a different way. After all, the code is free of charge and the contributors hardly solvent for the most part, so attempting to collect royalties is not a powerful incentive. However, firms with software patents may seek damages from large corporate and noncorporate users and firms that service open source software, as SCO is doing, or commercial competitors with software patents may sue open source software to enjoin further utilization of the code. It remains to be seen whether the open source movement will itself enter into defensive patenting, as large commercial vendors already do, or at least make a more concerted effort to forestall patenting by others by aggressively publishing. One intriguing new initiative is the Red Hat Assurance Plan, in which the Linux distributor is offering partial protection against intellectual property litigation.[14]

Another interesting area of study concerns the consequences of users paying royalties for an open source program that also included some commercially patented material. Such royalty demands might trigger "sweetheart" deals between firms, the splitting of open source projects into different branches (often termed "forking") and the privatization of blocks of code. The General Public License seeks to address these problems—and to discourage patent filings by firms working with open source projects—by prohibiting the incorporation of code that is encumbered by patent rights. As section 7 of the license states, "[I]f a patent license would

[12] Patent concerns have also slowed the adoption of Linux in the public sector: see, for instance, ⟨http://www.informationweek.com/story/showArticle.jhtml?articleID=26806464⟩ (accessed August 25, 2004) for a discussion of the impact of these concerns on the city of Munich's open source effort.

[13] See, for instance, ⟨http://news.zdnet.co.uk/business/legal/0,39020651,39116053,00.htm⟩ (accessed March 26, 2004).

[14] For a discussion, see ⟨http://www.redhat.com/about/presscenter/2004/press_blackduck.html⟩ (accessed August 24, 2004). One challenge is that the extent and dispersion of the patent holdings that may impact open source projects: the insurer Open Source Risk Management estimates that there are 283 patents that might be used in claims against the Linux kernel alone. See ⟨http://www.eweek.com/article2/0,1759,1631336,00.asp⟩ (accessed August 24, 2004).

not permit royalty-free redistribution of the Program by all those who receive copies directly or indirectly through you, then the only way you could satisfy both it and this License would be to refrain entirely from distribution of the Program." Many other types of open source licenses, however, do not address this issue.[15]

Another, less prominent, question relates to the impact of patents on the dynamics of information sharing and collaboration among open source contributors. To what extent will the ability of programmers to protect their discoveries with strong patent rights reduce their incentives to participate in open source projects?

To date, very little systematic analysis has examined the implications of patents for open source. However, a broader literature has scrutinized the impact of patenting on the generation and diffusion of scientific knowledge more generally. Since 1980, a series of reforms in the United States and elsewhere have greatly augmented the ability of academic institutions, government laboratories and non-profit institutions to patent their discoveries, even if governments originally funded the research. This literature has sought to understand the pervasiveness and consequences of the "anticommons" problem (Heller and Eisenberg, 1998): the concern that the patenting of scientific knowledge will lead to lower research productivity, and hence eventually to reduced economic growth. Much of the discussion of these questions to date has featured broad assertions and anecdotal examples (as in Bok, 2003). It is clear from these studies that institutions and researchers have responded to the increased incentives to commercialize products by engaging in more patenting and commercialization activities (for instance, Jaffe and Lerner, 2001; Lach and Schankerman, 2003). Whether these commercial activities have detrimental effects on research and social welfare is much more ambiguous.[16] Given this initial and somewhat contradictory evidence, our ability to draw conclusions for consequences of formal intellectual property rights for open source software is quite limited.

[15] A related danger is that programs will inadvertently infringe patents. Programmers may lack the incentives and skills needed to check whether their contribution infringes awards. As an effort to limit this problem, beginning in May 2004, Linux contributors were required to attest that they have the right to make that contribution. For a discussion, see ⟨http://www.computerworld.com/softwaretopics/os/linux/story/0,10801,93395,00.html⟩ (accessed August 8, 2004).

[16] For instance, Thursby and Thursby's (2003) study of six major research universities suggests that while the probability that a faculty member will indicate to his university's technology transfer office that he has made a new discovery has increased ten-fold over the past decade, research productivity in basic research journals has remained constant. On the other hand, Murray and Stern (2003) have shown that papers published in the journal *Nature Biotechnology* are somewhat less likely to be cited in other articles once the corresponding patent application issues. They find that the papers with corresponding patents are initially more heavily cited than those without, but then their citation rate declines more sharply over time.

A Broader Research Agenda

The open source process poses numerous interesting issues that extend well beyond the software industry. In this section, we'll highlight three of these. The first issue is the extent to which the open source model can move beyond software into other industries. Second, we'll discuss the way in which firms can accomplish many of the key goals of open source while employing other arrangements. Finally, we'll explore the parallels between open source software and academic research.

Can Open Source Work Beyond Software?

An interesting question is whether the open source model can be transposed to other industries. Could automobile components be developed in an open source mode, with General Motors and Toyota performing an assembler function similar to that of Red Hat for Linux? Many industries involve forms of cooperation between commercial entities in the form of for-profit or not-for-profit joint ventures. Others exhibit user-driven innovation or open science cultures. Thus, a number of ingredients of open source software are not specific to the software industry. Yet no other industry has yet produced anything quite like open source development.

Although some aspects of open source software collaboration (such as electronic information exchange across the world) could easily be duplicated, other aspects would be harder to emulate. Consider, for example, the case of biotechnology. It may be impossible to break up large projects into small manageable and independent modules, and there may not sufficient sophisticated users who can customize the molecules to their own needs. The tasks that are involved in making the product available to the end user involve larger expenditures than simply providing consumer support and friendlier user interfaces as in software. The costs of designing, testing and seeking regulatory approval for a new drug are enormous.

More generally, in many industries, the development of individual components requires large-scale teamwork and substantial capital costs, as opposed to (for some software programs) individual contributions and no capital investment (besides the computer the programmer already has). Another obstacle is that in mass-market industries, users are numerous and rather unsophisticated, and so deliver little peer recognition and ego gratification. These characteristics suggests that the open source model may not easily be transposed to other industries, but further investigation is warranted.

Can Firms Realize the Benefits of Open Source in Other Ways?

Corporations may emulate some of the benefits attached to open source production either by getting involved in open source themselves or by adopting institutional arrangements that deliver some of these benefits. First, using open source technology encourages users that they will not be "held up" by a future price increase after adopting a technology and that they will always be able to tailor their technology to their own particular needs. Second, open source avoids the problem of a "patent thicket" when multiple firms have overlapping intellectual property rights and at least one party attempts to extract a high fee for its particular contribution. Third, a firm might make a technology open source as a way of trying to certify a technological standard, in which case firms may contribute software to open source to benefit from the endorsement of such a standard, as the Hewlett Packard case discussed above illustrates.

Firms can also address these problems in non-open-source ways, such as patent pools, standard-setting organizations and self-imposed commitments. In a patent pool, firms blend their patents with those of other firms. These pools allow users to access a number of firms' patents simultaneously, thereby avoiding the "patent thicket." In many cases, the pooling agreements also specify the pricing schedule in the agreement that establishes the pool, assuring that no party attempts to extract very high fees or to increase its fees after users are locked in. To be certain, patent pools raise a risk that they can be used to hinder entry, but these concerns can in part be addressed through a careful design of the pool (Lerner and Tirole, 2004a; Lerner, Strojwas and Tirole, 2003).

Standard-setting organizations offer an alternative path for the certification of new technologies. Often firms can choose between standard-setting organizations, and they can seek an endorsement for an emerging technology from an independent and prestigious organization or use a more complacent one (Lerner and Tirole, 2004b). These bodies also help address the other concerns, frequently asking contributors of the key technologies to commit to license the technology on "reasonable and non-discriminatory" terms or to make various other concessions.

Self-imposed commitments can serve much the same role. For instance, firms can commit to license technologies at a given price schedule, or they can commit to provide sufficient information so that users can tailor the technology. An example of the latter is Microsoft's Shared Source Initiative, through the firm shares source code with customers, partners and governments. One open question about many of these self-imposed programs is the extent to which the commitments can be enforced if the firm subsequently changes its design.[17]

Open source production may seem like a unique and idiosyncratic realm. However, many of the issues are seen elsewhere in high-technology industries: when and how to share technology, how to set common standards, and how to combine freely available and commercial components arise both in the open source and the commercial realm. Open source projects and traditional firms can borrow from each other innovative approaches to the underlying problems.

Open Source and Academia

Open source and academia have many parallels. The most obvious parallel relates to motivation. As in open source, the direct financial returns from writing

[17] This is also a question for other commitments as well. For one illustration in a standard setting context, see *Rambus Inc. v. Infineon Techs. AG*, 318 F.3d 1081 (Fed. Cir. 2003).

academic articles are typically nonexistent, but career concerns and the desire for peer recognition provide powerful inducements.

Other similar dynamics are also at work. Consider, for instance, the discussion of motivation for programmers when choosing to which open source project they should contribute. As we highlight above, a critical goal is the selection of a project that is likely to continue to be successful, so that the programmers' contributions are widely recognized, yet which at the same time has interesting and challenging programming challenges to be addressed. These criteria should be familiar to anyone who has advised a doctoral student on the choice of a thesis topic!

However, there are also some substantial differences between the two realms. Here, we will highlight two areas where academic economists could learn from the open source realm. The first of these relates to the incentives to create public goods. Open source contributors often create substantial bodies of code, which are made widely available when completed. Far too often in academic economics, however, we do not see similar dissemination.[18] For instance, an author—after creating a unique dataset for a project—may simply save this information on a personal computer hard disk, rather than making it publicly available. Similarly, while there are some examples of efforts to create shared resources that can be widely used by the economics community—the NBER Patent Citations Database created by Bronwyn Hall, Adam Jaffe and Manuel Trajtenberg is a recent important example—far too often these efforts are neglected because the returns to the project leaders are low. Why it is not commonplace to see economists frequently seeking to establish their reputation by creating original, widely accessible datasets is an interesting question. (Akin to open source, we might anticipate that this strategy might be especially effective for those at smaller and less centrally located institutions.) One explanation might be that data collection is often inspired by what analyses one wants to perform, so it is harder to separate data collection and analysis. In any case, the design of mechanisms that successfully encourage such investments is an important challenge for academic economists.

A second area relates to access to published work. Contributors to open source projects seem to be powerfully spurred by the provisions of these licenses. The assurance that contributions—and subsequent contributions that build on it—will remain publicly accessible incentivizes programmers to write code. By way of contrast, in academic economics, it is standard to assign the copyright to one's work to a commercial publisher. In other areas of academia, this approach is under increasing attack. For instance, recent years have seen the rise of "open access" journals such as the *Public Library of Science*, which make all articles freely accessible and distributable. In response to this challenge, a number of established science journals, such as the *Proceedings of the National Academies of Sciences*, have not only begun providing free access to older issues, but even allowing authors to opt to have

[18] Data archiving policies, such as the *American Economic Review*'s, seek to address this problem, but are more the exception than the rule.

their articles immediately publicly accessible with the payment of an additional fee.[19] It is an interesting question as to whether open access will have the same appeal for the economics community.

Final Thoughts

This paper has reviewed our understanding of the growing open source movement. We have highlighted how many aspects of open source software appear initially puzzling to an economist. Our ability to answer confidently many of the issues raised here questions is likely to increase as the open source movement itself grows and evolves.

At the same time, it is heartening to us how much of open source activities can be understood within existing economic frameworks, despite the presence of claims to the contrary. The labor and industrial organization literatures provide lenses through which the structure of open source projects, the role of contributors and the movement's ongoing evolution can be viewed.

■ *We thank the National Science Foundation and Harvard Business School's Division of Research for financial support. The Institut D'Economie Industrielle receives research grants from a number of corporate sponsors, including France Telecom and the Microsoft Corporation. We thank Christophe Bisiere, Jacques Cremer, Alexandre Gaudeul, Justin Johnson, Hal Varian and the editors for helpful comments.*

[19] See, for instance, ⟨http://www.plos.org/about/openaccess.html⟩ and ⟨http://www.pnas.org/cgi/content/full/101/23/8509⟩ (accessed August 10, 2004).

References

Aghion, Philippe and Jean Tirole. 1997. "Formal and Real Authority in Organizations." *Journal of Political Economy.* 105:1, pp. 1–29.

Anderson, Ross. 2002. "Security in Open versus Closed Systems—The Dance of Boltzman, Coase and Moore." Unpublished working paper, Cambridge University.

Arrow, Kenneth J. 1962. "Economic Welfare and the Allocation of Resources for Invention," in *The Rate and Direction of Inventive Activity: Economic and Social Factors.* Richard R. Nelson, ed. Princeton, N.J.: Princeton University Press, pp. 609–26.

Bessen, James. 2002. "Open Source Software: Free Provision of Complex Public Goods." Unpublished working paper, Research on Innovation.

Bessen, James and Robert M. Hunt. 2003. "An Empirical Look at Software Patents." Working Paper 03-17, Federal Reserve Bank of Philadelphia.

Bok, Derek. 2003. *Universities in the Marketplace: The Commercialization of Higher Education.* Princeton, N.J.: Princeton University Press.

Boston Consulting Group. 2003. *Boston Consulting Group/OSDN Hacker Survey.* Boston: Boston Consulting Group.

Caillaud, Bernard. 2003. "La Propriété Intellectuelle sur les Logiciels." *Propriété Intellectuelle.* Conseil D'Analyse Economique, Rapport 41, pp. 113–71.

Casadesus-Masanell, Ramon and Pankaj Ghemawat. 2003. "Dynamic Mixed Duopoly: A Model Motivated by Linux vs. Windows." Strategy Unit Working Paper 04-012, Graduate School of Business Administration, Harvard University.

Dessein, Wouter. 2002. "Authority and Communication in Organizations." *Review of Economic Studies.* 69:4, pp. 811–38.

European Commission, Interchange of Data between Administrations. 2001. "Study into the Use of Open Source Software in the Public Sector." June; Available at ⟨http://europa.eu.int/ISPO/ida/jsps/index.jsp?fuseAction=showDocument&documentID=333&parent=chapter&preChapterID=0-17-134⟩.

Farrell, Joseph and Michael L. Katz. 2000. "Innovation, Rent Extraction, and Integration in Systems Markets." *Journal of Industrial Economics.* 48:4, pp. 413–32.

Franke, Nikolaus and Eric von Hippel. 2003. "Satisfying Heterogeneous User Needs via Innovation Tool Kits: The Case of Apache Security Software." *Research Policy.* 32:7, pp. 1199–215.

Gaudeul, Alexandre. 2004. "Competition between Open-Source and Proprietary Software: The (L^)TEX case Study." Unpublished working paper, Universities of Toulouse and Southampton.

Graham, Stuart and David C. Mowery. 2003. "Intellectual Property Protection in the Software Industry," in *Patents in the Knowledge-Based Economy: Proceedings of the Science, Technology and Economic Policy Board.* Wesley Cohen and Steven Merrill, eds. Washington, National Academies Press.

Greenwald, Bruce C. 1986. "Adverse Selection in the Labour Market." *Review of Economic Studies.* 53:3, pp. 325–47.

Hahn, Robert W. and Scott J. Wallsten. 2003. "A Review of Bessen and Hunt's Analysis of Software Patents." Unpublished working paper, American Enterprise Institute-Brookings Joint Center for Regulatory Studies.

Hammerly, Jim, Tom Paquin and Susan Walton. 1999. "Freeing the Source: The Story of Mozilla," in *Open Sources: Voices from the Open Source Revolution.* Chris DiBona, Sam Ockman, and Mark Stone, eds. Cambridge, Massachusetts: O'Reilly, pp. 197–206.

Hann, Il-Horn, Jeff Roberts, Sandra Slaughter and Roy Fielding. 2004. "An Empirical Analysis of Economic Returns to Open Source Participation." Unpublished working paper, Carnegie-Mellon University.

Haruvy, Ernan E., Fang Wu and Sujoy Chakravarty. 2003. "Incentives for Developers' Contributions and Product Performance Metrics in Open Source Development: An Empirical Investigation." Unpublished working paper, University of Texas at Dallas.

Heller, Michael and Rebecca Eisenberg. 1998. "Can Patents Deter Innovation? The Anticommons in Biomedical Research." *Science.* 280: 5364, pp. 698–701.

Holmström, Bengt. 1999. "Managerial Incentive Problems: A Dynamic Perspective." *Review of Economic Studies.* 66:1, pp. 169–82.

Jaffe, Adam B. and Josh Lerner. 2001. "Reinventing Public R&D: Patent Law and Technology Transfer from Federal Laboratories." *Rand Journal of Economics.* Spring, 32, pp. 167–98.

Johnson, Justin P. 2002. "Open Source Software: Private Provision of a Public Good." *Journal* *of Economics and Management Strategy*. 11:4, pp. 637–62.

Johnson, Justin P. 2004. "Collaboration, Peer Review and Open Source Software." Unpublished working paper, Cornell University.

Kuan, Jennifer. 2001. "Open Source Software as Consumer Integration into Production." Unpublished working paper, Stanford University.

Lach, Saul and Mark Schankerman. 2003. "Incentives and Invention in Universities." Discussion Paper No. 3916, Centre for Economic Policy Research.

Lakhani, Karim and Eric von Hippel. 2003. "How Open Source Software Works: 'Free' User-to-User Assistance." *Research Policy*. 32:6, pp. 923–43.

Lerner, Josh and Jean Tirole. 2002. "Some Simple Economics of Open Source." *Journal of Industrial Economics*. 52:2, pp. 197–234.

Lerner, Josh and Jean Tirole. 2004a. "Efficient Patent Pools." *American Economic Review*. 94:3, pp. 691–711.

Lerner, Josh and Jean Tirole. 2004b. "A Model of Forum Shopping, with Special Reference to Standard Setting Organizations." NBER Working Paper No. 10664.

Lerner, Josh and Jean Tirole. 2005. "The Scope of Open Source Licensing." *Journal of Law, Economics, and Organization*. 21, forthcoming.

Lerner, Josh, Marcin Strojwas and Jean Tirole. 2003. "Cooperative Marketing Agreements between Competitors: Evidence from Patent Pools." NBER Working Paper No. 9680.

"Microsoft at the Power Point." 2003. *Economist*. September 11.

Murray, Fiona and Scott Stern. 2003. "Do Formal Intellectual Property Rights Hinder the Flow of Scientific Knowledge? Evidence from Patent-Paper Pairs." Unpublished working paper, Massachusetts Institute of Technology and Northwestern University.

Open Source Development Labs. 2004. "OSDL Announces First Chinese Member." January 30; Available at ⟨http://www.osdl.org/newsroom/press_releases/2004/2004_01_30_beaverton.html⟩.

President's Information Technology Advisory Committee, Panel on Open Source Software for High End Computing. 2000. "Developing Open Source Software to Advance High End Computing." October; Available at ⟨http://www.hpcc.gov/pubs/pitac/pres-oss-11sep00.pdf⟩

Raymond, Eric. 1999. *The Cathedral and the Bazaar: Musings on Linux and Open Source by an Accidental Revolutionary*. Cambridge: O'Reilly.

Saint-Paul, Gilles. 2003. "Growth Effects of Non-Proprietary Innovation." *Journal of the European Economic Association: Papers and Proceedings*. 1:2-3, pp. 429–39.

Schmidt, Klaus and Monika Schnitzer. 2003. "Public Subsidies for Open Source? Some Economic Policy Issues of the Software Market." Discussion Paper No. 3793, Centre for Economic Policy Research.

Shapiro, Carl and Hal R. Varian. 2004. "Linux Adoption in the Public Sector." Unpublished working paper, University of California.

Thursby, Jerry and Marie Thursby. 2003. "Has Licensing Changed Academic Research? Issues of Productivity, Faculty Incentives, and Public Policy." Unpublished working paper, Emory University and Georgia Institute of Technology.

Waldman, Michael. 1984. "Job Assignments, Signaling, and Efficiency." *Rand Journal of Economics*. 15:2, pp. 255–67.

[14]

Open Source Software: Private Provision of a Public Good

Justin Pappas Johnson
Johnson Graduate School of Management
Cornell University
Ithaca, NY 14853

A simple model of open source software (as typified by the GNU-Linux operating system) is presented. Individual user-programmers decide whether to invest their own effort to develop a software enhancement that will become a public good if so developed. The effect of changing the population size of user-programmers is considered; finite and asymptotic results are given. Welfare results are presented. It is shown that whether development will increase when applications have a modular structure depends on whether the developer base exceeds a critical size. Potential explanations of several stylized facts are given, including why certain useful programs don't get written.

1. Introduction

As of late 2000, studies by Netcraft and E-Soft suggest that the web server Apache powers about 59% of all web pages.[1] In 1998, the operating system of choice on 17% of all new commercial servers was GNU-Linux.[2] This is rather striking because both Apache and GNU-Linux are now, and have always been, freely available for all.

There is a myriad of examples of free software.[3] Much of this software was written in a decentralized fashion by a large number of individual programmers scattered across the world. The sum of these efforts has produced an impressive collection of useful, reliable,

This paper is an extension of a chapter from my 1999 M.I.T. Ph.D. dissertation. I thank Daron Acemoglu, Travis Broughton, Jonathan Dworak, Frank Fisher, David P. Myatt, two anonymous referees, and a coeditor for helpful comments and advice. I especially thank Glenn Ellison for his extensive and concise remarks.

1. See www.netcraft.com/survey and www.securityspace.com for details. The methodologies are somewhat controversial. In particular, servers behind firewalls are not counted.

2. *Red Herring*, June 1999.

3. See sourceforge.org, freshmeat.net, and opensource.org to better appreciate the sheer scope and depth of open source activity. See www.perl.org and www.php.net for specific examples of two premier scripting languages that are open source.

Journal of Economics & Management Strategy, Volume 11, Number 4, Winter 2002, 637–662 and free software. Moreover, the source code of much free software also is freely available.[4]

Such software is commonly referred to as open source software. A competent programmer who has the source code of a program can, given time, figure out exactly how the program works. He or she can modify the program to suit his or her own preferences, correct bugs in the program, or use the components of the program to build a new or extended application.

In contrast, most software that one buys is available only as binary code. It can be difficult to invert such an executable to obtain the underlying source code.[5] Also, most firms restrict the rights of end users to modify software. Hence, much proprietary software cannot be modified usefully by anyone other than the original developer. Software for which the source code is not generally available is called closed source software.

Some computer and software companies are acknowledging the open source movement. In 1998, Netscape (now owned by AOL) opened the source code of its web browser, while Sun Microsystems has released the source code of its StarOffice program, and IBM has released an open source version of its popular AFS filesystem.[6] There are many more examples.

In Section 2, open source software development is modeled as the private provision of a public good. Section 3 examines the influence of the size of the developer base on welfare, development probability, and the distribution of effort and costs. Both finite and asymptotic results are presented.

In Section 4, the open source model is compared to traditional closed source (or profit-driven) software development. Neither system coincides with the socially optimal informationally decentralized solution. Relative to this solution, the open source paradigm exhibits both inefficient levels and distribution of development, but it benefits, as the closed source solution does not, from the fact that individuals know their own preferences better than a firm does and also from the fact that a greater skill set (that belonging to the community of programmers as a whole) can be exploited.

4. The source code of a program is the sequence of actual typed common-language words entered by the programmer that constitutes the logical structure of the program.

5. The difficulty depends on several factors, including the language in which the program is written. Also, generated source code may not match the original code. Thus, it may be difficult to work with generated source code.

6. See www.mozilla.org, openoffice.org, and www.openafs.org, respectively, for details. Technically, IBM has forked the AFS code into an open source version and a proprietary version.

In Section 5, several stylized facts are explained in the context of the model. In particular, it is argued that a reason the open source community has been able to build immensely complex software objects, such as operating systems, yet arguably has been less successful in building other useful applications, such as word processors of quality comparable to proprietary versions, is that a natural correlation between human capital and production technology leads those most able to build applications to build ones that are most useful in their own work.

The importance of the potential for incremental development of an open source application is addressed. In agreement with received wisdom in the open source community, it is shown that the possibility of incremental improvement is valuable when the developer base is large but that incremental development leads to less development when the developer base is small.

Also in Section 5, the stylized fact that open source applications tend to be less complete than their proprietary counterparts is considered. It is shown that this is a natural consequence of profit maximization when development costs are highly correlated across tasks and when reservation prices are additive across different program features.

Before addressing these issues, a very brief discussion of the legal aspect of open source software is in order. In particular, open source licenses are discussed. Also, the related literature is discussed briefly.

1.1 Open Source Software Licenses

The source code of open source software is freely available. Despite this, open source programs are commonly distributed under very precise licensing agreements. While there are many such licenses, only one will be discussed in the interest of saving space.

The GNU General Public License (GPL) is one of the most common and stringent of all such licenses. Most of the software mentioned so far is distributed under the GPL license. The GPL grants specific legal rights and responsibilities to those who use and modify products licensed under the GPL.

The GPL does not prohibit charging a positive price for a program covered by the license. However, it grants customers the right to obtain the source code. Moreover, anyone who lawfully obtains a program covered by the GPL automatically inherits the full rights to use, copy, modify, or distribute the program and source code in any manner desired, subject only to the terms of the GPL itself (Stallman, 1996). Thus, legally, all source code that incorporates GPL source code becomes open source code itself. Thus, while individuals are free to modify programs covered by the GPL, such modifications must be distributed under the terms of the License itself if they are to be distributed at all. Moreover, modifications or redistributions of such open source software must make the terms of the License apparent to others who might obtain the software.

1.2 Related Literature

Open source software development is modeled as the private provision of a public good. Such models of public-good provision have been studied by many people, including Chamberlin (1974), Palfrey and Rosenthal (1984), Bergstrom et al. (1986), and Bliss and Nalebuff (1984). The present paper differs from the existing literature both in the focus of the basic model and in the fact that the model is extended to address issues of relevance to the open source development regime.

In particular, the analysis considers not only whether a project will be successful, but also whether the composition of effort supplied is efficient. Further, the distribution of redundant effort is considered, since much open source development occurs with little or no coordination. Also, the open source regime is compared both to an informationally decentralized social planner's solution and to the solution of a profit-maximizing firm. Finally, the basic analysis places strong emphasis on a number of asymptotic results [other papers, for example Chamberlin (1974), do address asymptotic issues].

The extensions of the basic model also distinguish the current paper. For example, in Section 5 the importance of being able to make small contributions is related to the size of the pool of potential participants.

Lerner and Tirole (2000) also explore the economics of open source software. They provide a very broad discussion of a number of issues, emphasizing the relevance of the existing literature on labor economics, especially career concerns. The central distinguishing features of the present paper are as follows. First, their work is informal, unlike the present paper, which, for example, presents precise welfare results and precise comparative statics. Second, the present paper is focused entirely on the analysis of a public-goods game and its extensions, while their work explains how various different models each can aid the understanding of different issues. For example, both papers address the fact that it seems certain types of software are more likely to be developed than others, but their explanation is based on signaling, while the one given here is based on the basic public-goods model defined below. Third, the present paper shows in

Section 5 that a modular structure for development need not enhance the level of contributions, while Lerner and Tirole argue informally that modularization is likely required for success. Finally, the present work provides a simple potential explanation for why closed source firms might include more features in their products than an open source community would.

2. A Model of Open Source Software

Consider the following simultaneous-move game. There are n user-developers in the Internet community.[7] Each knows that an enhancement of a preexisting software application, the source code of which is open, can potentially be developed. Developing the enhancement of the software takes time, effort, and ingenuity. These costs are summarized for each agent by his or her privately known cost of development, c_i.

Each agent independently decides whether to develop the new application. Any agent i who chooses to develop bears the cost c_i. As long as at least one agent so chooses, the development will occur. Any developed software can be freely provided over the Internet to the other user-developers and will be so provided if developed.[8]

If the enhancement is developed, all agents receive their own privately known valuations v_i. If the software is not developed, all payoffs equal zero.

Suppose that all agents' costs and valuations are independent, identical draws from the joint distribution function $G(c, v)$ with support on the finite rectangle defined by $\{(c, v) : c_L \leq c \leq c_H, v_L \leq v \leq v_H\}$, where $c_L > 0$ and $v_H \geq 0$. Assume this is a smooth function and that it is strictly increasing on its support.

The first object of analysis is the optimal response of any agent i to the strategies of the other agents. Suppose that the agent believes that the probability that the development will take place if he or she does not innovate is π^i. A strategy for this agent is a decision to develop with some probability, conditional on his or her own realized cost and valuation, and given his or her beliefs about what other agents are doing (summarized by the value π^i). More precisely,

7. Note that the agents in this model could be firms instead of individuals. In fact, some firms do pay their employees to work on open source software that will be directly beneficial to the firm.

8. As noted above, most open source licenses do not prohibit the selling of open source software, although the GPL for instance does guarantee any purchaser strong rights to redistribution, and therefore might vastly restrict developing agents' ability to profit. Hence, the present analysis does not explain why so many agents simply give away developments they have made to open source projects.

a strategy for each agent i is a function ψ^i taking each of that agent's potential value-cost pairs (v_i, c_i) into the unit interval [0, 1].

An equilibrium of this game is a set of strategies and beliefs $\{(\psi^i, \pi^i)\}_{i=1}^n$ such that each strategy is optimal given that agent's beliefs, and such that each agent's beliefs are consistent with the strategies of the other agents. That is, Bayesian Nash equilibria are considered.

Optimality for agent i requires that ψ^i solve

$$\max_{\psi \in [0,1]} \left[v_i(\pi^i + \psi - \pi^i \psi) - c_i \psi \right].$$

Consistency requires that

$$\pi^i = \Pr\{\text{At least one agent } j \neq i \text{ chooses to develop}\},$$

where the probability on the right is computed using the underlying distribution $G(c, v)$ and the strategies of agents $j \neq i$.

An agent optimally chooses to develop the program with probability one if

$$v_i - c_i > \pi^i v_i,$$

which can be rearranged to yield

$$\frac{v_i}{c_i} > \frac{1}{1 - \pi^i}, \tag{1}$$

so it is clear that the optimal response is to invest in development with probability one, so that $\psi^i = 1$, if the value-to-cost ratio is sufficiently high. When inequality (1) is reversed, it is optimal never to develop, so that $\psi^i = 0$. When (1) is exactly satisfied, the agent is indifferent among all personal development probabilities. Given the smoothness of $G(c, v)$, this is a measure zero event. Since consistency implies that equilibrium beliefs are independent of such events, it is without loss of generality that one can assume agents who are indifferent choose to develop.

Throughout this entire paper only symmetric equilibria are considered. Let $\hat{q}$ denote the critical value-to-cost ratio. Also, let $F(q)$ be the induced distribution of the value-to-cost quotients;[9] that is,

$$F(q) = \Pr\left\{\frac{v}{c} < q\right\}.$$

9. The value-to-cost distribution is not taken as primitive, because later the performance of a closed source system will be compared to that of an open source one. To do so, the joint distribution of v and c will be needed.

Denote the upper bound of the support by

$$q_H = \frac{v_H}{c_L} < \infty.$$

It will also be convenient to define

$$\gamma = \Pr\{\text{No agent develops}\} = F(\hat{q})^n.$$

Given these definitions, the probability (from an individual agent's perspective) that none of the remaining agents develops is

$$1 - \pi = F(\hat{q})^{n-1} = \gamma^{(n-1)/n},$$

where π is the common value of the π^i. Hence one can determine from the agent's optimality condition that he will only be indifferent between developing and not when

$$q_i = \frac{1}{1 - \pi} = \gamma^{(1-n)/n},$$

which of course must equal $\hat{q}$ in equilibrium. Given this, inspection of the definition of γ (i.e., the probability that no agent develops) reveals that it is an equilibrium value if

$$\gamma = F\left(\gamma^{(1-n)/n}\right)^n, \tag{2}$$

which has a unique solution unless the distribution function F places no mass above 1, in which case there is no interior solution to this equation and the unique equilibrium exhibits no development. To avoid this boring case, assume that $F(1) < 1$, or equivalently that $q_H > 1$. Under this assumption, the above condition is both necessary and sufficient for γ to be an equilibrium value.

The straightforward manner in which the Bayesian Nash equilibrium[10] can be computed in the basic model has been explained. In the following sections a number of different issues are addressed in the context of the basic model.

Before proceeding, a few comments on the choice of the model detailed above are in order. One issue is that some user-developers might prefer to develop the software rather than have someone else do it. These people could be trying to signal how clever they are, perhaps out of vanity or the desire to obtain a better job in the future. In fact, the present model captures some of this quite easily. One must merely reinterpret the cost of development to be the net cost,

10. As mentioned previously, throughout this entire paper only symmetric equilibria are considered.

after factoring in other gains beyond mere direct utility from the use of the program.

Another issue is the choice between a static and a dynamic model. Clearly, both approaches capture much the same concept; the current approach allows one to discuss whether an innovation occurs or not, while a dynamic model in the spirit of Bliss and Nalebuff (1984) allows one to consider the issue of delay.

Of course, there are strong limitations to the static approach. In particular, analysis of such a model cannot capture adequately the incentives of an initial programmer to release her work under an open source license. Furthermore, it strongly relies on the emergence of equilibrium beliefs. Also, a static approach precludes study of how an open source development community acts over time as various improvements and new opportunities for development arrive.

Finally, an alternative to the present framework is a game in which agents have perfect information about the values and costs of all users. Assuming agents were identical, the symmetric equilibrium would exhibit mixed strategies. This approach would then resemble, for example, the work of Dixit and Shapiro (1986), which considers industry entry and exit.

3. The Number of User-Developers

Some open source projects have a greater number of potential developers in the community than others do. Here the influence of the population size on the open source environment is investigated. Both finite and asymptotic results are given.

3.1 Finite-Population Results

Finite results are presented here. Increasing the size of the developer base can lead to a lower overall probability of development. It is shown, however, that any decrease cannot be very large and that in any event all agents prefer having more potential developers.

Suppose that the number of user-developers increases. If individuals continued to use their original threshold rules, then clearly development would be more likely. However, when more individuals are present, the incentive to free-ride is raised, so that any individual will be less likely to develop the application herself in equilibrium. Whether the overall probability of development falls or rises as a result of including more agents is therefore ambiguous.[11]

11. An example in which the development probability always falls with increasing population size is when the value-to-cost distribution function is given by $F(q) = q^2/4$.

While the movement of the development probability is ambiguous, the likelihood π_n that at least one of the other $n - 1$ agents develops must increase (where subscripts are now used to denote the equilibrium values for a given population size n). This must be true because if the probability of at least one of the other agents developing were to fall with a growth in the population, then each agent optimally would choose to develop more frequently. This would be a contradiction, since if each agent develops more frequently, the probability of at least one agent developing in any subset of agents must also increase.

LEMMA 1: *The equilibrium probability that at least one of the first $n - 1$ agents develops is increasing in n. That is, π_n is increasing in n. Also, $\hat{q}_n$ is increasing.*

Proof. Recall that an individual agent i is indifferent between developing and not when $q_i = (1 - \pi_n)^{-1}$. In equilibrium, it is the case that

$$\pi_n = 1 - F(\hat{q})^{n-1} = 1 - F\left(\frac{1}{1 - \pi_n}\right)^{n-1}.$$

For each value of x the function $F(x)^{n-1}$ is decreasing in n. Therefore, the point π_n at which the above condition holds is strictly increasing in n (since $\hat{q}_n$ can never equal q_H in equilibrium). This fact plus inspection of the agent's optimization problem reveals that $\hat{q}_n$ is also increasing. □

Conceptually, each agent contributes only a small amount to the probabilistic chance of development when the number of developers is not too small. Since the preceding lemma shows that, from the standpoint of a given agent, the chance of at least one of the other agents developing is increasing, it stands to reason that the overall development probability cannot go down by very much when the size of the developer base is not too small. The following theorem makes this precise.

THEOREM 1: *If the population of user-developers is n, then any decline in the development probability resulting from adding one more user-developer is less (in magnitude) than $1/[(n - 1)e]$.*

Proof. Letting p_n denote the probability that any given agent develops in equilibrium when there are a total of n developers, the change in the development probability is

$$\begin{aligned}
&(1-\gamma_{n+1})-(1-\gamma_n)\\
&\quad=\gamma_n-\gamma_{n+1}=(1-p_n)(1-\pi_n)-(1-p_{n+1})(1-\pi_{n+1})\\
&\quad\geq(1-p_n)(1-\pi_n)-(1-p_{n+1})(1-\pi_n)=(1-\pi_n)(p_{n+1}-p_n)\\
&\quad\geq -p_n(1-\pi_n)=-p_n(1-p_n)^{n-1}\\
&\quad\geq \min_{p\in[0,1]}[-p(1-p)^{n-1}]\\
&\quad=-\frac{1}{n}\left(\frac{n-1}{n}\right)^{n-1}>\frac{-1}{(n-1)e},
\end{aligned}$$

where the last inequality follows from the fact that $[(n-1)/n]^n$ converges monotonically to e^{-1} from below. □

This bound on the possible decrease in the development probability converges rapidly to zero. This suggests that for large projects there is little chance that growth in the developer base will lead to fewer developments.

Lemma 1 also implies that each agent is better off in expectation when the population increases. Agents are better off because, in equilibrium, higher values of n deliver higher option values of doing nothing.

Insofar as social welfare can be expressed as the sum of individual welfares, society is better off in expectation as well. It is not true, however, that individuals or society are better off in each state of nature.[12]

THEOREM 2: *Expected social welfare is increasing in n. Moreover, the expected welfare of each user is increasing in n.*

Proof. Denote the expected payoff to agent i, conditional on his or her type and the total number of agents n, by $x_i(v_i, c_i, n)$. Then

$$x_i(v_i,c_i,n)=\max[v_i\pi_n,v_i-c_i]\leq\max[v_i\pi_{n+1},v_i-c_i]=x_i(v_i,c_i,n+1),$$

since $\pi_n \leq \pi_{n+1}$.

12. For example, there are states in which the addition of another user results in the project not being developed when it would have been developed in the absence of the marginal user. This is true precisely because the threshold $\hat{q}_n$ is rising with n. However, individuals are better off in states of the world where the marginal user develops and they themselves do not, but would have otherwise.

Hence, agent i's payoff is increasing in n conditional on his or her type. But since this is true for every type of i, his or her *ex ante* payoffs are also increasing in n. Finally, observe that payoffs are never negative.

It follows that expected social welfare with n agents can be expressed as

$$\sum_{i=1}^{n} \mathrm{E}x_i(v_i, c_i, n) \leq \sum_{i=1}^{n} \mathrm{E}x_i(v_i, c_i, n+1) \leq \sum_{i=1}^{n+1} \mathrm{E}x_i(v_i, c_i, n+1),$$

where the last summation is the expected social welfare with $n+1$ agents. This proves the theorem. □

3.2 Limiting Results

One of the major arguments for why the open source paradigm should be successful is that open source code permits an extremely large labor force (potentially the entire Internet community of programmers) to bring its skill and insight to bear on a problem.[13] The notion that the open source method can marshal considerable intellectual power seems to be taken seriously by some major firms. Consider the following excerpt from an internal Microsoft document, which assesses the threat of open source software (OSS below):[14]

> The ability of the OSS process to collect and harness the collective IQ of thousands of individuals across the Internet is simply amazing.... Linux and other OSS advocates are making a progressively more credible argument that OSS software is at least as robust—if not more—than commercial alternatives.[15]

It is thus natural to explore the behavior of the model as the pool of user-developers grows large. The limiting probability of innovation is investigated first. Then, the issue of the distribution of costs and redundant effort is considered.

13. In the case of bug fixing, this notion is captured by *Linus' law*, which states, "Given enough eyeballs, all bugs are shallow."

14. These so-called Halloween documents can be read at opensource.org. Their authenticity has been confirmed by Microsoft itself at www.microsoft.com/ntserver/nts/news/mwarv/linuxresp.asp.

15. As a practical matter, it is not clear exactly how successful the open source paradigm is either in absolute terms or relative to proprietary alternatives. Much evidence is merely anecdotal. However, Miller et al. (1998) found that failure rates of commercial versions of UNIX utilities ranged from 15% to 43%, in contrast to failure rates of 6% for GNU utilities (which are open source).

It is important to note that another major argument for why the open source system should be successful is that it engenders interactions and synergies between developers. These are explicitly ruled out in this model.

3.2.1 Development Probability. Consider what happens to the probability $1 - \gamma_n$ of development and the probability π_n that at least one of any subset of $n-1$ users develops the software when the population grows large. The following is immediate.

Theorem 3: *Both π_n and γ_n have limiting values π^* and γ^*, respectively. In particular,*

$$\gamma^* = \lim_{n\to\infty} \gamma_n = \frac{1}{q_H},$$

$$1 - \pi^* = \lim_{n\to\infty} (1 - \pi_n) = \frac{1}{q_H}.$$

Proof. In fact, each of the above limits implies the other, since, by definition, $1 - \pi = \gamma^{(n-1)/n}$. Hence, only the first limit will be derived. It has already been shown that a unique symmetric equilibrium exists for each n. Hence, all that needs to be demonstrated is that for any $\varepsilon > 0$ there exists an N such that for $n > N$ the equilibrium value of γ_n lies in $(\gamma^* - \varepsilon, \gamma^* + \varepsilon)$.

Let $\varepsilon > 0$ be given. It is clear that $1/(\gamma^* + \varepsilon) < q_H$, and hence for some N_1 it is the case that $n > N_1$ implies $(\gamma^* + \varepsilon)^{(1-n)/n} < q_H - \eta_1$ for some $\eta_1 > 0$.

Since $F(q_H) = 1$ and F is strictly increasing on its support, it must be that for $n > N_1$

$$F\left[(\gamma^* + \varepsilon)^{(1-n)/n}\right] < 1 - \eta_2$$

for some $\eta_2 > 0$, which implies that

$$F\left[(\gamma^* + \varepsilon)^{(1-n)/n}\right]^n$$

converges to zero. In particular, there is an N_2 such that (2) cannot be satisfied at $\gamma^* + \varepsilon$, or for any greater value, when $n > \max[N_1, N_2]$. This is so because F is an increasing function and because the map $x \mapsto x^{(1-n)/n}$ is decreasing.

Now consider $\gamma^* - \varepsilon$. There is some N_3 such that $n > N_3$ implies that $(\gamma^* - \varepsilon)^{(1-n)/n} > q_H$ and hence that $F[(\gamma^* - \varepsilon)^{(1-n)/n}]^n = F(q_H) = 1$, since F is a distribution function. This implies that neither $\gamma^* - \varepsilon$ nor any point less than it can satisfy (2).

One can now conclude that for $n > \max[N_1, N_2, N_3]$ it must be the case that $\gamma_n \in (\gamma^* - \varepsilon, \gamma^* + \varepsilon)$. Since ε was arbitrary, the result follows. □

This is intuitive because, in the limit, only the agents with the highest value-to-cost ratios will develop the software. Hence, the asymptotic probability of no development must be such that it keeps an agent of type q_H indifferent. This type of result also appears in previous works on the public provision of private goods, e.g., Chamberlin (1974).

This result is robust to many modifications of the model. For example, if people received slightly higher values when they wrote the program themselves, or if the underlying distributions were different, the conclusion that the limiting probability of development does not equal one would still hold.

On the other hand, the bounded support of the distribution of value-to-cost ratios is important. If the value-to-cost distribution were unbounded, then development would take place with arbitrarily high probability as the population size grew large. To see that this must be so, suppose for the sake of contradiction that the limiting probability of development were less than one. From an individual agent's viewpoint, this implies that the probability that one of the other agents develops is less than one. For an agent with a sufficiently high value-to-cost ratio, it is suboptimal to not develop independently. This implies that the probability that an individual agent develops does not converge to zero, a contradiction.[16]

3.2.2 Costs and Redundancy. Here the potential for wasteful duplication of effort is considered. This issue is considered by Raymond (1999) in response to the assertion of Brooks (1995) that adding more programmers to most software projects only delays completion, resulting in unbounded waste in the limit.[17]

In agreement with Raymond (1999), it can be shown that redundant efforts and costs do not grow without bound in the present environment. To this end, define p_n to be the probability that any individual in a population of size n chooses to develop. For a fixed population of size n, the expected number of development efforts equals np_n.

Theorem 4: *The expected number of development efforts converges as the population grows. Precisely,*

$$\lim_{n\to\infty} np_n = \log(q_H).$$

16. Technically, this argument should be made using the lim sup of the probability of no development. It follows then that the lim sup converges to zero, so that the limit exists and equals zero.

17. This is a version of *Brooks' law*. The idea is that many projects comprise tasks that must be performed sequentially and that, task by task, more programmers need not hasten progress. The model presented in the present paper clearly is not sequential and thus cannot be taken literally as a response to Brooks (1995).

Proof. It has already been shown that $\gamma_n = (1-p_n)^n$ converges to $1/q_H$ and so continuity of the natural logarithm implies that $n \log(1 - p_n)$ converges to $-\log(q_H)$. A first-order Taylor expansion of the logarithm around 1 reveals that

$$n \log(1 - p_n) = -n \frac{p_n}{1 - \hat{p}_n}$$

for some $\hat{p}_n \in (0, p_n)$. Since p_n converges to zero, it follows that np_n converges to $\log(q_H)$. □

The incentive to free-ride is strong enough to bound the amount of redundant effort in the limit. Selfish agents willingly choose to restrict redundant effort. While perhaps a cynical conclusion, this theorem provides positive support to the open source paradigm. It is also true that total costs are bounded, and that in the limit only the least-cost programmers develop.

Theorem 5: *The total expected costs of development borne by the open-source community converge to* $c_L \log(q_H)$.

Proof. It is the case that $\hat{q}_n$ converges to q_H. This is clear, since it has been previously demonstrated that the limiting probability of development is less than one, and since that result is incompatible with agents having nonnegligible *ex ante* development probabilities in the limit. Moreover, the limit of $\hat{q}_n$ must exist, since it is an increasing bounded sequence. Suppose for the sake of contradiction that it is not the case that only the agents with the lowest possible cost develop in the limit. Then, for some $\varepsilon > 0$, the sequence $\{\bar{c}_n\}$ with elements defined by $\bar{c}_n = \sup\{c : v/c \geq \hat{q}_n\}$ contains an infinite number of elements that are greater than $c_L + \varepsilon$. This implies that $\hat{q}_n < v_H/(c_L + \varepsilon)$ an infinite number of times, which is incompatible with the fact that $\hat{q}_n$ converges to $q_H = v_H/c_L$. □

This is in accordance with the perception in the open source community that those who find particular problems easy or interesting end up solving them. Of course, this theorem is a limiting result; in general, those who develop should not be expected to be those with the lowest costs.[18]

Again, the assumption of bounded support for F is critical. If the support of F were unbounded, the amount of redundant effort

18. It is important to note that this result relies heavily upon the rectangular support of $G(c, v)$. If the region of support were, for example, circular, then it would not be true that the highest possible values of v/c correspond to the lowest values of c.

would become unbounded as n grew. The reason is that users with extreme value-to-cost ratios would not find it optimal to tolerate even a tiny probability of no development, and hence would invest their own resources.

It is possible to say a bit more about the distribution of redundant efforts. Theorem 4 also implies that, regardless of the underlying joint distribution of values and costs, the (random) number of development efforts follows a well-defined distribution asymptotically.

COROLLARY 1: *The number of development efforts converges to a Poisson random variable with mean* $\log(q_H)$.

Proof. For each n, the number of development efforts can be expressed as the sum of n independent binomial variables with success probability p_n. It is the case that $p_n \to 0$ and $np_n \to \log(q_H)$. It is known that the limiting distribution is therefore Poisson. See, for example, Ash (1972, p. 348). □

4. Comparing Open Source To Closed Source

In this section the performance of an open source system is compared to that of a closed source one and also to that of an informationally decentralized social planner's solution (described in more detail below). To set a closed source benchmark, imagine as before that there are n agents, but that one of them has proprietary control over a software project whose source code is closed to the other $n-1$ agents. The interpretation is simply that one of the agents is effectively a software company with exclusive access to the source code and sole rights to distribution. Suppose further that the other $n-1$ agents already possess the basic software program, and that there is now a potential product enhancement that the firm can develop at some cost. If the firm develops the enhancement, it will be able to use it internally and also to offer it on the market to the other $n-1$ agents. If W is the profit the firm expects to earn from selling the development on the market, then the firm will choose to develop the enhancement if and only if $c_f \leq v_f + W$, where v_f and c_f represent the firm's (randomly realized) internal valuation and development cost, respectively.

Now consider a social planner who wishes to maximize the expected sum of values less costs in the community. Assume that the social planner must assign each agent a rule to follow, and that agents will follow whatever rule is assigned (this is discussed in more detail below). Each agent's rule tells the agent whether to develop or not, conditional only on his or her own private value and cost. These rules must be assigned prior to the determination of any randomness. Thus, the social planner is constrained by the fact that all information is private.

Attention is also restricted to deterministic, symmetric rules. Given these restrictions, the planner instructs each agent to develop if and only if her value-and-cost pair (v, c) lies in some development region Δ.

THEOREM 6: *If a social planner is constrained to offer each agent the same deterministic decision rule, then there are constants $a, b > 0$ such that each agent i is instructed to develop if and only if*

$$c_i \leq a + bv_i.$$

Proof. This can be deduced by considering the action of an agent whose decision has no net impact on social welfare in expectation (given their valuation and cost). Consider a single person, say agent 1, on the boundary of Δ. If she develops, social welfare is

$$-c_1 + v_1 + \mathrm{E}\sum_{i=2}^{n} v_i - (n-1)pc^*, \tag{3}$$

where p is the probability that any other individual agent's value-cost pair lies in Δ, and c^* is the expected cost of that agent conditional on being in Δ. If this agent instead does not develop, welfare is given by

$$\left[1 - (1-p)^{n-1}\right]\left(v_1 + \mathrm{E}\sum_{i=2}^{n} v_i^*\right) - (n-1)pc^*, \tag{4}$$

where v_i^* is the valuation of agent i given that at least one of the last $n-1$ agents does in fact develop. Of course, the values p, c^*, and v_i^* are endogenous, in that they depend upon the rule that has been assigned. This does not influence the present analysis.

Rewrite (3) in the following manner:

$$-c_1 + v_1 + \left[1 - (1-p)^{n-1}\right]\mathrm{E}\sum_{i=2}^{n} v_i^* + (1-p)^{n-1}\mathrm{E}\sum_{i=2}^{n} v_i^{**} - (n-1)pc^*,$$

where v_i^{**} is the value of agent i given that none of the last $n-1$ agents develops. Since agent 1 is presumed to be on the boundary of Δ, expected social welfare should be invariant to her decision. Equating (3) and (4) yields

$$(1-p)^{n-1}v_1 + (1-p)^{n-1}\mathrm{E}\sum_{i=2}^{n} v_i^{**} = c_1. \tag{5}$$

Letting $a = (1-p)^{n-1}\mathrm{E}\sum_{i=2}^{n} v_i^{**}$ and $b = (1-p)^{n-1}$ completes the proof. □

It is important to note that the social planner's problem as defined above is somewhat unusual. The reason is that the social planner is assumed to be able to force agents to follow decision rules based on agents' private information, but cannot extract such information from the agents. Therefore, the decision rules above will be referred to as the socially optimal informationally decentralized decision rules.

Note further that the decision rules above are not incentive-compatible. Instead, they can be thought of as representing what an altruistic community would achieve if it were unable to share information or coordinate. This benchmark is consistent with earlier analysis in this paper, since it continues to restrict agents to act only on their own private information. Thus, this informationally decentralized social planner's problem highlights the importance of incentive effects in the standard open source environment analyzed earlier, as made clear by the following theorem.

THEOREM 7: *When agents obey the socially optimal informationally decentralized decision rules, the overall probability of innovation is higher than it is in the equilibrium of the open source regime.*

Proof. Let $\hat{\pi}$ denote the probability that at least one agent of any group of $n-1$ agents will develop under the informationally decentralized social planner's regime, and let π be the corresponding equilibrium probability under the open environment. Agent i of type (c_i, v_i) will be instructed to develop whenever $c_i \leq a + bv_i$. Given the definition of a and b defined in the proof of Theorem 6, and bearing in mind that $(1-p)^{n-1} = 1 - \hat{\pi}$, this condition is

$$c_i \leq (1-\hat{\pi})\sigma + (1-\hat{\pi})v_i, \tag{6}$$

where $\sigma > 0$. Also recall that agent i of type (c_i, v_i) would develop under the open source regime if

$$c_i \leq (1-\pi)v_i. \tag{7}$$

Suppose for the sake of contradiction that $\hat{\pi} \leq \pi$. It straightforward to see that inequality (6) describes a strictly larger region of the support of $G(c, v)$ than inequality (7) does. Since the distribution function $G(c, v)$ is strictly increasing on its support, it follows that each agent obeying the optimal informationally decentralized decision rule develops with strictly higher probability than an agent in the open regime. However, if each agent individually develops with higher probability in this social planner's scheme than in the open regime, then the

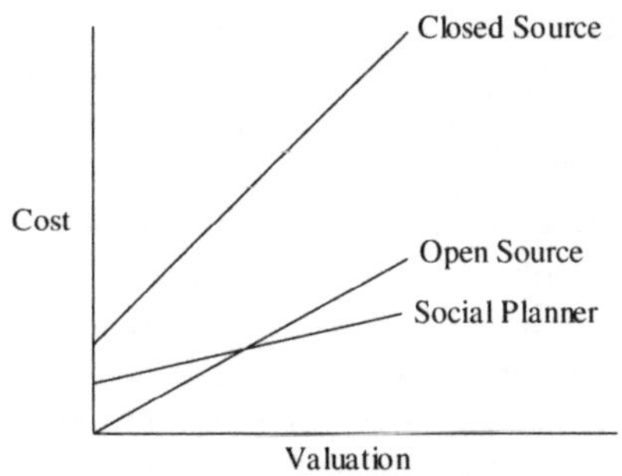

FIGURE 1. COMPARISON OF THE THREE SYSTEMS

probability that at least one member of a group of $n - 1$ agents will develop must be higher in that scheme as well; that is, it must be that $\hat{\pi} > \pi$. This contradiction establishes the theorem. □

Relative to the informationally decentralized social optimum, the level of development is too low in the open environment. Furthermore, the distribution of effort is inefficient in the sense that some types that develop under the open regime might not develop under this social planner's solution. These will be types with high values and high costs. Facing free riding (and the lower probability that someone else will develop) in the open regime compels these agents to innovate themselves. The social planner, however, will not want very high-cost agents to develop. Such agents are compensated, so to speak, by the fact that the planner establishes a regime in which the probability that other agents develop is higher than in the open regime.

Figure 1 provides a comparison of the three possible systems.[19] Suppose that valuations are measured on the horizontal axis and costs on the vertical axis. The decision rules that would be followed under the three systems can be shown graphically. Each development region is the area underneath a particular ray in the value-cost space. The closed source rule is a ray emanating from a point above the origin with a slope of one. The open source rule is a ray emanating from the origin at a slope less than one, and the socially optimal informationally decentralized rule is a ray emanating from a point above the origin at a slope less than that of the open source rule.[20]

19. This diagram assumes that the intercept term a in the decision rule assigned by the social planner is less than W, the expected profits the firm will accrue by selling the development. However, this assumption has no bearing on the subsequent discussion.

20. More precisely, the slope of the open source rule is $1 - \pi$ and the slope of the rule assigned by this social planner is $b = (1 - p)^{n-1} < 1 - \pi$, where the inequality follows from Theorem 7.

Some heuristic comments are in order. The resources of the firm are limited in that it cannot access the entire talent pool of the Internet. This is an assumption of the model, but there are several reasons why it might be so in reality. First, when source code is closed, it is not even possible for individuals to know what their costs would be, much less for the monopolist to know. This is certain to complicate contracting efforts. Also, as a practical matter, some open source programmers are already employed and choose to work on open source projects in their spare time. Their costs might include a random opportunity-cost component that depends on their workload at their primary place of employment. Hence, even if it is clear who the best engineer is for a given task, it might not be clear whether he or she will be available to perform it. Third, a firm might believe that revealing its source code widely might provide an edge to any competitors, present or future.

The open source system, in contrast, exploits the potential of all the users. This can (but need not) result in only low costs being borne. Another plus for open code is that more information is being used. This is meant in the following sense. Each agent has access to his or her private information and could end up writing the software. In contrast, in the closed source regime only the firm can exploit its information, and it does not have access to the information of other agents. More information is being "conditioned on" (although the information is not aggregated) when everyone has access to the code.

One might simply say that firms don't always know what people want, but people usually do. When source code is unavailable publicly, the human capital and insight present in the community as a whole cannot be harnessed.

A good example appears to be the Apache web server. This was developed from the original NCSA web server beginning around 1995. The people who developed Apache found that many changes to the NCSA were needed. Evidently, no firms were supplying these changes at prices that many webmasters were willing to pay. One might think that the dramatic changes taking place on the World Wide Web were such that the webmasters had vastly superior information about their own needs. Arguably, the open nature of Apache allowed important developments to occur more rapidly than otherwise would have been possible.

5. Other Open Source Issues

The following three subsections use the basic model to explore some other issues related to open source software.

5.1 An Empirical Puzzle

A puzzle in the open source community is why some obviously useful software does not get written (or is not fully developed). For example, while open source word processors and spreadsheets do exist, it is fair to say that only recently have they begun to be comparable in quality to, for example, Microsoft Office.[21] On the other hand, hundreds of other free utilities and applications exist. In this section it is argued that a natural correlation between the human capital and the production technology of workers will tend to lead to the production of certain types of programs (like networking utilities) but not others (like word processors and spreadsheets).

An argument put forth by Eric S. Raymond[22] is that open source programmers wish to establish a reputation for ingenuity in the greater hacker community (Raymond, 1999). Thus, projects that are considered more exciting are more likely to be developed.

The model developed here admits a simple alternative explanation. Consider two possible applications, an enhancement of a word processor and an addition to a networking utility. Inasmuch as people who are most likely to value the networking utility are also most able to write the addition, a natural negative correlation exists between value and cost. Not surprisingly, such negative correlation can easily lead to heightened levels of development.

Figure 2 displays numerically generated results when value and cost have a joint lognormal distribution with the correlation coefficient of $\log(v)$ and $\log(c)$ given by ρ, and with value and cost having positive means satisfying $\mathrm{E}\log(v) - \mathrm{E}\log(c) = 1$, and with both $\log(v)$ and $\log(c)$ having unit variance. Two populations sizes are considered, $n = 5$ and $n = 50$. Changing the correlation coefficient does not alter either marginal distribution, but influences the distribution of the value-to-cost ratio. As the correlation between value and cost falls, the open source community performs better, as measured by the increase in the development probability.

Another consideration is that programs geared toward nonspecialists may require extensive and costly usability testing. If those at great ease with software are writing programs for themselves, they may neglect to include certain friendly features. Also, usability engineering may require training in human-computer interaction that most professional programmers lack.

21. For example, the home pages of open projects like Gnumeric and KOffice admit that a lot more development is needed. This again highlights a limitation of a static model with a single project rather than a dynamic one with varying degrees of progress.

22. Eric S. Raymond is a programmer and well-known open source software advocate. He was influential in Netscape's 1998 decision to release its browser source code.

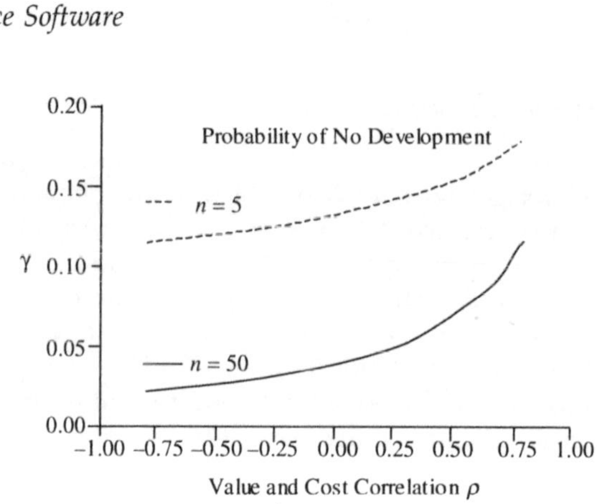

FIGURE 2. RELATION BETWEEN VALUE AND COST CORRELATION AND DEVELOPMENT

5.2 Modularity and Incremental Development

Many open source projects receive code contributions that are individually quite small. As a whole, the sum of these contributions might be quite valuable. Prevalent among open source proponents is the notion that one reason the open environment can be successful is that there are many small tasks that can be completed for any particular project. With many small tasks, the argument runs, it becomes more likely that any individual will find it worthwhile to contribute, increasing aggregate development.

Here the issue of whether scope for incremental innovation should lead to heightened development is investigated by extending the basic model. Two different open environments are considered, one of which is *modular* and the other *nonmodular*. As will be clear, the modular environment admits incremental innovation while the nonmodular environment does not.

Suppose that there are k tasks or projects. Each user-developer receives an independent draw from $G(c, v)$ for each of these projects. Define the modular environment to be one which is a k-replica of the standard model. That is, individuals simultaneously decide which if any of the projects to complete. As long as at least one agent chooses to develop a particular project, all agents receive their valuations for that project.

Define the nonmodular environment to be one in which agents receive their valuations for a project only if at least one user has individually completed all k tasks. That is, the entire collection of projects is worthless unless a single developer has completed each of them by herself. Hence, each agent must decide *ex ante* whether to develop all or none of the projects. It is straightforward to show that this implies that the decision rule of each agent is to develop all k projects if and only if

$$z_i^k = \frac{\sum_{j=1}^k v_i^j}{\sum_{j=1}^k c_i^j}$$

is sufficiently large. It turns out to be the case that whether a modular environment will generate more development in expectation depends critically on the size of the developer base.

THEOREM 8: *Define N^* as follows:*

$$N^* = 1 + \frac{\log(\frac{\mathrm{E}c}{\mathrm{E}v})}{\log(F(\frac{\mathrm{E}v}{\mathrm{E}c}))}.$$

For any fixed $n > N^*$ there exists some K such that for all $k > K$ the probability that (all k components of) the nonmodular project will be completed is less than the probability that any one of the k modular projects will be completed. For any fixed $n < N^*$, there exists a K' such that for $k > K'$ the probability that (all k components of) the nonmodular project will be completed exceeds the probability that any one of the k modular projects will be completed.

Proof. Let π_{mod}^n denote the probability that any of $n-1$ users develops any one given project in the modular case (this is independent of k), and let $\pi_{\mathrm{nmod}}^{n,k}$ denote the probability that the development is made in the nonmodular environment (that is, that all k tasks are undertaken together by at least one agent of the $n-1$).

To prove the theorem, it need only be shown that when $n > N^*$ there exists a K such that for $k > K$ it is the case that $\pi_{\mathrm{nmod}}^{n,k} < \pi_{\mathrm{mod}}^n$, and that when $n < N^*$ there exists a K such that for $k > K$ it is the case that $\pi_{\mathrm{nmod}}^{n,k} > \pi_{\mathrm{mod}}^n$.

It will be shown that as k grows large the distribution function of z_i^k places arbitrarily large probability on a neighborhood around $\mathrm{E}v/\mathrm{E}c$. Having shown this, it will follow that the nonmodular environment's limiting equilibrium, obtained by letting k grow large and holding n fixed, is identical for each n. This will in turn allow the two environments to be compared for a given population.

Observe that z_i^k can be expressed as

$$z_i^k = \frac{\frac{1}{k}\sum_{j=1}^{k} v_i^j}{\frac{1}{k}\sum_{j=1}^{k} c_i^j},$$

so that the law of large numbers implies that the corresponding distribution places arbitrarily high probability on any given neighborhood of $\mathrm{E}v/\mathrm{E}c$ as k grows large.

The equilibrium of the nonmodular environment converges to one in which $\pi = 1 - \mathrm{E}c/\mathrm{E}v$. Since z_i^k is converging in probability to $\mathrm{E}v/\mathrm{E}c$ for each user, any solution to the equation

$$\pi = 1 - F_k\left(\frac{1}{1-\pi}\right)^{n-1}$$

must be arbitrarily close to $1 - \mathrm{E}c/\mathrm{E}v$, since the distribution function $F_k(z_i^k)$ is converging to a function that places an atom at $\mathrm{E}v/\mathrm{E}c$. Therefore, for fixed n, $\pi_{\mathrm{nmod}}^{n,k}$ converges to $1 - \mathrm{E}c/\mathrm{E}v$ as k grows large.

Next, observe that $\pi_{\mathrm{mod}}^{n} > \pi_{\mathrm{nmod}}^{n,k}$ if and only if $n > N^*$. The proof is simple. If

$$1 - \pi > F\left(\frac{1}{1-\pi}\right)^{n-1},$$

then it must be that $\pi_{\mathrm{mod}}^{n} > \pi$, whereas the opposite conclusion holds otherwise. Letting $\pi = 1 - \mathrm{E}c/\mathrm{E}v$, it is clear by directly solving for n that

$$n = 1 + \frac{\log\left(\frac{\mathrm{E}c}{\mathrm{E}v}\right)}{\log\left(F\left(\frac{\mathrm{E}v}{\mathrm{E}c}\right)\right)} = N^*$$

will exactly satisfy the above inequality. This proves the theorem. □

When the number of potential developers is large enough, the modular environment will outperform the nonmodular one. It is better to work with a large number of upper tails that correspond to smaller projects than to work with a small number of averages that correspond to larger projects.

However, when the number of potential developers is small, the nonmodular environment does better in terms of development. The reason is that developers know that the project has no functionality unless all of the components are present. There may be parts of the whole that are of high cost or low value to a given user. That user might nonetheless be willing to put extra effort in to be sure that the aggregate product, which she does value, will exist.

Thus nonmodularity will sometimes temper the free-riding present in the open source development system.

Raymond (1999) asserts that good open source projects need to be developed initially by a small group and only later released to the general community for further improvement. Heuristically, developers need to have something sizable to "play with" before the open source model can be expected to do well.

5.3 The Completeness of Open Source Software

Some people are reluctant to experiment with open source software because there is an impression that such software tends to be less complete than corresponding closed source applications. It often seems that proprietary software is easier to learn, has more features and better documentation, and is more user-friendly on the whole.

In this section, the modular framework introduced above will be adapted to provide a theoretical explanation of this observation, in an admittedly restrictive environment. Consider the following two conditions, which describe a special case of the model developed so far.

Condition 1: In the modular environment, for each agent i the cost of developing project $j = 1, 2, \ldots, k$ is given by c_i, an independent and identical draw from some random variable with support on $[c_L, c_H]$, where $c_L > 0$.

One interpretation of Condition 1 is that each agent has a single, privately known, and innate skill level that solely determines his or her cost of working on projects. Condition 2 removes any uncertainty and asymmetry regarding agents' valuations of projects.

Condition 2: In the modular environment, each agent places value v on each component $j = 1, 2, \ldots, k$, where v is a commonly known constant such that $v > c_L$.

Theorem 9: *Suppose that Conditions 1 and 2 hold, and that the marginal cost of distributing software is zero. Then the probability that an open source community develops all k of the possible projects approaches zero as k grows large. However, as k grows large there is a strictly positive limiting probability that a profit-maximizing firm will develop all of the possible projects.*

Proof. The probability that any one of the developments is made by the open source community is independent of k. Call this probability $1 - \gamma < 1$. It is obvious that the probability of all developments occurring is $(1 - \gamma)^k$, which clearly converges to zero as k becomes large.

On the other hand, if a firm has developed r components, it can charge rv for a program containing all of them. Doing so is clearly optimal, since such pricing extracts the entire valuation from each consumer. The firm is able to consume any component internally, and also sell it to the other $n-1$ agents. Hence the net gain that accrues to a firm producing r components is $r(nv - c_f)$, where c_f is the realized cost level of the firm (constant for it across all projects by Condition 1). Since $v > c_L$ by assumption, there is some $\varepsilon > 0$, which is independent of r, such that for any $c_f \in [c_L, c_L + \varepsilon]$ it is the case that $r(nv - c_f) > 0$. For realized costs in this interval, it is clearly optimal for the firm to develop all k possible components, since its profits are increasing in the number of components produced. Since there is a strictly positive probability that the firm will have a cost in $[c_L, c_L + \varepsilon]$, and since this probability does not depend on k, the result follows. □

6. Conclusion

The open source software movement is not new. However, only with the striking success of GNU-Linux, coupled with the decisions of major firms such as IBM and Sun Microsystems to open their source code, has it attracted widespread attention.

It is striking that a paradigm for costly investment based upon the absence of property rights has produced such a wide variety of useful and reliable software. A simple model of open source software has been presented to facilitate understanding of the phenomenon, and to enable efficiency comparisons between it and the traditional, profit-driven method of development.

It has been shown that the superior ability of the open source method to access the Internet talent pool, and to utilize more private information, provides an advantage over the closed source method in some situations. Nonetheless, free riding implies that some valuable projects will not be produced, even when the community of developers becomes large. However, this same free riding also curbs the amount of redundant effort in the limit.

Potential explanations for several stylized facts have been presented, including why some simple programs are not written while other very complex programs are, and why proprietary programs tend to be more complete than open source programs. Also, the advantage of the possibility of incremental development has been shown to depend on whether the developer base exceeds a critical mass or not; this provides a theoretical explanation for why open source is a good development model when a base product has already been completed but not a good means of producing the base product itself.

The open source movement is gaining attention. Many questions concerning the movement remain unanswered. In this paper the seemingly prior question of how well an open source community will function given that it exists has been addressed. The answers provided hopefully will aid in the investigation of other aspects of open source software.

References

Ash, R.B., 1972, *Real Analysis and Probability,* New York: Academic Press.

Bergstrom, T., L. Blume, and H. Varian, 1986, "On the Private Provision of Public Goods," *Journal of Public Economics,* 29, 25–49.

Bliss, C. and B. Nalebuff, 1984, "Dragon-slaying and Ballroom Dancing: The Private Supply of a Public Good," *Journal of Public Economics,* 25, 1–12.

Brooks, F.P., 1995, *The Mythical Man-Month: Essays on Software Engineering,* Reading, MA: Addison-Wesley.

Chamberlin, J., 1974, "Provision of Collective Goods as a Function of Group Size," *American Political Science Review,* 68, 707–716.

Dixit, A. and C. Shapiro, 1986, "Entry Dynamics with Mixed Strategies," in L. Thomas, III, ed., *The Economics of Strategic Planning: Essays in Honor of Joel Dean,* Lexington, MA: Lexington Books.

Lerner, J. and J. Tirole, 2000, "The Simple Economics of Open Source," NBER Working Paper No. 7600.

Miller, B.P., D. Koski, C.P. Lee, V. Maganty, R. Murthy, A. Natarajan, and J. Steidl, 1998, "Fuzz Revisited: A Re-examination of the Reliability of Unix Utilities and Services," University of Wisconsin Computer Science Working Paper.

Palfrey, T.R. and H. Rosenthal, 1984, "Participation and the Provision of Discrete Public Goods: A Strategic Analysis," *Journal of Public Economics,* 24, 171–193.

Raymond, E.S., 1999, *The Cathedral and the Bazaar,* O'Reilly Books.

Stallman, R.M., 1996, *GNU Emacs Manual, Version 19.33,* Boston: Free Software Foundation.

Name Index

The International Library of Critical Writings in Economics

1. Multinational Corporations
Mark Casson
2. The Economics of Innovation
Christopher Freeman
3. Entrepreneurship
Mark Casson
4. International Investment
Peter J. Buckley
5. Game Theory in Economics
Ariel Rubinstein
6. The History of Economic Thought
Mark Blaug
7. Monetary Theory
Thomas Mayer
8. Joint Production of Commodities
Neri Salvadori and Ian Steedman
9. Industrial Organization
Oliver E. Williamson
10. Growth Theory
(Volumes I, II and III)
R. Becker and E. Burmeister
11. Microeconomics: Theoretical and Applied (Volumes I, II and III)
Robert E. Kuenne
12. The Economics of Health
(Volumes I and II)
A.J. Culyer
13. Recent Developments in Macroeconomics
(Volumes I, II and III)
Edmund S. Phelps
14. Urban and Regional Economics
Paul C. Cheshire and Alan W. Evans
15. Modern Public Finance
(Volumes I and II)
A.B. Atkinson
16. Exchange Rate Economics
(Volumes I and II)
Ronald MacDonald and Mark P. Taylor
17. The Economic Value of Education: Studies in the Economics of Education
Mark Blaug
18. Development Economics
(Volumes I, II, III and IV)
Deepak Lal
19. The New Classical Macroeconomics
(Volumes I, II and III)
Kevin D. Hoover
20. The Economics of the Environment
Wallace E. Oates
21. Post Keynesian Theory of Growth and Distribution
Carlo Panico and Neri Salvadori
22. Dynamic Labor Demand and Adjustment Costs
Giorgio Galeazzi and Daniel S. Hamermesh
23. The Philosophy and Methodology of Economics (Volumes I, II and III)
Bruce J. Caldwell
24. Public Choice Theory
(Volumes I, II and III)
Charles K. Rowley
25. Evolutionary Economics
Ulrich Witt
26. Economics and Psychology
Shlomo Maital and Sharone L. Maital
27. Social Choice Theory
(Volumes I, II and III)
Charles K. Rowley
28. Non-Linear Dynamics in Economic Theory
Marc Jarsulic
29. Recent Developments in Experimental Economics
(Volumes I and II)
John D. Hey and Graham Loomes
30. Monopoly and Competition Policy
(Volumes I and II)
F.M. Scherer
31. The Economics of Technical Change
Edwin Mansfield and Elizabeth Mansfield
32. The Economics of Exhaustible Resources
Geoffrey Heal
33. The Economics of Institutions
Geoffrey M. Hodgson
34. The Economics of Transport
(Volumes I and II)
Herbert Mohring

35. Implicit Contract Theory
Sherwin Rosen
36. Foundations of Analytical Marxism (Volumes I and II)
John E. Roemer
37. The Economics of Product Differentiation (Volumes I and II)
Jacques-François Thisse and George Norman
38. Economic Growth in Theory and Practice: A Kaldorian Perspective
John E. King
39. Markets and Socialism
Alec Nove and Ian D. Thatcher
40. Recent Developments in the Economics of Education
Elchanan Cohn and Geraint Johnes
41. The Theory of Inflation
Michael Parkin
42. The Economics of Location (Volumes I, II and III)
Melvin L. Greenhut and George Norman
43. Financial Intermediaries
Mervyn K. Lewis
44. The Political Economy of Privatization and Deregulation
Elizabeth E. Bailey and Janet Rothenberg Pack
45. Gender and Economics
Jane Humphries
46. Macroeconomics and Imperfect Competition
Jean-Pascal Bénassy
47. Labor Economics (Volumes I, II, III and IV)
Orley C. Ashenfelter and Kevin F. Hallock
48. The Economics of Altruism
Stefano Zamagni
49. The Economic Analysis of Rent Seeking
Robert D. Tollison and Roger D. Congleton
50. Economics and Biology
Geoffrey M. Hodgson
51. The Economics of Ageing
John Creedy
52. Fiscal and Monetary Policy (Volumes I and II)
Thomas Mayer and Steven M. Sheffrin
53. The Economics of Information (Volumes I and II)
David K. Levine and Steven A. Lippman
54. Transaction Cost Economics (Volumes I and II)
Oliver E. Williamson and Scott E. Masten
55. Agricultural Economics
George H. Peters
56. International Debt (Volumes I and II)
Graham Bird and P. Nicholas Snowden
57. Economics and Discrimination (Volumes I and II)
William A. Darity, Jr
58. Business Cycle Theory
Finn E. Kydland
59. International Trade (Volumes I and II)
J. Peter Neary
60. The Money Supply in the Economic Process
Marco Musella and Carlo Panico
61. Small Firms and Economic Growth (Volumes I and II)
Zoltan J. Acs
62. Producer Cooperatives and Labor-Managed Systems (Volumes I and II)
David L. Prychitko and Jaroslav Vanek
63. Ethics and Economics (Volumes I and II)
Alan P. Hamlin
64. The Economics of the Family
Nancy Folbre
65. The Economics of Training (Volumes I and II)
Orley C. Ashenfelter and Robert J. LaLonde
66. Chaos Theory in Economics: Methods, Models and Evidence
W. Davis Dechert
67. General Equilibrium Theory (Volumes I, II and III)
Gérard Debreu
68. Economic Growth: Theory and Evidence (Volumes I and II)
Gene M. Grossman
69. Long Wave Theory
Christopher Freeman

70. The Economics of Communication and Information
Donald M. Lamberton
71. The Foundations of Public Finance (Volumes I and II)
Peter Jackson
72. The Theory of the Firm
Mark Casson
73. The Economics of Uncertainty (Volumes I and II)
John D. Hey
74. The Economics of Global Warming
Tom Tietenberg
75. The Development of Ecological Economics
Robert Costanza, Charles Perrings and Cutler Cleveland
76. Economic Growth in the Long Run: A History of Empirical Evidence (Volumes I, II and III)
Bart van Ark
77. The Economics of Productivity (Volumes I and II)
Edward N. Wolff
78. The Economics of Population: Key Modern Writings (Volumes I and II)
Julian L. Simon
79. Political Business Cycles
Bruno S. Frey
80. Cultural Economics: The Arts, the Heritage and the Media Industries (Volumes I and II)
Ruth Towse
81. Law and Economics (Volumes I, II and III)
Richard A. Posner and Francesco Parisi
82. Independent Central Banks and Economic Performance
Sylvester Eijffinger
83. Culture, Social Norms and Economics (Volumes I and II)
Mark Casson
84. Industrial Policy and Competitive Advantage (Volumes I, II and III)
David B. Audretsch
85. The Economics of Housing (Volumes I and II)
John M. Quigley
86. Economic Demography (Volumes I and II)
T. Paul Schultz
87. Trade and the Environment: Economic, Legal and Policy Perspectives
Alan M. Rugman and John J. Kirton with Julie A. Soloway
88. The Economics of Fiscal Federalism and Local Finance
Wallace E. Oates
89. Price Theory and its Applications
Bernard Saffran and F.M. Scherer
90. Women in the Labor Market (Volumes I and II)
Marianne A. Ferber
91. Market Process Theories (Volumes I and II)
Peter Boettke and David Prychitko
92. Input–Output Analysis (Volumes I, II and III)
Heinz Kurz, Erik Dietzenbacher and Christian Lager
93. Mathematical Economics (Volumes I, II and III)
Graciela Chichilnisky
94. The Foundations of Regulatory Economics (Volumes I, II and III)
Robert B. Ekelund, Jr.
95. The Economics of Marketing
Martin Carter, Mark Casson and Vivek Suneja
96. Service Industries in the Global Economy (Volumes I and II)
J.R. Bryson and P.W. Daniels
97. Economic Justice (Volumes I and II)
Giorgio Brosio and Harold M. Hochman
98. Foreign Exchange Intervention: Objectives and Effectiveness
Sylvester C.W. Eijffinger
99. Economic Anthropology
Stephen Gudeman
100. Consumer Theory
Kelvin Lancaster
101. The Economics of Famine
Jean Drèze
102. Microeconomic Theories of Imperfect Competition
Jean J. Gabszewicz and Jacques-François Thisse

103. The Economics of Executive Compensation
(Volumes I and II)
Kevin F. Hallock and Kevin J. Murphy
104. The Foundations of Long Wave Theory
(Volumes I and II)
Francisco Louçã and Jan Reijnders
105. The Economics of Commodity Markets
David Greenaway and C.W. Morgan
106. Corporate Governance
(Volumes I, II, III and IV)
Kevin Keasey, Steve Thompson and Mike Wright
107. Economic Welfare: Concepts and Measurement
(Volumes I and II)
John Creedy
108. Economic Forecasting
Terence C. Mills
109. Recent Developments in Game Theory
Eric S. Maskin
110. The Economics of Increasing Returns
Geoffrey Heal
111. The Economics of Corruption and Illegal Markets
(Volumes I, II and III)
Gianluca Fiorentini and Stefano Zamagni
112. The Economics of Price Discrimination
George Norman
113. The Economic Theory of Auctions
(Volumes I and II)
Paul Klemperer
114. The Economics of Regional Policy
Harvey W. Armstrong and Jim Taylor
115. Economic Integration and International Trade
Carsten Kowalczyk
116. The Political Economy of Science, Technology and Innovation
Ben Martin and Paul Nightingale
117. The Economics of Science and Innovation
(Volumes I and II)
Paula E. Stephan and David B. Audretsch
118. Innovation, Evolution of Industry and Economic Growth
(Volumes I, II and III)
David B. Audretsch and Steven Klepper
119. The Economics of Energy
(Volumes I and II)
Paul Stevens
120. Privatisation in Developing Countries
(Volumes I and II)
Paul Cook and Colin Kirkpatrick
121. The Economics of Tourism
(Volumes I and II)
Clem Tisdell
122. The Economics of Unemployment
(Volumes I, II, III and IV)
P.N. Junankar
123. Privatisation and Corporate Performance
David Parker
124. Income Distribution
(Volumes I, II and III)
Michael Sattinger
125. International Finance
(Volumes I and II)
Robert Z. Aliber
126. Welfare Economics
(Volumes I, II and III)
William J. Baumol and Charles A. Wilson
127. The Theory of Trade Policy Reform
Carsten Kowalczyk
128. The Economics of Defence
(Volumes I, II and III)
Keith Hartley and Todd Sandler
129. The Economics of Property Rights
(Volumes I and II)
Svetozar Pejovich
130. Gender and Development: Theoretical, Empirical and Practical Approaches
(Volumes I and II)
Lourdes Benería with Savitri Bisnath
131. The Economics of Politics
(Volumes I and II)
Dennis C. Mueller
132. Economic Theory and the Welfare State
(Volumes I, II and III)
Nicholas Barr
133. The Regulation and Supervision of Banks
(Volumes I, II, III and IV)
Maximilian J.B. Hall
134. The Political Economy of Monetary Union
Paul De Grauwe

135. The Economics of Sport
(Volumes I and II)
Andrew Zimbalist
136. The Economics of Advertising
Kyle Bagwell
137. Regulation, Economics and the Law
Anthony I. Ogus
138. The Economics of Barter and Countertrade
Rolf Mirus and Bernard Yeung
139. The Economics of Technology Transfer
Sanjaya Lall
140. The Political Economy of Development
(Volumes I, II and III)
Amitava Krishna Dutt
141. Macroeconomics and the Environment
Mohan Munasinghe
142. Happiness in Economics
Richard A. Easterlin
143. Speculation and Financial Markets
(Volumes I and II)
Liam Gallagher and Mark P. Taylor
144. Public Procurement
(Volumes I and II)
Sue Arrowsmith and Keith Hartley
145. The Economics of Intellectual Property
(Volumes I, II, III and IV)
Ruth Towse and R.W. Holzhauer
146. Forecasting Financial Markets
(Volumes I and II)
Terence C. Mills
147. The Economics of Labor Unions
(Volumes I and II)
Alison Booth
148. New Developments in Exchange Rate Economics
(Volumes I and II)
Lucio Sarno and Mark P. Taylor
149. Long Term Trends and Business Cycles
(Volumes I and II)
Terence C. Mills
150. The Economics of Language
Donald M. Lamberton
151. The Economics of Migration
(Volumes I, II, III and IV)
Klaus F. Zimmermann and Thomas Bauer
152. Cost–Benefit Analysis
Arnold C. Harberger and Glenn P. Jenkins
153. The Economics of Budget Deficits
(Volumes I and II)
Charles K. Rowley, William F. Shughart II and Robert D. Tollison
154. Alternative Theories of the Firm
(Volumes I, II and III)
Richard Langlois, Tony F. Yu and Paul Robertson
155. The Distribution of Tax Burdens
Don Fullerton and Gilbert E. Metcalf
156. International Financial Integration
(Volumes I and II)
Sylvester C.W. Eijffinger and Jan J.G. Lemmen
157. The Economics of Structural Change
(Volumes I, II and III)
Harald Hagemann, Michael Landesmann and Roberto Scazzieri
158. The Economics of Poverty and Inequality
(Volumes I and II)
Frank A. Cowell
159. The Economics of Schooling
(Volumes I and II)
Eric A. Hanushek
160. Intra-Industry Trade
Peter J. Lloyd and Herbert G. Grubel
161. Economic Analysis of Regional Trading Arrangements
Richard Pomfret
162. The Principal Agent Model: The Economic Theory of Incentives
Jean-Jacques Laffont
163. The Economics of Business Strategy
John Kay
164. Recent Developments in Transport Economics
Kenneth Button
165. The Economics of Higher Education
Clive R. Belfield and Henry M. Levin
166. Constitutional Political Economy
(Volumes I and II)
Stephan Voigt
167. Economics and Religion
(Volumes I and II)
Paul Oslington
168. The Economics of Conflict
(Volumes I, II and III)
Todd Sandler and Keith Hartley
169. Cognitive Economics
(Volumes I and II)
Massimo Egidi and Salvatore Rizzello

170. Comparative Law and Economics (Volumes I, II and III)
Gerrit de Geest and Roger Van Den Bergh
171. Personnel Economics (Volumes I and II)
Edward P. Lazear and Robert McNabb
172. Empirical Industrial Organization (Volumes I and II)
Paul L. Joskow and Michael Waterson
173. Multinationals and Public Policy (Volumes I and II)
Stephen Young
174. Complexity in Economics (Volumes I, II and III)
J. Barkley Rosser, Jr.
175. Time in Economic Theory (Volumes I, II and III)
Stefano Zamagni and Elettra Agliardi
176. The Economics of Affirmative Action
Harry J. Holzer and David Neumark
177. Recent Developments in Environmental Economics (Volumes I and II)
Michael Hoel
178. The Economics of Natural Hazards (Volumes I and II)
Howard Kunreuther and Adam Rose
179. Recent Developments in Growth Theory (Volumes I and II)
K. Daron Acemoglu
180. The Political Economy of Environmental Regulation
Robert N. Stavins
181. The Economics of Nonprofit Enterprises
Richard S. Steinberg
182. Recent Developments in Urban and Regional Economics
Paul C. Cheshire and Gilles Duranton
183. The Economics of Public Private Partnerships
Darrin Grimsey and Mervyn K. Lewis
184. New Economic Geography
J. Vernon Henderson
185. Recent Developments in International Trade Theory
Rod Falvey and Udo Kreickemeier
186. New Developments in Economic Sociology (Volumes I and II)
Richard Swedberg
187. The Psychology of World Equity Markets (Volumes I and II)
Werner De Bondt
188. Spatial Economics (Volumes I and II)
Masahisa Fujita
189. The Economics of Deflation (Volumes I and II)
Pierre L. Siklos
190. Real Options and International Investment
Alan M. Rugman and Jing Li
191. Open Economy Macroeconomics
Norman C. Miller
192. Imperfect Competition, Nonclearing Markets and Business Cycles
Jean-Pascal Bénassy
193. Recent Developments in Economic Methodology (Volumes I, II and II)
John B. Davis
194. Modern Classics in the Economics of Education (Volumes I and II)
Clive Belfield
195. The Economics of Crime (Volumes I, II and III)
Isaac Ehrlich and Zhiqiang Liu
196. The Economics of Public Utilities (Volumes I and II)
Ray Rees
197. The Economics of Patents (Volumes I and II)
John Cantwell
198. The Economics of Biotechnology (Volumes I and II)
Maureen McKelvey and Luigi Orsenigo
199. The Economics of the Mass Media
Gillian Doyle
200. The Economics of Leisure (Volumes I and II)
Clem Tisdell
201. Cartels (Volumes I and II)
Margaret C. Levenstein and Stephen W. Salant
202. New Developments in the Economics of Population Ageing
John Creedy and Ross Guest
203. Recent Developments in the Economics of Training (Volumes I and II)
Francis Green

204. Recent Developments in Behavioral Economics
Shlomo Maital
205. Recent Developments in Cultural Economics
Ruth Towse
206. Islamic Finance
M. Kabir Hassan and Mervyn K. Lewis
207. Recent Developments in Labor Economics (Volumes I, II and III)
John T. Addison
208. The International Monetary Fund and the World Economy (Volumes I and II)
Graham Bird and Dane Rowlands
209. New Developments in Experimental Economics (Volumes I and II)
Enrica Carbone and Chris Starmer
210. International Taxation
James R. Hines Jr.
211. The Foundations of Credit Risk Analysis
Willi Semmler and Lucas Bernard
212. Economic Integration and Spatial Location of Firms and Industries (Volumes I, II and III)
Miroslav N. Jovanovic
213. Innovation and Economic Development
Lynn K. Mytelka
214. The Economics of Modern Business Enterprise (Volumes I, II and III)
Martin Ricketts
215. The Economic Theory of Invention and Innovation
Albert N. Link
216. The Economics of Hazardous Waste and Contaminated Land
Hilary Sigman
217. Recent Developments in Monopoly and Competition Policy
George Norman
218. Financial Crises
Franklin Allen and Douglas Gale
219. Developments in the Economics of Privatization and Regulation
Michael Crew and David Parker
220. Applied Welfare Economics
Richard E. Just, Darrell L. Hueth and Andrew Schmitz
221. The Economics of Networks
Mark Casson and Marina Della Giusta
222. The Economics of Innovation Policy (Volumes I and II)
Albert N. Link
223. The Economics of Health Behaviours (Volumes I, II and III)
John Cawley and Donald S. Kenkel
224. Recent Trends in the Economics of Copyright
Ruth Towse and Richard Watt
225. Incomplete Markets
Michael Magill and Martine Quinzii

Future titles will include:

Segmented Labor Markets and Labor Mobility (Volumes I and II)
Michael Reich

The Economics of the Hidden Economy (Volumes I and II)
Friedrich Schneider

The Economics of Contracts
Patrick Bolton

Neuroeconomics
Paul J. Zak

Feminist Economics
Lourdes Benería, Ann Mari May and Diana L. Strassman

Recent Developments in Monetary Policy
Alec Chrystal and Paul Mizen

The Economics of Knowledge
Robin A. Cowan

Path Dependence
Paul A. David

The Economics of Gambling and National Lotteries
William R. Eadington

The Economics of Transfer Pricing
Lorraine Eden

Equality and Economic Growth
Oded Galor

Economics of Water Resources
R. Quentin Grafton

The Economics of Vouchers
Caroline M. Hoxby

The Economics of Free Trade
Douglas A. Irwin and Arvind Panagariya

The Economics of Organisation and Bureaucracy
Peter M. Jackson

Computational Economics
Kenneth L. Judd

New Developments in Behavioral Economics
Elias L. Khalil

The Phillips Curve
Richard G. Lipsey, Robert Leeson and Edward Nelson

The Economic Role of the State
Steven G. Medema

Recent Developments in Law and Economics
Francesco Parisi and Robert Cooter

The New Evolutionary Economics
Jason Potts and Kurt Dopfer

The Knowledge Economy
Danny T. Quah

New Developments in Public Choice
Charles K. Rowley, Robert D. Tollison and William F. Shughart

The Economics of Traffic Congestion
Eric Verhoef

Controlling Public Expenditure
John Wanna

Tax Competition and Tax Harmonisation
David Wildasin

Recent Developments in Evolutionary Economics
Ulrich Witt

The Economics of Climate Change
Graciela Chichilnisky